Structure, Autonomy, and Policy Impacts of Local Public Administrations

Çiğdem Akman
Süleyman Demirel University, Turkey

Onur Kulaç
Pamukkale University, Turkey

IGI Global
Scientific Publishing
Publishing Tomorrow's Research Today

Vice President of Editorial — Melissa Wagner
Director of Acquisitions — Mikaela Felty
Director of Book Development — Jocelynn Hessler
Production Manager — Mike Brehm
Cover Design — Jose Rosado

Published in the United States of America by
IGI Global Scientific Publishing
701 East Chocolate Avenue
Hershey, PA, 17033, USA
Tel: 717-533-8845
Fax: 717-533-7115
Website: https://www.igi-global.com E-mail: cust@igi-global.com

Library of Congress Cataloging-in-Publication Data

Names: Akman, Çiğdem editor | Kulaç, Onur, 1984- editor
Title: Structure, autonomy, and policy impacts of local public administrations / Çiğdem Akman, Onur Kulaç.
Description: Hershey, PA : IGI Global Scientific Publishing, 2026. | Includes bibliographical references and index. | Summary: "This book explores how local public administrations are structured, their autonomy, and how these factors influence their ability to implement and shape policies. It examines the relationship between governance frameworks and the impact of local decision-making on public service delivery and community development"-- Provided by publisher.
Identifiers: LCCN 2025029859 (print) | LCCN 2025029860 (ebook) | ISBN 9798337355764 hardcover | ISBN 9798337355771 paperback | ISBN 9798337355788 ebook
Subjects: LCSH: Public administration--Cross-cultural studies | Local government--Cross-cultural studies | Political science--Decision making--Cross-cultural studies | Government accountability--Cross-cultural studies
Classification: LCC JF1351 .S865 2025 (print) | LCC JF1351 (ebook)
LC record available at https://lccn.loc.gov/2025029859
LC ebook record available at https://lccn.loc.gov/2025029860

British Cataloguing in Publication Data
A Cataloguing in Publication record for this book is available from the British Library.

Table of Contents

Detailed Table of Contents

civil servants, increased decentralization, and application of information technology are proposed. The book chapter affirms the important role of local government in sustainable development and the common prosperity of the whole country.

In this respect, the main purpose of this study is to analyze the local government system of Italy, a European country with a similar central government approach to Turkey. In this study, the functioning of these four levels of Italian local government and the functioning, powers and responsibilities of their subordinate bodies will be analyzed. In addition, the powers and duties of local administration types, their financial relations, audit practices and their comparison with Turkey are also included.

This study explores the relationship between the autonomy of local governments by drawing upon the theoretical frameworks of Montesquieu and Tocqueville. Within the context of Turkey's historical background and political culture, the study addresses the functionality of local administrations, deficiencies in public engagement, and the lack of transparency. Particular attention is given to issues such as the prevalence of corruption in local governments, the inadequacy of oversight mechanisms, and the low level of citizen involvement in governance processes. Grounded in Tocqueville's concept of "local liberties" and Montesquieu's principles of the separation of powers and democratic governance. It further offers concrete recommendations for how these practices might be adapted to the Turkish context. Finally, the study proposes reform initiatives aimed at enhancing local autonomy and outlines strategies to strengthen democratic participation. It argues that local self-governance and civic engagement should be more effectively integrated into the Turkish political system.

Both the United States and India serve as symbolic leaders of continuing democracy on the global stage. India, however, operates as a more cooperative federalist government that is neither purely federal nor unitary compared to the more rigid American federalist form of government. Differences in democratic philosophy between the two nations yield different policy outcomes at local levels in the context of federal influence. To address these distinctions, this chapter will provide narrative comparison of these two democratic systems through the lens of federal and local healthcare spending policies that attempt to combat opioid addiction as a primary public health concern. This chapter takes a step to develop an answer to the question of how decentralized, federalist systems of government impact local policies in the context of addiction and public health.

The study is dedicated to analyzing the current state of municipalities and local self-government bodies, their role within the system of public administration, as well as identifying the challenges and prospects for their development in the context of Azerbaijan. The research examines the specific features of interaction between state authorities and local self-governance institutions, including mechanisms for regulating powers, resource allocation, and the principles of subsidiarity. Particular attention is given to the legal framework, institutional stability, and the impact of state policy on the efficiency of municipal governance. The analysis has revealed shortcomings in legislative regulation, including unclear delineation of functions, the absence of accountability mechanisms, and limited opportunities for judicial protection. The study emphasizes the importance of financial and personnel stability for municipalities, the need to enhance the professional competence of municipal employees, and the active engagement of the population in local governance processes.

Local Self-Government (LSG) existed in a variety of forms throughout India. LSG was seen as an effective form of day-to-day management and administration in rural areas in India. This ensured a democratic form of administration even during the time of monarchs. Although it had a setback during the Muslim and British rulers period, it continued to exist. Gandhi raised his voice for increased decentralization

expected to see how collective capabilities can transform public education into a more inclusive direction in the long term.

Preface

In today's world, local governments are becoming increasingly functional as an indispensable part of social life and democratic governance. They attract attention not only with their increasing importance but also with the radical transformations in their structures and operations. This book, titled "Structure, Autonomy and Policy Impacts of Local Public Administrations", aims to examine this dynamic and constantly evolving field in depth.

One of the most striking changes observed in local governments over time is undoubtedly their increasing autonomy. Local governments have now become active actors who create their own budgets, manage their resources and implement policies that meet local needs. This process has also brought with it new responsibilities and expectations. Fundamental principles such as openness, accountability and efficiency have become central to the modern understanding of local government; comprehensive reform efforts have been implemented to ensure that these principles become operational all over the world.

OVERVIEW OF CHAPTERS

Chapter 1: The Structure of Local Governments in Egypt Historical and Contemporary Perspectives

This research explores the structure, evolution, and challenges of local government in Egypt, emphasizing its role in enhancing governance and decentralization. It begins with a historical overview, detailing the progression of administrative systems from ancient governance models to contemporary frameworks. Study examines the current organizational structure of local government, highlighting the hierarchical system of governorates, districts, and villages, and their interconnected responsibilities. Challenges such as bureaucratic inefficiencies, political centralization, and limited financial autonomy are analyzed, underscoring their impact on governance efficacy. Additionally, recent reforms and decentralization efforts are evaluated, offering insights into strategies for improving local government operations. Comparative analysis with global best practices highlights potential pathways for progress. This paper aims to contribute to the discourse on strengthening local governance in Egypt, emphasizing its significance in fostering sustainable development and inclusive governance

Chapter 2: Local Government Structure in Vietnam: Characteristics and Tasks

The book chapter provides a comprehensive view of local government in the state management system in Vietnam. The chapter emphasizes three main contents: organizational structure, characteristics, and local government tasks. Local government is organized into three levels, including province, district, and commune. The book chapter analyzes the main characteristics of local government. The local government is responsible for development planning, budget management, infrastructure development, security and order, public service provision, resource management, and anti-corruption. The book chapter raises challenges such as human resource shortages, pressures, transparency requirements, and uneven budget allocation. Directions for administrative reform, capacity building of local civil servants, increased decentralization, and application of information technology are proposed. The book chapter affirms the important role of local government in sustainable development and the common prosperity of the whole country.

Chapter 3: Italy's Local Government Structure, Functioning, and Practices

In this respect, the main purpose of this study is to analyze the local government system of Italy, a European country with a similar central government approach to Turkey. In this study, the functioning of these four levels of Italian local government and the functioning, powers and responsibilities of their subordinate bodies will be analyzed. In addition, the powers and duties of local administration types, their financial relations, audit practices and their comparison with Turkey are also included.

Chapter 4: The Autonomy of Local Governments: Democratization of Turkish Public Administration in the Light of Montesquieu and Tocqueville

This study explores the relationship between the autonomy of local governments by drawing upon the theoretical frameworks of Montesquieu and Tocqueville. Within the context of Turkey's historical background and political culture, the study addresses the functionality of local administrations, deficiencies in public engagement, and the lack of transparency. Particular attention is given to issues such as the prevalence of corruption in local governments, the inadequacy of oversight mechanisms, and the low level of citizen involvement in governance processes. Grounded in Tocqueville's concept of "local liberties" and Montesquieu's principles of the separation of powers and democratic governance. It further offers concrete recommendations for how these practices might be adapted to the Turkish context. Finally, the study proposes reform initiatives aimed at enhancing local autonomy and outlines strategies to strengthen democratic participation. It argues that local self-governance and civic engagement should be more effectively integrated into the Turkish political system.

Chapter 5: Federalism and Local Governments: India and the United States as Examples of How Federalism Impacts Local Spending

Both the United States and India serve as symbolic leaders of continuing democracy on the global stage. India, however, operates as a more cooperative federalist government that is neither purely federal nor unitary compared to the more rigid American federalist form of government. Differences in democratic philosophy between the two nations yield different policy outcomes at local levels in the context of federal influence. To address these distinctions, this chapter will provide narrative comparison of these two democratic systems through the lens of federal and local healthcare spending policies that attempt to combat opioid addiction as a primary public health concern. This chapter takes a step to develop an answer to the question of how decentralized, federalist systems of government impact local policies in the context of addiction and public health.

Chapter 6: State-Municipal Cooperation in Azerbaijan: Enhancing Governance Through Local-State Collaboration

The study is dedicated to analyzing the current state of municipalities and local self-government bodies, their role within the system of public administration, as well as identifying the challenges and prospects for their development in the context of Azerbaijan. The research examines the specific features of interaction between state authorities and local self-governance institutions, including mechanisms for regulating powers, resource allocation, and the principles of subsidiarity. Particular attention is given to the legal framework, institutional stability, and the impact of state policy on the efficiency of municipal governance. The analysis has revealed shortcomings in legislative regulation, including unclear delineation of functions, the absence of accountability mechanisms, and limited opportunities for judicial protection. The study emphasizes the importance of financial and personnel stability for municipalities, the need to enhance the professional competence of municipal employees, and the active engagement of the population in local governance processes.

Chapter 7: Local Self-Government in India: A Critical Analysis through the Lens of Democratic Decentralization

Local Self-Government (LSG) existed in a variety of forms throughout India. LSG was seen as an effective form of day-to-day management and administration in rural areas in India. This ensured a democratic form of administration even during the time of monarchs. Although it had a setback during the Muslim and British rulers' period, it continued to exist. Gandhi raised his voice for increased decentralization and self-rule of the villages. Although the Constitution did not provide such an option, many committees opined that local governance should be entrusted to the local people. Accordingly, LSG got constitutional recognition through the 73rd and 74th Amendments in 1992. It provided a three-tier system of governance at the regional level as well. Using analytical and critical lenses, this chapter examines the functioning of the constitutionally established LSG model through the lens of democratic decentralization to expose how far it has achieved its objective.

Chapter 8: Reinforcing Local Governance in India: The Impact of Judicial Oversight on Panchayati Raj Institutions

Judicial decisions of the Indian Judiciary on elections of Panchayat (local governance) reflect that the Indian Judiciary is one of the main authorities to be consulted in cases concerning democratic processes of local governance. This chapter dealt with some landmark judgments in matters concerning interference with candidacy, manipulation of voter lists, ballot secrecy, procedural adherence, and candidacy eligibility. It has shown devotion to the integrity and accountability of local governance. Indian Constitution made administration accountable to the people for any malpractices. Malpractice, as evidenced by many judicial pronouncements, often subverted this model. The intervention of the judiciary is needed to secure the integrity of elections. This chapter has advocated for a robust and transparent electoral system. Judicial intervention has highlighted systemic failures. Indian Courts have enthused the formulation of policies to reduce electoral malpractices. Policy innovations can deepen democracy by empowering local self-governments in a strong and decisive manner.

Chapter 9: Mental Health Support in Education: The Power of Policy in Knowledge Mobilization Efforts

This paper will contextualize the current state of the education system using a future-oriented lens to analyze mental health and the education system. Situated within the Canadian context (namely the province of Ontario), it calls on various scholarly dialogues to highlight the importance of knowledge mobilization. The function of policy in addressing mental health and the role of educators is emphasized, given the effectiveness of policy in making large-scale changes. It is suggested that a policy-based approach be taken within teacher education programs, to ensure that educators will be supported and equipped with future-oriented skills and competencies. Future studies should aim to collect qualitative and quantitative understandings of the impact of teacher education programs and the efficacy of courses aimed at bridging the gap between traditional teacher education programs and programs that include aspects of mental health training.

Chapter 10: Mapping Research Trends Digital Communication on Public Policy: A Systematic Literature Review

This study aims to examine the trend of scientific research related to digital communication on public policy. The research method used a systematic literature review based on 94 scientific articles from the Scopus. Data was collected from Scopus database and data analysis using the VOS viewer Application. The study revealed that with 94 scientific articles on Digital Communication on Public Policy that had gone through the review including data by year, by author, by country or territory, by subject area, issue clustering data and grouping. The chapter contributes to the development of driving forces for further research on Digital Communication on Public Policy. This article has limitations that only review articles sourced from the Scopus database. This study aids in the process of formulating and creating future policies.

Chapter 11: Collective Capabilities and Local Democratic Governance to Transform Public Education: A Case Study on The Brazilian State of Ceará

Amartya Sen's Capability Approach (CA) provides an alternative understanding of development, welfare, and democracy. Amartya Sen focuses on the non-material roots of welfare, such as agency freedom, and the material roots of economic development. However, his approach's liberal roots, which put individuals at the center of analysis, have been criticized in various aspects. The literature on collective capabilities provides arguments for filling these criticized gaps in CA. This study aims to discuss the role of social movements in transforming the power relations created by the neoliberal economic and political system, along with its relationship between education and deliberative democracy through collective capabilities, using the solid example of the Brazilian state of Ceará. By examining Ceará, it is expected to see how collective capabilities can transform public education into a more inclusive direction in the long term.

As a result of these reforms, local governments have become more autonomous, transparent, accountable and, most notably, able to guide public policies and become the engine of local development. However, each country's unique historical, cultural and political conditions have led to these transformation experiences manifesting themselves in different ways. For this reason, this book has given special importance to different country practices. Thus, it is aimed to present more clearly the differences and similarities in the structure, autonomy and policy effects of local governments and to provide a comparative perspective.

We sincerely hope that this study will serve as a comprehensive and reliable resource for academicians, policy makers, practitioners and all researchers and readers interested in this field. We hope that our book will contribute to current debates, theoretical approaches and practical analyses on local governments, thus providing a valuable basis for both academic literature and field applications. Our greatest wish is that the study will shed light on the dynamic problems faced by local governments and will contribute to the deepening of understanding in this field. We would like to express our deepest gratitude to all individuals and institutions who contributed to the preparation of this book and enriched the content of our study with their ideas and suggestions. In particular, the meticulousness, academic sensitivity and sharing approaches shown in the preparation of each chapter have increased the integrity and quality of the book. We would like to thank the academicians, experts, colleagues and valuable readers who contributed directly or indirectly to the process and would like to emphasize once again that this study is the product of a joint effort.

Chapter 1
The Structure of Local Governments in Egypt Historical and Contemporary Perspectives

Ossama Sayed Ramadan
https://orcid.org/0009-0004-2148-7820
Süleyman Demirel University, Isparta, Turkey

Çiğdem Akman
https://orcid.org/0000-0002-1936-6884
Süleyman Demirel University, Isparta, Turkey

ABSTRACT

This research explores the structure, evolution, and challenges of local government in Egypt, emphasizing its role in enhancing governance and decentralization. It begins with a historical overview, detailing the progression of administrative systems from ancient governance models to contemporary frameworks. Study examines the current organizational structure of local government, highlighting the hierarchical system of governorates, districts, and villages, and their interconnected responsibilities. Challenges such as bureaucratic inefficiencies, political centralization, and limited financial autonomy are analyzed, underscoring their impact on governance efficacy. Additionally, recent reforms and decentralization efforts are evaluated, offering insights into strategies for improving local government operations. Comparative analysis with global best practices highlights potential pathways for progress. This paper aims to contribute to the discourse on strengthening local governance

DOI: 10.4018/979-8-3373-5576-4.ch001

in Egypt, emphasizing its significance in fostering sustainable development and inclusive governance

INTRODUCTION

The Arab Republic of Egypt holds a pivotal place in the Middle East due to its evolving political, administrative, and cultural landscape. It has been the focus of extensive research given the history of political upheaval and its substantial economy. Prolonged occupations, administrative instability resulting from military coups, and dynamic national changes have hindered the advancement and development of local governments (Aksu & Akman, 2023, p. 58).

Local government is a critical component of decentralized governance, enabling communities to address specific needs through localized decision-making. It is vital for garnering citizen support, ensuring efficient public service delivery, and promoting sustainable development. In Egypt, local government has historically been central to managing urban and rural issues, functioning through a structured system of governorates, districts, towns, and villages. Despite its significance, the system remains highly centralized, limiting its capacity to function as an effective instrument for inclusive governance (Posner, 2011, p. 2).

The historical development of local government in Egypt reflects its colonial and post-colonial administrative trajectory. Its foundations trace back to the Ottoman period and were further shaped under British colonial rule, during which local authorities primarily served as instruments of control rather than empowerment. Post-independence, Egypt's local government system expanded its role in delivering essential services such as education, health, and infrastructure development. However, centralization has persisted as a defining characteristic, restricting the autonomy and effectiveness of local entities (Martinez & Timofeev, 2010, p. 7).

The 2014 constitution marked a significant turning point by emphasizing decentralization as a guiding principle for governance in Egypt. Articles like 176 stressed the need to transfer authority and resources to local entities to enhance their ability to address community needs. Despite these constitutional provisions, practical implementation has been inconsistent. Local councils, a vital component of participatory governance, have remained inactive, with elections suspended since 2011, creating a gap in citizen representation and accountability (Morsy, 2015).

Challenges facing Egypt's local government system include limited financial autonomy, over-reliance on the central government for funding and decision-making, and a lack of citizen engagement in local initiatives. Additionally, inefficiencies and corruption within local administrative bodies further undermine public trust and service delivery effectiveness. These issues highlight the need for comprehensive reforms to enable local governments to act as true agents of development and public accountability (Sayigh, 2019, p. 15).

1. CONCEPT AND PURPOSE OF LOCAL GOVERNMENT

Countries transitioning toward democracy often aim to diminish the authority and capacity of the central government by granting local and sub-government entities spanning executive, legislative, and judicial powers more autonomy. This process is known as decentralization, and the degree of centralization or decentralization depends on the extent to which the central government delegates powers to local governments.

Local government refers to administrative and political units established to manage public affairs within a specific, localized geographic area, such as cities, towns, or districts. Operating under the authority of a national or regional government, local governments play a crucial role in delivering services, maintaining infrastructure, and representing the interests of local residents. They are responsible for areas such as education, public transportation, waste management, and local law enforcement (Rondinelli & Nellis, 1986, pp. 3-23).

Local governments are typically overseen by elected officials, including mayors, council members, or commissioners, who are accountable to their constituents. The powers and responsibilities of local governments can vary significantly depending on the country's legal and political framework. For instance, in federal systems like the United States, local governments possess considerable autonomy and operate independently of state and federal authorities. In contrast, in unitary states like France, local governments are more directly controlled by the central government. Local governments play a critical role in fostering democratic governance by providing citizens with opportunities to engage directly in decision-making processes at the community level. They are essential for addressing the specific needs and preferences of their populations, thereby making governance more responsive and efficient (Shah, Shah, Heymans, & Steffensen, 2006, pp. 30-33).

Local government is considered the governing body that oversees a smaller geographical area within a state, such as a city, county, region, state, or province. The jurisdiction of one province's laws does not extend to another. This level of government is responsible for most, if not all, functions that the central national government perform (Cheema & Rondinelli, 2007, pp. 40-55).

Figure 1. Local governments advantages

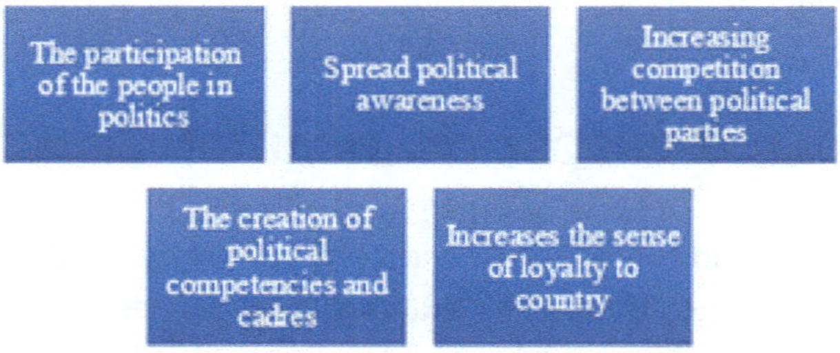

Source: (Prud'homme, 1995, pp. 201-220)

Source: (Prud'homme, 1995, pp. 201-220)

A sense of pride often emerges within individual citizens as they perceive their country as a large home that they contribute to organizing, protecting, and enhancing in all political, economic, and social spheres. Thus, local government represents the level of public administration closest to citizens, tasked with managing local affairs and ensuring that services meet the specific needs of communities (Miller, 2002, pp. 15-40).

Local government in Egypt plays a crucial role in the country's administrative, social, and economic structure. It serves as the link between the central government and local communities, ensuring the implementation of national policies while also managing essential services that directly impact citizens' lives. Local governments are responsible for critical services such as sanitation, health care, education, urban planning, and public safety.

They also play a key role in promoting economic development within neighborhoods by supporting local businesses, creating job opportunities, and managing public resources. Despite their vital role, local governments in Egypt face several challenges, including centralization of power, limited financial resources, bureaucratic inefficiency, and delays in local elections. These issues hinder the full realization of local governance and the effective delivery of services. Although the central government still retains significant control, there is potential for reform. Empowering local councils, increasing their financial and administrative autonomy, and holding regular elections could enhance the effectiveness of local government. By addressing these challenges, Egypt's local government could play a more transformative role in improving the quality of life for its citizens, promoting community engagement, and contributing to the overall development of the country.

Local governments play a vital role in addressing community needs by providing a range of essential services that contribute to the well-being of citizens. One of these fundamental functions is service delivery, where local governments provide key services such as education, healthcare, sanitation, and infrastructure development. These services are tailored to address the unique needs of the local community, ensuring that resources are allocated more efficiently (Kessy, 2013, p. 219).

Decentralization is a critical process wherein administrative responsibilities are transferred from central authorities to local governments. This shift reduces the burden on central authorities and enhances efficiency and responsiveness to local needs. Through decentralization, local governments become more capable of making informed decisions that align with the local context. Community engagement is also a crucial aspect of local government work, as it encourages citizen participation in decision-making processes that directly affect their lives. This engagement fosters transparency, accountability, and trust between citizens and government (Bardhan & Mookherjee, 2006).

1.1. Reason of Nearby Government

Local governments play a vital role in meeting the needs of communities by providing a range of essential services that contribute to the well-being of citizens. A fundamental function is service delivery, in which local governments offer key services such as education, healthcare, sanitation, and infrastructure development. These services are tailored to address the unique needs of the local community, thereby ensuring more efficient resource allocation (Harb & Atallah, 2020).

Neighborhood government is directly in touch with the daily realities of its citizens. Unlike central or regional governments, which may be disconnected from local issues, neighborhood councils are best positioned to address specific local needs such as sanitation, infrastructure, healthcare, education, and security. Their proximity to the community allows them to identify and address problems quickly and efficiently.

Neighborhood governments promote political participation and community engagement. They provide a platform for citizens to voice their concerns, participate in decision-making, and influence the policies that affect their lives. By electing representatives to local councils, residents can ensure that their interests are considered in the governance process, fostering a sense of empowerment and responsibility among the community.

Local governments are thus more capable of making informed decisions that align with local contexts. Community engagement is a critical aspect of their work, encouraging citizen participation in decision-making processes that directly affect their lives. This participation fosters transparency and accountability, helping to build trust between citizens and the government.

The decentralization of power to local authorities helps distribute decision-making, which reduces the burden on central governments and prevents excessive centralization. Local governments, including neighborhood councils, allow for more localized control over resources and services, ensuring that decisions are made closer to where they impact citizens. This decentralization also encourages accountability and transparency within local governance structures.

Neighborhood government plays a critical role in the efficient delivery of essential services. Services such as waste management, local policing, public health initiatives, and infrastructure maintenance are often better managed at the neighborhood level. Neighborhood councils can tailor their approach to meet the specific needs of their community, ensuring that services are responsive, timely, and effective.

Neighborhood governments play a key role in fostering a sense of community and belonging among local residents. By involving citizens in local decision-making, these governments help build social capital, encourage collaboration, and promote local identity. This, in turn, strengthens social cohesion, allowing residents to work together towards common goals and improving overall well-being.

Local governments are essential in driving economic development within neighborhoods. They can create a conducive environment for businesses, attract investments, and promote local economic initiatives. By supporting small and medium-sized enterprises (SMEs) and creating jobs, neighborhood councils can contribute to the economic growth of the area and ensure that development benefits the local population.

Neighborhood governments are essential for addressing challenges that are specific to local communities, such as urbanization, population growth, and environmental concerns. Local authorities are in a better position to develop strategies and policies that respond to these unique challenges, whether it be through improving infrastructure, providing adequate housing, or addressing public health issues.

Economically, local governments play a significant role in promoting growth by implementing local policies and programs that support small businesses, improve infrastructure, and create employment opportunities. Through these activities, local governments contribute to creating a conducive environment for economic development (Andrew, 2022).

2. AUTHENTIC IMPROVEMENT OF NEIGHBORHOOD GOVERNMENT IN EGYPT

This chapter explores the evolution of local administration in Egypt, providing an overview of its trajectory from ancient times through British occupation and Ottoman rule, and into the modern era. It also examines the contemporary Egyptian constitutions that regulate local administration and its powers.

2.1. Overview of Local Administration in Ancient and Modern Egypt

Local administration in ancient Egypt can be traced back to the earliest periods of Egyptian history, particularly during the Pharaonic era, when the kingdom was divided into administrative units known as nomes (or sepat). These were essentially provinces, each governed by a nomarch, a local governor who had significant authority over his region, including control over agricultural production, resources, and labor. The role of the nomarch was crucial for maintaining order and collecting taxes, and he reported directly to the Pharaoh, who was considered the supreme ruler.

Centralized Power: Although local governors had considerable autonomy within their nomes, they were still bound by the authority of the Pharaoh, who controlled the central administration from the capital city (e.g., Memphis or Thebes). The Pharaoh's role was that of a divine ruler, and his word was absolute, which ensured that local administration was deeply intertwined with the central authority.

Administrative Structure: The local administration was highly organized, with a hierarchical structure. In each nome, there were officials responsible for specific tasks, such as tax collection, maintaining public works (like irrigation systems), and ensuring military defense. These roles were often filled by individuals of high social standing, ensuring loyalty to the central government.

Economic Role: The local administrative units played an essential role in Egypt's economy, especially in managing agricultural production, which was the backbone of the state's wealth. The nomarchs, along with their subordinates, were tasked with managing the vast lands, organizing labor, and ensuring the smooth operation of the economy (Parkinson, 2002, pp. 50-70).

Local Administration in Modern Egypt:

In modern Egypt, the structure and function of local administration have undergone significant changes, particularly in response to the political, social, and economic transformations the country has experienced over time. While ancient Egypt's local administration was largely based on a hierarchical, centralized system under the Pharaoh, modern Egypt has moved through various stages of governance, including colonial rule, post-independence, and contemporary reforms.

Colonial Era (British Rule, 1882-1952): During British colonial rule, local administration in Egypt was heavily influenced by foreign control. The British implemented a centralizing model of governance that weakened the power of local authorities. However, they retained a local administrative structure at the municipal and provincial levels, which was still largely subordinate to the British government.

Post-Independence (1952-1970): After the Egyptian Revolution of 1952, which ousted the monarchy and led to the establishment of a republic, Egypt saw significant changes in its administrative structure. President Gamal Abdel Nasser pursued a policy of centralization, and local governments became more directly controlled by the central state. This period also saw the establishment of regional councils and increased involvement of the central government in local governance.

Nasser's Reforms: Nasser's policies aimed at unifying Egypt under a centralized government. Local administrative units were designed to promote economic and social reforms, and power was concentrated in the hands of the central government. Governors were appointed by the central government, and local councils were given limited power.

Post-Nasser Era (1970s - Present): Following Nasser's death, Egypt's political landscape shifted, but centralization continued under the regimes of Anwar Sadat and Hosni Mubarak. In the modern era, local governments still largely depend on the central government for funding, authority, and decision-making. However, efforts towards decentralization have been introduced in recent decades to promote local autonomy and improve governance (Bassiouni, 2012, pp. 245-266).

Decentralization Efforts: In the 1990s, Egypt began experimenting with decentralization to improve local governance and service delivery. This included giving local councils more responsibilities in areas such as education, health, and urban planning, but with limited fiscal autonomy. However, the central government still holds considerable power over local authorities.

Recent Reforms (2010s - Present): Under President Abdel Fattah el-Sisi, there has been an increased focus on improving the efficiency of local governments, though reforms remain limited in scope. The government has emphasized the importance of modernizing local governance structures to respond to urbanization and growing population demands, but local governments still struggle with insufficient funding, lack of coordination, and bureaucratic inefficiencies.

Local Government Structure: In modern Egypt, local administration is divided into governorates (provinces), each headed by a governor appointed by the president. Each governorate is further divided into districts and cities, which are governed by councils. Local councils are elected, but their power is often limited, with the central government maintaining strong oversight.

Challenges: Despite efforts to reform, the local administration still faces several challenges, including corruption, lack of transparency, and limited authority to enact significant policy changes. The central government's tight control over local resources and decision-making has hindered local development and efficient public service delivery. (Kurun, 2015, pp. 185-190).

2.2. Key Legislative and Constitutional Milestones

Local governance in Egypt has undergone several significant legislative and constitutional changes throughout its history. These milestones reflect the evolving political, social, and economic circumstances in the country, influencing how power is distributed between central and local authorities. The following outlines some key legislative and constitutional milestones in the development of local governance in Egypt:

1. The British Colonial Period (1882–1952): During the British colonial era, local governance in Egypt was heavily influenced by British administrative practices. The British established a system of local councils, which, while not fully autonomous, allowed for some level of local participation in governance, primarily in urban areas. The Local Councils Act of 1883: This act established the framework for local councils in Egyptian cities and towns. These councils had limited powers and were essentially advisory bodies that reported to the central government. While local councils were formed, they had little real influence and were controlled by the British authorities. The focus of this act was on urban governance and municipal management. The 1913 Administrative Code: This code was an important development in the structure of local government, organizing local administration into regions and districts. However, real power still resided with the British authorities, and local councils continued to have minimal authority. (Bassiouni, The Law of Egypt: Local Governance and Decentralization p 245-266, 2012).
2. Post-Independence Era (1952–1970): Following the 1952 revolution, Egypt underwent significant changes in governance, and the country's local administration was reshaped to align with the central government's policies under President Gamal Abdel Nasser. The 1956 Constitution: The 1956 Constitution, drafted after the revolution, established Egypt as a republic and formally abolished the monarchy. It introduced the concept of centralization, where local authorities were subordinate to the central government. While it set the stage for local governance, it emphasized national unity and control over local resources, limiting the powers of local authorities. Law No. 43 of 1979 (The Local Administration Law): This law established the structure of local administration in Egypt and

aimed to decentralize some powers to local councils. The law defined the role of governorates, cities, and villages, and provided for the election of local council members. However, despite its intentions, local councils still faced considerable limitations in terms of budget control and administrative independence, as the central government maintained tight oversight (Elgohary, 2008).

3. The Mubarak Era and Further Centralization (1981–2011): Under President Hosni Mubarak, local governance in Egypt became increasingly centralized. Despite this centralization, some laws attempted to allow for more local representation and participation. Law No. 43 of 1979 (Revised in 2000): This law was revised in 2000 to give local councils more responsibilities, but it was still under the heavy influence of the central government. Local councils were expected to provide services such as education, healthcare, and infrastructure, but central government control over funding and decision-making remained strong. The 2005 Amendment to the Local Administration Law: The 2005 amendment aimed to improve local governance by enhancing the electoral process for local councils. It introduced measures to encourage greater political participation, such as allowing multi-candidate elections. However, the government retained control over key decisions, and the amendments failed to empower local councils in a meaningful way, as the executive branch still had significant power over local authorities (Kabbani, 2014).
4. The Post-Revolution Period (2011–Present): The 2011 Egyptian revolution, which led to the ousting of Mubarak, brought about significant changes in the political landscape of Egypt. This period saw the drafting of new constitutional frameworks and attempts at both centralization and decentralization. The 2012 Constitution: Following the revolution, Egypt adopted a new constitution in 2012, which included provisions related to local governance. It called for the creation of a more decentralized administrative system and gave local councils more autonomy, although real power remained with the central government. The 2012 constitution recognized the importance of local governance and promised reforms to give local entities more control over local development and resources. The 2014 Constitution: The 2014 constitution, which replaced the 2012 version, reaffirmed Egypt's commitment to decentralization and local governance but still maintained a strong central government. The 2014 constitution stipulated that local councils should be elected through a multi-candidate system, and it encouraged local participation in political life. However, the central government retained significant authority over local matters, especially in terms of budgeting and administrative powers (Abouelazm, 2014). The 2017 Local Elections Law (Law No. 108 of 2017): This law governs the elections of local councils and defines the powers and functions of these councils. It also introduced more detailed regulations for the election of local representatives and created a frame-

work for improving local governance, but once again, the central government retains oversight of the process. This law was seen as an attempt to balance local representation with central government control, although many critics argued it did not go far enough in decentralizing power.

5. Current Trends and the Sisi Administration (2013–Present): Under President Abdel Fattah el-Sisi, there has been a renewed focus on both administrative reform and the centralization of power. Despite promises of decentralization, local governance continues to be largely controlled by the central government.

Recent Local Governance Reforms (2014–Present):

While local elections were originally planned to take place soon after the 2011 revolution, they were delayed multiple times. The Sisi administration has introduced some reforms to improve local governance, including the creation of new governorates and greater emphasis on infrastructure development at the local level. However, the actual decentralization of power remains limited, and the central government continues to have a significant say in the functioning of local councils (Hanna, 2023).

Local Governance Challenges:

One of the significant ongoing challenges is the financial dependence of local governments on the central government. Local councils have limited fiscal autonomy, and local development is often contingent on the central government's allocation of resources. In addition, local authorities face challenges in managing large urban populations and rural areas with differing needs, requiring more efficient decentralization and local empowerment. (Erdoğan, 2019, pp. 170-190).

3. STRUCTURE AND ORGANIZATION OF NEIGHBORHOOD GOVERNMENT IN EGYPT

Neighborhood governance in Egypt has evolved through several phases, influenced by various political regimes. From the era of the Pharaonic state to the Ottoman Empire, and later under British colonial rule, the concept of local government was mostly centralized, with minimal involvement of local communities in decision-making.

During the Pharaonic period, local administration was highly centralized. Local communities, including neighborhoods, were often governed by appointed officials, such as nomarchs, who acted as intermediaries between the local population and the central government. These officials were responsible for ensuring the collection of taxes and the implementation of royal decrees.

The Ottoman Empire decentralized certain aspects of governance, leading to the creation of local councils in some areas. However, these councils were still controlled by the central government, and their role was largely advisory. During British rule, the colonial administration introduced local councils, particularly in urban areas. These councils were not autonomous and had very limited powers, as they were primarily responsible for sanitation, public health, and urban planning.

The Arab Republic of Egypt is divided into seven regions, encompassing a total of 27 governorates. Each governorate has a capital and is subdivided into centers, divisions, or a combination of both. Administrative centers are typically found in governorates with rural areas, with each center divided into local units. The capital of the center is usually the largest city in its area. If the center comprises more than one city, the capital of each local unit might be a main village or city. The main village is supported by a number of smaller villages, and each village may have subordinate hamlets or smaller settlements.

When the capital of a center is a large city, the city is further divided into several sections, each led by a head known as the head of the neighborhood. If the city is comprised of a single section, its leader serves as the head of the city and employs divisional structures such as smaller neighborhoods or sheikhs. The head of the city appoints leaders for these subdivisions (El-Gamal, Ismail, & El Bagoury, 2025, pp. 325-330).

Local administrative units in Egypt operate within a centralized framework, with decision-making authority heavily concentrated at the governorate level. Areas act as intermediaries between governorates and towns, facilitating policy implementation and service delivery. Each area is managed by an appointed official who coordinates efforts between towns and the governorate. At the grassroots level, towns address immediate community needs, focusing on services like sanitation, water supply, primary education, and healthcare.

Local councils are designed to enhance citizen representation and align national policies with regional contexts. They oversee the management of public services, including sanitation, healthcare, and education. Nonetheless, financial and administrative constraints often impede their effectiveness (Sims D., 2012, pp. 70-120).

Figure 2. The administrative divisions of Egypt

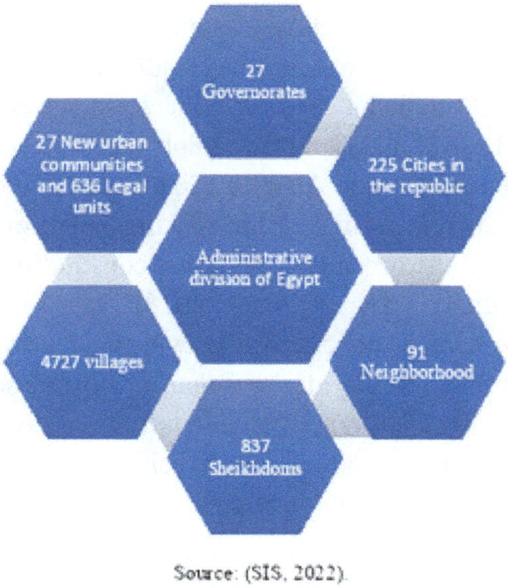

Source: (SIS, 2022).

4. CHALLENGES FACING LOCAL GOVERNMENT IN EGYPT

This chapter addresses the challenges local governments in Egypt face in carrying out their work, as outlined by the Constitution. These challenges include the centralization of power in the hands of the president, issues with funding, and the weakness of civil society.

4.1. Issues of Decentralization and Implementation

Despite various attempts to decentralize, power in Egypt remains largely centralized in the hands of the national government. Local governments and neighborhood councils often lack the authority to make independent decisions regarding key matters such as budget allocation, urban planning, and the implementation of national policies. The central government retains significant control over local administrations, with local leaders frequently appointed rather than elected. This centralization undermines the intended benefits of decentralization and limits the capacity of local governments to address local needs effectively.

Decentralization in Egypt has been a persistent challenge, particularly since 2008. The centralized administrative structure has traditionally concentrated decision-making authority at the national level, leaving local governments with limited autonomy. The 2014 Egyptian Constitution emphasizes the need for administrative and fiscal decentralization through Articles 176 and 242, which advocate granting local units greater independence in decision-making and resource allocation. However, subsequent legislation to operationalize these constitutional mandates has been lacking, resulting in limited progress (Saleh, 2018).

The centralized system of governance is evident as governors and key local officials are appointed directly by the president or central authorities, reflecting a persistent top-down approach. This framework diminishes the capacity of local councils to act independently or address the specific needs of their constituencies. Local councils often function as implementers of national policies rather than autonomous bodies (Shantir, 2022).

Many local governments in Egypt lack the necessary administrative capacity to implement decentralization policies effectively. This includes the shortage of qualified personnel, inadequate training, and insufficient technical expertise within local government institutions. As a result, local councils struggle to manage resources efficiently, plan and execute projects, and maintain the quality of public services. Additionally, local officials often face bureaucratic obstacles that impede their ability to take swift and effective action. The lack of a skilled and professional workforce at the local level is a significant barrier to successful decentralization and efficient local governance.

Efforts toward decentralization are further hindered by bureaucratic inertia and a lack of coordination among various levels of government. Frequent changes in legislation and unclear administrative structures create instability, complicating long-term planning for effective local governance. Additionally, local authorities often lack the technical expertise, training, and regulatory capacity to fully exercise their limited powers, weakening their ability to develop and implement policies tailored to their communities' needs (Ibrahim, 2024, pp. 54-53).

Another challenge in decentralization is the lack of public awareness and participation. In many communities, citizens may not fully understand the role of local government or how they can engage in decision-making processes. Without adequate civic education and public outreach, local governments may struggle to gain the trust and cooperation of the public. Furthermore, citizens may not actively participate in local elections or in the planning and implementation of policies, which weakens the accountability of local governments. Encouraging public engagement and creating awareness about the benefits of decentralization is essential for its successful implementation.

4.2. Resource Constraints and Financial Dependence

Local governments have limited mechanisms to generate their own revenue. Taxation powers, such as property or municipal taxes, are either weakly enforced or centrally controlled, resulting in inadequate local income streams. Moreover, inefficiencies in collecting fees or taxes exacerbate financial challenges, leaving local councils with insufficient resources to invest in infrastructure or public services.

Local governments in Egypt rely heavily on transfers from the central government for their operational budgets. This financial dependency limits their ability to make independent decisions or prioritize local needs effectively. Local councils often do not have enough revenue-generating mechanisms, such as local taxes or fees, to fund their operations or development projects. Consequently, most local governments depend on financial allocations from the central government to cover essential services such as healthcare, education, infrastructure maintenance, and public safety. This system of financial dependency creates inefficiencies, as local governments have limited control over the allocation and utilization of funds.

Infrastructure deficiencies, inadequate funding hampers local governments' ability to develop essential infrastructure, such as roads, schools, healthcare facilities, and water systems (Reuters, 2024). Many rural and marginalized areas suffer from chronic underinvestment, perpetuating disparities in public service delivery between urban and rural regions.

Local governments in Egypt face challenges in generating sufficient revenue from local sources. While they are responsible for managing public services at the neighborhood level, they often lack the ability to raise funds through taxes or other local revenue-generating mechanisms. Local taxes, such as property taxes, are either not adequately collected or are too low to support the needs of local governments. This reliance on external funding restricts the financial autonomy of local councils and limits their ability to plan long-term projects or respond to emerging needs in their communities. The lack of a diversified and reliable revenue base also leads to disparities in service delivery, as wealthier regions may generate more local revenue while poorer areas remain underfunded.

Local governments often face delays in receiving financial transfers from the central government, which can disrupt the timely delivery of services and development projects. Bureaucratic obstacles, such as cumbersome approval processes and slow fund disbursement mechanisms, can lead to inefficiencies and delays in implementing local programs. This slow and bureaucratic process further exacerbates the challenges faced by local governments, particularly in high-need areas where urgent interventions are required.

Dependency on External Support, in some instances, international aid and development grants supplement local government budgets. While helpful, such funding is often tied to specific projects or outcomes, limiting its utility in addressing broader or long-term community needs. Impact on Decentralization Goals, financial dependence undermines decentralization efforts by perpetuating central government control over local affairs. Without financial independence, local governments cannot effectively exercise the powers envisioned under constitutional reforms or meet the demands of their constituents (Mulder, 2023, pp. 5-7).

4.3. Weak Civic Participation and Transparency

Civic engagement and transparency are crucial components of a well-functioning local government. However, both have been limited in Egypt, contributing to inefficiency and a lack of accountability in local governance.

Constraints on Political Freedoms and Civil Society, political freedoms and civil society organizations in Egypt have faced numerous restrictions, particularly in the past decade. Laws regulating non-governmental organizations (NGOs) have been prohibitive, hindering their ability to mobilize and advocate for local issues. This limits the avenues through which citizens can organize, raise their concerns, and participate meaningfully in governance. In addition, the lack of a free media has stifled public discourse on government accountability, weakening local governments' ability to be transparent and responsive to citizen expectations (Rutherford, 2013, pp. 315-325).

Transparency and Accountability in local government activities remain significant concerns in Egypt. Despite laws requiring transparency, there are gaps in implementation. The central government maintains tight control over information, and local governments often operate with limited access to data concerning budgets, planning reports, and policy decisions. This opacity makes it difficult for citizens to hold local authorities accountable, fostering a climate of corruption and inefficiency. The slow progress of decentralization reforms has also meant that many local governments still lack the resources and structures necessary for effective engagement in transparent governance (Elsharkawy, 2022).

Impact of Weak Civic Participation and Transparency, the lack of transparency has led to a disconnect between local governments and the populations they serve. Local leaders are often seen as unaccountable to the public, diminishing confidence in the effectiveness of local governance. Without robust mechanisms for participation and oversight, it is challenging for local governments to address the diverse and evolving needs of their communities, which may include issues like housing, education, and public services (Awad, 2022).

5. FUTURE PROSPECTS AND RECOMMENDATIONS FOR LOCAL GOVERNMENT IN EGYPT

The future of local government in Egypt depends on addressing the challenges and leveraging the opportunities presented by decentralization and local governance reforms. While there are significant obstacles to overcome, including financial dependence, bureaucratic inefficiency, and the centralization of power, there are also pathways toward improving local governance, enhancing service delivery, and empowering communities. Below are the future prospects and recommendations for strengthening local government in Egypt.

5.1. Enhancing Administrative and Financial Independence

Enhancing administrative and financial independence is foundational for effective decentralized governance. In Egypt, centralization has historically restricted local authorities' ability to effectively address region-specific challenges. Improving this autonomy requires a multifaceted approach to empower local councils and improve governance. Key components for ımprovement are:

- **Decentralization of Resources**: Egypt's local governments heavily rely on funding from the central government, often leading to delays and inefficiencies. Decentralizing financial resources would provide local authorities with the flexibility to address local needs promptly. Allocating a portion of national revenues directly to governorates and local councils, as observed in other successful countries, can facilitate decentralization (kohli, 2004, pp. 143-180).
- **Local Revenue Generation**: Introducing mechanisms for generating local revenue, such as property taxes, business fees, or tourism-related charges, can help local governments achieve financial independence. This autonomy reduces reliance on central allocations and allows for more region-specific investments.
- **Administrative Independence**: Granting local councils more decision-making authority in areas such as urban planning, public services, and education is crucial. This would require legal reforms to redefine the relationship between local and central governments, delegating significant administrative responsibilities to the local level.

- **Capacity Building**: Enhancing independence also involves strengthening the capacity of local officials through training in budgeting, financial management, and governance (Werr & Lewis, 2023).
- **Monitoring and Accountability**: Establishing robust monitoring systems ensures accountability. Clear performance metrics, audits, and oversight mechanisms are essential to prevent resource misuse and corruption.

Challenges to implementation are:

- **Resistance from Central Authorities**: Central authorities in Egypt may resist relinquishing control due to political and institutional inertia.
- **Inadequate Infrastructure**: Many local councils lack the infrastructure or expertise needed to effectively manage independent resources and responsibilities. Addressing this gap requires significant investment in training and technological tools.
- **Legal and Regulatory Obstacles**: Current laws often impose strict limitations on local governments, necessitating comprehensive legal reforms to truly empower local councils (Helbawy, 2024, p. 25).

5.2. Promoting Civic Engagement and Transparency

Civic engagement and transparency are essential pillars of effective governance, particularly in enhancing accountability and inclusivity of local governments. In Egypt, efforts to improve these aspects face significant challenges but also offer substantial opportunities for progress.

- **Transparency**: Ensures that citizens have access to information about government decisions, resource allocations, and public expenditures. This involves publishing budgets, contracts, and progress reports online or through accessible channels.
- **Building Trust Through Accountability**: Transparency mechanisms, coupled with accountability systems like anti-corruption units and independent audits, can reduce instances of mismanagement and build public trust (Reuters, 2024).
- **Utilizing Technology for Engagement**: Digital platforms and social media tools can enhance civic participation and transparency by providing accessible forums for discussion and information sharing. Apps and e-government services, already implemented in some sectors, could be expanded to improve interaction between local authorities and citizens.

Challenges in promoting engagement and transparency are:

- **Low Public Awareness and Political Culture**: Many citizens lack understanding of their rights to participate in local governance. This stems from a historical top-down governance model that discourages bottom-up civic involvement (Monks, 2017).
- **Restrictive Legal Frameworks**: Egyptian laws related to freedom of information and association collectively limit citizens' ability to engage with and monitor local authorities effectively.
- **Digital Divide**: While technology offers solutions, access remains unequal, especially in rural areas. Limited internet penetration and digital literacy hinder broader public participation.
- **Legal Reforms**: Enhancing legislation to ensure freedom of information and protect citizen rights to monitor and participate in local governance is crucial.
- **Investing in Digital Solutions**: Expanding e-governance tools and providing free internet access to underserved areas would bridge the digital divide and facilitate better engagement (AlAshry, 2022, p. 2).

5.3. Integrating Technology for More Efficient Governance

The adoption of technology has the potential to revolutionize local governance in Egypt, addressing inefficiencies and enhancing citizen engagement. By leveraging digital tools, local authorities can streamline operations, improve transparency, and foster inclusivity.

- **Digital Platforms**: Reduce bureaucracy and enhance accessibility. However, their reach is limited due to uneven internet penetration and technological literacy.
- **Electronic Payment Systems**: The integration of electronic payment systems for municipal services has begun, aiming to ensure transparency and reduce corruption. This aligns with Egypt's national digital transformation strategy (Ministry of Communications and Information Technology).
- **Geospatial Information Systems (GIS)**: GIS is increasingly used in urban planning and resource allocation, particularly in Cairo and Alexandria, to optimize service delivery and monitor development projects (Lewis N., 2024).

With increasing reliance on digital platforms, safeguarding sensitive government data and securing against cyberattacks are critical but under-addressed issues.

- **Infrastructure Investments**: Investments in infrastructure, especially in underserved areas, can bridge the digital divide and ensure equitable access to e-governance tools.
- **Public-Private Partnerships (PPPs)**: Collaborating with private-sector innovators can accelerate the development and deployment of advanced technologies, such as AI and IoT, for governance applications.
- **Data Management Practices**: Establishing robust cybersecurity measures and privacy controls can build public trust in digital governance (Bellamy, 2023).

CONCLUSION

The local government system in Egypt has faced significant challenges and undergone various changes over the past few decades. Historically centralized, Egypt's local administration structures have struggled with issues of independence, resource distribution, and transparency. Since the early 2000s, several legislative decentralization initiatives have been introduced, but their implementation has often been slow and inconsistent. Despite constitutional mandates and political will, local governments remain highly dependent on central authorities for decision-making and funding, limiting their ability to effectively address local needs. Furthermore, there exists a noticeable gap between the theoretical frameworks for decentralization and their practical application in Egypt's local administration.

One of the most pressing challenges facing local governance in Egypt is the lack of financial autonomy for local authorities. The central government's control over local budgets and expenditures stifles the capacity of local governments to invest in development, infrastructure, and services. Local councils, often heavily reliant on central allocations, struggle with insufficient resources to meet the growing demands of their populations. This dependence is particularly evident during times of economic strain when financial allocations to local governments are inadequate to address fundamental needs such as education, healthcare, and infrastructure development.

Additionally, civic participation in local governance remains weak. Despite efforts to enhance political engagement through municipal elections, low voter turnout and limited public awareness of local governance processes hinder effective democratic participation. This lack of engagement contributes to a transparency deficit in local governments, where corruption and mismanagement can often go unchecked. The failure to fully empower local councils with decision-making authority, coupled with a lack of robust civic participation, has created a situation where many Egyptians feel disconnected from the political process at the local level.

While Egypt's local government system faces significant challenges, the potential for reform remains high. The key to overcoming these obstacles lies in adopting more effective decentralization strategies, empowering local governments, and promoting active civic engagement. Only through these measures can Egypt aspire to create a more responsive, transparent, and accountable local governance system that meets the needs of its diverse and growing population.

REFERENCES

Aksu, D., & Akman, Ç. (2023). Mısır Arap Cumhuriyeti'nin Yerel Yönetim Yapısı: Karşılaştırmalı Bir Analiz. *Karadeniz Sosyal Bilimler Dergisi, 15*(28), 57–76. DOI: 10.38155/ksbd.1246159

AlAshry, M. S. (2022). A critical assessment of the impact of Egyptian laws on information access and dissemination by journalists. *Cogent Arts & Humanities, 9*(1), 2115243. DOI: 10.1080/23311983.2022.2115243

Andrew, S. (2022). *This town of 170,000 replaced some cops with medics and mental health workers. It's worked for over 30 years*. CNN.

Awad, H. (2022). *Centralised and Decentralised: The Authoritarian Upgrading of the Egyptian System of Local Governance*. Academic.

Bardhan, P., & Mookherjee, D. (2006). *Decentralization and Local Governance in Developing Countries: A Comparative Perspective*. The MIT Press. DOI: 10.7551/mitpress/2297.001.0001

Bellamy, F. D. (2023). *U.S. data privacy laws to enter new era in 2023*. Reuters.

Cheema, G. S., & Rondinelli, D. A. (2007). *Decentralizing Governance*. Brookings Institution Press.

El-Gamal, A. A., Ismail, M. M., & El Bagoury, A. A. (2025). The Role of Coordination Mechanisms Between the central Government and Local Administration Units. In *Improving the Performance of the Local Administration Bodies in Egypt* (pp. 325–330). Arab Journal of Administration.

Elsharkawy, S. (2022). *Decentralization in Egypt: More than 10 years of a stumbling path*. Arab Forum for Alternatıves.

Hanna, N. (2016). *The State and its Servants: Administration in Egypt from Ottoman Times to the Present*. American University in Cairo.

Harb, M., & Atallah, S. (2020). *Local Governments and Public Goods: Assessing Decentralization in the Arab World*. London College of Professional Studies.

Helbawy, H. E. (2024). *Decentralization as a Tool for Service Delivery and Development The Egyptian and Dutch Experience*. Urban Library.

Ibrahim, A. H. (2024). *Decentralization and its Impact on Improving Public Services*. University of North Maluku. DOI: 10.21744/ijss.v7n2.2278

Kessy, A. (2013). Decentralization and Citizens' Participation: Some Theoretical and Conceptual Perspectives: 219. Brill. kohli, A. (2004). State-Directed Development: Political Power and Industrialization in the Global Periphery p143-180. Cambridge.

Kurun, İ. (2015). *Democratisation in Egypt From A Historical Perspective: Problems, Pitfalls and Prospects*. Yönetim ve Ekonomi.

Lewis, N. (2024). A new city is rising in Egypt. But is it what the country needs? CNN world .

Martinez, J., & Timofeev, A. (2010). *Decentralizing Egypt: Not Just Another Economic Reform: 7-8*. International Center for Public Policy.

Miller, D. (2002). *The Regional Governing Of Metropolitan America*. Routledge.

Monks, K. (2017). Egypt plans new controls on social media. CNN world.

Morsy, A. (2015). *A Delayed Transition: Egypt's Suspended Elections*. Middle East Institute.

Mulder, F. (2023). The paradox of externally driven localisation: A case study on how local actors manage the contradictory legitimacy requirements of top-down bottom-up aid. *Journal of International Humanitarian Action*, *8*(1), 5–7. DOI: 10.1186/s41018-023-00139-0

Posner, P. W. (2011). *Democratization in Egypt: The Potential Role of Decentralization: 2-3*. The Urban Institute.

Reuters. (2024). Egypt PM says Saudi's planned $5 bln investment independent of cenbank deposit. Reuters.

Rondinelli, D. A., & Nellis, J. (1986). Assessing Decentralization Policies in Developing Countries: The Case for Cautious Optimism p3-23. Development policy review- Oxford.

Rutherford, B. K. (2013). *Egypt after Mubarak: Liberalism, Islam, and Democracy in the Arab World*. Princeton University Press.

Saleh, A. (2018). Local Councils in Egypt: Decentralization and the Dream of Political Action. The legal agenda .

Sayigh, Y. (2019). *Behind the Veil: Managing the Finances: 15*. Carnegie Middle East Center.

Shah, A. (Ed.). (2006). *Local governance in developing countries*. World Bank Publications.

Shantir, M. A. (2022). Decentralization and Geographical Inequality in Egypt. Arab reform initiative .

Sims, D. (2012). *Understanding Cairo: the logic of a city out of control*. The American University in Cairo.

Werr, P., & Lewis, A. (2023). *Egypt asset sales face obstacles as state maintains grip*. Reuters.

Chapter 2
Local Government Structure in Vietnam: Characteristics and Tasks

Nguyen Chi Hai
https://orcid.org/0000-0002-5975-1824
An Giang University, Vietnam & Vietnam National University Ho Chi Minh City, Vietnam

ABSTRACT

The book chapter provides a comprehensive view of local government in the state management system in Vietnam. The book chapter emphasizes three main contents: organizational structure, characteristics, and local government tasks. Local government is organized into three levels, including province, district, and commune. The book chapter analyzes the main characteristics of local government. The local government is responsible for development planning, budget management, infrastructure development, security and order, public service provision, resource management, and anti-corruption. The book chapter raises challenges such as human resource shortages, urbanization pressures, transparency requirements, and uneven budget allocation. Directions for administrative reform, capacity building of local civil servants, increased decentralization, and application of information technology are proposed. The book chapter affirms the important role of local government in sustainable development and the common prosperity of the whole country.

DOI: 10.4018/979-8-3373-5576-4.ch002

INTRODUCTION

The chapter on local government structure in Vietnam - characteristics and tasks aims to provide a comprehensive and systematic view of the organization, role, and responsibility of local government in the state management structure in Vietnam. The mission of the chapter is to help readers understand how local governments operate, thereby realizing the important role of local governments in economic and social development and ensuring people's lives. The chapter focuses on three core elements.

- Organizational structure
- Characteristics of local government
- Tasks and powers of local government

The organizational structure will explain the decentralization of local government in Vietnam into three levels, including provincial, district, and commune levels, with each level undertaking different tasks. However, it aims to serve the interests of the community. This structure ensures that Government policies are implemented consistently, facilitating flexibility in management at each local level, to adapt to the different economic, cultural, and social characteristics of each region.

The chapter analyzes the main characteristics of the local government system in Vietnam. Local governments must comply with government regulations but still have a certain autonomy in management. This is important in the modern context when each locality must develop by its capacity and conditions (An, 2023). The connection between the Communist Party of Vietnam and local governments is emphasized because local governments operate under the leadership of the Communist Party of Vietnam, which helps ensure unity and stability in the implementation of policies.

The chapter delves into the specific tasks that local governments must perform, including developing development plans, managing the budget, ensuring security and order, developing infrastructure, and providing public services such as health care, education, and environmental protection. These tasks help ensure people's lives and support the country's sustainable development. Understanding these tasks, readers can see the importance of local governments in maintaining and developing economic and social life in each region (Dao & Nguyen, 2015).

The main concern of the book chapter is how local governments can overcome current challenges such as human resource shortages, pressure from urbanization, and the need for transparency in management. The book chapter provides some orientations to improve and develop local governments, including administrative reform, increased decentralization, and capacity building for civil servants. The recommendations aim to help localities operate more effectively, creating a government that is close, transparent, and trustworthy to the people (Binh & Giai, 2021).

The mission of the book chapter is to build a solid knowledge foundation and help readers gain a deeper understanding of the local government system in Vietnam, its unique characteristics, and the necessary factors to develop a strong and sustainable local government, contributing to development.

OVERVIEW OF LOCAL GOVERNMENT IN VIETNAM

Local government in Vietnam plays an important role in the political system and state management, acting as a bridge between the central government and the people at the grassroots level. According to the Constitution of the Socialist Republic of Vietnam, local government is organized into three levels, including provincial level (including provinces and centrally run cities), the district level (including districts, towns, and provincial cities), and the commune level (including communes, wards, and towns). This system ensures unity in state management while allowing flexibility in meeting the requirements of socioeconomic development and administrative management in each specific area (Jutting et al., 2005).

Local government is the agency that implements the Party's guidelines and policies, the State's policies and laws in areas such as economy, culture, education, health, national defense, and security. In Vietnam, the local government system is not only built for management but also to develop social activities, protect the common interests of the community, and promote people's participation in state management (Adger, 2000).

The highlight of the local government system in Vietnam is the clear decentralization of management. The provincial level focuses on planning development strategies and coordinating and managing large resources. The district level performs the intermediary function, supervising the implementation of policies and laws at the commune level and organizing the implementation of tasks assigned by the provincial level. The commune level, as the level closest to the people, is directly responsible for daily issues such as household registration, land management, rural infrastructure construction, and ensuring security and order (Amoatey & Hayibor, 2017).

The structure of local government in Vietnam is designed to ensure the coordination between state power and people's participation. The People's Council, the local state power agency, is directly elected by the people and is responsible for supervising and deciding on important local issues. Meanwhile, the People's Committee, the local administrative agency, is responsible for organizing the implementation of the resolutions of the People's Council and the tasks assigned by higher levels.

In the current context, local governments face many challenges. Uneven socio-economic development among regions, pressure from urbanization, and increasing demands for transparency and accountability in state management have posed many difficult problems for local governments. In many places, financial resources are limited, and the management and enforcement capacity of local officials and civil servants has not met development requirements. Issues such as corruption, abuse of power, and unreasonable budget allocation are also major obstacles to the effectiveness of local governments (Alm et al., 2011).

To overcome these challenges, local governments should be comprehensively reformed to enhance management efficiency. Administrative reform, including simplifying procedures, and improving transparency and accountability, will help increase people's trust in the government. At the same time, it is necessary to improve the capacity of local officials and civil servants through training, professional development, and the use of information technology in management (Bardhan & Mookherjee, 2006). In addition, local authorities need to promote decentralization, and delegation of power, and grant more autonomy in management and socio-economic development, so that localities can be more proactive in solving their specific problems (Besley & Burgess, 2002).

In the future, to meet the requirements of the development and international integration process, local authorities in Vietnam need to continue to innovate and modernize management activities and increase transparency and efficiency in implementing tasks. Building a strong local government system with enough capacity to respond to challenges and take advantage of opportunities from the globalization process not only contributes significantly to the sustainable development of each locality but also of the whole country (Fritzen, 2006).

Local authorities in Vietnam are an indispensable part of the state management system. With a reasonable organizational structure, outstanding characteristics, and important roles, local authorities are both a management tool of the state and a place to directly approach and serve the interests of the people. Although there are many challenges, with appropriate reforms and the right development orientation, local authorities can become a solid foundation for Vietnam to achieve comprehensive and sustainable development goals in the future (Hue & Tung-Wen Sun, 2022).

LOCAL GOVERNMENT ORGANIZATIONAL STRUCTURE

The local government system in Vietnam is organized into three levels, each level has its structure and functions to suit each geographical feature and management requirements of each area.

Figure 1. Local government organization in Vietnam

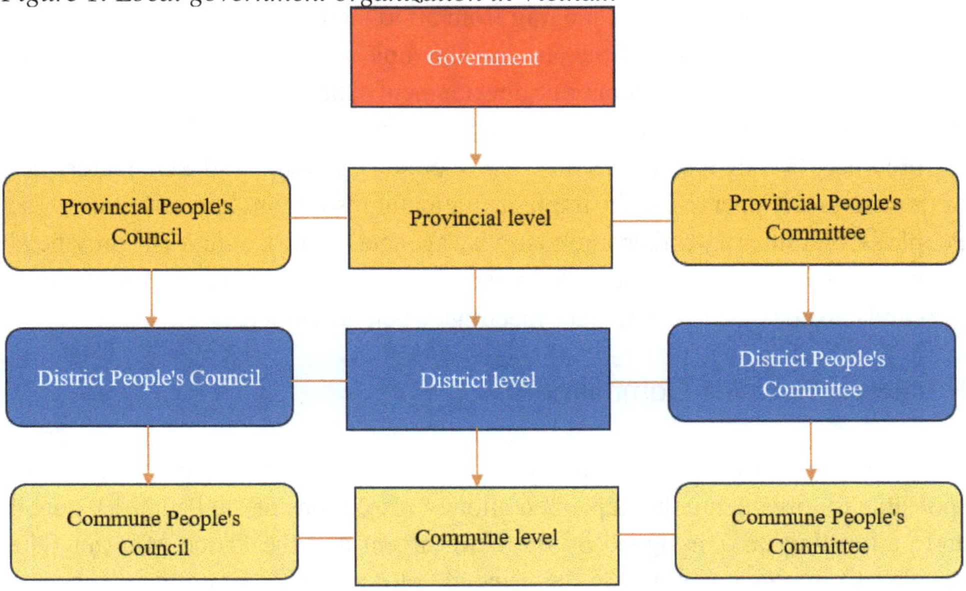

Provincial Level

The provincial local government in Vietnam is the highest level of management in the local government system, playing a strategic role in implementing the central government's policies and guidelines in localities and ensuring comprehensive socio-economic development within the province and centrally-run cities. According to the provisions of the 2013 Constitution and the 2015 Law on Organization of Local Government (amended and supplemented in 2019), the provincial government consists of the People's Council and the People's Committee.

Provincial People's Council

The People's Council is a local state power agency, directly elected by voters of the province. The provincial People's Council has the role of deciding on important issues of economy, culture, society, security, and national defense, as well as supervising the activities of the People's Committee and related agencies. The composition of the provincial People's Council includes people's representatives elected through universal suffrage. The number of delegates depends on the population size and characteristics of the province, ranging from 50 to 85 delegates.

The functions and tasks of the provincial People's Council include deciding on long-term and annual socio-economic development plans for the locality. Approving the local budget, and allocating financial resources to all levels of government in the province. Issuing resolutions on specific policies suitable to the characteristics of the province. Supervising the implementation of resolutions and activities of the People's Committee and other administrative agencies in the locality. The provincial People's Council operates under the plenary conference regime, meeting twice a year and can convene extraordinary meetings when necessary.

Provincial People's Committee

The Provincial People's Committee is a local state administrative agency, responsible for organizing the implementation of resolutions of the People's Council and performing tasks assigned by the Government and the Prime Minister. The People's Committee operates on the principle of democratic centralism, ensuring effectiveness and timeliness in administrative management. The composition of the Provincial People's Committee includes the Chairman of the People's Committee, Vice-Chairmen, and Members. The number of Vice Chairmen of the People's Committee ranges from 2 to 5 people, depending on the type of administrative unit (province, centrally-run city) and the socio-economic characteristics. The members of the People's Committee are leaders of the departments, branches, and sectors under the province.

The functions and tasks of the Provincial People's Committee include administrative management, and operating state administrative activities in the fields of economy, culture, health, education, environment, security, and national defense. Implementing the budget and managing public finance, organizing budget revenue and expenditure, and managing capital sources from the central and local levels to serve infrastructure development and public services.

The People's Council and the People's Committee at the provincial level have a close relationship, supporting each other to ensure effective state management at the local level. The People's Council plays a decisive and supervisory role, while the People's Committee is responsible for organizing implementation. The resolutions of the People's Council are the legal basis for the People's Committee to deploy programs and action plans. The People's Committee must periodically report on the implementation of tasks to the People's Council and is subject to the supervision of this agency.

The provincial government has a special role in coordinating between the Central Government and lower levels of local government, ensuring consistency in the implementation of national policies while still flexibly adapting to the characteristics of each province. Provinces such as Hanoi, Ho Chi Minh City, and Da Nang have made good use of the autonomy mechanism at the provincial level to promote socio-economic development, creating momentum for the whole country.

District Level

The district-level local government in Vietnam is an intermediate level in the administrative management system, playing a connecting role between the provincial and communal governments. According to the 2013 Constitution and the 2015 Law on Organization of Local Government (amended and supplemented in 2019), the district level includes districts, towns, provincial cities, and equivalent administrative units. The district-level government is organized with two main bodies: the People's Council and the People's Committee, which undertake the functions of administrative management and socio-economic development in the area.

District-Level People's Council

The District-level People's Council is a local state power agency, directly elected by voters in the district. The District-level People's Council has the role of deciding important issues within its management scope while supervising the activities of the People's Committee and related agencies. The composition and number of district-level People's Council delegates depend on the population size of each district, usually ranging from 30 to 50 delegates. The composition of district-level People's Council delegates includes individuals representing the local people, elected through universal, direct, and secret elections.

District People's Committee

The District People's Committee is a local state administrative agency, responsible for organizing the implementation of resolutions of the People's Council and performing tasks assigned by the Provincial People's Committee and the Government. The composition of the District People's Committee includes the Chairman of the People's Committee, who is the head, responsible for leading and directing all activities of the People's Committee and is responsible to the People's Council, the Provincial People's Committee, and the law. The Vice Chairman of the People's Committee is in charge of specific areas such as economy, culture - -society, and national defense - security. The members of the People's Committee are leaders of specialized departments such as the Department of Finance - Planning, the Department of Education and Training, the Department of Natural Resources and Environment, and other agencies.

Functions and tasks of the District People's Committee including Administrative management, organizing the implementation of legal policies and resolutions of the People's Council, and directing and operating administrative activities throughout the district. Managing the budget and public finance, making estimates, allocating budgets to communes and wards, and supervising the use of the budget. Socio-economic development, building and implementing development programs suitable to local characteristics, focusing on agriculture, industry, services, and trade. Managing land and resources, issuing land use rights certificates, protecting natural resources, and supervising exploitation activities.

Commune Level

The commune-level local government is the lowest and most basic level in the administrative system in Vietnam, close to the people, and plays an essential role in policy implementation, administrative management, and public service provision. According to the 2013 Constitution and the 2015 Law on Organization of Local Government (amended and supplemented in 2019), the commune-level government includes communes, wards, and towns. The commune-level government has two main bodies: the People's Council and the People's Committee, which undertake the functions of administrative management, operation, and socio-economic development within the locality.

Commune-Level People's Council

The commune-level People's Council is the state power agency in the locality, elected by voters on the principle of universal, direct, and secret ballot. The commune-level People's Council is the bridge between the government and the people, ensuring that management decisions are consistent with the aspirations of the community. The composition and number of delegates to the People's Council at the commune level ranges from 15 to 30 people, depending on the population size and natural area of the locality. The delegates to the People's Council at the commune level are trusted people, representing the will and aspirations of the community.

The functions and tasks of the People's Council at the commune level are to make resolutions on socio-economic development, security, national defense, budget, and other important issues within the commune. Supervise the activities of the People's Committee at the commune level, specialized agencies, and the implementation of resolutions. Decide on plans for infrastructure development, social welfare, and issues directly affecting people's lives. The People's Council at the commune level meets regularly twice a year and holds extraordinary meetings when necessary to resolve urgent issues.

Commune People's Committee

The Commune People's Committee is a local state administrative agency, responsible for organizing the implementation of resolutions of the People's Council and tasks assigned by the People's Committee at a higher level. The composition and structure of the Commune People's Committee includes the Chairman of the People's Committee, Vice Chairmen of the People's Committee, and members of the People's Committee. The Chairman of the People's Committee is the head, responsible for operating all activities of the People's Committee. The Vice Chairmen assist the Chairman in specific areas such as economics, culture-society, or security-defense. The members are leaders of departments and branches such as justice, finance accounting, land administration, culture-society, and military.

The functions and tasks of the Commune People's Committee include administrative management, handling administrative procedures related to household registration, granting land use right certificates, birth and death registration, and other public procedures. Manage budget and finance, organize commune budget revenue and expenditure, manage revenue sources from public services, and fees, and periodically report financial information. Develop socio-economic, organize agricultural and fishery extension activities, and promote production and business by local conditions.

The People's Council and the People's Committee at the commune level coordinate closely to ensure effective local governance. The People's Council decides on important issues through resolutions, while the People's Committee implements those resolutions. The People's Council has the right to supervise and request the People's Committee to report on the implementation of its tasks. This coordination helps maintain transparency and accountability in governance.

The commune-level government plays a special role in addressing people's daily issues, from basic administrative procedures to community development activities. In particular, in rural and remote areas, the commune level is the closest level of government to the people, playing an important role in implementing poverty reduction policies, economic development, and protecting traditional culture. The commune-level government is an important link in the local government system, contributing to maintaining unity from the central to the grassroots level and ensuring people's lives.

CHARACTERISTICS OF LOCAL GOVERNMENT IN VIETNAM

Local government in Vietnam is an important component of the state government system, with distinct characteristics reflecting the operating mechanism, role, and relationship with central government levels. These characteristics are shaped by the organizational structure, laws, and management practices in localities across the country.

Consistency in the Local Government System

Consistency is one of the outstanding and core characteristics of the local government system in Vietnam. This is an important principle to ensure a close connection between government levels, from central to local, helping to effectively implement the policies, laws, and guidelines of the Party and State nationwide.

Organizational Consistency

The local government system in Vietnam is organized into three levels, including provincial, district, and communal levels. Although each level of government has its functions and tasks, all operate under a common legal framework stipulated by the 2013 Constitution and related legal documents, such as the Law on Organization of Local Government 2015 (amended and supplemented in 2019). This ensures that local governments are organized and operated according to the same principles and legal framework.

At the provincial level, local governments focus on strategic planning, resource coordination, and comprehensive management.

At the district level, local governments assume the role of intermediary, implementing and monitoring policies from the provincial level down to the commune level.

At the commune level, local governments directly approach and solve issues related to the people, ensuring the implementation of policies in a specific and practical manner.

Unified Implementation of Laws and Policies

Local governments in Vietnam are under the overall leadership of the Communist Party of Vietnam and the centralized management of the State. Local governments at all levels are under the direct command of local Party organizations. This ensures that Party policies are implemented consistently, creating stability and unity in the political system. Local governments must strictly comply with the instructions, resolutions, and policies from the central level, ensuring that all local decisions are consistent with the overall development goals of the country. For example, socioeconomic development programs, such as the New Rural Development Program or the Sustainable Poverty Reduction Program, are implemented synchronously from the central to local levels, with unified implementation methods but still suitable to the specific conditions of each locality.

Unified Administrative Management

Local governments operate on the principle of clear decentralization and delegation of power, but must still ensure centralized control and management from the central government (Gaventa, 2004). This helps the central government to monitor, supervise, and promptly adjust the activities of local governments, avoiding arbitrary changes or lack of synchronization between levels.

Each level of local government has its authority in areas such as planning, budget management, and socio-economic development (Faguet, 2014). However, important decisions must be approved by a higher-level agency or by the national strategy. Local governments are subject to supervision by both the legislative (People's Council) and executive (People's Committee at a higher level), ensuring that all local activities are within the legal framework.

Unified local government systems play a key role in maintaining stability, efficiency, and synchronization in state management. Thanks to unity, major policies of the Party and State, such as economic development, environmental protection, or administrative reform, can be implemented synchronously and effectively nationwide. At the same time, unity also helps to minimize conflicts, overlaps, or contradictions between levels of government (Fukuyama, 2013).

Unity in the local government system in Vietnam is an important factor in ensuring cohesion and effectiveness in state management. Despite facing challenges such as regional differences and diverse development requirements, unity is still the foundation for the local government system to operate smoothly and contribute to the sustainable development of the country (Ngo et al., 2019).

High Autonomy in Local Management

Autonomy in local management in Vietnam is an important feature of the local government system, stipulated in the 2013 Constitution and the 2015 Law on Organization of Local Government (amended and supplemented in 2019). Autonomy helps local governments at all levels, including provinces, districts, and communes, to be flexible and proactive in making decisions and managing areas by the socioeconomic, cultural, and geographical characteristics of their localities. This is an important factor in promoting balanced, sustainable development appropriate to each region.

Autonomy in Policy-Making and Planning

Local governments have the right to formulate and implement socio-economic development plans by the overall strategy of the whole country but still meet the specific needs of the locality. The People's Councils at the provincial, district and communal levels have the authority to issue resolutions on important issues such as land use planning, infrastructure construction, cultural development, education, health care, and environmental protection. These resolutions are developed based on consultation with relevant parties and public opinions, ensuring feasibility and suitability to the actual situation (Gainsborough, 2003).

Financial Autonomy

One of the most obvious manifestations of autonomy is the ability to establish and manage a budget. Local governments have the authority to determine sources of budget revenue, including taxes, fees, charges, and revenues from public services. At the same time, localities have the right to decide on budget allocation for priority programs and projects such as infrastructure development, support for the poor, or improvement of public services. Financial autonomy not only increases the efficiency of resource use but also creates conditions for localities to develop according to their potential and strengths (Hill, 2024).

Autonomy in Personnel Management

Local governments have autonomy in recruiting, appointing, and using cadres and civil servants. This right allows localities to select personnel suitable to specific conditions and job requirements while promoting the improvement of capacity and efficiency of administrative apparatus.

Local governments at all levels have autonomy in organizing and providing public services such as health, education, water supply and drainage, environmental sanitation, and traffic management (Henry, 2015). Local governments can develop and implement priority policies, such as tuition exemptions for poor students or medical support for people in disadvantaged areas, depending on resources and actual conditions (Hope, 2001).

Autonomy in local management brings many benefits, including enhancing the effectiveness of administrative management and public service provision. Promoting the potential and strengths of each locality. Encouraging creativity and initiative of local governments in solving arising problems. However, autonomy also poses significant challenges, especially for localities with limited resources. Disparities in management and financial capacity among localities can lead to imbalanced development. In addition, without close supervision, autonomy can be abused, leading to corruption or ineffective management (Ho, 2002).

Monitoring and Accountability Mechanisms

The monitoring and accountability mechanisms in local governance in Vietnam are two important factors to ensure transparency, efficiency, and trust in the operations of local governments. This is the foundation for local governments to exercise their powers properly, comply with the law, and meet people's expectations (Lawrence et al., 2015).

The local monitoring mechanism is implemented through three main channels, including the People's Council, the higher-level state agency, and the people. The People's Council is the local state power agency, the People's Council is responsible for monitoring the operations of the People's Committee, administrative agencies, and organizations in the area. People's Council delegates are directly elected by voters, and have the right to question, request reports, and propose remedial measures if violations are detected. The People's Council holds regular meetings to evaluate and monitor the implementation of resolutions and tasks of the People's Committee.

Accountability is the requirement for local authorities to report and clarify their decisions, actions, and performance results to supervisory agencies and the people. Accountability in Vietnam is implemented through forms such as the People's Committee must present a report on the performance of its tasks to the People's Council at regular meetings or when there is a special request (Nguyen et al., 2017).

The monitoring and accountability mechanism helps to improve transparency, limit abuse of power and corruption, and increase people's trust in local authorities. Monitoring and accountability mechanisms in local governance in Vietnam are important tools to ensure that the government operates transparently, effectively, and by the law (Nguyen & Nguyen, 2022).

Aiming to Serve the People

In the local government system in Vietnam, aiming to serve the people is a basic and important principle, reflected in policies, management activities, and public service provision. Local governments at all levels (province, district, commune) play a central role in solving people's daily problems, ensuring that people's rights, needs, and aspirations are given top priority.

Local governments, especially the commune level, are the level closest to the people, directly responsible for handling basic administrative procedures such as birth registration, granting land use right certificates, household registration, and other public services. According to the report of the Ministry of Home Affairs in

2023, more than 70% of people's administrative requests are resolved at the commune level. This affirms the important role of grassroots governments in quickly and promptly responding to essential needs.

Local governments are responsible for providing essential public services, ensuring welfare, and improving the quality of life of the people (Birkmann et al., 2010). Key areas including Local primary health care systems, such as commune health stations, play an important role in primary health care, disease prevention, and implementation of national health programs. Local governments manage public schools, ensuring children in all localities have access to basic education, especially in remote and isolated areas. Construction and maintenance of roads, water supply, drainage systems, and public works to meet the living and economic development needs of the people (Kerkvliet, 2004).

To ensure that management decisions are consistent with the aspirations and interests of the community, local governments have increased channels of contact and dialogue with the people. Resident meetings, voter meetings, and online feedback mechanisms help people participate in contributing their opinions to local development policies, plans, and projects. Serving the people is the goal and principle of operation throughout local management in Vietnam (Marr, 2004).

DUTIES AND POWERS OF LOCAL GOVERNMENTS

Local governments in Vietnam are assigned a number of specific duties and powers to ensure effective state management in localities. These duties and powers aim to ensure effectiveness in administrative management, promote socio-economic development, ensure national defense and security, and meet the needs of people in each locality.

Making Socio-Economic Development Plans and Planning

Making socio-economic development plans and planning is one of the most important tasks of local governments in Vietnam. This is the process of orienting comprehensive and long-term development for localities, aiming to achieve economic, cultural, social, national defense, and security goals within the framework of the State's general laws and policies. This process is implemented synchronously from the commune, and district to provincial levels, ensuring compliance with the national development strategy while still meeting the specific characteristics and potentials of each locality (Faguet & Shami, 2008).

The main objective of planning and planning is to orient sustainable development and ensure economic growth associated with environmental protection, social security, and preservation of local cultural identity. Create conditions to maximize the exploitation of economic potential, natural resources, and local human resources. Meet the needs of infrastructure development, improve people's lives, and sustainably reduce poverty (Cuadrado-Ballesteros, 2014).

The planning and planning process is carried out through steps including data collection and assessment of the current situation, local authorities conduct surveys and collect data on the economy, population, resources, infrastructure, and other areas to serve as a basis for planning (Leonardsson & Rudd, 2015). Determining development goals, based on the national development strategy and local characteristics, local authorities determine priority goals, such as developing agriculture, industry, tourism, or services. Making detailed plans, specific programs and projects are built to achieve the set goals, including plans for developing transport infrastructure, improving the education system, health care, and environmental protection (Betsill & Bulkeley, 2021). Consultation and approval, local authorities organize meetings and workshops to consult with stakeholders, including people, businesses, and social organizations, before submitting the plan to the People's Council for approval. The main contents of local socio-economic development planning and plans often include

Land allocation for purposes such as agricultural production, infrastructure construction, nature conservation, and urban development.

Planning the construction of transport works, water supply and drainage, electricity, telecommunications, and public facilities.

Proposing measures to support poor households, promote vocational training, and create jobs.

Integrating solutions to protect natural resources, manage waste, and respond to climate change.

Developing programs to improve the quality of education, and health care, and promote cultural values.

The People's Council plays a decisive role in approving development plans and plans. The People's Committee is responsible for organizing the implementation and deployment of specific programs and projects and monitoring the progress and effectiveness of implementation. The People's Committee also coordinates with higher-level agencies and mobilizes the participation of people and businesses in the implementation process. Planning and making socio-economic development plans is an important task to help local authorities promote sustainable development, balancing economic growth, environmental protection, and improving the quality of life.

Public Budget and Financial Management

Public budget and financial management is an important task of local governments in Vietnam, aiming to ensure financial resources for socio-economic development activities, improve people's lives, and implement local public policies. This task is stipulated in the 2013 Constitution and the 2015 State Budget Law, ensuring that local governments at all levels manage their budgets effectively, transparently, and by the law.

Local governments prepare annual budget estimates, including revenue and expenditure estimates, in accordance with the socio-economic development orientation and financial policies of the State (Callanan, 2005). Budget estimates are built on the main sources of revenue, including taxes, fees, charges, and revenues from public services or local resources. The People's Councils at the provincial, district, and commune levels have the right to discuss, approve, and supervise the implementation of these estimates.

Local budgets are allocated to priority areas such as Infrastructure construction, investment in transportation, electricity, water, schools, hospitals, and public works. Socio-economic development, funding poverty reduction programs, supporting people in remote areas, and promoting the development of key economic sectors. Security and defense, ensuring security and order, national defense, and natural disaster prevention (Bonsón et al., 2015). Social welfare, investment in health, education, culture, and environmental protection. Local authorities have autonomy in deciding on budget allocation but must comply with the provisions of the State Budget Law and ensure the effective use of financial resources.

Local authorities implement budget revenues and expenditures in the locality according to approved plans (Meekel, 2008). Budget revenues include revenues from taxes, personal income tax, value-added tax, and non-agricultural land use tax. Revenues from fees, such as environmental protection fees, household registration fees, and household registration fees. Revenues from resources, revenues from natural resource exploitation, land use, or public services.

Local budget management activities are subject to supervision from many sides, including the People's Council which has the right to supervise, question, and request reports on budget implementation. The State Audit conducts inspections, evaluates budget implementation, and detects violations. Citizens can monitor and reflect on public financial management through information disclosure channels. Local administrative agencies must publicly disclose periodic financial reports, including budget estimates, budget settlements, and reports related to the use of public resources (Boex & Yilmaz, 2010).

Ensuring Social Security and Order

Ensuring social security and order is a key task of local authorities in Vietnam, aiming to maintain political stability, and community safety, and create a favorable environment for socio-economic development. Local authorities at all three levels (province, district, commune) closely coordinate with functional forces to deploy measures to maintain security and order and prevent threats to social stability.

Local authorities play a central role in organizing, managing, and coordinating activities to ensure security and order in the area. This is the level closest to the people, helping to promptly detect and prevent violations of the law and maintain a safe living environment. Local authorities not only carry out the tasks assigned by higher-level authorities but also proactively develop plans suitable to the specific situation of each locality (Fisher, 2022).

Local authorities regularly coordinate with police, military, and militia forces to carry out tasks of ensuring security and order. Activities include crime prevention, organizing patrols, controlling the area; detecting and handling violations of the law, such as theft, drug trafficking, and other crimes. Managing residence, monitoring the population situation, handling issues related to household registration, temporary residence, and temporary absence, contributing to crime prevention, and maintaining public order. Maintaining rural and urban security, coordinating the resolution of land disputes, complaints, and conflicts within the community, and avoiding major conflicts that affect local security (Cheema & Rondinelli, 2007).

Local authorities play an important role in disseminating and educating the law, raising people's awareness of their responsibility to maintain social order. Programs to disseminate the law, mobilize the masses to participate in maintaining security and order, and build the movement "All people protect national security" have been widely deployed in localities. Local authorities are responsible for organizing and operating response activities in emergencies such as natural disasters, fires, epidemics, or security incidents. Authorities closely coordinate with relevant agencies to minimize damage and quickly restore normal life for people.

Development and Management of Public Infrastructure

Development and management of public infrastructure is an important task of local governments in Vietnam, aiming to meet people's needs, promote socio-economic development, and improve people's quality of life. Public infrastructure includes transportation systems, water supply and drainage, electricity, telecommunications, schools, hospitals, and other public works. Local governments, with their close role to the people, undertake this task through planning, resource mobilization, implementation, and supervision (Dekker et al., 2015).

Local governments are responsible for developing infrastructure development plans by the local socio-economic development strategy and the national master plan. Water supply and drainage systems, developing clean water supply facilities, wastewater treatment, and drainage systems, ensuring environmental sanitation and public health. Education and health infrastructure, building schools, hospitals, and health centers in localities, especially in remote areas, to ensure equitable services for all people (Dick-Sagoe, 2020). Socialized sources, attract the participation of businesses, organizations, and communities in investing in infrastructure projects. International support, taking advantage of aid, loans, or international cooperation to invest in infrastructure development. Local authorities need to ensure transparent and effective use of resources, avoiding waste or loss (Fan et al., 2020).

Local authorities play a role in organizing the implementation of infrastructure projects from approval, and implementation, to construction supervision. During the implementation process, measures to control quality, progress, and costs are always given top priority. Supervision is not only carried out by management agencies but also through community participation to ensure that the project meets the actual needs of the people. Developing and managing public infrastructure is an essential task of local governments, contributing significantly to improving the quality of life and promoting sustainable development (McCarty, 2001).

Handling Complaints, Denunciations, and Preventing Corruption

Handling complaints, denunciations, and preventing corruption is a key task in the state management activities of local governments in Vietnam. This task aims to protect the legitimate rights of the people, enhance transparency and responsibility in management, and maintain social order and discipline. This is also an important tool to enhance people's trust in the government.

Local governments are responsible for receiving, considering, and handling complaints and denunciations from individuals and organizations in the area according to the provisions of the law, especially the Law on Complaints 2011 and the Law on Denunciations 2018. This process is carried out through the following steps: Initial reception and processing, complaint and denunciation petitions are submitted to the People's Committees at all levels. The officer in charge receives, classifies, and forwards the dossier to the competent authority for settlement. Local authorities conduct investigations and verifications of complaints and denunciations to draw accurate and objective conclusions. Resolve and notify the results. After coming to conclusions, local authorities notify the people of the results and take remedial measures. Local authorities also organize direct dialogues with people in complicated cases, thereby finding reasonable solutions and limiting prolonged conflicts (Morgan & Trinh, 2017).

Local authorities coordinate with relevant agencies such as the Inspectorate and the State Audit to inspect and supervise the implementation of tasks with high risks of corruption, such as land management, project bidding, and budget use. Officials who commit corrupt acts will be strictly handled according to the provisions of the law, thereby deterring and preventing corruption. Resolving complaints and denunciations and preventing corruption are key tasks of local authorities, contributing to maintaining social order, protecting people's rights, and building a clean state apparatus.

CHALLENGES AND FUTURE DEVELOPMENT DIRECTIONS

Local governments in Vietnam play a central role in implementing central policies and ensuring sustainable development in each locality. However, in the context of globalization, urbanization, and rapid technological development, local governments are facing many major challenges, requiring appropriate development directions to improve management efficiency and serve the people (Pham et al., 2022).

Human Resource Issues

Human resources are a key factor determining the operational efficiency and sustainable development of local governments in Vietnam. However, in the context of innovation and international integration, the issue of quality and quantity of human resources in local governments has become one of the biggest challenges, requiring clear and effective development directions in the future (Yilmaz & Venugopal, 2013).

The cadres and civil servants in localities also face challenges in improving their professional qualifications, management skills, and use of information technology. With the increase of modern management requirements, such as e-government, digital governance, and digital tools, many officials are still limited in applying technology to their work, affecting the effectiveness of management and service to the people (Ola, 2021).

The problem of human resources in local governments stems from many causes. Limitations in training and fostering civil servants, many localities lack continuous and in-depth training programs for cadres and civil servants, leading to a failure to update new knowledge and skills promptly. The remuneration policy is not attractive for recruitment, income and remuneration in disadvantaged localities are not competitive enough to attract talent, especially young, highly qualified cadres

(Nguyen et al., 2018). In remote areas, opportunities for promotion and learning of cadres are often limited, leading to a mentality of not wanting to work long-term in the locality. Uneven socio-economic development between regions causes human resources to be concentrated in large cities, causing imbalance.

Local authorities should improve their remuneration policies, and apply attractive salary and bonus policies, allowances, and financial support to retain talent, especially in disadvantaged areas. Invest in building modern facilities and equipment at local government agencies to create a more favorable and professional working environment (Ostrom, 2010).

Human resources are a decisive factor for the success of local authorities in implementing policies, meeting people's needs, and promoting socio-economic development. To address current challenges, local authorities should focus on training innovation, improving remuneration policies, and creating career development opportunities for officials and civil servants (Painter, 2003). Effective investment in human resources not only helps improve local management capacity but also contributes to building a strong local government system that meets the requirements of the integration and development period.

Pressure from Urbanization and Economic Development

Urbanization and economic development are taking place at a rapid pace in Vietnam, bringing many opportunities but also creating great pressure on local authorities in management and sustainable development. Vietnam's urbanization rate reached about 41% in 2023 (General Statistics Office), and is expected to continue to increase strongly in the coming years, as large cities and suburban areas become economic centers, attracting labor and investment. However, this process poses many challenges for local authorities in infrastructure management, social security, the environment, and the balance between economic growth and cultural preservation.

Urbanization puts great pressure on urban infrastructure systems and the management capacity of local authorities. Rapid population growth in large cities leads to serious overload in traffic, water supply and drainage, waste treatment, and housing. For example, traffic congestion in Hanoi and Ho Chi Minh City is a serious problem, causing great economic and quality of life losses. Urbanization is often concentrated in economically developed areas, while rural, remote, and isolated areas are left behind, leading to imbalances in resource and labor allocation. The process of migration from rural to urban areas increases social problems such as lack of housing, schools, medical facilities, and the risk of slum formation (Rhodes, 2018).

Developing satellite urban areas and economic zones in rural areas to create local jobs and reduce pressure on migration to cities (Rodríguez-Pose & Kroijer, 2009).

Urbanization and economic development pose great challenges but also open up development opportunities for localities in Vietnam. Local authorities need to orient sustainable development, balance economic growth and environmental protection, invest in infrastructure and public services, and promote people's participation in urban management. Only by properly addressing the pressures from urbanization and the economy can local authorities ensure a sustainable development future and improve the quality of life for the community.

Corruption and Transparency

Corruption and transparency are important issues in administrative management and socio-economic development, especially at the local government level. Corruption not only undermines people's trust in the management apparatus but also wastes resources, hinders development, and increases social inequality. In the context of Vietnam promoting administrative reform and building a rule-of-law state, addressing corruption and enhancing transparency are urgent tasks, requiring strong commitment and synchronous solutions from local governments.

The cause of this problem is the lack of an effective monitoring system, inspection and examination work in some localities is still formalistic, and not strong enough to detect and handle corrupt acts. Lack of transparency of information, work procedures, and information related to land management, public finance, and investment projects are often not fully disclosed, making it difficult for people to monitor. Some local officials and civil servants lack a sense of responsibility and take advantage of loopholes in legal regulations for personal gain. Corruption handling measures are not strict, leading to low prevention effectiveness (Rodríguez-Pose & Ezcurra, 2010).

To address corruption and enhance transparency, local governments need to implement clear and effective development orientations. Local governments need to increase the disclosure of information related to planning, budgets, and public investment projects on local electronic information portals, creating conditions for people and businesses to easily access. Apply technology platforms such as e-government and digital databases to manage more transparently and reduce direct contact between officials and people, thereby reducing the risk of corruption. Develop a mechanism to protect the safety and rights of those who report corruption, ensuring that they are not retaliated against or discriminated against (Woodside, 2020).

Uneven Budget Allocation

Budget allocation is one of the important tasks of local governments to ensure financial resources for socio-economic development activities and improve the quality of life of the people. However, in Vietnam, the budget allocation among localities is still inadequate, with clear differences between economically developed regions and poor areas, especially remote areas. This situation not only causes difficulties for disadvantaged localities but also creates major challenges in ensuring balanced and sustainable development nationwide (Wescott, 2003).

This leads to an imbalance in infrastructure development, public services, and poverty reduction programs. Rich localities are able to invest in large projects, improving the quality of life for people, while poor localities have difficulty meeting basic needs, from building roads, and schools to providing health and education services.

To address the uneven budget allocation, local and central governments need to implement specific development orientations, focusing on improving the financial decentralization system and increasing the efficiency of budget use. Reform the budget allocation system, build a fairer allocation mechanism, and ensure that poor localities receive sufficient financial resources to develop infrastructure and basic public services, while still encouraging rich localities to promote their financial autonomy. Use an electronic financial management system to monitor budget allocation and use, minimize losses, and ensure transparency (Robinson, 2015).

Implement separate financial support programs for poor, remote, and isolated areas to build infrastructure and develop the economy. Support poor localities to improve the quality of human resources, creating conditions for sustainable economic development. Promote investment attraction, tax reform, and development of local economic sectors to increase budget revenue. Local authorities need to develop specific budget use plans, prioritizing high-benefit projects and minimizing waste. Strengthen the role of People's Councils, Inspectorates, State Auditors, and the community in monitoring budget allocation and use (Smoke, 2015).

The uneven allocation of budget is one of the major challenges for local authorities in Vietnam, hindering balanced development between regions. To overcome this, it is necessary to build a more equitable, transparent, and effective budget allocation mechanism while increasing support for poor localities and promoting financial autonomy. Only by solving this problem can local authorities ensure comprehensive and sustainable development, contributing to narrowing the socio-economic gap between regions and building a country with even development.

Promoting Administrative Reform and Information Technology Application

Administrative reform and information technology application are becoming one of the key development orientations of local governments in Vietnam in the context of strong international integration and digital transformation. This is not only an important solution to improve the efficiency of state management, but also the key to improving the quality of public services, creating convenience for people and businesses, while enhancing transparency and minimizing corruption in the administrative apparatus (Shah & Thompson, 2004).

Administrative reform in localities has achieved many positive results in recent years. According to the 2023 Administrative Reform Index Report, many provinces and cities such as Quang Ninh, Da Nang, Hanoi, and Ho Chi Minh City are in the leading group in terms of management efficiency and administrative procedure reform. However, in reality, some localities, especially in remote areas, still face many difficulties such as cumbersome administrative procedures, slow processing time, and lack of transparency.

The application of information technology (IT) in local state management has also developed significantly. As of 2023, 98% of provincial administrative agencies have deployed online public service portals, and 85% of commune-level administrative procedures have been digitized. However, the application of IT is still uneven, many places still lack infrastructure, and the qualifications of staff do not meet the requirements of using technology, leading to low efficiency.

Administrative reform and IT applications play an important role in improving the efficiency of local government operations. It helps simplify administrative procedures, cut unnecessary procedures, shorten the time to process records and create convenience for people and businesses. Administrative reform and IT application are inevitable trends to improve the efficiency of local government operations and better meet the needs of people and businesses in the digital transformation period. However, to achieve this goal, local authorities need to invest heavily in technology infrastructure, improve human resource capacity, and build appropriate policy mechanisms. When implemented synchronously, administrative reform and IT not only help improve the quality of public services but also create momentum for the sustainable development of localities, contributing to building a modern, transparent, and effective administration in Vietnam (Vu & McIntyre-Mills, 2008).

Strengthening People's Participation

People's participation in local management and development activities is one of the core factors in building a transparent, effective, and community-friendly local government. In the context of Vietnam promoting administrative reform and sustainable development, strengthening people's participation is not only a requirement but also an important development orientation of local governments in the future (Stoker, 2017).

To promote the role of people in local development, the government needs to build a transparent and accessible participation mechanism. The government needs to make information related to planning, budgets, and development projects transparent, making it easy for people to access and understand so that they can participate in contributing their opinions. Increase the use of online channels such as electronic information portals and mobile applications to receive people's opinions, especially in areas with good technology infrastructure (Thanh & Canh, 2019).

Encourage people to participate in organizations that monitor public projects, land management activities, and budget spending at the local level. There should be a mechanism to encourage people to report violations and corruption in management while protecting the rights of whistleblowers. The government needs to disseminate knowledge about the law, rights, and obligations of citizens in participating in local management, especially in rural areas and ethnic minorities (Trung et al., 2023). Organize courses and seminars so that people, especially young people, can better understand the state management process and how to participate effectively.

Increasing people's participation helps create more appropriate public policies, minimizing the risk of waste and loss of resources. At the same time, it strengthens people's trust in the government, creating a close, consensual relationship between the government and the community. When people actively participate, they also become an important factor in monitoring and enhancing the transparency and accountability of local governments (Saito, 2008).

CONCLUSION

Local governments in Vietnam play an important role in maintaining order, developing the socio-economy, and ensuring the welfare of people in each region. In the context of the country promoting innovation, international integration, and digital transformation, local governments are not only a bridge between the Central Government and the people but also a key force in implementing development policies and programs effectively and practically. However, to fulfill their mission, local governments must face many challenges and require strong innovation.

The chapter has clarified the organizational structure, characteristics, and role of local governments in the state management system in Vietnam. With a three-level structure: province, district, and commune, local governments operate under the unified leadership of the Communist Party of Vietnam, ensuring consistency in policy implementation while still being flexible to meet the specific needs of each locality. Important tasks such as planning for socio-economic development, budget management, ensuring security and order, developing infrastructure, and providing public services are carried out by local authorities to achieve the goal of sustainable development and improving the quality of life of the people.

The local government system is still facing many challenges such as the disparity in resources between localities, pressure from urbanization and economic development, corruption, and lack of transparency, as well as the need for administrative reform and improving management capacity. These issues require more synchronous and effective development orientations and solutions in the future.

Local government is an important link in the state management system, playing an irreplaceable role in promoting the development of each region and the whole country. Although there are still many challenges, with the right orientation and determination to reform, local government is fully capable of developing strongly, contributing to the prosperity and stability of the country. This chapter hopes to provide a comprehensive and in-depth view of local government in Vietnam while suggesting feasible solutions to build a more effective, transparent, and sustainable management system in the future.

REFERENCES

Adger, W. N. (2000). Institutional adaptation to environmental risk under the transition in Vietnam. *Annals of the Association of American Geographers, 90*(4), 738–758. DOI: 10.1111/0004-5608.00220

Alm, J., Buschman, R. D., & Sjoquist, D. L. (2011). Rethinking local government reliance on the property tax. *Regional Science and Urban Economics, 41*(4), 320–331. DOI: 10.1016/j.regsciurbeco.2011.03.006

Amoatey, C., & Hayibor, M. V. K. (2017). Critical success factors for local government project stakeholder management. *Built Environment Project and Asset Management, 7*(2), 143–156. DOI: 10.1108/BEPAM-07-2016-0030

An, D. T. (2023). The Role of Local Government in Private Investment Intentions: A Case Study in Vietnam. *International Journal of Sustainable Development and Planning, 18*(2), 439–446. DOI: 10.18280/ijsdp.180212

Bardhan, P., & Mookherjee, D. (2006). *Decentralization, corruption, and government accountability: An overview. Handbook of Economic Corruption*. Edward Elgar Publishing. DOI: 10.4337/9781847203106.00013

Besley, T., & Burgess, R. (2002). The political economy of government responsiveness: Theory and evidence from India. *The Quarterly Journal of Economics, 117*(4), 1415–1451. DOI: 10.1162/003355302320935061

Betsill, M. M., & Bulkeley, H. (2021). Cities and the multilevel governance of global climate change. In *Understanding Global Cooperation* (pp. 219–236). Brill. DOI: 10.1163/9789004462601_014

Binh, N. T., & Giai, N. Q. (2021). Study on Citizen participation in local governance in Vietnam. *NISPAcee Journal of Public Administration and Policy, 14*(2), 87–109. DOI: 10.2478/nispa-2021-0016

Birkmann, J., Garschagen, M., Kraas, F., & Quang, N. (2010). Adaptive urban governance: New challenges for the second generation of urban adaptation strategies to climate change. *Sustainability Science, 5*(2), 185–206. DOI: 10.1007/s11625-010-0111-3

Boex, J., & Yilmaz, S. (2010). An analytical framework for assessing decentralized local governance and the local public sector. *Urban Institute Working Paper*.

Bonsón, E., Royo, S., & Ratkai, M. (2015). Citizens' engagement on local governments' Facebook sites. An empirical analysis: The impact of different media and content types in Western Europe. *Government Information Quarterly*, *32*(1), 52–62. DOI: 10.1016/j.giq.2014.11.001

Callanan, M. (2005). Institutionalizing participation and governance? New participative structures in local government in Ireland. *Public Administration*, *83*(4), 909–929. DOI: 10.1111/j.0033-3298.2005.00483.x

Cheema, G. S., & Rondinelli, D. A. (Eds.). (2007). *Decentralizing governance: Emerging concepts and practices*. Brookings Institution Press.

Cuadrado-Ballesteros, B. (2014). The impact of functional decentralization and externalization on local government transparency. *Government Information Quarterly*, *31*(2), 265–277. DOI: 10.1016/j.giq.2013.10.012

Dao, T. H. M., & Nguyen, T. A. T. (2015). Citizen-centered local governance in Vietnam: The participation at local level. *Citizen Participation in Selected Local Governance of Asia Pacific Countries*, 111-128.

Dekker, R., Emilsson, H., Krieger, B., & Scholten, P. (2015). A local dimension of integration policies? A comparative study of Berlin, Malmö, and Rotterdam. *The International Migration Review*, *49*(3), 633–658. DOI: 10.1111/imre.12133

Dick-Sagoe, C. (2020). Decentralization for improving the provision of public services in developing countries: A critical review. *Cogent Economics & Finance*, *8*(1), 1804036. DOI: 10.1080/23322039.2020.1804036

Faguet, J. P. (2014). Decentralization and governance. *World Development*, *53*, 2–13. DOI: 10.1016/j.worlddev.2013.01.002

Faguet, J. P., & Shami, M. (2008). Fiscal decentralization and local government performance. *World Development*, *36*(9), 1653–1679.

Fan, X., Qiu, S., & Sun, Y. (2020). Land finance dependence and urban land marketization in China: The perspective of strategic choice of local governments on land transfer. *Land Use Policy*, *99*, 105023. DOI: 10.1016/j.landusepol.2020.105023

Fisher, R. C. (2022). *State and local public finance*. Routledge. DOI: 10.4324/9781003030645

Fritzen, S. A. (2006). Probing system limits: Decentralisation and local political accountability in Vietnam. *Asia Pacific Journal of Public Administration*, *28*(1), 1–23. DOI: 10.1080/23276665.2006.10779312

Fukuyama, F. (2013). What is governance? *Governance: An International Journal of Policy, Administration and Institutions, 26*(3), 347–368. DOI: 10.1111/gove.12035

Gainsborough, M. (2003). *Changing political economy of Vietnam: the case of Ho Chi Minh City*. Routledge. DOI: 10.4324/9780203222317

Gaventa, J. (2004). Participatory development or participatory democracy? Linking participatory approaches to policy and governance. *IDS Bulletin, 35*(2), 1–11. DOI: 10.1111/j.1759-5436.2002.tb00020.x

Henry, N. (2015). *Public administration and public affairs*. Routledge.

Hill, D. M. (2024). *Democratic theory and local government*. Taylor & Francis. DOI: 10.4324/9781003583561

Ho, A. T. K. (2002). Reinventing local governments and the e-government initiative. *Public Administration Review, 62*(4), 434–444. DOI: 10.1111/0033-3352.00197

Hope, K. R. (2001). The new public management: Context and practice in Africa. *International Public Management Journal, 4*(2), 119–134. DOI: 10.1016/S1096-7494(01)00053-8

Hue, T. H. H., & Tung-Wen Sun, M. (2022). Democratic governance: Examining the Influence of citizen participation on local government performance in Vietnam. *International Journal of Public Administration, 45*(1), 4–22. DOI: 10.1080/01900692.2021.1939713

Jutting, J., Corsi, E., & Stockmayer, A. (2005). Decentralization and poverty reduction. *OECD Development Centre Working Paper*, 236.

Kerkvliet, B. J. T. (2004). Surveying local government and authority in contemporary Vietnam. *Beyond Hanoi: local government in Vietnam*, 1-27.

Lawrence, J., Sullivan, F., Lash, A., Ide, G., Cameron, C., & McGlinchey, L. (2015). Adapting to changing climate risk by local government in New Zealand: Institutional practice barriers and enablers. *Local Environment, 20*(3), 298–320. DOI: 10.1080/13549839.2013.839643

Leonardsson, H., & Rudd, G. (2015). The 'local turn' in peacebuilding: A literature review of effective and emancipatory local peacebuilding. *Third World Quarterly, 36*(5), 825–839. DOI: 10.1080/01436597.2015.1029905

Marr, D. G. (2004). A brief history of local government in Vietnam. *Beyond Hanoi: local government in Vietnam*, 28-53.

McCarty, A. (2001, March). Governance institutions and incentive structures in Vietnam. In *Conference on Building Institutional Capacity in Asia: Public Sector Challenges and Government Reforms in South East Asia;* 12 March; Jakarta.

Meekel, T. (2008). Local government finance in Serbia. In *Local public finance in Central and Eastern Europe* (pp. 364–390). Edward Elgar Publishing. DOI: 10.4337/9781035305124.00022

Morgan, P. J., & Trinh, L. Q. (2017). Fiscal decentralization and local budget deficits in Viet Nam: An empirical analysis. In *Central and Local Government Relations in Asia* (pp. 333–368). Edward Elgar Publishing. DOI: 10.4337/9781786436870.00019

Ngo, H. V., Edelenbos, J., & Gianoli, A. (2019). Community participation and local government capacity in Vietnam: Conditions for coproduction. *Public Administration and Development, 39*(2), 104–118. DOI: 10.1002/pad.1844

Nguyen, B., Mickiewicz, T., & Du, J. (2018). Local governance and business performance in Vietnam: The transaction costs' perspective. *Regional Studies, 52*(4), 542–557. DOI: 10.1080/00343404.2017.1341625

Nguyen, T. B., & Nguyen, Q. G. (2022). Transparency in Local Government in Vietnam. *Scientific Papers of the University of Pardubice. Series D. Faculty of Economics and Administration, 30*(2).

Nguyen, T. V., Bach, T. N., Le, T. Q., & Le, C. Q. (2017). Local governance, corruption, and public service quality: Evidence from a national survey in Vietnam. *International Journal of Public Sector Management, 30*(2), 137–153. DOI: 10.1108/IJPSM-08-2016-0128

Ola, R. O. (2021). *Local administration in Nigeria.* Routledge. DOI: 10.4324/9781003209546

Ostrom, E. (2010). Beyond markets and states: Polycentric governance of complex economic systems. *The American Economic Review, 100*(3), 641–672. DOI: 10.1257/aer.100.3.641

Painter, M. (2003). Public administration reform in Vietnam: Problems and prospects. *Public Administration and Development, 23*(3), 259–271. DOI: 10.1002/pad.249

Pham, T. H., Hoang, T. T. H., Thalassinos, E. I., & Le, H. A. (2022). The impact of quality of public administration on local economic growth in Vietnam. *Journal of Risk and Financial Management, 15*(4), 158. DOI: 10.3390/jrfm15040158

Rhodes, R. A. W. (2018). *Control and power in central-local government relations.* Routledge. DOI: 10.4324/9780429463518

Robinson, R. I. (2015). *Postwar Market for State and Local Government Securities*. Princeton University Press.

Rodríguez-Pose, A., & Ezcurra, R. (2010). Does decentralization matter for regional disparities? *Journal of Economic Geography*, *10*(5), 619–644. DOI: 10.1093/jeg/lbp049

Rodríguez-Pose, A., & Kroijer, A. (2009). Fiscal decentralization and economic growth in Central and Eastern Europe. *Growth and Change*, *40*(3), 387–417. DOI: 10.1111/j.1468-2257.2009.00488.x

Saito, F. (2008). *Foundations for local governance: Decentralization in comparative perspective*. Springer. DOI: 10.1007/978-3-7908-2006-5

Shah, A., & Thompson, T. (2004). Implementing decentralized local governance: A treacherous road with potholes, detours, and road closures. *World Bank Policy Research Working Paper*, *3353*, 1–27.

Smoke, P. (2015). Rethinking decentralization: Assessing challenges to a popular public sector reform. *Public Administration and Development*, *35*(2), 97–112. DOI: 10.1002/pad.1703

Stoker, G. (2017). *Transforming local governance: from Thatcherism to New Labour*. Bloomsbury Publishing.

Thanh, S. D., & Canh, N. P. (2019). Local governance: Impacts of fiscal decentralization on government size and spending composition in Vietnam. *Asian Economic Journal*, *33*(4), 311–340. DOI: 10.1111/asej.12189

Trung, N. S., Phuong, D. T., Thanh, B. T., & Dien, B. X. (2023). The organization of local government in Vietnam. *Russian Law Journal*, *11*(3), 1010–1017.

Vu, M. T. T., & McIntyre-Mills, J. J. (2008). Towards local government strategic planning in Vietnam: Systemic governance interventions for sustainability. *Asian Social Science*, *4*(2), 91–105.

Wescott, C. G. (2003). Hierarchies, networks and local government in Viet Nam. *International Public Management Review*, *4*(2), 20–40.

Woodside, A. B. (2020). *Vietnam and the Chinese model: A comparative study of Vietnamese and Chinese government in the first half of the nineteenth century* (Vol. 140). BRILL.

Yilmaz, S., & Venugopal, V. (2013). Local government discretion and accountability in Philippines. *Journal of International Development*, *25*(2), 227–250. DOI: 10.1002/jid.1687

Chapter 3
Italy's Local Government Structure, Functioning, and Practices

Hasibe Ceyhan
https://orcid.org/0000-0002-6551-0787
Karamanoğlu Mehmetbey Üniversitesi, Karaman, Turkey

ABSTRACT

In this respect, the main purpose of this study is to analyze the local government system of Italy, a European country with a similar central government approach to Turkey. In this study, the functioning of these four levels of Italian local government and the functioning, powers and responsibilities of their subordinate bodies will be analyzed. In addition, the powers and duties of local administration types, their financial relations, audit practices and their comparison with Turkey are also included.

INTRODUCTION

The profound change and transformation in the understanding of public administration in the globalizing world has also affected local government processes. With this process of change, important reforms have been realized in local governments, and the capacity to respond to social and social needs that will ensure effectiveness at the international level has been established. This process has made significant contributions to the integration of Europe and, of course, Turkey, and opened the door to a change in the understanding of local government and major reforms. It is widely accepted that the most important changes that can be expected from the reforms are the development of local interests, the enhancement of tools and capacities that will enable local governments to be effective on the international stage,

DOI: 10.4018/979-8-3373-5576-4.ch003

and the improvement of their capabilities in public-private partnerships. While these developments have further increased the quality and efficiency of the services provided by local governments to the public, they have also brought to the fore the establishment of measurement and evaluation systems and performance measurement in local governments, which are necessary in terms of savings.

In order to make their central structures stronger, world states have sought a series of policies that aim to provide solutions to local governments, which are shaped according to the wishes and needs of the people, both administratively, financially and politically. In particular, the policies adopted by European states have been shaped in a way to strengthen the principle of subsidiarity on the axis of participatory governance. This administrative structuring, in which the wishes and expectations of the people are taken into account to a great extent, has made it necessary to evaluate the needs of the society within the framework of development, effectiveness, fast and efficient service delivery, economy and frugality criteria. In this framework, the administrative structure, functioning mechanism and management approach of local governments in the Republic of Italy, which is the main subject of this chapter, have changed over time. After the establishment of national unity in Italy in 1870 and the dictatorial regime after the Second World War, the transformation to a democratic regime was realized with the referendum held in 1948 and the existence of local administration structures consisting of regions, provinces and municipalities was also accepted. In this respect, the main purpose of this study is to analyze the local government system of Italy, a European country with a similar central government approach to Turkey.

In presenting our study, we first aim to give a general information about the main social indicators, political, administrative and economic structure of Italy. In our study By looking at the administrative structure of Italy from a historical perspective, the constitutional and legal foundations of its administrative structure will be briefly examined. In addition, local government units, which will constitute the main part of our study, will be discussed separately. With the 1948 Constitution, Italy defined its local governments as three-tier, and later on, with the amendment made in the 1990 Constitution, it increased its local governments to four tiers. These four levels are composed of municipalities that provide social services, economic development services and regulatory services, provinces, whose function has recently weakened due to the strengthening of regions and municipalities, metropolitan cities, and regions, which have an important role because they work in cooperation with the central structure. In this study, the functioning of these four levels of Italian local government and the functioning, powers and responsibilities of their subordinate bodies will be analyzed. In addition, the powers and duties of local administration types, their financial relations, audit practices and their comparison with Turkey are also included.

1. GENERAL INFORMATION ABOUT ITALY AND ITS HISTORICAL DEVELOPMENT

Officially known as the Republic of Italy, Italy is located on a peninsula stretching from the south of Europe to the Mediterranean Sea in a northwest-southeast direction, with a surface area of 301,338 km2. Italy borders France to the northwest, Switzerland and Austria to the north, Slovenia to the northeast, the Mediterranean Sea to the south and west, the Adriatic Sea to the east and the Alps to the north. The islands of Sicily and Sardinia in the Mediterranean Sea and many islands around the peninsula belong to Italy, while the town of Campione on the shores of Lake Lugano is officially recognized as Italian territory, although it is completely separate from Italian territory. In addition, there are two independent countries within its territory, the Vatican State in Rome, which is the religious capital of the Catholic sect, with an area of 0.44 km2, and the Republic of San Marino, the oldest living republic in Europe, with an area of 481 km2 (T.C. Ministry of Trade Italy Country Profile, 2024: 3). As of 2024, Italy has a population of 58,819,000, its capital is Rome, its currency is the Euro (€), its language is Italian and its form of government is the Republic, which operates as a multi-party and parliamentary democracy (T.C. Ministry of Foreign Affairs, 2025). As Italy has a geography stretching from north to south, the climate varies from region to region. Although temperatures vary from region to region during the winter months, almost all parts of the country are sunny except for the high areas in the north in summer and the highest temperatures during the day are around 30 degrees (T.C. Ministry of Trade Italy Country Profile, 2024: 4). Italy, a country experiencing population growth, is one of the countries with the lowest birth rate in the world. Italy has the world's oldest population after Japan and Germany, with population growth driven by immigration from abroad. The country's ethnic structure consists of Italians, Romanians, North Africans, Africans (Sub-Saharan), Albanians, Asians, Chinese, Ukrainians, Latin Americans. The ratio of the number of unemployed in the country to the total labor force was determined as 7.7% in 2023, and in addition, the ratio of immigrants to the total population is expected to double to 13.6% in 2030. Moreover, looking at the sectoral distribution in the country, 3.9% of the population is employed in agriculture, 28.3% in industry and 67.8% in the services sector (Republic of Turkey Ministry of Trade Italy Country Profile, 2024: 4-5). With a GDP of USD 2.328 trillion as of 2024, Italy is the 4th largest economy in Europe and the 8th largest in the world. Italy is a founding member of the European Union and its main trading partners are Germany, France, the USA, Spain, China, the Netherlands and the UK. The organizations it is a member of are international organizations such as the UN, EU, NATO, OSCE, G-7, G-20, which operate in the world and Europe, as well as technical regulatory bodies. Italy's main export products are machinery and transportation vehicles, chemical products, fertilizers and plastic materials, pharmaceuticals and pharmacology products, textiles, products derived from refined petroleum and automobile and motor vehicle accessories. Imports include transport equipment, crude oil, chemical products, fertilizers and plastic materials, pharmaceuticals and pharmacological products, precious metals and natural gas. Italy is at the forefront of pumice, pozzolana and feldspar production. Another important underground resource is marble, in particular the world-famous white Carrara marble from the Massa and Carrara quarries in Tuscany. In the last decade, Italy has become one of the world's largest producers of renewable energy, second largest in the European Union after Germany and ninth in the world (Ministry of Foreign Affairs, 2025). In addition, the manufacturing sector, which is very strong in the Italian economy, has been the second largest producer in Europe and the sixth largest in the world for the last 30 years. Major industrial products include automotive, shipbuilding, chemicals, furniture, clothing and textiles, leather goods and footwear, food processing, ceramic products, parts and machinery. Italy is Europe's second largest producer of machinery after Germany and the third largest producer in the pharmaceutical industry (Ankara Chamber of Commerce, 2020). Our country realized a trade volume of approximately 26 billion dollars with Italy in 2022 and approximately 27.3 billion dollars in 2023. Italy is Turkey's 5th largest exporter and 6th largest importer, and more than 1,500 companies with Italian capital operate in Turkey. In 2023, 600 thousand Italian tourists visited Turkey. As one of the leading countries supporting Turkey's EU membership, Italy is one of Turkey's most important trade partners (Republic of Turkey Ministry of Foreign Affairs, 2025). In terms of the historical process, political unity in Italy was achieved as a result of the War of Independence led by Garibaldi in 1866, following the re-establishment of the Kingdom of Italy (Risorgimento) in 1861. Following the Prussian-French War of 1870-71, an independent nation-state was established with the expulsion of the last remaining French forces (Republic of Turkey Ministry of Foreign Affairs, 2025). Italy, one of the favorite countries of the West, has been a country of wars and revolutions throughout history. In the XIIth century, 'City States' with their own military power, their own assemblies and elected leaders developed. Italy gained its national unity as a member of the Napoleonic Empire in 1802 but lost it again when the empire collapsed. Italy was under dictatorship for nearly twenty years during the first and second world wars, It ensured its political integrity by taking the French public administration system as a model (Koçak, 1996: 58). Since June 2, 1946, Italy, which has been governed as a democratic republic, abolished the royal system in the country as a result of a referendum and the Italian Constitution entered into force on January 1, 1948. In the Italian Republic, the executive, headed by the president, is carried out by the council of ministers. The legislative branch is carried out jointly by the national assembly and the council of ministers, and the judiciary carries out its work independently of the legislative and executive branches

(Arıkboğa, 2021: 505). The international organizations of which Italy is a member are the European Union (EU), World Trade Organization (WTO), United Nations (UN), Council of Europe, North Atlantic Treaty Organization (NATO), International Monetary Fund (IMF), Organization for Economic Cooperation and Development (OECD) (Republic of Turkey Ministry of Trade Italy Country Profile, 2024: 4-5).

2. POLITICAL AND ADMINISTRATIVE STRUCTURE OF ITALY

Historical events have shaped the administrative structure of Italy, which has been home to many European civilizations for centuries. The Renaissance movement was born in the Tuscany region of Italy and spread throughout Europe from there. In addition, Rome, the capital of Italy, has been the center of Western civilization and the Catholic Church for centuries (Larousse, 1981). Italy, a unitary state governed by a democratic parliamentary system, can be divided into three administrative and political periods. The first is the liberal period, which started with the establishment of the kingdom and the declaration of independence in 1861 and continued until 1922. The second one is the fascist period, which started in 1922 when Mussolini came to power and lasted until 1943. The third period is the reconstruction period, which covers the period after 1943. The main principles regarding the political and administrative structure of the country were regulated by the Constitution that entered into force in 1948 (Koşar, 2013: 328). Article 5 of the Italian Constitution states that "*The one and indivisible Republic recognizes and strengthens local autonomy; it fully implements administrative decentralization in the services subordinate to the State; it harmonizes its legislation, principles and methods with the requirements of autonomy and decentralization*". Within the framework of this constitutional provision, Italy is a unitary state that includes elements of political decentralization (Tortop, 1996: 63). Under the Constitution, the President is appointed by the Parliament and the legislature is composed of two chambers, the National Assembly and the Senate. The President appoints the Prime Minister and the cabinet, which must receive the vote of confidence of both houses (Küçük, 2019: 10). In Italy, which has a bicameral parliamentary structure as the National Assembly and the Senate, members of parliament are elected by the people every five years. Members of the National Assembly, with 630 representatives, are elected on a national basis, while members of the Senate, with 315 representatives, are elected on a regional basis in proportion to the population of the region in question. The President of the Republic is elected for seven years by a committee consisting of delegates from both houses (Arıkboğa, 2021: 505). The duties and powers of the President, who is the head of state, can be listed as follows: "*to dissolve Parliament or one of the two chambers after consultation with the presidents of the chambers, to issue orders for the election of new chambers, to appoint ministers on the recommendation of the prime minister, to issue decrees and by-laws, to fix the dates of meetings, to authorize the submission of draft laws to the chambers, 'to promulgate laws, to appoint state officials in cases specified by law, to hold referendums, to ratify international agreements with parliamentary approval, to declare war with parliamentary approval, to grant amnesty, to reduce penalties, to award various ranks and decorations"* (Şan, 2011: 92). In this context, the functioning of the legislative, executive and judicial powers is organized as follows. First of all, the laws that come before the Senate and the National Assembly, which are elected and have similar responsibilities within the sphere of action of the legislature, must be passed by both houses. Members of the Senate are elected every five years and the voting age for the Senate is 25 and the election age is 40. Elections for members of the National Assembly are held every five years and the country is divided into 32 electoral districts for parliamentary elections. In addition, according to the proportional representation system, between 4 and 50 members of parliament are elected in each electoral district (Şan, 2011: 92). While the executive system in Italy is based on a parliamentary structure, the judicial system operates under the Ministry of Justice. In the judicial system guaranteed by Article 104 of the Constitution, the judiciary is administered by civil and criminal courts, the Council of State in Rome is the appellate authority for the decisions of administrative courts, and the Court of Accounts is the judicial authority for public accounts. A Supreme Council of the Judiciary has been established to regulate and supervise the functioning of the judiciary, and the constitutional judicial function is carried out by the Constitutional Court in Italy (Şan, 2011:92).

3. ITALY'S LOCAL GOVERNMENT SYSTEM AND LEGAL FOUNDATIONS

The history of local governments in Italy, which completed its national unity later than other countries on the European continent, dates back to the 12th century. The functioning of both local and central government was determined through the Bonapartist administrative structure established during the Napoleonic period from 1802 to 1814 (Toksöz et al., 2009: 97). Italy, which is a unitary state, is a regional state and autonomy is provided to regional governments by giving them legislative authority. Despite the autonomous structure, Italy is not a federal country and regional governments are local government units (Raffer & Padovani, 2019:142). Until regional governments gained a legal basis in Italy, they faced many obstacles due to the fear that the centralist governance structure could be threatened by regional governance. The concern over the deterioration of national unity was seen as a threat by most of the ruling elites and regional governments were opposed (Olivetti,

2014: 148). Over time, the autonomy granted to regional governments by the central government in Italy was built from the top down. Regional governments were given the power to make laws except for the issues that are within the competence of the central government (Baldini & Baldi, 2014: 90-97). In this respect, local governments in Italy are regulated in the fifth chapter of the Constitution, Articles 114 - 133, which states that "The Republic is divided into regions, provinces and communes. Communes, provinces, metropolitan cities and regions are autonomous organizations with their own statutes, powers and responsibilities, according to the principles laid down in the Constitution" (Italian Constitution of 1948, art. 114). The Italian Constitution defines local governments as regions, provinces and communes, while preserving the unity and indivisibility of the State. According to the principles enshrined in the Constitution, local government units are autonomous, with their own status, powers and specific spheres of action and functions. Although Italy is divided into regional administrative levels, the power of government is mostly centered in Rome (Kelly, 1998: 232). Local government units, which were defined in three levels by the 1948 Constitution of the Republic of Italy, were strengthened by the Law on Local Authorities enacted in 1982 (Ulusoy and Akdemir, 2006: 127), and later, with the reform of the Constitution in 1990, local governments were strengthened by including metropolitan cities in the local government level. Law No. 142/1990 aimed to expand the scope of autonomy by granting local governments significant administrative and financial powers (Iannello, 2002: 2). In 1990 and 1999, important laws were passed on the establishment of metropolitan cities, but no results were achieved. In 2001, a constitutional amendment gave metropolitan cities a constitutional status as a unit of local government. The Delrio Law, passed in 2014 and enacted in 2015, made it possible to establish metropolitan cities, but the establishment of metropolitan cities remained on paper for 14 years. The Delrio Law of 2014 is a revolutionary law in terms of the restructuring of local governments and is extremely important in terms of its wide range of powers and responsibilities and its vertical and horizontal redistribution. In addition to the establishment of metropolitan cities, it also includes the reshaping of provincial governments and municipal unions, the reduction of small municipalities, changes in the election procedure of provincial government bodies, and the transformation of some provincial governments into metropolitan governments. After the law came into force, the president and council members of the provincial administration were not elected directly by the people, but by the municipal councils within the provincial borders through elections among themselves. Many activities performed by the provincial administration were transferred to regional administrations and municipal unions, and although the law aimed to abolish the provincial administration completely, it was not possible (Arıkboğa, 2021: 506-507).

In Italy, a large part of public services are carried out by municipalities, provinces and regions in a broad and effective decentralization, and governors, who serve as the representative of the central government, work at the provincial and regional level (Toksöz et al, 2009: 92). As a result, the Constitution of the Republic of Italy defines the state as single and indivisible, accepts local autonomy and ensures the widest application of decentralization principles in the fulfillment of public services.

3.1. Local Government Units and Institutional Structures in Italy

With the 1948 Constitution, Italy defined local governments as three levels (regions, provinces and municipalities) and with an amendment made in the 1990 Constitution, metropolitan cities were included in the local government level. Today, the number of regional administrations in Italy is 20, the total number of provincial administrations and metropolitan cities is over 100, and the number of municipalities is over 7900 (Toksöz, 2009: 91).

There are four levels of local government in Italy: Regions, Provinces, Metropolitan cities and Municipalities.

Regional (Region) Government: Regions are of great importance in the formation of the central state in Italy in 1861. This is because the historical process that the regions have gone through has led them to form an autonomous structure. There are twenty regions in Italy, 5 with special status and 15 with ordinary status. Regional administrations have three main organs: the president, the regional assembly and the executive box. The legislative and decision-making body of the regional administration is the regional assembly, which is elected at the provincial level by different competing lists. The number of members in the regional assembly varies between 30-80, proportional to the population of the region, and is elected directly by the people every 5 years. The regional assembly has a government commissioner who coordinates between the services provided by the region and the tasks of the center. The regional assembly also has the power to dismiss the president and the executive council. The president is elected by the people of the region, but in regions that have not accepted popular election of the president, the president is elected by the regional assembly. The president issues regional laws and regulations, sets regional policies, presides over meetings of the regional assembly and the regional executive board, appoints members of provincial and municipal control committees, and represents the region vis-à-vis the central administration. In regions where the president is directly elected by the people, the president appoints the members of the councillors. There is no requirement to be a member of parliament to be a councillor.

The municipal budget is approved by the regional assembly. Another body of the regional administration is the board of directors (Giunta). The members of this board, the executive body of the regional administration, are elected by majority vote. It is composed of the president and officials appointed by the president for a five-year term. The general duties of the Board of Directors are to manage the properties of the region within the framework of the law, to control the administrative organization of the region, to take necessary actions and to accompany the decision taken by the regional assembly (Koşar, 2013: 332-333).

In addition, the duties of the Board of Directors, which is the executive body, can be listed as follows (Erbay & Akgün, 2017:5-6)

- Implement the laws and policies adopted by the Regional Assembly,
- Prepare the budget and annual balance sheet of the region sent to the Assembly, and make transfers between certain parts of the budget when necessary,
- To ensure the realization of public works projects in the region,
- Enter into contracts with other legal entities on behalf of the region,
- To carry out the necessary work on disposals, sales and other issues related to the assets and debts of the Region,
- To carry out all financial and other planning and programming related to the region,
- To take the necessary initiative to determine whether any regional or State Law is constitutional.

Regional administrations have the authority to take and execute regulatory actions within the framework of legal regulations. In this context, it is possible to list the duties of regional administrations within the framework of Article 118 of the Italian Constitution as follows (Ulusoy & Akdemir, 2006:127-128):

- Health and social assistance services,
- Local museum and library services,
- Tourism and hospitality industry services,
- Intra-regional transportation and urban planning services,
- Agriculture and forestry,
- Urban and rural police services,
- Fire brigade and marketplace services,
- Occupational Health Safety
- Health protection, sport, food
- Urban planning, large and small scale transportation networks
- Other duties assigned by law.

Legislative power, one of the most important powers for the functioning of regional governments, is limited by the Constitution, European Union rules and international obligations. The regional assemblies legislate within the framework of the basic principles of the laws enacted by the Italian Parliament, with a primary concern for the national interest, provided that they do not infringe the interests of the other regions. Regions can determine and change their own status and can apply to the national parliament for legislation. The regions elect the President of Italy, with three elected members of each regional assembly voting together with the parliament in the election of the president. Regions have absolute authority over their own budgets and municipal unions as well as municipal consortia are supervised by the region. In terms of local participation and the functioning of local democracy within the framework of the governance structure of the regions, citizens living in the region have the right to hold referendums and, if necessary, to initiate referendums on laws and administrative decisions concerning the region. How these rights are exercised is determined within the authority of the regional administration (Toksöz, 2009: 97-98).

Provincial Governments: Although provinces in Italy have lost their importance in the face of the gradual strengthening of municipalities and regions, they continue to play a role in the state mechanism due to political functioning. The provincial administration, which constitutes the weakest link among local government units, has a governor appointed by the Council of Ministers, who is responsible for the functioning of decentralized state services in the provinces, supervises and coordinates state affairs. The governor has the authority to ensure public security and order, to enforce the laws enacted throughout the country, to follow certain public health affairs, and to control the legality of the decisions of the provincial general assembly (Geray, 1997:62-65).

There are three organs of provincial government: the Provincial Assembly, the Provincial Council and the Provincial President. The 2014 Delrio Law introduced a system of direct popular election of the provincial president and the provincial council. was abolished. After the Delrio Law, the function of the provincial government was significantly reduced and many of its functions were transferred to metropolitan cities, municipalities or regional governments under the necessary legislation. The provincial council is the decision-making body of the province and is elected by universal suffrage for a term of 4 years. The number of members varies between 24-45 depending on the population of the province and the provincial assembly elects a president and a councillor from among its members. Seats in the assembly are allocated according to the proportional representation system, which gives weight to the majority party. The provincial council is the executive body of the province, consisting of a president, a vice-president and other members. The maximum number of members of the provincial council is 8. The provincial council determines the policies of the provincial administration and approves the budget, within the scope of its powers granted to it by law. It submits its work to the parliament annually and may also submit proposals to the parliament. The provincial mayor is elected for a four-year term by the mayor and councillors within the province. The provincial president carries out activities within the scope of action permitted by law. He also ensures and supervises the fulfillment of the functions assigned by the municipality and regional administration (Küçük, 2019: 17).

The duties of the provincial administration can be listed as follows (Vesperini, 2011: 6):

- Budget setting and management,
- Determination of tax and fee rates,
- Supporting middle and high schools,
- Construction and repair of roads, planning of public transportation
- Environmental planning, protection and social services,
- Ensuring public order.

Metropolitan Cities: In the local government reform in Italy in the 1990s, the idea of establishing a metropolitan city system in large urban settlements instead of provincial governments was put forward (Italian Constitution, art.114), but with the constitutional amendment in 2001, metropolitan cities were included in the Constitution as a local government unit. Metropolitan cities, which are based on the idea of a stronger urban structure in which large municipalities merge with neighborhoods and economic and social integration is achieved, have never been established due to deficiencies in the law, the electoral system and the management structure of metropolitan cities not being fully determined, and the lack of interest of regional governments (Boggero, 2016: 4). With Law 42/2009 of 2009, metropolitan cities, like other local government units, have financial resources, revenue and expenditure autonomy and independent financial resources (Italian Constitution, art. 119). In the following process, the Delrio Law 56/2014 of 2014 established metropolitan city governments in 10 cities, including Milan, Venice and Rome, and these metropolitan cities had to take over the tasks carried out by the provincial governments delegated to them by the law. In 2009, the Reggio Calabria region became a metropolitan city, Palermo, Messina and Catania in 2015 and Cagliari in 2016. Article 142 of the 1948 Italian Constitution granted metropolitan city status to the provinces of Turin, Milan, Genoa, Bologna, Florence, Rome, Bari, Naples and Cagliari. By the autonomous regions individualized metropolitan areas are Trieste in the Firuli-Venezia Giulia region, Cagliari, Catania, Messina in Sardinia and Palermo in Sicily (Küçük, 2019: 15). Among these, the Metropolitan Cities covering the largest area are Turin (6,827 km2) and Rome (5,363 km2), while at the other extreme are Milan (1,576 km2), Genoa (1,834 km2) and Naples (1,179 km2). Turin and Milan cover 315 and 134 municipalities, respectively, compared to 42 and 41 for Bari. In terms of wealth generated, Milan, Rome and Turin rank highest for value added (Coşkun et al, 2019: 308).

In metropolitan cities, the decision-making body is the metropolitan city council and the executive body is the Metropolitan Giun ta, as in provincial local governments. Certain rules, such as the process of formation and election of the metropolitan city council, have been adopted in the same way. The metropolitan government is headed by the metropolitan mayor, who is elected in a similar way to the election procedure for the mayor of the provincial government. The president represents the metropolitan administration, makes appointments and additionally chairs the Giunta council. The metropolitan council takes basic decisions, directs the administrative unit and carries out the necessary inspections (Tortop, 1996: 66).

It is possible to list the duties of metropolitan cities as follows (Arıkboğa, 2021: 513-514):

- Roads, traffic, transportation, planning, protection of environmental values within the city's infrastructure services,
- Management of the communication network, as well as water and electricity services,
- Annual revision of the three-year master plan and economic development,
- Regional planning and health services in wider areas,
- Coordination of vocational training, school services and urban service activities
- Determination of taxes and fees.

Municipalities: Although the history of municipalities in Italy dates back to the period of the royal constitution, the current boundaries of the municipalities were drawn in 1861 and became autonomous according to the constitution implemented in 1947. As decentralized institutions, municipalities are authorized in areas outside the competence of central government, regional governments, provincial governments and metropolitan cities in line with the principles of differentiation and competence of the Italian Constitution (Governo Italiano, 2025).

Municipalities have three organs. These are: The mayor, the municipal council and the city board. The mayor is elected directly by the people for a five-year term and is the head of the municipal council administration. He is responsible for the implementation and supervision of decisions taken by the city council and the city board, contracts signed and other municipal affairs. The mayor may delegate some of his or her duties to his or her self-appointed deputies and sets the agendas of the council and the board of directors. The mayor presides over the meetings of the municipal council, represents the municipality in court, publishes the laws, regulations and proclamations of the state since he is an official of the central government. The mayor also appoints the members of the municipal council (Tortop, 1996: 67). The municipal council is elected by the population for a five-year term. The municipal council is the decision-making body of the municipality and is responsible for the activities of municipal affairs planning and control over matters falling within its sphere is ensured by the municipal council. In addition, the municipal budget is approved by the municipal council. The number of councillors varies according to the size of the municipality, with proportional representation in municipalities over five thousand inhabitants. The Municipal Council acts as the executive body of the municipality and is also called the "Municipal Giunta". The Municipal Council is composed of the mayor and members. The number of members of the municipal council varies according to the population of the municipality and is obliged to implement the decisions taken by the municipal council (Ulusoy and Akdemir, 2013: 155).

The duties and powers that municipalities must fulfill within the framework of the law are as follows (Arıkboğa, 2021: 513):

- Local security, police services
- Education Services (construction of school buildings, school bus services)
- Social Assistance Services (Shelters, disability assistance, etc.)
- Urban planning (Housing land registry, construction and trade permits)
- Cultural and entertainment services (museums, theaters, exhibition halls, etc.)
- Economic development (making the necessary plans for trade)

In addition, the scope of action of municipalities includes economic development services and supervision of commercial activities, development of tourism and agriculture, registration of births, marriages and deaths, and military service.

3.2. Financial Structure and Control of Local Government Units in Italy

The functioning of local government finances in Italy is generally characterized by fiscal autonomy. According to the constitutional amendment of 2001, it is mandatory to establish a financing system for local government revenues that will enable them to fulfill the tasks assigned to them. In this respect, local governments in Italy are financed by taxes, aids, borrowing and other sources. In other words, the main sources of income of local government units in Italy are taxes, funds provided by the central government and revenues from citizens' expenditures. These revenues constitute 87% of the total budget of local government units (Bohlooli Zamani and Dessì, 2017).

Article 119 of the Italian Constitution regulates the sources of revenue of local governments, and the main principles are set out as follows (Governo Italiano, 2020):

> *"Municipalities, provincial governments, metropolitan cities and regions have revenue and expenditure autonomy. Communes, provinces, metropolitan cities and regions shall have independent financial resources. They may impose taxes and collect their own revenues in accordance with the Constitution and according to the principles of coordination of state finances and the tax system. They receive a share of the tax revenues related to their territory".*

The law ensuring fiscal autonomy has put into practice the necessary arrangements regarding the revenues of local governments within the framework of the following three principles (Toksöz et al., 2009: 100):

1. Local authorities may impose taxes and fees in accordance with the principles of public finance provided for by law.
2. An administration may receive a share of national taxes collected in its geographical area.
3. A stabilization fund could be established for local governments in underdeveloped regions with weak financial capacity, from which resources could be transferred to local governments in these regions.

In Italy, where the 2003 Financing Law put into effect, which put into practice important laws that could interfere with the above-mentioned local government autonomy, the rate of regional tax on productive investments and the rate of additional tax on national income tax levied through regions and municipalities were frozen, but the gap between revenues and expenditures was compensated through aids (Tortop, 2011:67-70). Implemented in 2009, the "Fiscal Federalism Law" is considered as a turning point for the country, which aims to improve the sphere of influence, responsibility and fiscal autonomy of local and regional governments and to provide adequate revenue sources for the needed issues. In addition, more of the allocated own tax revenues and shares from national taxes were transferred to local governments (Arıkboğa, 2021: 513).

In Italy, the most important source of taxation for regional governments is the regional tax on economic activity, called IRAP (imposta regionale sulle attivita produttive), but there is also a share of central government taxes, as well as additional taxes and state aid to local governments. Autonomous regions, on the other hand, can only impose taxes in areas authorized by law, and regions can receive a share of the Value Added Tax collected in that region to finance the health sector. Other examples of regional government revenues include fees for the authorization of the use of public goods, fees for phytosanitary activities, university tuition fees, and fees for professional activity permits (Council of Europe, 2017: 48-49).

Unlike regional governments, the revenues of provincial administrations in Italy are regulated by law and are granted more limited fiscal autonomy compared to other units of government. As a result of the reforms undertaken in the country, the main revenues of provincial governments include state aid, independent tax revenues, shared taxes, additional taxes and borrowing. The tax source of provincial governments consists of additional taxes added to both central government taxes and municipal taxes. These taxes include vehicle registration tax, tax on the use of public lands, taxes on services provided to citizens in the provinces, and environmental protection. Moreover, the authority to determine the rates of these taxes belongs to the provincial government and provinces in Italy follow the same borrowing procedure as municipalities (Arıkboğa, 2004:87).

Regulations on municipal revenues were made within the framework of laws, just like in the provinces. The ability of municipalities to establish their own tax system is limited. While municipalities do not have autonomous taxing powers as provinces and regions do, the rate and base of taxes collected by municipalities are determined at the national level. Municipal revenues Tax revenues account for 60% of municipal revenues and have a significant share. These taxes include IMU (impostamunicipalepropria) levied on property owners as part of the property tax, TASI (tax for indivisible services) public tax on lighting and street cleaning, TARI (tassa sui rifiuti, tax on refuse) garbage tax on waste collection and disposal, municipal advertising and promotion taxes on public advertisements, and revenues from the additional rate added by municipalities to the national income tax. Another important revenue for municipalities is fees, and municipalities are given more freedom to determine the rate of fees compared to tax revenues. Fees on the use of public lands and fees on public advertisements constitute the revenues that municipalities receive from fees. Another important source of revenue for municipalities to fulfill their duties is aid, and the aid system of provincial governments shares the same characteristics with municipalities. Municipalities receive three types of transfer revenues: recurrent funds that finance basic ordinary services, conditional funds that finance special expenditures, and matching funds that aim to adjust local differences in the tax base (Arıkboğa, 2004:88).

The sources of revenue of metropolitan city governments are different for each region across the country, but the general practice is that revenues consist of funds transferred from the Italian central government. At this point, the constitution grants local governments both revenue and expenditure autonomy and the authority to impose taxes. The Italian central government basically manages the financial resources by collecting income taxes and distributing these revenues to different levels according to the needs (Coşkun et al., 2019: 311).

Regarding the supervision of local governments, Article 125 of the Italian Constitution states that "*Guardianship control over the operations of the territory shall be exercised by the organs of the State in accordance with the procedures and principles established by the laws of the Republic, and for this purpose administrative judicial bodies shall be established*". This law reinforces the idea that there is a heavy administrative tutelage over local governments. This is due to the fact that Italy has a unitary structure. Again, based on Article 125 of the Constitution, the actions and practices of local administrations in Italy are controlled by the central administration or through commissions established on its behalf in terms of compliance with the law. The administrative acts of the regions are supervised by an audit commission chaired by the regional governor and composed of judges, civil servants and experts, while the administrative acts of provinces and municipalities are carried out by a regional body, the regional audit committee. This commission is selected by the regional ambassador from among experts such as law professors, civil servants, judges, etc., and the commission checks the legality of administrative acts through parliamentary decisions. Only decisions taken by assemblies are subject to control. Decisions of the executive body are subject to review at the request of the executive committee of the local government assembly or a number of its members. These decisions are considered to have entered into force if they are not annulled by the committee within 20 days. Constitutional reforms have changed the mechanism of supervision (Koşar, 2013: 343-344).

As a result, both the delegation of authority from the central government to local governments and all kinds of public services carried out by local governments within the framework of their partial autonomy have been carried out in a way to take into account the wishes and welfare of the people. In this framework, local In 2002, the autonomy of regional taxes was frozen, reducing the tax burden by freezing the autonomy of regional taxes and cutting transfers to the government, which was reinstated in 2006. Subsequently, local autonomy was regulated by parliament, allowing for the determination of expenditures and the liberal provision of local services.

4. COMPARISON OF LOCAL GOVERNMENT SYSTEMS IN ITALY AND TÜRKIYE

When comparing the local government systems of Italy and Turkey, it is important to provide information about Turkey's political and administrative structure as well as its local government system. Since the above-mentioned topics provide information about Italy's political and administrative structure as well as its local governments, we can briefly mention the following information for Turkey.

In terms of Turkey's political and administrative structure, Turkey is a unitary state and while the parliamentary government system was in effect before 2018, the presidential government system has been in effect since 2018. In Turkey, where a centralist approach to governance prevails, the legislature is unicameral (the Turkish Grand National Assembly), the executive is dual-headed (the President and the Council of Ministers) in the pre-2018 period and unicameral executive (the President) in the post-2018 period, and the judicial system is dualist. State organization in Turkey is carried out in the form of centralized administration and decentralized administration in accordance with the principle of integrity of administration (Usta, 2021: 44-45). When we look at Turkey's local administration, local government organizations are included in the country's administrative integrity. Local governments, which have almost a century and a half of history in the country, carry out services under three headings as Special Provincial Administration, Municipality and Village and have an important role in the development of democratic life. There are also "local administrations" which are similar to local governments but do not have legal personality. The principles of establishment of local governments, their fields of action regarding their duties and powers, and their financial systems are determined by legislative bodies and local governments are not included in the hierarchical structure of the central government. Local governments are controlled by the central government for compliance with the law and the rules that local governments must comply with in terms of national integrity are also determined by the central government (Kavruk, 2021)

Article 123 of the 1982 Constitution states that "*the organization and functions of the administration shall be based on the principles of centralized administration and decentralization" and Article 127 of the 1982 Constitution states that "Local administrations are public legal entities whose principles of establishment are specified by law in order to meet the local, common needs of the people of a province, municipality or village, and whose decision-making bodies are constituted by the electorate, also specified by law.*" provisions guarantee local governments in Türkiye.

At this point, due to Turkey's unitary state structure, local governments are organized under the supervision and control of the central administration, which is referred to as tutelage control in the Constitutional provisions mentioned above (Kavruk, 2021).

Table 1. Comparison of local government structures in Italy and Turkey

	TÜRKİYE	**İTALYA**
Constitutional Basis of Local Governments	Articles 123 and 127 of the 1982 Constitution stipulate. "The administration is a whole with its organization and duties and is regulated by law. The organization and duties of the administration are based on the principles of central administration and decentralization"	Article 114 of the 1948 Italian Constitution.
Local Government	Special Provincial Administration, Municipality, Village.	Region, Metropolitan City, Provincial Government, Municipality
Local Government Units	**Special Provincial Administration** -Governor -Provincial General Assembly - Provincial Council **Municipality** -Mayor - Municipal Council -Municipality Council **Village** -Muhtar -Council of Elders -Village Association	**Region** -Head of the regional administration -Regional Assembly -Regional Council **Metropolitan City** -Metropolitan Mayor -Metropolitan City Council -Metropolis Giunta **Provincial Administration** -Provincial President - Provincial Assembly -Provincial Council **Municipality** -Mayor -Municipality Assembly -Municipality Council
General Activities of Local Governments	Infrastructure services, urban transportation, environment, housing, culture, education, health, trade, health, social services, etc.	Education, health care, culture and sport, water supply, sewerage, electricity, gas, environment and general cleaning, traffic and transport, urban planning, tourism, and other administrative tasks.
Revenues of Local Governments	Taxes, fees, shares obtained from general budget revenues, donations, participation shares in expenditures, borrowings	Taxes, fees, donations, contributions to expenditures, borrowings, revenues obtained according to the provisions of private law
Local Government Expenditures	General public expenditures, infrastructure and transportation services, social and cultural services, personnel costs	Expenditures on health, expenditures on general public services, expenditures on economic affairs, expenditures on environmental protection, expenditures on education, expenditures on housing, community welfare, culture and religion, expenditures on social security and social assistance.
Autonomy of Local Governments	Administrative and financial autonomy/ Limited autonomy	Administrative and financial autonomy/ It has a more autonomous structure compared to Turkey
Audit of Local Governments	Guardianship Supervision Financial Audit (Court of Accounts) Judicial Review Ethical Audit Ombudsman Inspection	Guardianship Supervision Financial Audit (Corte di Conti)) Judicial Review Public Opinion Audit Ombudsman Inspection

As seen in the table above, both Turkey's and Italy's local governments have a constitutional basis. Although the local government structure of both countries is different, in Turkey the mandate of local governments is more limited within the framework of certain laws, whereas in Italy local governments provide services in a much wider range of areas from education to infrastructure services. In Turkey, the most important share of local government revenues comes from taxes and general budget revenues. In Italy, on the other hand, taxes, fees, donations, contributions to expenditures, borrowings, revenues obtained according to the provisions of private law are the main sources of income of local governments. While the centralization of many policies in Turkey leads to a limited understanding of autonomy, it is concluded that Italy has a more autonomous structure in terms of administrative and financial autonomy compared to Turkey. It is possible to infer that Turkey and Italy have similar audit mechanisms in general.

CONCLUSION

Today, almost all countries have local governments with different administrative structures due to their different economic structures, spatial diversity and different population characteristics. Local governments, which have an important place in terms of the functioning of the administrative mechanism, are an important field in terms of finding effective, participatory, democratic and efficient solutions to local problems, providing representation and participation, contributing to the development of democracy within the political system, reaching citizens more quickly and providing efficient services.

Italy, a unitary state governed by a democratic parliamentary system, adopted a centralized governance model during the Risorgimento process as a country with different local structures, and with the restructuring period covering the period after 1943, it gave its final form to its political and administrative structure with the Constitution that came into force in 1948. Italy, which preferred an intensely centralized structure in order to ensure unity and integrity within the country, increased its tendency to make reforms over time. First, it legally recognized regional governments in 1963, then it carried out a local government reform that granted extensive powers to local governments, and then it granted significant powers to local governments starting in 1990.

Italy, which secured local and regional governments with the constitution with Article 114 of the 1948 Constitution, has given legislative authority to regional governments in addition to special status regions with the reform it made in 2001, after various reforms it has made since the 1990s, and ensured that metropolitan cities gained constitutional status as a local government unit n 2009, Italy enacted the

"Fiscal Federalism Law", which is important in terms of decentralization, increases the financial autonomy of local and regional governments, and increases the taxes allocated to local governments and their shares of national taxes. With the Delrio Law, which was put into effect in 2015, the functions of provincial governments were reduced, while the role of metropolitan cities and municipal unions was increased, and some provincial governments were transformed into metropolitan cities. At this point, the central and local The relationship between the central government and local governments has begun to change, and when we look at the division of duties between the central government and local governments, we see that most of the local services are carried out by regional and local governments. In Italy, there is equality between the central government and the regions and municipalities, and it is possible to say that there is a horizontal functioning rather than a vertical relationship between them.

It can be said that local governments, which relieve the central government's task burden, have a higher level of financial autonomy in Italy compared to Turkey. When the income structure of local governments in Italy is evaluated, while local governments can determine the rates of tax revenues within the framework of the lower and upper limits determined by the law, local governments in Turkey do not have the authority in this regard. Local government expenditures in Turkey are made on the axis of general public services, expenditures for the welfare of the society and environmental protection services. Local government expenditures in Italy primarily include health, social security and social assistance expenditures and other public service expenditures.

As a result, a strong local government approach prevails in Italy, where local governments have a wide area of action. In this direction, the fact that the duties and areas of application of Italian local governments are wide, that they have a strong financial structure, that the taxes collected, the donations made and other resources are autonomous, has caused the local government system to be less dependent on the center compared to Turkey.

REFERENCES

Arıkboğa. (2021), Dünyada Yerel Yönetimler ve Mali Yapıları "İtalya'da Yerel Yönetimlerin İdari ve Mali Yapısı", Nobel Yayınevi, s: 503-535

Arıkboğa, Ü. (2004), Yönetimler Arası Mali İlişkiler: Türkiye'de Merkezi Yönetim ile Büyükşehir Belediyeleri Arasındaki Mali İlişkilerin Niteliği Üzerine Bir Araştırma, İstanbul, Yaylacık Matbaası, s:1-284

Baldini, G.& Baldi, B. (2014), Decentralization in Italy and the Troubles of Federalization, Regional and Federal Studies,24(1), s:87-108.

Boggero, G. (2016), "The Establishment of Metropolitan Cities in Italy: An Advance or a Setback for Italian Regionalism?", Perspectives on Federalism, S.8(3), ss.1-22.

Bohlooli Zamani, M. A. H. S. A., & Dessì, S. (2017). Local governments' approach towards green bond. An opportunity for Italian municipalities to finance green projects in the public real estate sector.

Council of Europe. (2017), Local and Regional Democracy in Italy, https://www .coe.int/en/web/congress/-/local-and-regional-democracy-in-italy, (Erişim Tarihi: 03.02.2025)

Erbay, Y. & Akgün, H. (2017), Türkiye'de ve Avrupa'da Yerel Yönetimler, Yayımevi: Uluslararası İlişkiler Kütüphanesi, 2. Basım, s:832

Geray, C. (1997), Ülke Ülke Yerel Yönetimler(İtalya), Çağdaş Yerel Yönetimler Dergisi,Cilt6, sayı:1, s: 53-76.

Iannello, C. (2002) Italian Republic, United Cities and Local Governments- Co untry Public: Italy, University of Naples, https://www.gold.uclg.org/sites/default/files/Italy_0.pdf, (Erişim Tarihi: 07.01.2005)

Italiano, G. (2025), https://www.governo.it/it/costituzione-italiana/parte-seconda -ordinamen to-della-repubblica/titolo-v-le-regionile-province-e-i.Erişim Tarihi: 02.02.2025

Kavruk, H. (2021), Yerel ve Bölgesel Yönetimler-Yerel Yönetimler, Birlikler, Ajanslar, Özel Alan Yönetimleri, Ankara, Nobel Yayınevi, s:457

Kelly, M. J. (1998). Political Downsizing: The Re-Emergence Of Self Determination, and The Movement Toward Smaller, Ethnically Homoge nous States, HeinOnline. *Drake Law Review*, *49*, 209–397.

Koçak, H. (1996), "Ülke Ülke Yerel Yönetimler- İtalya'da Yerel Yönetimler" Çağdaş Yerel Yönetimler, cilt 5, sayı 4, Temmuz 1996, s:57-66

Koşar, N. (2013), "İtalya'da Yerel Yönetimler ve Merkezi Yönetim– Yerel Yönetimler Arası Mali İlişkiler", Uluslararası Yönetim İktisat ve İşletme Dergisi, Cilt 9, Sayı 18, s: 327-348

Küçük, H. (2019), 'Merkez-Çevre Teorisi Ve Yerelleşmeye Etkisi: İtalya Örneği', Journal of Political Administrative and Local Studies, cilt 2, sayı, s:1-26

Larousse, M. (1981), Meydan Gazetecilik ve Neşriyat, İstanbul, s:5970

Olivetti, M. (2014), ''Centralization vs. Decentralization: The Current Trends in Italy'', Korel Göymen ve Onur Sazlak (Ed.), Centralization Decentrali zation Debate Revisited, Sabancı Üniversitesi,İstanbul, s: 1-423

Raffer C.& Padovani,E.(2019), Local Public Finance in Europe:Country Reports, Gütersloh: Hertie School and Bartelsmann Stiftung, Italy, ss:141-153

Toksöz. (2009), Yerel Yönetim Sistemleri, TESEV Yayınları, İstanbul, s:1-148

Tortop, N. (1996), "İtalya'da Yerel Yönetimlerin Yapısı ve Son Düzenlemeler", Çağdaş Yerel Yönetimler Dergisi, Cilt:5, Sayı: 3, s: 63-70. Şan, G. (2011), "İtalya'da Yerel Yönetimler". http://www.yerelsiyaset.com/pdf, (Erişim Tarihi 05.01.2025): s.92.

Ulusoy, A., Akdemir, T. (2006). Mahalli idareler (teori/ uygulama/maliye), Seçkin Yayınları, Ankara, s: 528

Usta, S. (2021), Dünyada Yerel Yönetimler ve Mali Yapıları (Almanya'da Yerel Yönetimlerin İdari ve Mali Yapısı), Ankara, Nobel Yayınevi, s: 17-52

Vesperini, G. (2011) "Regional and Local Government in Italy: An Overview",Universita Degli Studi Della Tuscia, Viterbo- Italy, Università degli studi della Tuscia, Viterbo–Italy, ss:1-24 https://images.irpa.eu/wp-content/uploads/2011/06/vesperinig.pdf, (Erişim Tarihi: 01.02.2025)

Chapter 4
The Autonomy of Local Governments:
Democratization of Turkish Public Administration in the Light of Montesquieu and Tocqueville

Tanzer Çeliktürk
https://orcid.org/0000-0002-0219-5740
Pamukkale University Honaz Vocational School, Denizli, Turkey

ABSTRACT

This study explores the relationship between the autonomy of local governments by drawing upon the theoretical frameworks of Montesquieu and Tocqueville. Within the context of Turkey's historical background and political culture, the study addresses the functionality of local administrations, deficiencies in public engagement, and the lack of transparency. Particular attention is given to issues such as the prevalence of corruption in local governments, the inadequacy of oversight mechanisms, and the low level of citizen involvement in governance processes. Grounded in Tocqueville's concept of "local liberties" and Montesquieu's principles of the separation of powers and democratic governance. It further offers concrete recommendations for how these practices might be adapted to the Turkish context. Finally, the study proposes reform initiatives aimed at enhancing local autonomy and outlines strategies to strengthen democratic participation. It argues that local self-governance and civic engagement should be more effectively integrated into the Turkish political system.

DOI: 10.4018/979-8-3373-5576-4.ch004

1. INTRODUCTION

"Democracy, in order to function and to maintain its existence, must possess a culture of compromise. In a country where compromise cannot be achieved, the realization of democracy becomes impossible, or even if realized, it cannot be sustained" (Ağaoğulları, 2007, p. 99). As emphasized in this statement, which highlights the concept of compromise as a fundamental principle of contemporary democracy, democracy does not entail ignoring internal differences. On the contrary, one of its most crucial elements is the management of conflicts among those differences and their eventual reconciliation through mutual checks and balances.

Groups and individuals within society strive to protect their own interests and are ultimately compelled to reach some form of agreement in order to live together. Democracy, as the political system that emerges from this social structure, should not be viewed merely as a system of agreement. Rather, it is a system that includes differences and conflicts within itself (Ağaoğulları, 2007, p. 99). In current public administration literature, the autonomy of local governments has emerged as a core element of democratic governance. Local governments are not merely administrative bodies that provide services; they are also political spaces in which citizens participate directly, influence decision-making, and cultivate a sense of democratic responsibility (Elazar, 1987). For this reason, strengthening local governments at the subnational level, limiting centralization, and expanding participatory channels have become among the primary objectives of modern democracies. Democracy is now widely understood not only as an electoral mechanism but also as a governance approach rooted in societal consensus and civic engagement.

At the beginning of the modern era, Montesquieu, one of the leading political thinkers of the eighteenth century, and Tocqueville, an important representative of nineteenth-century Anglo-Saxon liberal democratic thought, both defended the institutionalization of frameworks that allow the clash of different social interests and enable their reconciliation through mutual restraint. Both thinkers asserted that the roots of democracy must be planted at the local level. According to Tocqueville (2017a), "Without town liberty, freedom cannot be imagined" (p. 68). Montesquieu (2016) similarly emphasized that "liberty is only possible in a system where individuals can act without fear" (Book XI, Chapter 6). They argued that local governments are not simply administrative units but also play a central role in fostering liberties, social participation, and individual responsibility. Montesquieu linked the spirit of the law to institutions that are designed to secure individual freedoms and ensure citizen participation. Tocqueville expressed that local governments offer individuals a unique opportunity to experience democracy in practice and to acquire their liberties through this process. Accordingly, a strong connection is established between local autonomy and democratic participation, and the necessity of maintaining oversight over powers at the local level is emphasized.

In the Turkish context, the centralized administrative tradition that originated during the Ottoman period continued into the Republican era. Concerns about national security, minority revolts, and the desire to preserve social cohesion institutionalized a cautious attitude toward local autonomy. In particular, the 1982 Constitution further strengthened the authority of the central government. Although the Constitution provided formal guarantees for local autonomy, these guarantees were limited by mechanisms such as administrative tutelage (Keleş, 2016; Özbudun, 2009). Taking into account Turkey's historical experience and political culture, it becomes apparent that a centralized model dominates rather than one based on genuine local autonomy. The centralized administrative mindset inherited from the Ottoman Empire persisted through the Republican era, during which the powers of local governments were kept under the control of the central state. This situation became even more entrenched in the southeastern regions of Turkey, where local governments were often associated with the PKK. Concerns about regional security and fears of social fragmentation frequently prevented the development of local autonomy, thereby intensifying the need for reform in Turkey's local governance system.

Local governments are among the essential pillars of democratic governance. Montesquieu and Alexis de Tocqueville, two major thinkers in French intellectual history, consistently argued that local governments are not only administrative entities but also key instruments in promoting individual liberties, social engagement, and civic responsibility. Montesquieu associated the spirit of laws with institutions designed to guarantee individual freedom and enable participation in governance. Tocqueville similarly emphasized that local governments provide a space where individuals can experience democracy directly and thus acquire a practical sense of freedom. These ideas reveal a strong relationship between local autonomy and democratic engagement and highlight the importance of maintaining accountability at the local level.

However, Turkey's local governance structure remains predominantly centralized, shaped by its historical background and political experience. The centralized model inherited from the Ottoman Empire continued during the Republican period, and the authority of local governments was consistently restricted by the central government. In southeastern regions especially, the association of local governments with separatist threats such as the PKK further reinforced this control. For this reason, concerns about regional security and the fear of social disintegration have frequently hindered efforts to enhance local autonomy. These factors have deepened the structural need for comprehensive reform in Turkey's approach to local governance.

A functioning system of local government not only strengthens civic participation and public trust but also contributes to the more efficient use of public resources and helps to prevent corruption. Nevertheless, local governments in Turkey face serious challenges in terms of administrative capacity, lack of oversight, and insufficient citizen engagement. Reports by the Court of Accounts indicate major deficiencies in local government budgeting, including unauthorized spending and inefficient resource management (Court of Accounts, 2021, pp. 147–151). Furthermore, according to data provided by the Turkish Statistical Institute, public participation in municipal decision-making processes remains below two percent (TÜİK, 2021). This indicates that public oversight in local governance is weak, and when combined with a lack of transparency, it creates a fertile ground for corruption.

Yet, policy tools such as participatory budgeting and digital citizens' assemblies, as seen in countries like Finland and Iceland, provide successful models that could be adapted to Turkey's local governance structure. In Finland, the municipality of Helsinki has implemented a participatory budgeting initiative called "OmaStadi," which enables citizens to propose and vote on projects and thereby participate in municipal decision-making (OECD, 2022, pp. 58–59). In Iceland, following the 2008 crisis, the "Better Reykjavik" platform allowed citizens to submit proposals directly to municipalities, which have subsequently influenced the delivery of public services in the city (OECD, 2022, pp. 60–61).

In this study, the views of two French thinkers who belonged to the aristocracy and lived in France during periods of significant transformation, although separated by a century, will be examined with respect to democracy, liberty, local democratic structures, the contributions of local governments to democracy, and ideal models of governance. Their perspectives will be evaluated within the context of their historical conditions, personal backgrounds, and most important works: "The Spirit of the Laws" by Montesquieu and "Democracy in America" by Tocqueville.

2. THEORETICAL FRAMEWORK: MONTESQUIEU AND "THE SPIRIT OF THE LAWS"

2.1. Montesquieu: "The Spirit of the Laws"

Upon returning from his journey to England in 1731, Montesquieu published what he considered the most important work of his life, *The Spirit of the Laws*, in Geneva in 1748. In his own words, the subject of this book is "the laws, customs, and traditions of all the peoples of the world." The author examines how institutions, as products of humanity, can be most appropriately addressed in both a general societal context and within specific societies. He frames this analysis within a universal understanding of law, investigating both physical and moral causes. Within this framework, Montesquieu explores which sociopolitical models are most effective, which are least harmful to society, and under what circumstances particular institutions and practices may lead to beneficial or detrimental outcomes (Ağaoğulları, Zabçı, and Ergün, 2009, p. 369).

In the opening pages of the work, Montesquieu states that, unlike the classical works of his era, he would not employ abstraction or the method of deductive reasoning. Instead, he adopts the method of observation and empirical analysis used in the positive sciences (Göze, 2007, p. 175). Accordingly, rather than merely examining the formal structure of laws as human constructs, he adopts a methodology that investigates how laws emerge, the conditions under which they arise, and the reasons behind their development, with the aim of uncovering what he refers to as the universal "spirit of the laws." According to Montesquieu, "Every law has a reason, because every law is tied to an element of physical, moral, or social reality. Every law implies a relationship, and the spirit of the laws is the network of these relationships" (Göze, 2007, p. 176). When examining social laws, Montesquieu regarded them not only as legal constructs but also sought to place them on a universal foundation by relating their formation and evolution to sociopolitical, economic, and geographic factors, and by using common scientific concepts (Ağaoğulları, Zabçı, and Ergün, 2009, p. 376).

Montesquieu makes a clear distinction between laws themselves and what he calls their spirit, stating: "I am not studying the laws, but the spirit of the laws. This spirit is found in the various relationships laws have with other things" (Ağaoğulları, Zabçı, and Ergün, 2009, p. 376). In Montesquieu's view, laws are closely related to their origins, the intentions of the lawmakers, the historical events upon which they are based, the way of life of the people, the geographic structure of the country, the customs and religious understanding of the society, as well as the constitution and conception of liberty within that society. It is necessary to assess political systems, along with civil laws and all other forms of legislation, by taking these factors into account (Montesquieu, 1998, p. 56).

According to Montesquieu, laws emerge as a result of the deterioration of equality when people begin living in organized societies, and when individuals start to compete for the advantages provided by the collective. The relationships among peoples are regulated by international law, the relationships between rulers and the ruled by political law, and interpersonal relationships by civil law. These laws are, in general, products of human reason and are specific to the societies in which they are created. Therefore, it is unlikely that the laws of one nation would be fully applicable to another (Montesquieu, 1998, pp. 54–56).

2.2. The Forms of Government Envisioned by Montesquieu and Their Characteristics

Montesquieu, who asserted that it is impossible for a society to exist without governance, emphasized the necessity of political authority. However, he also stated that he was not concerned with the question of which form of government is the best. While he acknowledged that each form of government is closely related to the "spirit" of the nation to which it belongs (Montesquieu, 1998, p. 55), he maintained that the most reasonable form of government would be the one that reflects human inclinations and secures "peace, liberty, and the safety of life." Montesquieu classified forms of government based on the virtues expected of citizens, the number of individuals holding sovereign power, and the manner in which governance is exercised. Although this classification seems to treat political systems as pure and ideal types, it is evident that Montesquieu implicitly favored monarchy over other systems (Ağaoğulları, Zabçı, and Ergün, 2009, p. 396).

In *The Spirit of the Laws*, Montesquieu argued that both legal systems and political regimes are shaped by a variety of factors, including climate, geography, religion, customs, economic conditions, and historical development. According to him, the "spirit of the laws" is a synthesis of these elements, and every society's specific conditions necessitate different types of governance.

Within this classification, Montesquieu identified three principal types of government: republic, monarchy, and despotism. A republic is defined as a system in which sovereignty is held either by the entirety of the people or by a portion thereof. It can be further divided into two subtypes: democracy, where sovereignty rests with the majority of the people, and aristocracy, where power is concentrated in the hands of a limited elite. Despotism refers to a regime in which all power is concentrated in a single individual, who governs arbitrarily and without adherence to any established legal framework (Montesquieu, 1998, p. 57).

In addition to this tripartite classification, Montesquieu also categorized governments as either "moderate" or "despotic." The key criterion he used in making this distinction was the presence or absence of liberty. In despotic regimes, liberty does not exist, whereas in moderate governments, liberty is established and can flourish (Montesquieu, 1998, pp. 80–82). Montesquieu associated moderate governments especially with monarchies. He argued that limiting monarchical power through honor-based laws and the institutional constraints placed upon rulers fosters individual freedom and enables effective executive governance (Montesquieu, 1998, p. 82). Behind this linear association between moderate government and liberty lies Montesquieu's preference for the English model of monarchy, which he regarded as the ideal form of moderate governance (Ağaoğulları, Zabçı, and Ergün, 2009, p. 397).

Montesquieu did not hold a particularly favorable view of republican regimes, especially the democratic and aristocratic variants. He regarded democracy as a form of government suited only to ancient times and small-scale societies. According to Montesquieu, the essential principle of democracy is "virtue," which he defined as the citizens' respect for equality and their willingness to subordinate personal interests to the common good. However, he believed that the wealth and luxury produced by growing commerce had eroded this principle of virtue and thus weakened democratic governance (Montesquieu, 1998, pp. 72–74). Montesquieu treated democratic virtue and liberty as distinct concepts and prioritized liberty. For this reason, he did not consider democratic and aristocratic regimes to be free governments, which set him apart from Aristotle, who regarded liberty as the central principle of democracy (Raynaud and Rials, 2003, p. 603).

Montesquieu, who understood democracy only in terms of the direct democracy practiced in ancient Greece, rejected both democracy and aristocracy due to their tendency to concentrate unlimited power either in the hands of the people or the nobility. He believed that such concentration of power posed a fundamental threat to the liberty of citizens.

2.3. Political Liberty According to Montesquieu

According to Montesquieu, liberty is primarily a political concept and can only emerge within a political society. In the absence of such a society, one may speak not of liberty, but only of independence. While independence refers to the ability of an individual to act according to personal desires and passions, liberty is defined as the right to do only what is permitted by law (Ağaoğulları et al., 2009, p. 419). Since liberty consists in the ability to act within the limits of the law, an individual must neither be forced to do what the law does not permit nor prevented from doing what the law allows (Montesquieu, 1998, pp. 232–233). In this respect, Montesquieu's concept of liberty is closely aligned with the notion of negative liberty as understood in liberal thought.

Montesquieu assumes the existence of laws that do not contradict universal principles of justice and that prevent individuals and groups within society from oppressing one another. From this assumption, he concludes that political liberty can only be achieved within regimes that are moderate in nature and governed by such laws. He identifies the existence of law as a prerequisite for liberty, and further argues that the second requirement is the establishment of a "moderate government" (Montesquieu, 1998, p. 233).

Montesquieu maintained that in order to establish the moderate government necessary for political liberty, a system must be created in which powers are reconciled, softened, regulated, and set into motion, and where the balance of power is maintained through mutual restraints (Montesquieu, 1998, p. 123). Given that all holders of power tend to abuse it, the absence of limitations on authority poses a threat to liberty, even in states governed by constitutional order. Therefore, every country must establish and sustain a constitution and a constitutional order that ensures power is constrained by counterbalancing power, in accordance with its own social and political context (Montesquieu, 1998, p. 233).

Montesquieu claimed to have found such a constitutional order, designed explicitly to guarantee political liberty, in England. According to him, the secret of liberty in England lies in the structure of its political system. Valuing individual freedom, private property, and aristocratic privilege above all else, Montesquieu may be described as a liberal aristocrat. He was particularly impressed by the English system, in which monarchy (represented by the king's executive role), aristocracy (represented by the House of Lords as both a legislative chamber and a supreme court), and democracy (represented by the House of Commons as a legislative body) were merged into a single political framework. In this system, each center of power serves to limit and balance the others (Ebenstein, 2003, p. 390).

2.4. Montesquieu and the Concept of Decentralized Governance

Montesquieu (1689–1755) is one of the most influential political thinkers of the French Enlightenment. The political climate of the eighteenth century was characterized by the dominance of absolute monarchies, yet it was also a period during which intellectual efforts toward liberty and the rule of law intensified. Through the political theories he developed during this period, Montesquieu laid the foundations for both the idea of the constitutional state and the modern conception of local governance. In particular, his seminal work *The Spirit of the Laws* (1748) introduced the principle of the separation of powers, which entails not only the classical division among the legislative, executive, and judicial branches but also a balance and oversight mechanism among different tiers of administration. In this respect, Montesquieu's approach to local government is directly related to the principles of contemporary governance and decentralization (Montesquieu, 2016, pp. 154–158). He observed the oppressive effects of centralized absolutism in France and was inspired by the constitutional monarchy and separation of powers in England.

"The independence of the judiciary, the parliamentary tradition, and the functioning of local communities in England were the primary sources shaping his understanding of local liberty and balance. In England, liberty derives from the structure of government. The legislative, executive, and judicial powers are separated and monitor one another. The legislative power resides in a parliament composed of representatives of the people and the nobility; the executive power belongs to the king; and the judiciary is exercised by independent judges. This separation ensures that no branch completely dominates the others, and in this way, liberty is preserved. The English system prevents the abuse of power by counterbalancing it with power" (Montesquieu, 2017, pp. 156–158). "In England, the privileges of the nobility are protected through the House of Lords, which prevents the monarchy from slipping into despotism. At the same time, the representatives of the people share legislative power in the House of Commons. This balance prevents both the king and the nobility from possessing absolute authority, and liberty is guaranteed within this moderate governmental structure" (Montesquieu, 2017, pp. 162–163).

His most important work, *De l'esprit des lois* (*The Spirit of the Laws*), established the foundations of liberty and the rule of law by linking the functioning of political institutions to variables such as climate, tradition, economy, and religion. According to Montesquieu, individual liberty is possible only through the limitation of political power. In this context, the separation of powers he proposed became the cornerstone of the modern constitutional state. However, Montesquieu's concept of separation of powers implies not only horizontal division, but also vertical distribution—that is, a balance between central and provincial authority. He stated that "in order for liberty to exist in a state, the legislative, executive, and judicial powers must be independent from one another, and none must be subject to the will of another" (Montesquieu, 2016, p. 221). This principle positions the idea of decentralization not merely as an administrative matter but as a safeguard for liberty itself.

His assertion that "political liberty is not merely equality before the law; it is also security against arbitrary rule" underlines the importance of enabling citizens to participate directly in decision-making processes. For Montesquieu, liberty can only be achieved by limiting arbitrary rule, which requires power to be constrained and distributed. Based on this view, he argued that the concentration of power in a single authority inevitably leads to despotism. For Montesquieu, liberty can only be safeguarded by the distribution of power both horizontally and vertically. The vertical distribution of authority forms the basis of decentralization. According to him, the functionality of decision-making at the local level is not only a matter of administrative efficiency, but also a guarantee of individual freedoms and political participation (Montesquieu, 2016, pp. 210–215).

Montesquieu identified the centralization of power as the most prominent characteristic of despotism and authoritarianism. Therefore, liberty must be preserved through a sharing of power not only among the legislative, executive, and judicial branches but also between central and local governments. He viewed local governments as instruments for cultivating civic consciousness and political education. According to him, when local communities manage their own affairs, it not only improves administrative efficiency but also fosters public responsibility. This approach is considered a precursor to today's concept of multi-level governance. In summary, Montesquieu believed that individual liberty and political legitimacy can be achieved only by limiting central authority, recognizing local powers, and ensuring the supremacy of law. His political philosophy relates not only to institutional structures but also to the development of civic consciousness. According to him, legal rules alone are insufficient to protect individuals against the state; the state itself must also be constrained. The most fundamental method of achieving this is through the distribution of power. In this respect, local governments represent a domain in which citizens can directly interact with governance and have a say in decisions that affect their own lives. Montesquieu emphasized that only through active civic engagement can liberty move from being a mere abstract ideal to becoming a concrete reality (Montesquieu, 2016, pp. 222–224).

Montesquieu generally discussed local governments in monarchies within the context of "intermediate powers." These were institutions such as nobles, local councils, or municipalities that played a crucial role in balancing the king's absolute authority and ensuring local autonomy. According to him, local governments in monarchies function as a buffer against arbitrary practices of the central authority and contribute to the protection of liberties. In despotic regimes, however, such autonomy does not exist, as all power is concentrated in a single authority. "In monarchies, due to the nature of the government, there exist intermediate, dependent, and secondary powers. Nobility, clergy, privileged cities, and municipalities constitute the core structure of monarchy. These intermediate powers not only balance royal authority but also enable a degree of autonomy in the implementation of laws at the local level. If such powers are eliminated, monarchy transforms into despotism, for there remains no buffer between the king and the people, and all is subjected to arbitrary rule" (Montesquieu, 2017, pp. 22–23).

Montesquieu regarded local autonomy as essential for the protection of liberties. The parliamentary system in England and the local assemblies within the feudal structures of Europe were, for him, concrete examples of local freedoms. Local autonomy is directly linked to the authority of individuals and communities to manage their own affairs, and this serves as a shield against arbitrary government. Montesquieu maintained that local liberties, consistent with the spirit of laws, are shaped by the historical and cultural conditions of societies. "Liberty can only exist in a governmental structure in which citizens feel secure. This sense of security is made possible through the authority to manage one's own affairs at the local level. In European monarchies, the privileges of cities and municipalities are the foundation of this local autonomy. For example, in Gothic governments, cities had their own assemblies, which acted as a counterweight to royal authority. Such autonomy does not exist in despotic regimes, because the despot seeks to concentrate all power in his own hands" (Montesquieu, 2017, pp. 159–160). "The power of local governments enables citizens to participate in the legislative process, and this participation is one of the cornerstones of liberty. In England, the House of Commons consists of representatives elected at the local level, and their participation in legislation plays a critical role in safeguarding liberty" (Montesquieu, 2017, p. 162).

Montesquieu praised England as the country where local autonomy and liberty were best practiced. For him, the parliamentary system in England, the legislative participation of locally elected representatives in the House of Commons, and the autonomy of local institutions such as municipalities and local courts formed the foundation of liberty. These local governments established a counterbalance against central authority and supported citizens' right to self-governance. "In England, liberty is protected through the power of local governments and representatives. The House of Commons is composed of representatives elected at the local level, and these representatives are part of the legislative power. Local courts and municipalities operate independently of royal authority, thereby safeguarding the citizens' right to manage their own affairs. This system prevents the abuse of power and protects liberty at every level" (Montesquieu, 2017, pp. 161–162). "In the English system, local liberties are ensured by the right of the people to elect their own representatives and by the autonomy of local governments. This structure prevents the monarchy from descending into despotism and guarantees the security of every individual" (Montesquieu, 2017, p. 164).

One of Montesquieu's most significant contributions was his recognition that different forms of government may develop depending on the geographic, cultural, and historical conditions of different societies. In *The Spirit of the Laws*, he examined in detail the influence of climate, religion, tradition, and social structure on political institutions, and argued that no single regime could be universally applied to all societies. He stated that "a legislator must consider the spirit of the people, for laws that are suitable to one nation may bring disaster to another" (Montesquieu, 2016, p. 33). He also emphasized the influence of geography and culture in shaping political structures. According to him, every political regime must be in harmony with the historical and cultural context of its society. This perspective highlights that centralization is not a one-size-fits-all solution and that governance must be sensitive to local diversity. In this sense, Montesquieu opposed the idea of a single model of governance and advocated for governance rooted in local foundations. Today's models of multi-level administration under the concept of "governance" institutionalize Montesquieu's early proposals.

This perspective guided Montesquieu's assessment of multinational and religiously diverse empires such as the Ottoman Empire. Montesquieu observed the need for centralized administrative structures to maintain authority across the vast territories of the Ottoman Empire, and acknowledged the resulting bureaucratic apparatus as historically inevitable. "In the government of the Turks, local authorities are subordinate to the absolute power of the sultan. Governors and other local officials act as representatives of the sultan and do not possess any real autonomy. This is a fundamental characteristic of despotic regimes: all power is concentrated in a single hand, and no local liberties or intermediate institutions exist" (Montesquieu, 2017, p. 43). From this angle, Montesquieu's culturally and geographically sensitive approach provides an important analytical framework for evaluating the deficiencies in local autonomy in modern Turkey. According to this perspective, in societies like Turkey with a historically centralized state tradition, the institutionalization of local democracy is expected to be a gradual process and one that may encounter cultural resistance. However, this reality does not suggest abandoning the goal of local autonomy. On the contrary, it necessitates a carefully planned and socially informed transition.

Montesquieu's concept of local governance is not only a safeguard for individual liberties but also a guarantee of political balance and social stability. He regarded local institutions as schools of civic participation that shape the political culture of society and prepare citizens for engagement in governance. For this reason, the presence of local assemblies is not merely a technical or administrative choice but a moral and political necessity. Local administration, when organized effectively, possesses the capacity both to recognize diversity and to manage pluralism. This capacity reflects Montesquieu's vision of political pluralism. "Liberty can only exist in a government where citizens feel secure. This sense of security is achieved through the authority to manage affairs at the local level. In European monarchies, the privileges of cities and municipalities constitute the basis of local autonomy. For example, in Gothic governments, cities had their own councils, which acted as a counterweight to the king's authority. Such autonomy is never found in despotic governments, because the despot seeks to consolidate all power in his own hands" (Montesquieu, 2017, pp. 159–160).

3. THEORETICAL FRAMEWORK: TOCQUEVILLE AND "DEMOCRACY IN AMERICA"

Alexis de Tocqueville, one of the most prominent political thinkers of the nineteenth century, made groundbreaking observations regarding the functioning of democracy. In his seminal work *Democracy in America* (1835), he offered a detailed analysis of the American local government system and its influence on individual liberties. According to Tocqueville, local governments serve as the foundational pillars of democracy; they are structures that enhance both political participation and the awareness of individual freedom (Tocqueville, 2017, pp. 60–63). Through *De la démocratie en Amérique* (*Democracy in America*), Tocqueville became not only a political observer but also a key figure who shaped the evolution of liberal democracy. His ideas were profoundly influenced by the political experiences of his time. The political shifts following the French Revolution of 1830, class conflicts, and growing distrust in centralization reinforced his search for liberty. During his travels in the United States, he carefully studied practices such as federalism, town governments, elected officials, and direct citizen participation, describing these structures as "the school of democracy."

The small local units Tocqueville referred to as "American townships" are characterized by direct citizen involvement in governance, including budgeting, electing public officials, and managing local affairs. He asserted that "when a people becomes accustomed to managing its own affairs, it acquires a sense of liberty" (Tocqueville, 2017, p. 102). According to this view, local governments are not merely service units but institutions that establish the societal foundations of democracy. Tocqueville regarded town meetings as the first space in which citizens become acquainted with political life. This form of local participation helps individuals develop awareness of collective problems and shared responsibilities.

For Tocqueville, centralization isolates the individual, increases political passivity, and diminishes interest in public affairs. In contrast, decentralization transforms the people into active political agents and encourages the development of democratic habits. As he stated, "the further citizens are removed from governance, the less liberty thrives, and the more obedience becomes a matter of habit" (Tocqueville, 2017, p. 133). In his view, equipping individuals with the experience and responsibility to manage their immediate environment is a prerequisite for cultivating democratic consciousness at the national level. Thus, Tocqueville's understanding of local democracy can be seen as a forerunner of modern participatory democracy and governance models.

One of Tocqueville's most striking comparisons is that between the practices of local governance in continental Europe and in the United States. In his words, "in Europe, government is the master of the town; in America, the town is a partner of the government." In France, local governments function as hierarchical units that implement the central authority's commands, thereby distancing citizens from public affairs. In contrast, in the United States, people participate directly in decision-making at the local level, and this participation fosters civic identity. Tocqueville wrote, "without town life, liberty remains an abstract idea; it is never put into practice," thus emphasizing that democracy can only be internalized when it is institutionalized at the local level.

Tocqueville's emphasis on local democracy is not merely a proposal for institutional reform. It also represents a strategy for strengthening civil society, promoting voluntary associations, and building social capital. In this respect, he anticipated the theoretical framework later developed by Robert Putnam (1993) in his concept of "social capital." For Tocqueville, a free society is sustained not only through laws and elections but also through the everyday relationships formed among citizens.

Tocqueville's approach to local governance offers a distinctive perspective not only in terms of political participation but also with regard to moral responsibility and the capacity for social solidarity. When citizens become accustomed to managing their affairs collectively at the local level, they develop not only political habits but also key societal values such as trust, voluntarism, and mutual responsibility. As Tocqueville observed, "Americans immediately form associations to confront social issues; they seek solutions without referring everything to the state" (Tocqueville, 2017). This approach reduces dependence on the state and contributes to the construction of a robust civil society.

Tocqueville also argued that local assemblies instill political identity in individuals. In his view, a person who assumes even a minor role in town affairs learns responsibility, accountability, and how to serve the public interest. Therefore, the governance experience acquired at the local level lays the cultural and intellectual foundation required for national democracy. This perspective later inspired scholars such as Elinor Ostrom, who developed concepts such as "common governance" and "community-based decision-making" (Ostrom, 1990).

In conclusion, Tocqueville argued that local governments play a central role in counteracting the alienating effects of centralization. He saw them as essential for developing political socialization, a culture of responsibility, and a spirit of voluntarism. Drawing from the American example, he emphasized that active participation of citizens in governance is the fundamental element that sustains democracy. Through these insights, Tocqueville became one of the most influential intellectual sources for contemporary democratic theory.

3.1. Tocqueville's Analysis of the American Model of Government

Tocqueville viewed the American model of governance as the direct antithesis of the French regime. According to him, the fundamental flaw of the French system was not merely unchecked monarchical sovereignty but an extreme centralization of authority. In contrast, the American context revealed a different reality, where democracy replaced absolute monarchy and locally autonomous institutions took the place of centralized structures. Shortly after the July Revolution of 1830 established a constitutional regime in France, Tocqueville decided to visit the United States together with his friend Gustave de Beaumont. Although the official purpose of the trip was to examine the American penal system, their true objective was to study what Tocqueville believed to be a model of universal significance that had found a secure and established expression in America. His intention was not solely to analyze the political and administrative structures, but also to investigate the entire socio-political fabric of the United States, the spirit of democratic thought, its social reflections, and both the hopes and fears inspired by this new model (Ebenstein, 2003, p. 298).

Tocqueville begins *Democracy in America* by clearly articulating the central insight of the book:

> *"Among all the new things that drew my attention during my stay in America, nothing struck me more than the general equality of conditions. I quickly recognized its immense influence on the course of society. I saw that this same factor extended its influence far beyond laws and political customs, that it reached civil life as well, shaping opinions, generating feelings, suggesting customs, and modifying everything that it did not create" (Tocqueville, 1962, p. 1).*

As this introduction suggests, Tocqueville recognized that the equality of conditions, which formed the basis of American life, prevailed not only in the political and administrative spheres but also in civil society. He understood that it prescribed a particular way of life and fundamentally shaped socio-political dynamics. Tocqueville came to realize that the French and American Revolutions did not occur as isolated events but were instead components of a global transformation that affected the entire world (Ebenstein, 2003, p. 299).

> *"Everywhere we see particular events in the life of nations contributing to the advancement of democracy. Everyone, knowingly or unknowingly, is serving this cause. The gradual development of equality of conditions, therefore, bears the marks of a divine process. It is universal and enduring, and it cannot be prevented by human effort. All men and all events contribute to its progress" (Tocqueville, 1962, p. 4).*

Tocqueville was also clear-sighted regarding the fate of the social class to which he belonged. In his view, aristocracy is a class that begins to die the moment it is born, and he expressed no particular affection for it. He acknowledged that the idea of a privileged class dominating governance was no longer acceptable and had no future.

> *"There is a country in the world where this great social revolution, which I have described, has reached its natural limits. This revolution took place in America in a simple and straightforward way. I am convinced that, like the Americans, we too will soon achieve nearly complete equality of conditions" (Tocqueville, 1962, p. 11).*

Although Tocqueville admired American democracy and the internalization of equality, he also recognized potential threats to individual liberty that could emerge from this system. As a result, he refrained from presenting the American political and administrative model as an ideal.

"I do not conclude that we will necessarily achieve the same political outcomes as the Americans from a similar social condition. I do not believe that they have discovered the only possible form of government in a democracy" (Tocqueville, 1962, p. 11).

While praising American democracy, Tocqueville simultaneously criticized its weaknesses. In his view, despite the dangers to liberty posed by excessive equality, democracy could not be replaced by any alternative regime and must therefore be embraced (Schmidt, 2002, p. 80). Tocqueville regarded democracy not merely as a political regime but as a way of life grounded in the principle of equality (Ebenstein, 2003, p. 300).

He expressed concern that the American democratic and legal systems had a tendency not only to establish but to render irresistible the power of the majority. Tocqueville argued that the direct and absolute sovereignty of the people in America often led to the suppression of minority groups. Unlike in other countries, where popular sovereignty might be indirect, symbolic, or ineffective, in America it was deeply embedded in customs, laws, administrative practices, and even in the daily lives of individuals (Tocqueville, 1962, pp. 24, 62–63).

3.2. Precautions Against the Tyranny of the Majority

According to Tocqueville, the power of the majority, which establishes absolute control over freedom of thought, imposes not physical punishments on dissidents but rather social exclusion, alienation, and isolation. Although he recognized that the use of power in the United States was, in its current form, relatively benevolent, he also argued that the irresistible power of the majority penetrated the entire socio-political sphere. He believed this favorable usage was merely coincidental and insisted that such unchecked authority should be limited through certain socio-political institutions and relationships (Tocqueville, 1962, p. 69).

In Tocqueville's view, the tyranny of the majority finds its foundation in the idea of a singular and centralized authority. As democracy leads to the equalization of conditions, individuals become more satisfied with their material well-being, yet increasingly indifferent to political affairs. In democratic societies, people value equality more than liberty, and societal inequalities tend to provoke unrest and polarization. As a result, the state assumes the responsibility of compensating for the harms caused by inequality, and individuals begin to seek refuge in state power. As citizens withdraw from the political realm, the state fills the vacuum. This growth of state power eventually extends to cultural and economic life. The state begins to intervene in religion, education, social practices, culture, and even economic affairs. This dynamic further consolidates state authority after the tyranny of the majority, creating a system that limits individual freedoms (Çetin, 2007, p. 52).

"Such a power does not destroy, but it prevents one from living. It does not tyrannize, but it compresses, enervates, extinguishes, and stupefies a people until each nation is reduced to nothing more than a herd of timid and industrious animals, of which the government is the shepherd" (Tocqueville, 1962, p. 97).

3.3. Tocqueville's Conception of Decentralized Governance

Tocqueville's understanding of democracy is grounded in the belief that the individual must not only be a figure who casts votes during elections, but also an actively engaged citizen who participates in governance. Highlighting the town meetings in New England, which function through direct popular participation, Tocqueville argued that such institutions encourage citizens to assume public responsibility and take ownership of political processes. As he famously stated, "Without town liberty, freedom cannot be imagined" (Tocqueville, 2017, p. 68).

According to Tocqueville, local governments are not merely administrative units responsible for service delivery. They are also schools in which political liberties and civic virtues are cultivated. He explained how town institutions transform the individual from a passive subject into an active citizen with the following words: "The more local the sphere in which one participates in public affairs, the deeper one's passion for liberty becomes" (Tocqueville, 2017, p. 73).

Tocqueville's admiration for American local government was not based solely on its functioning but was also shaped by his disillusionment with French centralism. Criticizing the overly centralized French administrative system, he observed: "As administration in France becomes more centralized, citizens grow more distant from political life and come to accept all decisions as descending from an impersonal, top-down authority" (Tocqueville, 2017, p. 114). He believed that this condition led citizens to disengage from public life and contributed to the formation of a state in which all decisions were made by a distant and dominant authority.

In contrast, the American system was characterized by local institutions in which the public exercised direct authority. Tocqueville articulated this difference as follows: "In America, township life is the place where citizens take their first step into political life. This experience not only builds trust in government but also allows individuals to perceive themselves as truly free" (Tocqueville, 2017, p. 69).

In this context, Tocqueville's democratic theory is directly linked to the development of social capital and civil society at the local level. He emphasized that associations, neighborhood organizations, and networks of volunteerism foster interpersonal trust and create the invisible bonds that hold society together (Tocqueville, 2017, pp. 92–95). As Tocqueville noted, "Americans are constantly forming associations, and they naturally expect every public issue to be addressed by some community group" (Tocqueville, 1835/2017, p. 98). He believed this tendency added depth and substance to democracy.

Tocqueville's thesis has been confirmed by contemporary research, most notably in Robert D. Putnam's *Making Democracy Work* (1993). In that study, Putnam compared levels of social capital and public service performance across different regions of Italy and found that where civil society was strong, democratic participation was more widespread and public services were delivered more effectively (Putnam, 1993, pp. 85–120). Similarly, Daniel Elazar supported Tocqueville's views within the framework of federalism theory. According to Elazar, a decentralized structure is essential not only for administrative efficiency but also for the development of political participation and civic consciousness (Elazar, 1987, pp. 49–52).

4. MONTESQUIEU AND TOCQUEVILLE: A COMPARATIVE THEORETICAL ANALYSIS OF COMMON GROUND AND DIVERGENCES

Both Montesquieu and Tocqueville, two influential French thinkers, shared a critical stance against despotism and emphasized the importance of reconciling societal conflicts through balanced governance. A key point of convergence between them is their engagement with the Anglo-Saxon liberal model of governance. Montesquieu idealized the English political system, which had established political liberalism following the relatively stable Glorious Revolution of 1688. In contrast, Tocqueville focused on the American model, which he viewed as the successor to eighteenth-century English governance. Although he praised American-style democracy as a universal and inevitable development, unlike Montesquieu, he did not idealize it and openly critiqued its weaknesses.

Both thinkers belonged to the aristocratic class and lived during periods of intense socio-political transformation in France, marked by class conflicts and power struggles among monarchs, nobles, bourgeoisie, and emerging social groups. Unlike the relatively evolutionary and conciliatory transitions in England and the United States, political change in France was often radical, violent, and deeply divisive. These experiences significantly shaped both philosophers' search for a political system that could reconcile conflicts and establish checks and balances among competing forces.

From the perspective of contemporary democratic theory, Montesquieu might not be considered a democrat in the modern sense. He emphasized the importance of aristocracy and advocated for a constitutional parliamentary monarchy based on the separation of powers. Within this system, political freedom was to be achieved through institutionalized compromise and mutual restraint among conflicting societal forces.

A century later, Tocqueville lived in a France where the old regime had collapsed, yet the new regime remained unstable, swinging between absolute monarchy and the tyranny of the majority. The rise of the working class and the legacy of the French Revolution's destructive experiences further motivated Tocqueville to focus on the American system, where Montesquieu's theory of the separation of powers had been successfully institutionalized. Just as Montesquieu prioritized political liberty over egalitarianism, Tocqueville also rejected absolute equality and instead championed intermediary institutions and a separation of powers framework that extended into social life as safeguards against majority tyranny.

Both thinkers placed a strong emphasis on individual liberty and the limitation of power, yet the solutions they proposed were shaped by the conditions of their respective eras. As keen observers of social dynamics, Montesquieu and Tocqueville provided rigorous analyses of the forces shaping their societies. Because concepts such as democracy, individual liberty, and equality were not yet widespread in Montesquieu's time, he placed greater importance on the aristocracy to counter-balance monarchical power. While this stance would not be considered democratic by today's standards, it reflected the influence of England's strong aristocracy on Montesquieu's thinking. He sought to expand liberty within the framework of the French monarchy by strengthening aristocratic institutions.

Tocqueville, by contrast, lived in a time when the aristocratic class, in his own words, was "already dead." He acknowledged the irreversibility of popular sovereignty and criticized Montesquieu for attempting to revive aristocracy. Though he too came from the aristocracy, Tocqueville neither defended the old order nor fully endorsed the American model of democracy. His primary concern was to design a democratic system in which individual liberties would be protected and the people would be meaningfully involved.

Tocqueville, who drew attention to the weaknesses of democracy and its potential to threaten individual freedoms, became a crucial figure for modern democratic thought through the practical suggestions he offered. His remarks on safeguarding liberty remain highly relevant:

"To establish broad but visible and stable limits on the activity of government; to grant individuals certain rights and ensure they can be exercised without generating conflict; to preserve the original power, strength, and independence of individuals; to elevate them from the margins of society and sustain them in that position—these, to me, are the primary goals of legislation in the age we are entering" (Tocqueville, 1962, p. 105).

Both Montesquieu and Tocqueville argued that decentralization holds not only instrumental but also intrinsic value in the process of democratization. In their thought, local government is not merely a matter of administrative autonomy; it is the fundamental sphere in which citizens encounter the political system, form political identities, and internalize a consciousness of liberty. Accordingly, local governance processes are essential not only for service provision but also for constructing political culture and cultivating civic freedoms.

Montesquieu's theory is more structurally oriented, focusing on constitutional design and the formal separation of powers. Tocqueville, on the other hand, centered his analysis on local practices, participatory habits, and cultural patterns. While Montesquieu identified institutional balance and limited authority as the primary mechanisms for preserving liberty, Tocqueville believed that liberty could only be sustained through an active civic consciousness.

For example, Montesquieu's admiration for the English constitutional system reflected his belief in legal security rooted in institutional equilibrium. In contrast, Tocqueville saw the participatory practices in American townships as "the first threshold of democracy." Montesquieu, as an elite theorist, emphasized top-down constitutional architecture, whereas Tocqueville linked decentralization to the people's practical capacity for self-governance.

Nevertheless, both thinkers agreed that centralization was the principal source of political oppression and the erosion of liberty. Each argued that empowering local governments was essential to promote individual freedom, enhance political legitimacy, and foster public responsibility. As Tocqueville observed, "Without town life, liberty remains an idea; it is never put into practice."

5. CENTRALIZATION AND THE STRUCTURE OF LOCAL GOVERNANCE IN TURKEY

Tocqueville's admiring observations of American local governance underscore the crucial role that local democratic institutions play in fostering individual liberty and civic responsibility. As he famously asserted, "Free peoples learn the art of freedom in their townships" (Tocqueville, 2017, p. 68). Similarly, Montesquieu emphasized that the separation of powers and decentralization are vital guarantees of liberty, stating that "Liberty can exist only in a society in which the individual can act without fear" (Montesquieu, 2016, Book XI, Chapter 6). However, when examining the structure of public administration in Turkey, one observes the dominance of a deeply rooted tradition of centralization rather than a framework of democratic local autonomy.

Turkey's approach to local governance is historically grounded in a strong tradition of centralization. This tradition was shaped during the Ottoman Empire, primarily to preserve state continuity, public order, and territorial integrity. In the Ottoman system, provincial institutions consisted of officials appointed by and acting on behalf of the Sultan. Local populations had limited opportunities to participate directly in decision-making processes (Ortaylı, 2000). Rather than expressing genuine local autonomy, this administrative structure functioned as an extension of central authority.

Following the French Revolution, the rise of nationalist ideologies posed a threat to multiethnic empires, including the Ottoman state. As separatist movements emerged, the empire adopted reforms intended to restructure the social and political order, often at the expense of weakening local powers and strengthening central authority. One consequence of the modernization efforts during the so-called Tanzimat era of the nineteenth century was the emergence of a powerful non-Muslim bourgeoisie, particularly within minority communities. At the same time, the rise of provincial notables through the ayan movement challenged the dominance of central rule. The increasing political and economic influence of these local actors hastened the empire's fragmentation. The autonomy gained by the ayan class and the strengthening of the minority bourgeoisie led to rising demands for independence among non-Muslim communities (Akça, 2007, p. 60).

During the Republican era, centralization became institutionally entrenched at the constitutional level and emerged as a defining characteristic of the administrative system. The 1982 Constitution, in particular, preserved extensive powers for the central government. Although it formally recognized the legal status of local governments, it simultaneously imposed significant limitations through mechanisms of administrative guardianship (Özbudun, 2000). Article 127 of the Constitution clearly states that local governments are subject to tutelary oversight. This clause provides a legal basis for central authorities to intervene in local decision-making processes.

Control over local governments is exercised not only through legal channels but also through administrative, financial, and political means. The authority of the Ministry of the Interior to suspend mayors and appoint trustees has become a major point of contention regarding local autonomy. These practices are incompatible with the principles of subsidiarity articulated in the European Charter of Local Self-Government (1985). Although Turkey ratified the Charter in 1992, it did so with several reservations, which remain in effect. For example, Article 8 of the Charter calls for "only proportional and legal supervision of local authorities," a principle that is insufficiently applied in Turkey (Council of Europe, 2017).

Moreover, Turkish legislation concerning local governance is frequently amended by central authorities, further undermining the autonomy of local governments. Although the Metropolitan Municipality Laws enacted in 2004 and 2012 aimed to resolve coordination issues in local service delivery, they also enhanced the reach of central control (Keleş, 2016). Law No. 6360, in particular, expanded the boundaries of metropolitan municipalities to cover entire provinces, thereby weakening mechanisms of local participation in rural areas.

This centralist structure produces political, administrative, and social consequences. Administratively, it limits the capacity of local authorities to develop policies that respond to community-specific needs, slows decision-making processes, and narrows the channels for public participation. Socially, it weakens citizens' habits of political engagement and impedes the development of civic consciousness.

Yet, as Tocqueville emphasized, the institutionalization of democracy at the local level reinforces individuals' sense of belonging to the political system and enables the internalization of liberty (Tocqueville, 2017). Montesquieu's principle of constitutional equilibrium based on the separation of powers also applies not only at the horizontal level but also at the vertical level in the relationship between central and local authorities (Montesquieu, 2016). In this context, enhancing the autonomy of local governments in Turkey is not merely a technical reform. It is also a strategic necessity for fostering a democratic culture and expanding participatory governance.

5.1. Historical Fear of Fragmentation and Its Impact on Local Democracy in Turkey

One of the most significant historical obstacles to the development of local autonomy in Turkey is the persistent "fear of fragmentation" inherited from the Ottoman Empire. This fear deepened in response to events such as minority uprisings, foreign interventions, and the Balkan Wars during the late imperial period. Consequently, centralization became institutionalized as a national strategy to preserve territorial integrity and unity (Karpat, 1985, pp. 104–106). This historical trauma also permeated the mentality of Republican-era administrators, who frequently perceived the concept of local autonomy as a threat to the indivisibility of the state (Keyman and Koyuncu, 2005, p. 114).

The Treaty of Sèvres, signed in 1920, played a pivotal role in reinforcing this perception. Provisions in the treaty proposing the establishment of Armenian and Kurdish states in various parts of Anatolia embedded a permanent fear of national disintegration within the state's political mindset (Oran, 2001, pp. 356–358). This perception continued into the Republican era, especially following key events such as the Sheikh Said Rebellion (1925), the Dersim operations (1937–38), and the rise of PKK terrorism. These developments shaped a state reflex that viewed the expansion of local government authority as a national security risk (Mete, 2020, p. 70).

As a result, debates around local democracy and autonomy in Turkey have transcended mere administrative concerns and have become entangled with issues of territorial integrity, national security, and internal stability. Considering Turkey's geographic, ethnic, and historical complexities, implementing a model of local democracy such as the one envisioned by Tocqueville has been constrained by ongoing perceptions of risk. Tocqueville's idealized "township democracy" presupposes the existence of a strong civil society and a low-security-risk environment. In contrast, countries like Turkey—characterized by plural identities, traumatic historical memory, and ongoing terrorist threats—face considerable obstacles in applying such a model effectively (Çarkoğlu and Kalaycıoğlu, 2009, p. 112).

Montesquieu offers a more flexible theoretical foundation in this context. He argues that each society's system of governance should be shaped by its unique climate, economy, religion, culture, and social structure (Montesquieu, 2016, pp. 33–35). According to this approach, instead of replicating European models wholesale, a localized concept of autonomy should be developed that reflects Turkey's distinct historical and cultural context. Montesquieu's principle of the "spirit of the laws" emphasizes that legal and administrative frameworks must align with societal realities.

In this regard, the ongoing presence of ethnically motivated demands and armed separatist movements in Southeastern Anatolia has often been invoked to justify the sustainability of a centralized state structure. The state's security reflex has frequently evolved into a mechanism that suppresses demands for local democratization. This outcome stems from a dominant mindset that automatically links local autonomy with ethnic representation (Yıldız, 2012, pp. 201–203).

Additionally, the construction of national identity in Turkey has been strongly shaped by the ideology of a "unitary structure" and the concept of a "single nation." This paradigm fosters resistance to multicultural models of governance and often conflates local demands with separatist threats (Kadıoğlu, 2005, pp. 362–364). In both political discourse and media representation, local autonomy is frequently framed as a threat to national unity, which has fostered widespread public mistrust of the concept (Çınar, 2011, p. 5).

However, contemporary democratic governance models reject security-based reasoning as the sole justification for centralization. Properly regulated and monitored local autonomy can be implemented without undermining national unity. In this context, European countries such as Spain and Italy, which are not federal states but maintain strong traditions of local governance, offer meaningful examples for Turkey (Loughlin, Hendriks, and Lidström, 2011, pp. 19–23). In these cases, local autonomy has not led to ethnic or regional disintegration but has instead strengthened the capacity for effective governance. Similarly, within the United Kingdom, flexible autonomy models have been developed for culturally distinct regions such as Scotland and Wales, even within a unitary system (Keating, 2009, p. 145).

Montesquieu's ideas offer a valuable theoretical framework for striking such a balance. His concept of the "spirit of the laws" implies that governance structures must be developed in accordance with each society's historical experience, social fabric, and security perceptions. For Montesquieu, liberty is not merely a product of institutional design but must be safeguarded through practices that resonate with a society's core values. Accordingly, the evolution of local governance in Turkey should be grounded not in the direct transplantation of European models but in a context-specific system that accounts for historical trauma and present-day security concerns.

Thus, the direct adaptation of Tocqueville's "township democracy" to the Turkish context must be approached with caution. Tocqueville's model was built upon a homogeneous cultural structure, minimal security risks, and a robust foundation of civil society. Turkey's multilayered ethnic, cultural, and religious composition, along with its prolonged conflicts and societal polarization, prevents the replication of this model in its original form. However, Tocqueville's core principle of citizen participation in governance remains relevant. Within the Turkish context, this principle can be reinterpreted through the creation of new participatory mechanisms and local reforms that are sensitive to security concerns.

5.2. The Autonomy of Local Governments in Turkish Public Administration

The centralist tradition inherited from the Ottoman Empire was institutionalized as a security reflex against minority uprisings and territorial losses. This tendency was reinforced in the early years of the Republic through events such as the Sheikh Said, Ağrı, and Dersim rebellions. In the present day, the activities of the PKK terrorist organization and the association of some local governments with this group have generated a climate of distrust toward local autonomy. This situation necessitates a delicate balance between democratization and security.

In academic circles, it is frequently argued that Turkey lacks the political and historical foundations required for a transition to federalism. For instance, Fuat Keyman states that Turkey's political culture, low levels of societal trust, and historical attachment to centralism render the adoption of a federal structure highly unlikely (Keyman, 2010, p. 33). Similarly, Ergun Özbudun asserts that the unitary state model constitutes the cornerstone of Turkey's political tradition, and that federalism is incompatible with this legacy (Özbudun, 2009, p. 74).

Although Article 127 of the Turkish Constitution defines local governments, it also imposes strict limitations on their decision-making, resource management, and representative authority through administrative tutelage mechanisms. Furthermore, the administrative capacity of local governments remains a significant obstacle to the practical realization of autonomy. Reports by the Court of Accounts and academic research indicate that many municipalities lack sufficient technical infrastructure, qualified personnel, and fiscal discipline. According to the 2021 report of the Court of Accounts, budget discipline has not been achieved in a significant number of municipalities, personnel expenditures have increased uncontrollably, and irregular procurement practices are widespread.

At the root of these problems lie the lack of citizen participation and the weakness of civil oversight mechanisms. In Turkey, public engagement in local governance is extremely limited. According to data from the Turkish Statistical Institute (TÜİK, 2021), citizen participation in municipal council meetings is below two percent. Additionally, public information systems are not effectively used, and decisions by local governments are not communicated transparently.

This demonstrates that Tocqueville's notions of "civil society" and "conscientious citizenship" remain underdeveloped in the Turkish context. Tocqueville attributed the success of American democracy to voluntary associations, freedom of the press, and the influence of local public opinion on governance (Tocqueville, 2017, pp. 112–117). In contrast, civil society organizations in Turkey possess limited influence due to both legal restrictions and cultural obstacles.

The weak administrative capacity of local governments and the lack of effective public oversight create fertile ground for corruption. According to the 2022 Turkey Report by Transparency International, 38 percent of complaints regarding municipal tenders were based on irregularities and preferential treatment of certain companies. The frequent misuse of direct procurement and negotiated tendering procedures, when combined with weak oversight, has led to systemic corruption (Transparency International, 2022).

Sait Bayraktar summarizes this condition as follows: "Autonomy granted without sufficient administrative capacity becomes a tool in the hands of local rent-seeking networks" (Bayraktar, 2007, p. 18). Similarly, Akıllı and Akıllı (2014) emphasize that when transferring authority to local governments, financial oversight systems must be simultaneously strengthened.

Robert Putnam's theory of social capital also reveals significant limitations when applied to the Turkish context. In his comparative study of Italian regions, Putnam found that areas with high levels of social capital exhibited more effective and ethical public service delivery (Putnam, 1993, p. 172). In Turkey, however, low interpersonal trust and limited civic participation hinder the effectiveness of local governance.

In conclusion, while the theoretical frameworks offered by Tocqueville and Montesquieu provide a valuable vision for local democracy and individual liberties, numerous structural barriers persist in the Turkish context. The ideas of federalism or high-level local autonomy remain constrained by historical, political, administrative, and cultural factors. Therefore, local government reforms in Turkey must be approached incrementally, with an emphasis on oversight and civic participation.

5.3. The Relationship Between Local Autonomy and Democratic Participation: Challenges and Opportunities for Development

Local autonomy is not merely an administrative mechanism but a fundamental component of democracy. Alexis de Tocqueville described local governments as the foundation for citizens' acquisition of political competence. "The true school of political liberty is the township," he wrote, adding, "If local liberties are not safeguarded, the central government inevitably becomes oppressive" (Tocqueville, 2017, pp. 78–79). His praise for local administration in America stemmed from the high level of citizen participation, the public's oversight over local officials, and the widespread culture of voluntary association. Similarly, Montesquieu emphasized that individual liberty can only be secured by checking central power, declaring, "The spirit of laws gains meaning through public participation and the mutual control of powers" (Montesquieu, 2016, Book XI, Chapter 6).

In the Turkish context, however, these theoretical ideals have not been effectively translated into practice. According to 2021 data from the Turkish Statistical Institute (TÜİK), the rate of citizen participation in municipal decision-making processes is only 1.6 percent. The Council of Europe's 2021 report titled *Local and Regional Democracy in Turkey* also noted that participatory democratic tools are not widely used and that citizens generally lack access to municipal decision-making mechanisms (Council of Europe, 2021, p. 14).

Low levels of democratic participation also negatively affect the efficiency of public services. The United Nations Development Programme's 2020 report *Local Governance in Fragile Contexts* highlighted that countries with low participation rates tend to exhibit higher levels of local corruption and lower levels of public satisfaction (UNDP, 2020, p. 32).

Tocqueville made another critical observation: the alienation of citizens from governance leads to arbitrary rule. "As the citizen withdraws from governance, he also relinquishes his liberty" (Tocqueville, 2017, p. 133). In Turkey, this is reflected in the lack of transparency and accountability in local government. According to Transparency International's 2022 report, more than 40 percent of corruption complaints involving municipalities concern procedural violations in public procurement, the transfer of resources to favored firms, and allegations of partisan hiring practices (Transparency International, 2022, pp. 11–14).

Montesquieu's emphasis on oversight mechanisms is also relevant here. "Security is the guarantee of liberty. Power without oversight inevitably leads to corruption" (Montesquieu, 2016, Book XI, Chapter 4). Yet both administrative and citizen-based oversight mechanisms are notably weak in Turkey. The 2021 audit reports of the Court of Accounts revealed widespread irregular expenditures, off-the-record transactions, and unmonitored extrabudgetary activities in many municipalities (Court of Accounts, 2021, pp. 147–151).

These issues are not limited to institutional oversight failures. Citizens' inability to directly intervene in governance prevents the emergence of a natural check against local corruption. Robert Putnam's theory of social capital offers a compelling explanation: in societies with low levels of social capital, citizens lack the reflex to question public authority, and political responsibility remains underdeveloped (Putnam, 1993, pp. 175–177).

According to data from the Ministry of the Interior, as of 2023, there are 121,000 registered associations in Turkey. However, the vast majority are concentrated in Istanbul, Ankara, and Izmir, while representation in rural areas remains limited. Moreover, only 12 percent of these associations are actively functioning, according to the Directorate of Associations. This illustrates the restricted scope of voluntary civic engagement.

Municipal councils, likewise, often fail to serve as effective deliberative bodies. According to Çukurçayır and Eroğlu, in 85 percent of municipal councils in Turkey, genuine debate and pluralism are virtually nonexistent. Most decisions are made unanimously, and local opposition is underdeveloped (Çukurçayır and Eroğlu, 2011, p. 61).

Article 3 of the European Charter of Local Self-Government affirms that citizen participation in local decision-making processes is a fundamental right. However, in Turkey, this right is not effectively guaranteed by legal frameworks. Instruments of direct democracy such as citizens' assemblies, referendums, and participatory budgeting are extremely limited in both law and practice.

In conclusion, the essential balance between local autonomy and democratic participation has not been achieved in Turkey. As Tocqueville warned, "In a system where the local is neglected, liberty remains merely a promise on paper" (Tocqueville, 1835/2017, p. 148). Low participation, weak transparency, ineffective oversight, and an unstructured civil society constitute major obstacles to the realization of functional local autonomy in Turkey.

6. CONCLUSION AND EVALUATION

The classical intellectual legacies of Montesquieu and Tocqueville emphasize that local governments are not merely administrative units but fundamental arenas for the construction of liberty and democratic culture. Montesquieu advocated for a model of decentralization in which decision-making and oversight mechanisms are also independent at the local level. He emphasized, "If power is concentrated in one hand, liberty disappears," underlining that individual freedom can only be preserved within a dispersed system of power (Montesquieu, 1748/2016, Book XI, Chapter 6). Similarly, Tocqueville highlighted the democratic depth of local governance, stating, "Americans are a people who have learned to solve their own problems with their own hands" (Tocqueville, 2017, p. 81).

In the Turkish context, a clear divergence exists between Montesquieu's decentralist model and the structure of Turkish public administration. For decades, Turkish governance has been shaped by a centralized paradigm, where local governments operate largely under the supervision and control of the central authority. The 1982 Constitution further entrenched this centralism. Although Article 127 of the Constitution grants local administrations legal personality, it also confers upon the central government the authority of administrative tutelage, which severely limits local autonomy in practice (Keleş, 2016, p. 83).

Turkey ratified the European Charter of Local Self-Government in 1992, committing to its principles. However, many legal provisions and administrative practices still deviate significantly from the Charter. For instance, the authority of the Ministry of the Interior to dismiss elected mayors demonstrates the central government's ability to override local democratic mandates. This situation clearly contradicts Montesquieu's ideal of liberty through decentralized governance.

According to the OECD's *Decentralisation and Local Public Finance in Europe* report (2020), Turkey ranks among the lowest countries in terms of fiscal decentralization. Local governments account for only 10 percent of total public spending, whereas this figure is 44 percent in Sweden, 25 percent in Germany, and 19 percent in France (OECD, 2020, pp. 18–20). These statistics reveal that local autonomy in Turkey remains limited not only at the constitutional level but also in practice.

Additionally, the personnel systems of local governments are defined by the central administration. Recruitment, dismissal, and salary arrangements for municipal staff are subject to approval by the central authority. This narrows the scope of action for locally elected officials and generates continuous friction between local administrations and the central government. Such a system undermines Montesquieu's principle that "every power must be balanced by another power," thereby reducing the democratic depth of governance in Turkey.

Montesquieu's decentralist model is valuable not only in terms of administrative efficiency but also for promoting democratic stability and fostering civic culture. Turkey can move closer to this vision through constitutional and administrative reforms. Specifically, local governments' areas of responsibility must be redefined, their financial resources expanded, and administrative tutelage powers curtailed. These measures would operationalize Montesquieu's principle that "liberty can only be guaranteed by limiting power."

Thus, Montesquieu's theory of local governance offers not merely a normative framework but a concrete roadmap for democratic deepening. Direct citizen participation, widespread political accountability, and institutional pluralism all stem from the fundamental principles he articulated. In this regard, reengaging with Montesquieu's philosophy is crucial for reforming Turkish public administration into a more equitable, participatory, and pluralistic system.

In this light, Montesquieu's system-centered vision of constitutional liberty and Tocqueville's people-centered vision of practical democracy are complementary. Their combined insights continue to inform both institutional design and civic engagement within modern multi-level governance frameworks. In centralized states like Turkey, a dual-track transformation involving constitutional reform and the cultivation of participatory culture is both necessary and feasible.

Despite the formal constitutional recognition of local governments in Turkey, their functional autonomy remains limited. The centralized legacy inherited from the Ottoman Empire, minority uprisings during the early Republican period, and the continuing security concerns due to PKK terrorism have often led to the suppression of local autonomy claims under the guise of protecting national unity. In particular, the association of certain southeastern municipalities with terrorist activities has prompted the central government to expand tutelary mechanisms. This historical reflex has created a widespread societal aversion to federal structures and has framed demands for local autonomy as political threats.

Moreover, the administrative capacity, accountability, and service delivery performance of Turkish local governments remain highly contested. Reports from the Court of Accounts reveal widespread procedural violations, inefficient use of public resources, and insufficient financial oversight (Court of Accounts, 2021, pp. 147–151). According to TÜİK data, public participation in municipal decision-making processes is below 2 percent, highlighting the weakness of public oversight (TÜİK, 2021).

Transparency International's 2022 report states that municipalities are among the most frequently reported institutions for corruption allegations in Turkey. This observation aligns with Tocqueville's warning: "When citizens lose interest in governance, it is not liberty but arbitrariness that prevails" (Tocqueville, 2017, p. 133). The lack of civic engagement undermines transparency and accountability, allowing local officials to act in pursuit of personal interests.

However, this situation does not imply that local autonomy is unfeasible in Turkey. Rather, it underscores the need for a healthier, more accountable local governance framework. Models of local governance implemented in advanced democracies provide valuable guidance. For instance, Helsinki's "OmaStadi" participatory budgeting initiative launched in 2019 allocated €8.8 million to citizen-proposed projects. In 2021, approximately 80,000 citizens participated in the process, and the selected projects were determined through direct online voting (OECD, 2022, pp. 58–59). Citizens propose projects via digital platforms, and after technical evaluations, eligible proposals are voted on publicly. Implementation stages are also transparently monitored online (Helsinki City Executive Office, 2021).

Similarly, Iceland's post-crisis digital platforms, "Better Reykjavik" and "Better Neighborhoods," have allowed citizens to submit policy suggestions year-round, enabling direct access to municipal governments. As of 2022, over 70,000 users were registered on Better Reykjavik, with an average of 500 citizen proposals implemented annually (Citizens Foundation, 2022).

Adapting such systems to Turkey is feasible, but requires the fulfillment of several preconditions:

1. **A democratic balance must be established that transcends security reflexes**, local autonomy and national unity should not be treated as inherently conflicting objectives.
2. **Mechanisms enhancing the accountability of local leaders must be reinforced.** Court of Accounts oversight should be made more independent, and municipal councils must evolve into platforms that genuinely reflect opposition.
3. **A culture of participation must be cultivated.** Local governance systems should integrate digital platforms for citizen proposals and voting, along with consultative councils and citizens' assemblies. As demonstrated by Finland and Iceland, platforms must be accessible, transparent, and user-friendly.
4. **Political parties must prioritize merit in nominating local candidates,** and the authority of mayors should be counterbalanced by robust oversight frameworks.

As Tocqueville famously remarked, "Towns are the cradle of liberty. A people who lose their town lose their habit of freedom" (Tocqueville, 1835/2017, p. 148). Montesquieu similarly emphasized, "Law must distribute power, involve the people in decisions, and diffuse responsibility in governance" (Montesquieu, 1748/2016, Book XI), indicating that liberty is safeguarded through participatory and decentralized local government systems.

In conclusion, Turkey's local governance system is in clear need of reform. This transformation must occur not only structurally but also culturally and intellectually. The theoretical framework offered by Tocqueville and Montesquieu conceptualizes local democracy as more than a mode of administration—it is a way of life. To move toward this vision, Turkey must strengthen civil society, institutionalize transparency, and foster a culture of civic participation.

In addition, the following reform proposals should be implemented:

- Making participatory budgeting processes legally mandatory in all metropolitan municipalities,
- Introducing local referendum mechanisms into legislation,
- Broadcasting municipal council sessions live and publishing decisions online,
- Forming independent municipal audit boards composed of qualified experts,
- Ensuring civil society representation in municipal advisory boards.

REFERENCES

Ağaoğulları, M. Ali. (2007). *Toplumsal-Siyasal Çatışmanın Erdemi: Machiavelli ile Montesquieu'den Alınacak Dersler*, "Mete Tunçay'a Armağan" içinde, (Derleyenler: Mehmet Ö. Alkan, Tanıl Bora, Murat Koraltürk), İletişim Yayınları, İstanbul.

Akça, G. (2007). *Osmanlı Millet Sisteminin Dönüşümü.* Doğu Anadolu Bölgesi Araştırmaları.

Akıllı, H., & Akıllı, H. S. (2014). Decentralization and Recentralization of Local Governments in Turkey. *Transylvanian Review of Administrative Sciences, 42E*, 5–24.

Bayraktar, S. (2007). *Türk kamu yönetiminde adem-i merkeziyetin sınırları: Yerel yönetimler ve reformlar.* TODAİE Yayınları.

Çarkoğlu, A., & Kalaycıoğlu, E. (2009). *The rising tide of conservatism in Turkey.* Palgrave Macmillan. DOI: 10.1057/9780230621534

Çetin, H. (2007). *Çağdaş siyasal Akımlar.* Orion Kitabevi.

Çınar, M. (2011). The Justice and Development Party and the Kemalist Establishment. *Turkish Studies, 12*(1), 1–16. DOI: 10.1080/14683849.2011.563181

Citizens Foundation. (2022). *Better Reykjavik Annual Report.* https://citizens.is

Council of Europe. (2017). *European Charter of Local Self-Government.* Strasbourg: Council of Europe Publishing. https://www.coe.int/en/web/conventions/full-list/-/conventions/treaty/122

Çukurçayır, M. A. & Eroğlu, H. (2011). "Belediye Meclisleri Üzerine Bir Değerlendirme." *Yerel Yönetim Araştırmaları Dergisi*, 1(2), ss. 56–75.

de Tocqueville, A. (2017). *Amerika'da Demokrasi* (M. Tüzel, Çev.). İstanbul: Türkiye İş Bankası Kültür Yayınları. (Orijinal eser 1835'te yayımlanmıştır.)

Ebenstein, W. (2003). *Siyasi Felsefenin Büyük Düşünürleri.* (Çeviren: İsmet Özel), Şule Yayınları, İstanbul

Elazar, D. J. (1987). *Exploring Federalism.* University of Alabama Press.

Göze, A. (2007). *Siyasal Düşünceler ve Yönetimler.* Beta Basım Yayın.

Helsinki City Executive Office. (2021). *OmaStadi Evaluation Report.* https://omastadi.hel.fi

Kadıoğlu, A. (2005). Denationalization of citizenship? The Turkish experience. *Citizenship Studies, 9*(3), 357–377.

Karpat, K. H. (1985). *Ottoman population, 1830–1914: Demographic and social characteristics*. University of Wisconsin Press.

Keating, M. (2009). *The Independence of Scotland: Self-government and the shifting politics of union*. Oxford University Press. DOI: 10.1093/acprof:oso/9780199545957.001.0001

Keleş, R. (2016). *Yerinden Yönetim ve Siyaset* (9. Baskı). İstanbul: Cem Yayınları.

Keyman, E. F., & Koyuncu, B. (2005). Globalization, alternative modernities and the political economy of Turkey. *Review of International Political Economy*, *12*(1), 105–128. DOI: 10.1080/09692290500049896

Keyman, F. (2010). *Modernleşme, Ulus-Devlet ve Demokrasi: Türkiye Üzerine Tezler*. İstanbul Bilgi Üniversitesi Yayınları.

Loughlin, J., Hendriks, F., & Lidström, A. (2011). *The Oxford Handbook of Local and Regional Democracy in Europe*. Oxford University Press.

Mete, H. (2020). Kürt Sorunu, Yerel Yönetimler ve Kayyum Politikaları: Eleştirel Bir Değerlendirme. *Toplum ve Demokrasi*, *14*(2), 67–92.

Montesquieu, C. (1998). *Kanunların Ruhu Üzerine I*, (Çeviren: Fehmi Baldaş), Toplumsal Dönüşüm Yayınları, İstanbul

Montesquieu, C. (2016). *Kanunların Ruhu Üzerine*. (Çev. Mehmet Ali Ağaoğulları). İstanbul: Türkiye İş Bankası Kültür Yayınları. Kitap XI. *Bölüm*, *4*, 6.

Montesquieu, C. (2017), *Kanunların Ruhu Üzerine*, (Çev. Berna Günen), Türkiye İş Bankası Kültür Yayınları, Kitap I, Bölüm 3.

OECD. (2020). *Decentralisation and Local Public Finance in Europe*. OECD Publications.

OECD. (2022). *Enhancing Public Participation in Local Governance: Comparative Country Studies*. OECD Publishing. ss.

Oran, B. (2001). *Türk Dış Politikası: Kurtuluş Savaşından Bugüne Olgular, Belgeler, Yorumlar (Cilt 1)*. İletişim Yayınları.

Ortaylı, İ. (2000). İmparatorluğun. In *Uzun Yüzyılı*. İletişim Yayınları.

Ostrom, E. (1990). *Governing the commons: The evolution of institutions for collective action*. Cambridge university press. DOI: 10.1017/CBO9780511807763

Özbudun, E. (2000). *Contemporary Turkish Politics: Challenges to Democratic Consolidation*. Lynne Rienner Publishers. DOI: 10.1515/9781626373174

Özbudun, E. (2009). *Türk Anayasa Hukuku.* Yetkin Yayınları.

Putnam, R. D. (1993). *Making Democracy Work: Civic Traditions in Modern Italy.* Princeton University Press.

Raynaud, P., & Rials, S. (2003). Siyaset Felsefesi Sözlüğü, (Çeviren.İsmail Yarguz, Necmettin Kamil Sevin, Emel ergun, Hüsnü Dilli), İletişim Yayınları, İstanbul

Schmidt, M. G. (2002). *Demokrasi Kuramlarına Giriş.* Vadi Yayınları.

Tocqueville, A. (1962). Amerika'da Demokrasi, (Çeviren: Taner Timur), Yenilik Basımevi, İstanbul.

Tocqueville, A. (2017). *Demokrasi Amerika'da.* (Çev. Gökhan Özcan). İstanbul: Türkiye İş Bankası Kültür Yayınları. ss. 78–81, 127, 133, 148.

Transparency International. (2022). *Türkiye Yolsuzluk Raporu.* Uluslararası Şeffaflık Derneği.

TÜİK. (2021). *Belediye Hizmetleri ve Katılım İstatistikleri.* Türkiye İstatistik Kurumu.

UNDP. (2020). *Local Governance in Fragile Contexts.* UNDP Publications.

Yıldız, A. (2012). *Ne Mutlu Türküm Diyebilene: Türk Ulusal Kimliğinin Etno-Seküler Sınırları (1919–1938).* İletişim Yayınları.

Chapter 5
Federalism and Local Governments:
India and the United States as Examples of How Federalism Impacts Local Spending

Georgia Leona Litle
https://orcid.org/0009-0006-8188-3651
University of Oklahoma, Goldsby, USA

ABSTRACT

Both the United States and India serve as symbolic leaders of continuing democracy on the global stage. India, however, operates as a more cooperative federalist government that is neither purely federal nor unitary compared to the more rigid American federalist form of government. Differences in democratic philosophy between the two nations yield different policy outcomes at local levels in the context of federal influence. To address these distinctions, this chapter will provide narrative comparison of these two democratic systems through the lens of federal and local healthcare spending policies that attempt to combat opioid addiction as a primary public health concern. This chapter takes a step to develop an answer to the question of how decentralized, federalist systems of government impact local policies in the context of addiction and public health.

DOI: 10.4018/979-8-3373-5576-4.ch005

I. INTRODUCTION

The concept of federalism exemplifies foundational principles inherent to effective democratic systems of government on local, state, and national levels. "Federalism's importance is similar to natural law when it comes to defining justice and natural rights" (Trivedi, 2022, 974). Moreover, "[t]here are distinctive features in the type of federalism followed in almost every federal nation" (Trivedi, 2022, 972). To address distinctions between federalist systems, this chapter will provide a narrative comparison of two democratic structures, the United States and India, through the lens of federal and local healthcare spending policies that attempt to combat opioid addiction.

Both of these nations serve as symbolic leaders of continuing democracy on the global stage: India is the largest democracy in the world, and the United States is the oldest democracy. India, however, operates as a more cooperative federalist government that is neither purely federalist nor centralized. "It is difficult to imagine a diverse country like India following federalism without any compromises over sharing of decision-making powers and administrative responsibilities amongst various levels of government" (Trivedi, 2022, 974). "India is known as a federal nation, it has a lot of unitary features too, which sometimes contradicts its essence of federalism" (Trivedi, 2022, 974).

Differences in democratic philosophy between these two nations yield distinct policy outcomes at local levels in the context of federal influence. In the Indian context, transition to a more coalitional, multi-party-political environment catalyzed enhanced federalization. Another notable political phenomenon in India pertains to the idea that, although traditional grassroots democracy has failed to obtain systematic support in India, significant attempts have been made to strengthen localized, self-governing initiatives (Singh, 2001). "Indian federalism is considered very flexible, [and] the American system of federalism is more rigid" (Trivedi, 2022, 972). "The decentralization framework envisaged in the fiscal federalism literature emanating from western scholars does not easily fit into the Indian approach" (Ooman, 2015).

This case study will specifically address how local governments interact with federal and state entities in these two national contexts and how such interactions influence localized policy, including insight into gradations of federalist systems of government considering cultural, historical, and political idiosyncrasies. Because of the relevant nature of the opioid crises, case studies in this context are ripe for future use in academic discourse addressing effectiveness of use of federal funds in democratic societies rooted in federalist principles.

Looking at the modern opioid epidemic in particular, the opioid crises caused harmful addiction related outcomes in both nations; however, India's unique governmental structure and strategies for federal disbursement of funds to local governments provides contrast to the American federalist system of spending and federal disbursement. "Opioid use disorder (OUD) is a disabling disorder with high levels of morbidity and mortality that has devastated families and communities for decades" (Jalali et al., 2020). While much attention has been focused on the epidemic the United States, "the impact of opioid abuse and addiction in developing nations like India has been equally significant, [but] less publicized (Bhawalkar et al., 2024). This chapter's comparative analysis of the United States and India, coupled with practical examples in the health and addiction spending context, demonstrates the true complications inherent to issues of (i) the extent of cooperation in a system labeled as "cooperative federalism," and (ii) how cooperative federalist principles practically play out in unique national contexts. Effective governmental cooperation and federalism must be supported by a nuanced equilibrium of restrictive and idiosyncratic democratic conditions grounded in national identity and culture.

II. THEORETICAL FRAMEWORK

a. Cooperative Federalism

"Federalism can be traced back three thousand years, but the meaning [of the term] has changed and the concept has been modified over time" (Trivedi, 2022, 972). Concepts of decentralization and federalism have been treated in political economy literature as primary solutions to policy crises (Tripathi & Grigoriadis, 2023). However, "[a]lthough it is [a form] of non-centralization… federalism does not inevitably imply decentralization. This fundamentally implies the existence of numerous vertical and horizontal power centers [in a federalist government structure]" (Trivedi, 2022, 976). In most federalist systems, local governments can experience incongruity in both functions and financial support due local government dependency on intergovernmental transfers for financial support (Tripathi & Grigoriadis, 2023).

Some nations possess more decentralization of power in their democratic systems, which impacts diverse policy outcomes at the national, state, and local levels. Decentralization, as in pertains to governmental expenditures, is generally viewed as supportive to economic policy development while maximizing efficiency (Tripathi & Grigoriadis, 2023). "Both the United States and India currently adhere to a [more] formal trends in the construction of federalism, [but] with [difference] in the institutionalist approach and… distribution of constitutional authorities" (Trivedi, 2022, 977).

Federalism is [generally] defined as "division of power between the [center government] and the state" (Trivedi, 2022, 972). Other definitions would define the term as mere "decentralization of power" (Trivedi, 2022, 972). Correspondingly, the comparative federalism literature essentially sorts governments into two categories (i) federations where the constitution chiefly assigns exclusive capabilities to different levels of government that administer policy independently (Scholtz, 2023). Courts in these systems operate to interpret boundaries of these governmental compartments (Scholtz, 2023).

In the second category, governments share competences and administrative power demonstrating cooperative federalism and softened administrative exclusivity (Scholtz, 2023). This theory of cooperative federalism is widely accepted today and explains a more flexible relationship between levels of government (Zimmerman, 2001). These flexible relationships exist in contrast to the former idea of dual federalism that implies division of purposes between governmental levels (Zimmerman, 2001). The concept of pure and effective dual federalism is in decline of acceptance in the academic community (Zimmerman, 2001). Research questions focus on extent of intergovernmental cooperation and how cooperative federalist systems are maintained in delicate equilibrium under potentially restrictive conditions (Scholtz, 2023).

b. Dual Federalism

In the American context, the concept of dual sovereignty is apparent and more legalistic in the sense of clear written formality providing for genuine intergovernmental authority. Arguably, the United States demonstrates a system deeply characterized by elements of dual federalism. For example, Alexander Hamilton in Federalist 32 provided for concepts of pure dual federalism in the sense that state governments retain sovereignty not exclusively delegated to the United States and focusing on delegation of rights to states instead of restriction of rights (Zimmerman, 2001). Moreover, the Tenth Amendment to the United States Constitution further provided that the federal government only had specific powers and all other powers are reserved to the states or to the people (Zimmerman, 2001). Although the United States demonstrates elements of dual federalism in its foundational texts, practicalities suggest elements of cooperative federalist tendencies suggesting a fascinating interplay between governmental levels rooted in complicated historical context. "When examining the key elements of American politics, it is impossible to ignore the state's appealing institutional and constitutional history that spans two centuries and travels a stepwise evolution in federalism" (Trivedi, 2022, 979).

c. Concepts of Administrative Autonomy

Most political environments take for granted the concept that administrative agencies are active in the policy creation and implementation process. Administrative agencies' power and resources place them at the heart of the policy processes. The American example provides an exceptional setting of administrative independence in the federal government, state entities, and local government. Administrators at all levels have substantial discretion in how to implement governmental policies. Moreover, state governments are essential catalysts for governmental growth at local and national levels (Choi et al., 2004). Essentially, administrative independence, and by extension independence at different levels of government in a federalist system, is a matter of degree Thus, the extent that a federalist system is dual or cooperative in nature is a matter of scale in contrast to an exclusive categorization.

III. THE UNITED STATES

a. History of the American Federalist System

In the American context, federal state conflict is a foundational component of national democracy. Similarities between the United States and India include "constitutionalism, an associative and functional system of federalism, a multifaceted and multiethnic trend, a multifaceted state of governance, multilingualism, an institutional hierarchy" (Trivedi, 2022, 976). In the United States, however, the federal government and states are in some respects perpetually struggling over relative power and autonomy" (Goelzhauser & Konisky, 2020, 312). In comparison to India, the American Constitution does not generally or clearly organize fiscal obligations among the different levels of government (Briffault, 1996). "The American Constitution is a political instrument that, at the Philadelphia Convention in 1787, helped the American people become more homogeneous" (Trivedi, 2022, 977). "Federalism was initially used in the state paradigm in Switzerland in the 12th century, and the United States of America included its first model of federalism—the balanced model—into its constitutional structure" (Trivedi, 2022, 973).

In practice, different levels of American government rely on different revenue sources and have different spending objectives and coordination. (Briffault, 1996). The American federal Constitution does not clearly establish state or local governments (Briffault, 1996). Consequently, in some contrast to the Indian model, American states and localities do not derive their powers to borrow, tax, or spend from the federal constitution or government; these rights are inherent (Briffault, 1996). States have more political autonomy in the American system with intrinsic powers to "borrow, tax, spend, and delegate those fiscal powers to their localities" (Briffault, 1996).

Accordingly, the American Constitution does impose as many limitations on states as the Indian system via constitutional omission. The Supreme Court provides a check on state authority and has interpreted the Commerce Clause, Privileges and Immunities Clause, and Equal Protection Clause of the Constitution to prohibit certain state regulatory behaviors, such as behavior that discriminates against non-residents or burden interstate commerce (Briffault, 1996). Moreover, the Due Process Clause limits state ability to tax out-of-state entities without nexus to the taxing state, and the Supremacy Clause protects federal property from state taxation (Briffault, 1996). "Federalism which is both balanced and structural is a distinctive and important aspect of [American] governance" (Trivedi, 2022, 978). "The constitution clearly explains two levels of authority" (Trivedi, 2022, 977).

States commonly enact statutes contradicting federal policy while the federal government commonly attempts to control state authority and policy. Policy strategy often catalyzes polarized political tensions when the federal government implements limitations on state policy decisions when disbursing federal funds (Goelzhauser & Konisky, 2020). In the opioid context, multi-district litigation against American pharmaceutical companies that are liable for wrongdoing during the opioid crisis provides a characteristic example of federal-state tensions (Goelzhauser & Konisky, 2020). States individually sued opioid related corporations, but a unitary federal settlement was reached to conclude the litigation with federal restrictions on disbursement of settlement funds.

From a comparative point of view, "[t]he federal system in the United States is more robust, appropriate, transparent, balanced, mature, negotiated, demos-friendly, and stable than it is in India" (Trivedi, 2022, 976). A foundational component of American federalism is the concept that the federal government has broad authority to raise and spend money, including control of federal taxation (subject to minimal limitation rooted in the Due Process Clause of the Fifth Amendment required non-discriminatory taxation amongst the states) and general manipulation of currency (Briffault, 1996). Turning to federal spending, the American Constitution broadly empowers Congress to provide for the common defense and general welfare, yet the federal government's Spending Power has substantially developed over the last two decades (Briffault, 1996). Specifically, the federal government can attach conditions to the release of federal funds to direct policy, even absent of Congressional approval (Briffault, 1996).

Specific factors impacting federal control over state and local spending in the American context includes size of the federal budget, focus on distribution of payments directly to individuals (instead of intergovernmental transfer to state or local governments), federal taxation as a revenue source (including individual, estate, social insurance, and corporate taxes), federal borrowing as a source of revenue, and the federal deficit (Briffault, 1996). "The federal share of total government spending has ranged between 62% and 70% and has accounted for between 48% and 58% of domestic spending, between 1959 and 1994" in the United States (Briffault, 1996, 537). Notably, these revenue sources are indicators of the predominantly *redistributive* financial function of the American federal government, especially considering expansion of related federal programs, such as Social Security and Medicare. (Briffault, 1996). "The [American] administrative structure has a [generally] standardized hierarchy" of redistribution (Trivedi, 2022, 978).

In the American system of federalism, states are generally cited as a localized model for adjustment of federal fiscal practices. Such state level spending and debt limitations have been presented as models for policymakers who seek to limit federal spending and "balance" the federal budget deficit (including Reagan, Bush, Clinton, Obama, and Trump) (Briffault, 1996). In contrast to federal policy, many state constitutions limit state taxation and spending, including requirements for a balanced budget, debt limitations, and line-item state gubernatorial authority (Briffault, 1996). Consequently, in the American context, debt plays a less prominent role in financing governmental operations at the state level in contrast to the federal level (Briffault, 1996). For example, some measures, such as California's Proposition 13, restrict localized taxation, which operates to restrain localized, community-based spending decisions (Briffault, 1996).

To summarize, federalism has shaped the political process for policy-making and access to healthcare (Beer, 2024). American federalism allows for more policy innovation and diversity among states but the Supreme Courts can limit this autonomy to help facilitate policy homogeneity (Beer, 2024). Patterns in policy are largely driven by interactions between state policy and Supreme Court rulings (Beer, 2024).

i. The Impact of Partisanship on the American Federalist System

"[P]olitical parties are crucial to the formation of federal character" (Trivedi, 2022, 978). To gain partisan political advantage, a false image of benign intergovernmental cooperation can yield to coercive federalism in which the national government seeks to force subnational governments to its will through financial withholding and regulation (Goelzhauser & Konisky, 2020). The American political environment, which is rooted in federalist tension, is infused with trends of immense political polarization. "[P]olarization is... a defining feature of contemporary American politics" (Goelzhauser & Konisky, 2020, 311). Federal coercion certainly plays a part in intragovernmental relations in the sense that the American federal government can and does utilize its powers to control state policy (Goelzhauser & Konisky, 2020). Partisan polarization has operated to supplement attempts at federal coercion through catalyzing politically spiteful responses between the federal and state governments. In other words, the federal government uses formal powers to punish or deter states in a form of "punitive federalism" (Goelzhauser & Konisky, 2020). Moreover, policy innovation occurs at the state level and can lead to policy adoption by other states and the federal government but such innovation and diffusion can be limited by hostility to polarizing political policies (Karapin 2020).

In the healthcare context, polarizing policy decisions usually center on issues pertaining to universal or expansion of healthcare coverage and economic tension between public and private healthcare markets (Goelzhauser & Konisky, 2020). For an example, state level Medicaid expansion demonstrates the importance of federal funding. "Under the ACA, states can extend health coverage under Medicaid to nonelderly adults with income up to 138 percent of the federal poverty level... [and] the federal government pays 90 percent of the costs in the year 2020" (Goelzhauser & Konisky, 2020, 327). These federal spending initiatives impact budget outcomes at all government levels, as well as vulnerable populations.

ii. Federalism and the Opioid Epidemic

In response to the opioid addiction crisis, states and local subdivisions sued pharmaceutical manufacturers, distributors, and pharmacy chains to recover billions of dollars in national settlement funds that are financial recourse to rectify harm from the opioid epidemic. In general, these large federal settlements, such as the opioid settlement fund, are created with the intention to counteract the harmful health outcomes perpetuated by malfeasant corporate actors. Such intentions echo the purpose of the historically large Tobacco Master Settlement Fund created in the late 1990s. Similar to opioid settlement fund proceeds, the purpose of the tobacco settlement was to allocate lifesaving tobacco prevention efforts in each [participating] state. In the case of the tobacco litigation, while some participating states took funds and established tobacco prevention and education programs in accordance with the intended purpose of the federal settlement fund, few states effectively funded tobacco prevention programs at federally recommended standards, and only two states funded these programs at these recommended levels as of 2023.

Much of the opioid settlement proceeds were placed in a federal settlement fund in which states could opt-in as participants to receive settlement proceeds subject to terms of a unitary federal settlement agreement. This federal settlement fund, which was the result of multi-district litigation actions or "MDLs" present issues pertaining to federalism. There is no "nationwide" jurisdiction in the American context for class action lawsuits, yet these MDLs appear to circumvent that fact by compelling state attorneys litigating cases to participate in a federal level settlement (Gluck, 2022). In the context of federalism, MDLs exert a sort of "nationalist" power over state and local jurisdictions to facilitate global settlement at the federal level without consideration of nuances in state law (Gluck, 2022).

Prior Supreme Court opinions suggested the need for a federal statute that provides additional guidance on MDLs (Gluck, 2022). Moreover, established public policy literature addressing two different theoretical concepts provide foundations for analysis of whether these opioid federal settlement funds are effectively utilized within a given to state to fight consequences of opioid addiction: (i) the concept of legalized accountability and utilizing class action litigation to influence policy change and (ii) analysis of the impact of legislative content on policy outcomes addressed in policy innovation, diffusion, and reinvention related literature.

iii. Local Spending in the Context of American Federalism

"An important feature of an effective system of fiscal federalism is the assignment of sufficient revenue powers to subnational governments so that there is a strong connection between revenues and expenditures" (Tripathi & Grigoriadis, 2023). Moreover, in the American situation, "state and local budgets as a percentage of GDP have grown largely due to the expansion in state and local taxation" (Briffault, 1996, 538). Similarly in India, "states are free to design and fund their policy agendas that explicitly address local needs and goals, which is crucial in a nation with India's level of socioeconomic and geographic diversity" (Trivedi, 2022, 975).

In the United States, states largely obtain revenue from sales and gross receipts and state individual and corporate income taxes (Briffault, 1996). In contrast, local governments obtain revenue from property tax (Briffault, 1996). Thus, while most federal spending is redistributive, American state and local spending is largely developmental to assist in advancement of physical and social infrastructure necessary for public improvement, such as education, highways, mass transit, and community safety (Briffault, 1996).

From a local spending perspective in the American context, state and local governments have disincentive to operate in a redistributive manner. "Open internal borders securing the flow of capital and labor throughout the United States relatively free from state or local interference" (Briffault, 1996, 539). Therefore, people are free to relocate: if a state or locality attempts redistribution from the rich to poor, more poor people may remain in the state or local jurisdiction, while the rich will likely depart reducing the tax base (Briffault, 1996). In essence, the American federal government is the epicenter of redistributive economic activity in the United States because it can redistribute funds without recourse from taxpayers or competitive from less redistributive jurisdictions (Briffault, 1996).

American states provide a type of intermediary position facilitating some developmental and some redistributive programs (compared to the federal governments more extreme redistributive nature and locality focus on development) (Briffault, 1996). Thus, the argument exists that localities are better positioned to create and administer developmental policies in the because smaller size of local governments enables resident oversight aligned to local preferences and need (Briffault, 1996). Consequently, the independence of state and localities in the American federalist context presents issues of disparity amongst jurisdictions that manifest substantial consequences for local and state spending decisions, most notably economic differences in individual wealth, and poverty rates (Briffault, 1996). Although diversity among state government programs is desirable from the standpoint of promoting local preference, such lack of uniformity can instigate conflict and negate efficiency prompting the need for greater government oversight (Briffault, 1996). Turning to the American Medicaid program in particular, this healthcare coverage program substantially impacts health and addiction treatment. Medicaid has transitioned from a restrictive program primarily attached to recipients on public assistance in the 1960s to more expansive coverage (Grogan, 2025). Medicaid is ambiguously provided for the "medically needy" but now operates as a more embedded healthcare payment system that serves diverse economic sectors beyond a population with lower income into the economic middle class (Grogan, 2025).

b. American Opioid Statistics

"Over the past six months, the Bipartisan Policy Center "BPC" conducted a detailed analysis of federal appropriations and identified 57 federal programs that, either entirely or significantly, fund efforts to curb the epidemic. In total, the federal government included nearly $11 billion for these programs in its FY2017 and FY2018 discretionary appropriations bills. This includes a 124 percent increase between FY2017 ($3.3 billion) and FY2018 ($7.4 billion). These programs span the continuum of care, including prevention, treatment, and recovery. In addition, funds are directed to research, criminal justice, public health surveillance, and supply reduction efforts. Between FY2017 and FY2018, funding specifically targeted to opioid use disorder treatment and recovery increased by $1.5 billion (from $599 million to $2.12 billion). Over three quarters (77 percent) of the appropriations to opioid programs are administered by the Department of Health and Human Services (HHS).

The report also examines how federal opioid investments are spent across five geographically diverse states: Arizona, Louisiana, New Hampshire, Ohio, and Tennessee. The average drug overdose death rate in the five case study states was nearly one and half times (144 percent) higher than the national average in 2017.

Each state case study takes an in-depth look at how these states are allocating the two largest federal opioid grants, the State Targeted Response and State Opioid Response grants. BPC's analysis also incorporates county-level maps of federal funding and drug overdose deaths from 2015 to 2017 for each of the selected states.

Three Phases of the Epidemic

The CDC has identified three waves of the opioid epidemic… beginning with deaths involving prescription opioids, followed by increases in heroin, and finally synthetic opioids or fentanyl. The years 1999 to 2006 saw 10 percent annual increases in overdose deaths, slowing to an increase of 3 percent per year from 2006 through 2014, followed by a jump to 16 percent annually from 2014 through 2017.

The **first wave** of the opioid epidemic was ushered in by the introduction of OxyContin onto the market in 1996. OxyContin, a long-acting opioid generically prescribed as oxycodone, was promoted as a medication capable of relieving pain for up to 12 hours and was labeled as nonaddictive.

The American Pain Society sought to enhance the treatment of pain during this same time period. In 2001, the Joint Commission on Healthcare Organizations (now the Joint Commission) issued new pain-management standards. Opioid prescribing rates subsequently increased sharply. In 2009, primary care physicians prescribed the majority of opioids. The combination of a highly addictive drug's introduction to the market, an emphasis on addressing pain, aggressive marketing, and over prescribing—as well as a lack of evidence-based treatment availability and training in addiction—laid the groundwork for the opioid epidemic.

At the same time, pain clinics with little legal or regulatory oversight sprang up in Florida and other states in the Southeast. The Drug Enforcement Administration (DEA) reported that 90 of the top 100 oxycodone prescribers in the nation were in Florida. In the face of an increasing number of "pill mills" and mounting overdose deaths, beginning in 2010 Florida state legislators passed several laws intended to shut down illegally operating pain clinics. As a result of the new legislation and enhanced law enforcement activities, overdose death rates began to fall in Florida.

Nationally, faced with increasing reports of overdose deaths, a new formulation of OxyContin was introduced in 2010. The product was reformulated to make it more difficult to be crushed and snorted. The new formulation, as well as an increased emphasis on proper opioid prescribing, led to the second wave of the epidemic.

The **second wave** was marked by increasing rates of heroin-involved overdose deaths. As prescription opioids became harder to access due to federal and state policies that encouraged the use of prescription drug monitoring programs and decreased opioid prescribing, individuals with opioid use disorders turned to a cheaper and more readily available opioid: heroin. Heroin users were increasingly residents of small urban or non-urban, predominantly white areas of the country compared to previous eras. Heroin users were also likely to have begun misusing prescription opioids before using heroin.

Today, the United States is in midst of the **third wave** of the epidemic, marked by the increasing availability of illicit fentanyl and fentanyl analogs and increasing rates of overdose deaths involving synthetic opioids. Illicit fentanyl available in the United States originates in China. This product is either shipped to Mexico or the United States and is sometimes mixed with heroin, or in some cases pressed into pills. Fentanyl is cheap and powerful, and DEA seizures are more prevalent east of the Mississippi River. In Washington, DC, the Office of the Chief Medical Examiner reported that 71 percent of overdose deaths in the District involved fentanyl or a fentanyl analog. West Virginia, Ohio, and New Hampshire had the highest death rates from synthetic opioids in 2017" (Bipartisan Policy Center, 2019).

c. Relevant Court Case and the Tenth Amendment

In 2018, the Supreme Court struck down a federal prohibition (PAPSA) of state authorization of sports gambling (Zambrano, 2001). In 2014, the National Basketball Association ("NBA"), National Football League ("NFL"), National Hockey League ("NHL"), Major League Baseball ("MLB"), and National Collegiate Athletic Association ("NCAA") sued to determine the constitutional issue of whether "a federal statute that prohibits modification or repeal of state-law prohibitions on private conduct impermissibly commandeer the regulatory power of States" (Zambrano, 2001). The Court found that PASPA's provision prohibiting state authorization of sports gambling schemes violated the Tenth Amendment because it dictated what a state legislature may and may not do (Zambrano, 2001). This Court decision demonstrated the importance of the anti-commandeering clause of the Tenth Amendment that powers not delegated to the United States by the Constitution, nor prohibited by it, are reserved to States (Zambrano, 2001). The federal government has certain enumerated powers and the states have all other legislative powers (Zambrano, 2001). The Court has declared laws unconstitutional for violation of the Tenth Amendment when the federal government commandeers states to action demonstrating limits to federal, enumerated powers (Zambrano, 2001). This interpretation operates as a constitutional protection of liberty and the heart of American federalist equilibrium.

IV. INDIA

a. Historical Context

"A western based political analysis cannot provide [an accurate] theoretical underpinning or philosophical rationale for the democratic decentralization currently [apparent] in India" (Ooman (2015, 5). When it comes in comparison to the United States Constitution, "the Indian Constitution is open to changes and amendments, which makes it much more flexible and unitary in features" (Trivedi, 2022, 974). "As in other aspects of federal relations, fiscal federalism in India has been heavily skewed in favor of centralization, thanks to the... constitutional distribution of functions and finances" (Singh, 2001). The [Indian] federated states "are derived from a written constitution, the lengthiest in the world" (Singh, 2001). The Fundamental Rights embodied in the [Indian] constitution are guaranteed to all citizens: Indian civil liberties include fundamental rights common to most liberal democracies, such as equality, freedom of speech, freedom of association and peaceful assembly, and freedom of religion. In addition, such rights abolish "untouchability" and prohibit discrimination on the grounds of religion or caste. India occupies one fifth of the world's population rendering its political system impactful to overall global progress.

"India's model of federalism was mainly created in the aftermath of Partition, a time when the creation and revision of federal systems in other nations were being influenced by the requirement for powerful central administrations" (Trivedi, 2022, 975). "The most unitary aspect of the Indian constitution is that, while it is intended to function as a federal system under normal circumstances, it is constructed in such a way that it can function as a unitary system during times of war" (Trivedi, 2022). However, although "[t]he word federalism does not appear in the constitutional text, it is considered to be federal to the extent it introduced a dual polity in which the [center government] and the states have their separate powers and the rights to exercise those powers" (Trivedi, 2022, 975).

A foundational element of India's governmental style is the expression of statutory constitutional authority via directedly elected parliamentary governments at the national and state level and directly elected local governments (Rao & Singh, 2001). From a broad perspective, India is comprised of twenty-nine states and seven centrally administered union territories "via a quasi-federal system of governance, whose unitary trait sometimes overshadows its federal functions" (Singh, 2001). The makers of the Indian Constitution sought to facilitate a robust center of government to encourage national unity (Singh, 2001). "The spirit of India's constitutional amendments.. push toward pursuing efficiency goals and stressing accountability at the local level" (Bahl et al., 2010).

In addition to historical context, political, institutional forces contributed to making the Indian form of government (Singh, 2001). "Unprecedented regionalization and diversification of the party system has given rise to a new political matrix in the country" (Singh, 2001). In contrast to the American bipartisan system, diverse political parties control the political system with parties in control at the center potentially in conflict with those at the state and local levels: this is a difference from historic control and Congress Party dominance (Singh, 2001). Moreover, recent participatory political movements in India catalyzed "activation of primordial identities and the unbridled personal ambition of… elites [to] produce… unprecedented fragmentation of political parties and a mushrooming of regional… parties (Singh, 2001). "This implies that fiscal federalism, Indian style, relies on a cooperative rather than competitive relationship between the federal center and the states, while underscoring the predominance of public spending over revenue collection at the state level" (Tripathi & Grigoriadis, 2023).

Correspondingly, regional parties play an impactful and balancing role in Indian politics (Singh, 2001). As opposed to American bipartisanship, Indian presidents and governors are generally elected or appointed with diverse party backgrounds based on inter-party composition (Singh, 2001). India's model of federalism lacks some of the benefits of competitive federalist systems, such as policy correction (Rao & Singh, 2001). In more competitive systems, subnational jurisdictions can influence the policy development and experimentation (Rao & Singh, 2001).

b. Revenue, Expenditure, and Federalism in India

India's tendency for central governmental power can cause overly uniform policy initiatives. For example, India's response to COVID-19 pandemic was to implement a national lockdown (Choutagunta, 2021). This nationalized approach failed to consider variations across states and local governments in resources, healthcare capacity, and incidence of COVID-19 and local governments could not tailer policy response to local desires (Choutagunta, 2021). Some states experienced benefit from the national lockdown while others experienced enormous economic harm despite low rates of COVID-19 found in the jurisdiction (Choutagunta, 2021).

Sector specific considerations are essential to proper considerations of localized spending (Gupta, 2025). A given state can nurture a specific economic sector to pursue domestic

and international market opportunities that benefit the state, locality and nation (Gupta, 2025). From a purely fiscal point of view, economic federalism is an arguably positive factor for economic performance (Tripathi & Grigoriadis, 2023). "Ideally, the intergovernmental transfers system should ensure that subnational governments have enough resources to raise, which in turn can ensure the perpetuation of hard budget constraints" (Tripathi & Grigoriadis, 2023). Decentralization, however, can facilitate unforeseen economic consequences because localities will try to attract commercial and economic activity, and, correspondingly, local judiciaries have temptation to act in a manner that encourages such economic development (Rao & Singh, 2001). The Indian government "is different from that of Germany or South Africa where the federal governments decide major polices and where the different [branches] of government are at best [only] 'implementing' agencies" (Ooman (2015)).

Division of revenue and expenditure powers are allocated among the three levels of Indian government (the central or union government, state governments, and local governments in the form of municipalities or *panchayats*) (Singh, 2001). Thus, in the Indian context, the federal center is theoretically a residual power of state level services and goods (Tripathi & Grigoriadis, 2023). Yet, this objective is practically limited. States in the Indian style of government have more responsibility to provide "services" creating a systematic imbalance in fiscal management (Singh, 2001). Notably, the Indian Constitution failed to overtly include "services" within the scope of states' sales tax authority (Rao & Singh, 2001).

Indian federalism embodies fiscal mismanagement both at the central as well as state level that facilitates structural deficits on an aggregate basis (Tripathi & Grigoriadis, 2023). An intergovernmental transfer mechanism, which does not incentivize fiscal discipline and own revenue generation efforts tends to result in fiscal imprudence by subnational governments (Tripathi & Grigoriadis, 2023). The center government has unlimited borrowing power, yet the states' power is limited by the center government in the event of their indebtedness, although these limitations are infrequently enacted (Singh, 2001).

Moreover, Indian state governments are generally dependent on financial transfers from the central government because the central government dominates revenue collection (Singh, 2001). "The central government holds control over two thirds of the entire revenue collection, while state governments have to meet two thirds of the overall governmental expenditures" (Singh, 2001). Discretionary financial transfers have historically been made by the Planning Commission. "[D]iscretionary transfers include allocation of institutional finances from Life Insurance Corporation, General Insurance Corporation and Unit Trust of India, loans, grants, [and] disaster relief' (Singh, 2001). A well-established criticism of the Indian system of federalism [was] the historic lack of clarity of roles between the Finance Commission and the Planning Commission (Singh, 2001).

To summarize, at the state level, Indian state governments have incentives to mitigate budget restraints and place costs on other state or the federal government as much as possible causing poor budget management despite attempted economic reform at the state level (Tripathi & Grigoriadis, 2023). Moreover, an expectation exists of federal bailout that can encourage underperformance and lack of financial discipline (Tripathi & Grigoriadis, 2023). Decentralized public spending is supplemented with heightened fiscal independence at a subnational level triggering coordination failure between central, state and local governments (Tripathi & Grigoriadis, 2023). "This type of transfer system is associated with common pool problems, moral hazard issues and soft budget constraints" (Tripathi & Grigoriadis, 2023). Although Indian revenue collection is arguably more coherent and harmonized between levels of government because state capacity to collect revenue is limited (Tripathi & Grigoriadis, 2023). Such harmonization fails to take of advantage of some benefits of local revenue collection, such as making local governments that raise revenue more accountable towards citizens and provide more local benefits (Tripathi & Grigoriadis, 2023).

Additional clarification on the rules of financial transfers from the center to state to local governments can make any problems more transparent (Rao & Singh, 2001). Connections between center and state governments may matter more in higher share intergovernmental financial transfers (Tripathi & Grigoriadis, 2023). "Fiscal transfers from the Centre to the states are made by the Government of India on the recommendations of the Finance Commission, which is appointed every five years by the president of India under Article 280 of the Constitution, and of the Planning Commission" (Singh, 2001). "The Finance Commission has generally enjoyed a considerable degree of legitimacy in federal relations as a constitutional body of mixed membership consisting of retired politicians, experts and bureaucrats" (Singh, 2001).

The 2017 Goods and Services Tax (GST) offered concurrent powers to the center and state governments to levy the GST (Singh, 2001). Such allocation negated a traditional principle of clear distinction between the roles of each level of government in terms of revenue collection to avoid conflict (Singh, 2001). Moreover, the Mahatma Gandhi National Rural Employment Guarantee Act (MGNREGA), which offers a legal guarantee for one hundred days of employment per financial year to rural households, "is the world's largest public employment generation scheme" (Tripathi & Grigoriadis, 2023). The program works to safeguard rural growth and wellbeing via "social protection, livelihood… and democratic empowerment" (Tripathi & Grigoriadis, 2023). Financial funding is based on transfer from the center government to the states and calculated dependent on employment demand to encourage state governments to advance the Act and meet the needs of the deprived (Tripathi & Grigoriadis, 2023). Planning decisions for the act are made at the grassroots level "in open assemblies of the *gram sabha* (GS) and ratified by the *gram panchayat*" (Tripathi & Grigoriadis, 2023). The Act helps enable rural communities that serve as the backbone of many essential services, "rural local governments in India provide essential services to over 70 percent of the national population" (Bahl et al., (2010)).

c. Local Spending and Funding in India

"It is important to place local governments in India's fiscal federal map from a wider theoretical backdrop" (Ooman, 2015, 3). "Rural local governments are a new and potentially important part of India's fiscal federalism" (Bahl et al., 2010). "Indications of growing federalization of the polity and economy are evident both in the civil society and the state" (Singh, 2001). There are generally three tiers of rural local governments, village, block and district (Rao & Singh, 2001). "The population per village government is extremely small, raising questions of economic efficiency" (Rao & Singh, 2001). "[E]xpenditures are significantly higher in less populated and more backward gram panchayats" (Bahl et al., 2010). However, s large variation [exists] among rural local governments in the level of per capita spending (Bahl et al., 2010).

One of the policy questions relevant to addressing fiscal change in rural communities is whether the appropriate size of rural local government in India is in fact the *gram panchayat* (average population of about 15,000) (Bahl et al., 2010). "If this is to remain the basic unit, then the spending level needs to be ratcheted up in order to draw voters more directly into the fiscal governance process" (Bahl et al., 2010). Populations per block are considerably larger and are used to create constituencies of Legislative Assemblies, which are the lower houses of the state legislatures (Rao & Singh, 2001). The district is "approximately the size of the constituency of the member of the Lok Sabha, the lower house of the national parliament" (Rao & Singh, 2001).

"A sizeable proportion of families in India are landless, houseless or those who cannot afford to move around and buy a house in an environment where you have all the basic goods and services to live in reasonable comfort" (Ooman, 2015, 5). Localized governments have increasingly encouraged the voice of these citizens to institute a system of "formal state-local transfers modeled on the component of the existing center-state system" (Rao & Singh, 2001). "Much of this amount is funded by conditional grants which limits the fiscal autonomy of rural local governments" (Bahl et al., 2010). "Subnational governments, [however], often do not take into account overall economic performance, which may have serious ramifications in the form of critical inefficiencies" (Tripathi & Grigoriadis, 2023). "Many observers of intergovernmental fiscal relations in India have noted the poor fiscal performance of rural local governments, the overdependence on intergovernmental transfers, and the limited capacity to increase own source revenues" (Bahl et al., 2010).

d. Additional Relevant Amendments

In 1993, the 73rd and 74th Amendment Acts of the Indian Constitution decentralized power in India by transferring power to local bodies. The 73rd Amendment Act constitutionally required State Governments to adopt the new system of Panchayati Raj. Gram Sabhas are the basic units of democratic system which consists of the people registered in the electoral rolls of the village within the area of the Panchayat (Gupta, 2025). The powers and functions of the Panchayats are derived from the State legislature, and the Panchayats prepare a plan for economic development for the people of the Panchayats (Gupta 2025).

e. Examples of Relations in Federal and Local Funding

An important aspect of the Indian constitution is the Directive Principles of State Policy. Directive Principles are not legally enforceable but fundamental concepts of guidance for creating social harmony based on political justice, liberty, and equality. Thus, although morally admirable, the Directive Principles articulate ambiguous goals that are mere policy objectives to aid disadvantaged sector of society without legal teeth.

Correspondingly, durable health systems that help promote healthcare access and equality rest on the effectiveness of their primary healthcare (PHC) system, which requires government financing (Kadarpeta, 2024). The Ayushman Bharat health reforms safeguard PHC services and enhance financial protection through increased government financing (Kadarpeta, 2024). This attempt to associate public financing to service delivery and health outcomes poses challenges presents additional financing needs as well as the need for the development of systems for public accountability (Kadarpeta, 2024). The PHC seeks to provide people-centered services through a functional referral system between primary and other levels of care. Service availability is also being improved through the PHC contracting health personnel. Medications are provided to the health facilities through free drugs and diagnostics initiatives (Kadarpeta, 2024). The program provides for community engagement via local institutional structures and community-level interventions.

The National Health Mission controls PHC financing. Government financing ensures that health services According to the National Health Policy 2017, financing for PHC should occupy 75% of total government health spending in the country. Allocation for federal grants involves the local health departments (Health and Gram Panchayat) in planning and decision-making (Kadarpeta, 2024). Correspondingly, challenge in fiscal decentralization are presented pertaining to coordination and harmonization Furthermore, the budget structure consists of numerous line-item codes and there is limited flexibility for reprograming between priorities and such limited flexibility of allocation undermines the idiosyncratic priorities and objectives of UHC.

V. THE OPIOID CRISIS AS CONTEXT: HOW SPENDING RELATED TO OPIOID ABATEMENT HIGHLIGHTS UNIQUE GOVERNMENT SPENDING PATTERNS

In the American context, "[w]hile various interventions have been implemented over time, they have generally been insufficient to slow the growth of non-fatal and fatal overdoses at a national level" (Jalali et al., 2020). Likewise, "Indian policy makers and academics are understandably divided on the question of which way to move, and about whether the potential gains from policy reform are worth the disruption of the institutional structure for rural finance that would be required" (Bahl et al., (2010)). The opioid crisis in India "presents a unique set of challenges and opportunities that are deeply rooted in the country's cultural, social, and economic fabric" (Bhawalkar et al., 2024). India has lower opioid use prevalence than the United States (Singh & Rao, 2024). "In 2017, approximately 12 million Americans misused opioids and more than 47,000 people died of opioid overdose" (Jalali et al., 2020). However, data for middle and low economic areas are generally less reliable in India than "higher-income" countries (Singh & Rao, 2024). The number of opioid-related overdose deaths are not completely available (Singh & Rao, 2024).

However, a 2019 study[REMOVED HYPERLINK FIELD]_showed that "the prevalence of opioid use in India is three times the global average… [and] about 2.1% of India's population use opioids" (Singh & Rao, 2024). In addition, legal changes made access to Indian medical markets easier: India's previously more rigorous Narcotic Drugs and Psychotropic Substances Act was amended in 2014 to allow easier access to 'essential narcotics' to include fentanyl, oxycodone, codeine and hydrocodone, all of which are prominent within the American opioid epidemic (Singh & Rao, 2024). The crisis in Western countries is generally the result of prescription misuse, whereas India's epidemic is based in more of an interplay of historical and cultural practices, including traditional opium use suggesting the need for efficient and innovative approaches that encompass considerations beyond those addressed in traditional Western models of addiction treatment (Bhawalkar et al., 2024). For example, an "integration of traditional Indian medicine and practices into opioid addiction treatment. Ayurveda, yoga, and meditation have shown potential in managing… underlying factors in opioid misuse" (Bhawalkar et al., 2024).

Accordingly, the Indian epidemic is also not as physician induced as the American context. In the American context "alarming rise in opioid misuse over the past two and a half decades has resulted in a public health crisis, characterized most prominently by a dramatic increase in drug overdose deaths" (Jalali et al., 2020). In India, the epidemic is largely due to heroin not prescription drugs through an informal drug market (Singh & Rao, 2024).

Moreover, Indian state and localities have severe variation in addiction and overdose statistics suggesting the need for additional focus on localized need (Singh & Rao, 2024). In India, "higher rates of opioid abuse are strongly linked to socioeconomic factors like low income, unemployment, and poor education" (Bhawalkar et al., 2024). A centralized program that operates similarly to the MGNREGA, and thus serving more localities, could assist more underserved communities. Interestingly, local variations also have significance in the American context: substantial difference in opioid abuse and mortality rates exists at the neighborhood level as well as regionally (the American South, Northeast and the Midwest) in patterns of opioid abuse and mortality rates (Singh & Rao, 2024). Such American discrepancies pose more questions around physician-based addiction inducements, which may be grounds for additional state and federal regulation of medical practices. These substantial geographic differences in the American context are so defined the issue is presented of whether 'this is an entirely physician induced... epidemic" (Singh & Rao, 2024).

Also in India, although women report more stress than men, their opioid use statistics are likely underreported (Singh & Rao, 2024). Moreover, "[i]n ethnographic and clinical work, findings suggest that heroin addicts in India, almost always continue to live within households with female primary caregivers" (Singh & Rao, 2024). Thus, many addicts survive because of continued care, which may speak to differentiation in neighborhood related statistics. India's strong family and community network, however, also presents potential treatment through family and community-based interventions and prevention programs. Leveraging social networks is especially essential in the Indian treatment context, including early identification and reducing stigma associated with treatment (Bhawalkar et al., 2024). The recent COVID pandemic exacerbated opioid use. In India, a lockdown triggered upheaval among the poor and lack of access to addiction care (Singh & Rao, 2024). Even absent the pandemic, the availability of outpatient, evidence-based treatment of opioid dependence is rare (Singh & Rao, 2024). Many treatment centers are unregulated or places of incarceration not requiring patient consent or charging high process causing cycles of debt, addiction, and incarceration (Singh & Rao, 2024).

In the United States, "[t]his overdose fatality rate reflects a sudden increase of 345% between 2001 and 2016," and opioid use has less essential cultural groundwork (Jalali et al., 2020). In contrast, the use of opioids, both licit and illicit, has a long history in India, dating back centuries to the use of opium in traditional medicine and cultural practices (Bhawalkar et al., 2024). Thus, types of opioid use varies between India and the United States. As is the case in other parts of South Asia, "a 2004 national survey showed opium, in its non-synthetic form, being the most common opioid used in India" (Singh & Rao, 2024). In contrast, a 2019 national survey showed heroin, a semi-synthetic opioid, "as the most common opioid used in India, followed by pharmaceutical opioids" (Singh & Rao, 2024). Potential prevention strategies for these more localized issues, include school-based interventions, community awareness campaign, early identification and screening questions, harm reduction strategies, pharmacological treatments, opioid agonist therapy, psychosocial interventions, cognitive behavioral therapy, motivational interviewing, family-based interventions, integrated care models (Bhawalkar et al., 2024). "[H]igher rates of literacy also are associated with higher levels of spending, suggesting an education effect" (Bahl et al., 2010). In addition, the rapid growth of technology most certainly presents opportunities for addiction treatment: telemedicine and mobile health applications improve access to treatment (Bhawalkar et al., 2024).

Stigma and discrimination, regulatory barriers, limited access to treatment, rural location, are barriers to seeking treatment and accessing services in India and require additional local expenditure (Bhawalkar et al., 2024). "Local governments [already] have to provide local public goods like street lighting, drinking water, sanitation, primary health care, primary education, waste management, link road connectivity" with little revenue (Ooman, 2015, 4). Moreover, "[t]here is no [exact]fiscal information system that will allow a tracking of rural local government expenditures and revenues" (Bahl et al., 2010). Considering the imbalance of government spending and revenue collection, additional procedures and efforts at the local level are required to provide these localized services. A central action, such as the MGNREGA could prove helpful in catalyzing flow of federal funds to localities while retaining local decision-making authority. Notably, "the implementation of a nation-wide social policy initiative, the MGNREGA program, is associated with higher levels of public spending" (Tripathi & Grigoriadis, 2023). Furthermore, medical costs have dramatically increased in India as provided in Table 1 demonstrating Consumer Price Index for Health in India (Organization for Economic Co-operation and Development, 2025):

Table 1. Consumer Price Index for Health in India

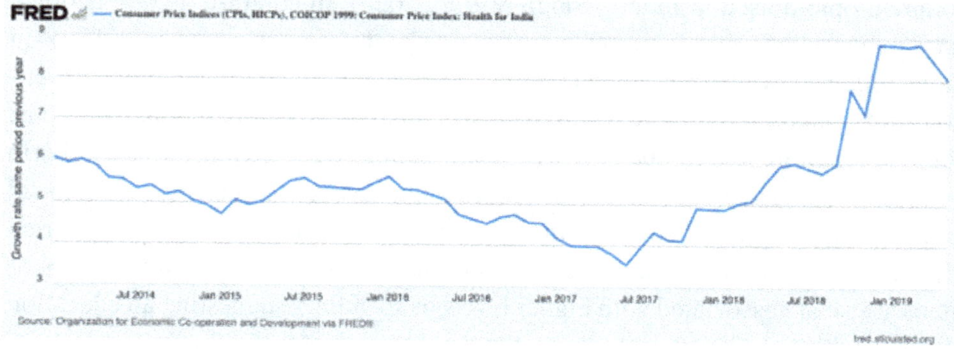

The nationalization of commercial banks in 1969 focused economic power in the center government, essentially monopolizing the financial sector (Rao & Singh, 2001). India experiences substantial socioeconomic disparity and healthcare infrastructure limitation (Bhawalkar et al., 2024). The central government may need to add resources to policy efforts for cohesive healthcare infrastructure while allocating resources to localities based on geographic need (which could improve reporting and incentive states to help citizens). "Any comprehensive strategy to address the opioid crisis [must]… strive to ensure equitable access to… treatment services across all segments of society" (Bhawalkar et al., 2024). Also, from the perspective of the central government, addressing the challenges surrounding addiction in the Indian context requires coordinated effort between multiple sectors, including healthcare, education, law enforcement, and social services (Bhawalkar et al., 2024). Additional central and local investment in training programs is also required to increase the number of healthcare professionals trained in addiction medicine (Bhawalkar et al., 2024).

In essence, the Indian opioid crisis requires increased national level coordination whenever justified by factors that are common across Indian state borders (Rao & Singh, 2001). "A constitutional amendment calls for a strengthening of the fiscal autonomy and service delivery importance of local governments" (Bahl et al., (2010)). In addition, unconditional grants to states and localities, likely determined by the Finance Commission, that do not distort states' fiscal incentives are necessary to fund local addiction treatment initiatives. Rural reform "might be done by a combination of factors such as increased assignment of expenditure responsibilities to rural local governments, a shift to unconditional grants that would give more discretion to local voters, and some additional capacity for local revenue mobilization' (Bahl et al., (2010)).

Notably, particularly in the Indian context, assignment of revenue raising authority is particularly important in determining the appropriate strategy for intergovernmental financial transfers (Rao & Singh, 2001). “The degree of poverty in rural areas, the deplorable level of local public services and the weak capacity of rural local governments are factors that push in the direction of more central and state government control over the budgets of rural local governments” (Bahl et al., (2010)). “Benefits of improvements [in the taxation system are likely to be large, not only because of the direct benefits of improvements in central information systems and institutions of enforcement, but also because these can provide a model for states to improve their tax administration” (Rao & Singh, 2001). The type of reform that most impact India’s federal system pertains to indirect taxes (Rao & Singh, 2001).

India has historically struggled with fiscal deficits, which has been essentially pushed down the federalism ladder to state governments (Rao & Singh, 2001). “Fiscal deficits at the state level have increased despite the central government’s apparent formal authority to strictly control state borrowing” because the central government uses discretionary loans as vehicles for political influence (Rao & Singh, 2001). Correspondingly, such central control of the financial system has allowed the government to park debts without printing money leading to inflation (Rao & Singh, 2001).

Table 2. Indian Central Government Debt as Total Percent of GDP for India

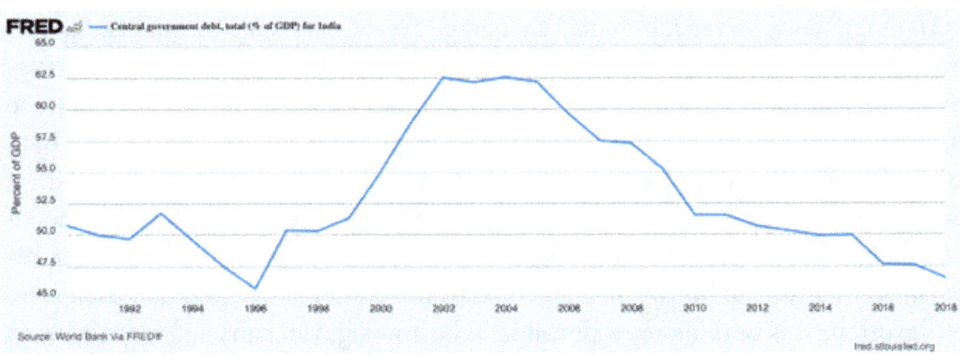

Table 3. General Government Gross Debt for India (% of GDP) for India

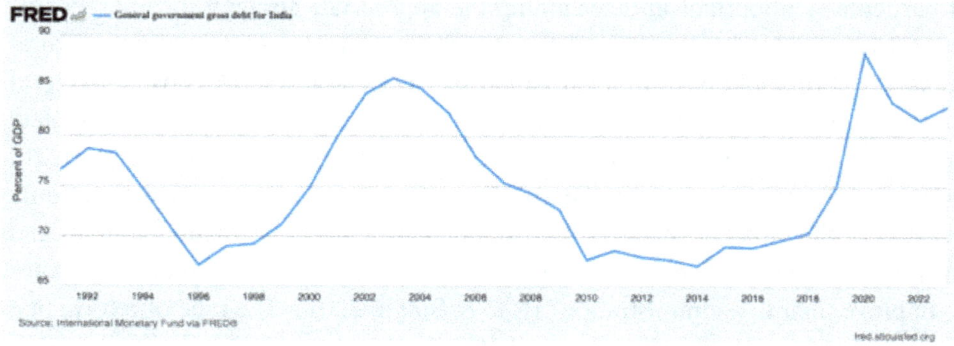

Decentralization and privatization can also enable higher-level governments to focus more clearly and directly on redistribution as an objective (Rao & Singh, 2001). Although little privatization has occurred recently in the Indian economic trajectory, privatization of public assets also provides a solution to funding addiction treatment in India (Rao & Singh, 2001). This type of reform differs "fundamentally from other aspects of reform, involving more than just reform within government or changing the nature and methods of regulating the private sector, instead explicitly shifting the boundary between private and public ownership" (Rao & Singh, 2001). Privatization can encourage efficiency and growth of the overall economic system and allow center-state transfers to meet more tailored objectives (Rao & Singh, 2001). Arguably, privatization may encourage greater interstate inequality, but this equality may be counterbalanced with more targeted central government disbursements to states and localities. "The danger in this strategy is the possible increase in fiscal disparities, which this research has shown to be already very large" (Bahl et al., (2010)). [S]pending is higher in less populated and more backward rural local governments, suggesting both a fixed cost effect, and that a considerable amount of equalization is built into the [Indian] system" (Bahl et al., 2010). Moreover, repayment of any state borrowing can come from additional taxes so that each level of government is both more responsible in borrowing decisions and responsive to constituent preferences to generate tax revenue (Rao & Singh, 2001).

VI. CONCLUSION

An appropriate equilibrium of federalist authority is a foundational component of a lasting democracy. "The meaning of federalism has greatly shifted over thousands of years and [this] foundation has somewhat been shadowed due to [idiosyncratic] political shifts" within specific nations (Trivedi, 2022, 972). India and the United

States are prime, globally impactful examples of progressively developed federalist systems rooted in unique cultural and historic influence.

This chapter utilizes the opioid health crises as a tool to analyze how these federalist systems impact local finding initiatives, "[t]he global opioid crisis has emerged as one of the most pressing public health challenges of the 21st century, with far-reaching implications for individuals, families, and societies" (Bhawalkar et al., 2024). The opioid crises in both the American and Indian contexts presents substantial public health challenges that require a comprehensive and coordinated response between national, state, and local governments.

"The Indian federation, which is sometimes characterized as a case of 'cooperative federalism' is different from similar patterns elsewhere in the world" in the sense that it focuses on central authority while also incorporating less strict or polarized federalist relations than found in the United States (Ooman, 2015, 3). The United States provides a contrasting example of a stricter federal system with clearer boundaries between national, state, and local authorities. This chapter provided historical and political context to the Indian and American federalist systems while suggesting how these federalist traditions operate to both help and hinder localized health funding. This analysis can provide suggestions for policy improvements based on federalist principles that can assist with health care spending at a local level.

REFERENCES

"2023 Supreme Court review: federalism." Supreme Court Observer. https://www.scobserver.in/journal/2023-supreme-court-review-federalism/ (April 19, 2025).

Bahl, R. W., Sethi, G., & Wallace, S. (2010). Fiscal decentralization to rural local governments in India: A case study of west Bengal state. *Publius*, *40*(2). https://scholarworks.gsu.edu/cgi/viewcontent.cgi?article=1320&context=econ_facpub

Beer, C. (2025). Judicial Federalism and Abortion in Mexico and the United States. *PS, Political Science & Politics*, *58*(1), 52–55.

Bhawalkar, J., Saraf, A., & Malik, M. M. (2024). The opioid crisis, preventing and managing substance abuse in India: A systematic review. *Cureus*, *16*(10), e70600. DOI: 10.7759/cureus.70600

Briffault, R. (1996). Public finance in the american federal system: basic patterns and current issues. Colum. J. Eur. L., 2, 533. https://scholarship.law.columbia.edu/faculty_scholarship/3575

Choi, Y. S., Cho, C. L., & Wright, D. S. (2004). Administrative autonomy among american state agencies: An empirical analysis of fragmentation and functionalism. *International Journal of Public Administration*, *27*(6), 373–398.

Choutagunta, A. (2025, April 19). G. P. Manish, and Shruti Rajagopalan. 2021. "Battling COVID-19 with dysfunctional federalism: Lessons from India.". *Southern Economic Journal*, *87*(4), 1267–1299. https://www.jstor.org/stable/27189159

Gluck, A. (2022). MDL nationalism, federalism, and the opioid epidemic. *De Paul Law Review*, *70*(2), 321. https://via.library.depaul.edu/law-review/vol70/iss2/5

Goelzhauser, G., & Konisky, D. M. (2020). The state of American federalism 2019–2020: Polarized and punitive intergovernmental relations. *Publius*, *50*(3), 311–343. DOI: 10.1093/publius/pjaa021

Grogan, C. M. (2025). Medicaid's Political Development since 1965: How a Fragmented and Unequal Program Has Expanded. *Journal of Health Politics, Policy and Law*, *50*(2), 137–164.

Gupta, S. (2025). Developing India's Food Processing Sector: Farm Politics, Federalism, and State-Directed Development. *Studies in Comparative International Development*, •••, 1–26.

Heitzman, J., & Worden, R. L. (1996, January). India: a country study. < bound method Organization. get_name_with_acronym of< Organization: Library of Congress>>.

Jalali, M. S., Botticelli, M., Hwang, R. C., Koh, H. K., & McHugh, R. K. (2020). The opioid crisis: A contextual, social-ecological framework. *Health Research Policy and Systems*, *18*(1), 87. DOI: 10.1186/s12961-020-00596-8

Kadarpeta, R. S. R., Anand, J. S., & Achungura, G. (2024). Strengthening Public Financing of Primary Healthcare in India: A Perspective. *Health Services Insights*, *17*, 11786329241249289.

Karapin, R. (2020). Federalism as a double-edged sword: The slow energy transition in the United States. *Journal of Environment & Development*, *29*(1), 26–50.

Oommen, M. A. (2015). Local governments in the fiscal space of Indian federalism: towards more rational arrangements, RULSG Occasional Paper, https://cds.edu/wp-content/uploads/RULSG2_MAOommen.pdf

Organization for Economic Co-operation and Development. (2025). Consumer price indices (CPIs, HICPs), COICOP 1999: Consumer Price Index: Health for India [INDCP060000GYM], retrieved from FRED, Federal Reserve Bank of St. Louis; https://fred.stlouisfed.org/series/INDCP060000GYM

Rao, M. G., & Singh, N. (2001). Federalism in India: political economy and reform. Stanford Center for International Development, 1-30. https://kingcenter.stanford.edu/sites/g/files/sbiybj16611/files/media/file/108wp_0.pdf

Scholtz, C., & Munteanu, A. (2023). How cooperative is "cooperative federalism"? The political limits to intergovernmental cooperation under a de facto concurrency rule. *Constitutional Political Economy*, *34*(1), 111–134.

Singh, B., & Rao, R. (2021). Is there an opioid epidemic in India? *Journal of Public Health*, *43*(Supplement_2), ii43–ii50. DOI: 10.1093/pubmed/fdab322

Singh, M. P. (2001). Towards a more federalized parliamentary system in India: Explaining functional change. *Pacific Affairs*, *74*(4), 553–568. DOI: 10.2307/3557806

Tracking Federal Funding to Combat the Opioid Crisis (March 2019). Bipartisan Policy Center. Tracking Federal Funding to Combat the Opioid Crisis.

Tripathi, P. K., & Grigoriadis, T. N. (2023). State capacity & the soft budget constraint: Fiscal federalism, Indian style. *Asia and the Global Economy*, *3*(2), 100058. DOI: 10.1016/j.aglobe.2023.100058

Trivedi, N. (2022). Federalism in India v USA: a comparative study. Jus Corpus Law Journal, 972-979. https://www.juscorpus.com/wp-content/uploads/2022/11/191.-Niyati-Trivedi.pdf

Vickers, J. (2010). A two-way street: Federalism and women's politics in Canada and the United States. *Publius*, *40*(3), 412–435.

Zambrano, P. A. (2020). Sports betting in Indiana: The proposed legislation after Murphy V. NCAA. *Indiana Law Review*, *53*, 743.

Zimmerman, J. F. (2001). National-state relations: Cooperative federalism in the twentieth century. *Publius*, *31*(2), 15–30.

Chapter 6
State-Municipal Cooperation in Azerbaijan:
Enhancing Governance Through Local-State Collaboration

Ulviyye Rzayeva
https://orcid.org/0000-0001-5881-6633
Azerbaijan State University of Economics, Baku, Azerbaijan

Rena Huseynova
https://orcid.org/0000-0001-5281-0556
Azerbaijan State University of Economics, Baku, Azerbaijan

ABSTRACT

The study is dedicated to analyzing the current state of municipalities and local self-government bodies, their role within the system of public administration, as well as identifying the challenges and prospects for their development in the context of Azerbaijan. The research examines the specific features of interaction between state authorities and local self-governance institutions, including mechanisms for regulating powers, resource allocation, and the principles of subsidiarity. Particular attention is given to the legal framework, institutional stability, and the impact of state policy on the efficiency of municipal governance. The analysis has revealed shortcomings in legislative regulation, including unclear delineation of functions, the absence of accountability mechanisms, and limited opportunities for judicial protection. The study emphasizes the importance of financial and personnel stability for municipalities, the need to enhance the professional competence of municipal employees, and the active engagement of the population in local governance processes.

DOI: 10.4018/979-8-3373-5576-4.ch006

INTRODUCTION

In the political and legal practices of modern states, there are generally three main models of the relationship between state authorities and local self-government: the Anglo-Saxon, the Continental, and the mixed model (Kim & Cho, 2019). The Anglo-Saxon model is characterized by the absence of direct subordination of local self-government bodies to state authorities, a high level of administrative decentralization, and the lack of central government representatives at the regional level, aligning with the model of relative autonomy. The Continental model, on the other hand, is distinguished by a high degree of centralization, direct control over local self-government bodies, and the integration of state administration and local self-governance within a single administrative-territorial unit, corresponding to the agency model. Finally, the mixed model combines elements of both the Anglo-Saxon and Continental models. According to Steenmans et al., in the modern world, it is challenging to observe these models in their pure form (Steenmans et al., 2023). In practice, different models may be applied in various situations within the same country.

The constitutional and municipal reforms in Azerbaijan, initiated in the mid-1990s, are largely based on a combination of the Continental (French) and, to some extent, the Anglo-Saxon models of local governance and self-government (Klimovský et al., 2010). Under this mixed system of local authority organization, local governance is carried out through municipalities, which are elected bodies of power, and through appointed heads and representatives of executive authorities.

Despite the existence of legislation aimed at regulating their activities, the weak implementation of the principles of decentralization and subsidiarity remains a pressing issue. This is reflected in the excessive dependence of municipalities on central government authorities, which hinders their ability to make independent decisions that align with regional needs and specificities (Atar & Kirboz, 2024).

The chapter aims to develop concrete recommendations for improving the interaction between state and local authorities in Azerbaijan, with particular attention to legal, institutional, and financial aspects of municipal autonomy. The objective is to identify specific policy and governance mechanisms that can enhance the capacity of municipalities to function more independently and effectively. The scope of the chapter includes the current legal framework, the institutional interaction between state and local levels, and practical challenges faced by municipalities. However, the study is limited to the analysis of structural and regulatory issues without an in-depth empirical survey of municipal practices.

To strengthen the practical relevance of the chapter and illustrate the key issues, it is important to highlight real-world manifestations of the challenges discussed. For example, in a number of municipalities, attempts to implement local development projects using internally generated funds failed due to the lack of legal instruments allowing municipal borrowing or independent budget formation. As a result, local governments had to defer even basic infrastructure improvements until subsidies were allocated from the central government. This case exemplifies the limitations of financial autonomy and underscores the structural imbalance in state-municipal relations.

Furthermore, although the Law on the Status of Municipalities was amended to expand their competencies, in practice, implementation has been hampered by the overlapping roles of municipalities and local executive authorities. These trends indicate a need for a clearer delineation of responsibilities and the establishment of effective coordination mechanisms.

The research also presents a series of proposals for reforming the lawmaking process to strengthen the autonomy of municipalities, as well as developing mechanisms to ensure their financial independence. The prospects for enhancing feedback between local authorities and the population are considered, including the implementation of transparency and accountability systems and the active involvement of citizens in decision-making processes.

An important component of the chapter is forecasting future scenarios for the development of relations between state and municipal authorities, along with identifying potential steps for adapting the national system of local self-government to European standards. Based on the analysis conducted, conclusions and practical recommendations are formulated to reinforce the institutional foundations of interaction between authorities at different levels and to enhance the effectiveness of governance in the interests of sustainable development in Azerbaijan's regions.

BACKGROUND

In democratic countries, the institution of local self-government is a key element in the implementation of the constitutional principle of the separation of powers, which serves as the foundation of state organization and governance. The principle of separation of powers, on which the concept of local self-government is based, encompasses both political and organizational dimensions. The political dimension is expressed in granting citizens the right to independently address local issues through elected bodies, which constitutes a fundamental component of democratic governance. Meanwhile, the organizational dimension involves the delineation of powers between different levels of government, ensuring the autonomy of municipal structures and their ability to operate independently of the central government within their jurisdiction. This contributes to the decentralization of power, making the governance system more flexible, efficient, and responsive to the needs of the population. The distribution of authority between national and local levels prevents excessive centralization and the concentration of power in a single entity, creating a system of checks and balances that ensures no level of government monopolizes decision-making processes. At the same time, the state retains a regulatory and coordinating role, establishing the legal framework for the functioning of local self-government without supplanting it. This mechanism also enhances civic engagement, as public participation in local governance provides individuals with a tangible opportunity to influence the quality of life in their communities. Furthermore, the local self-government system, being an integral part of the overall governance structure, plays a crucial role in implementing state policies at the local level, adapting them to the specific conditions of individual regions. Thus, local self-government is not merely an administrative structure but a fully-fledged level of public authority that contributes to strengthening democracy, fostering civil society, and improving the overall effectiveness of state governance (Salzberger, 1993).

In the Republic of Azerbaijan, local self-government is defined as a special form of public power at the local level, which operates outside the system of state authority (Huseynov, 2023). By law, local executive authorities and municipalities, which exercise the functions of local self-government, have delineated powers that, with rare exceptions, do not overlap or duplicate each other. Municipal authority is not part of state power, while local executive authorities represent the direct form of implementing state power at the local level. According to the "Regulation on Local Executive Authorities" approved by the Decree of the President of the Republic of Azerbaijan on June 16, 1999, local executive bodies are organized by the President of the country. Heads of local executive authorities are appointed by the President and are accountable to him, which emphasizes their direct connection with the central government (Decree of the President of the Republic of Azerbaijan on approval of the Statute on Local Executive Authorities, 2012).

As part of their activities, heads of executive authorities form advisory councils, the main goal of which is to consider and discuss issues related to local socio-economic and cultural development. However, the practice of appointing representatives of executive power in cities, towns, and villages often leads to the duplication of functions of local self-government bodies, which creates challenges in implementing the principle of municipal autonomy (Regulations on Local Executive Authorities, 2012).

Local self-government in Azerbaijan is a non-state system of organizing citizens, which allows them, within the framework of the law, to independently and freely address issues of local importance (Constitution of the Republic of Azerbaijan, 1995). This right is implemented through representative bodies – municipalities, the members of which are elected by free and secret voting. The term "municipality" encompasses not only local self-government bodies but also enterprises, institutions, and property related to their activities. To perform their functions, municipalities may create executive structures that are accountable to the elected bodies.

Thus, the local self-government system in Azerbaijan represents a complex mechanism that, despite having a clear legal framework, continues to face challenges related to the duplication of functions, dependence on central authorities, and the need to develop effective governance mechanisms at the local level. One of the key issues remains the insufficient autonomy of municipalities, which is manifested in limited financial and administrative capacities as well as strict oversight by state bodies. The formally established powers of local self-government often overlap with the functions of executive structures, leading to inefficient resource allocation and a lack of clear accountability for decision-making.

Despite the legal basis for the functioning of municipalities in Azerbaijan, in practice, there is a significant gap between their formal powers and their actual ability to independently manage local affairs. This gap is reflected in situations where local authorities cannot address even essential infrastructure needs without direct financial support from the state budget. Such examples illustrate the systemic nature of the problem and the need for reform.

In the context of ongoing centralization, municipalities largely depend on state subsidies, which restricts their ability to independently generate budgets and implement long-term socio-economic development programs. This, in turn, affects their capacity to respond effectively to the needs of the population and adapt to local challenges. Additionally, the institutional weakness of local authorities is reflected in the shortage of qualified personnel, the absence of sustainable mechanisms for interaction with civil society and the business sector, and insufficient transparency in decision-making processes.

The purpose of this chapter is to analyze the current state of cooperation between state and local authorities in Azerbaijan and to develop practical recommendations for enhancing its effectiveness. The main objectives include identifying institutional barriers to local self-governance, examining mechanisms of financial autonomy, and exploring citizen participation in local decision-making processes. The scope of the chapter is limited to legal, administrative, and institutional dimensions, without extensive empirical data from individual municipalities. The analysis focuses on the period from the establishment of the municipal system to the present day, with particular attention to contemporary challenges and reform opportunities.

MAIN FOCUS OF THE CHAPTER

The Legal Framework of Local Self-Government in Azerbaijan

The Republic of Azerbaijan is a unitary state with a distinctly centralized system of governance, in which the Nakhchivan Autonomous Republic holds a special administrative and legal status by the country's Constitution (Wienen & Mosler-Törnström, 2013). The organization of power is based on a rigid centralization principle, wherein key executive functions are concentrated in the hands of the President. The President determines the strategic direction of the state, appoints and oversees the activities of executive authorities, and possesses broad powers in domestic and foreign policy. The executive branch is structured so that central government bodies are responsible for the formulation and implementation of national policies, while local executive authorities operate within designated administrative territories, ensuring the execution of decisions made at the highest level.

The country's administrative division consists of 67 territorial units, including republics, cities of national significance, districts, and municipalities. Although formal institutions of local self-government, such as municipalities, exist, their powers remain limited, and real authority in the regions belongs to the local executive bodies appointed by the President (State Statistical Committee of the Republic of Azerbaijan. Classification of administrative territorial divisions, 2024). This governance model is shaped by historical, political, and economic factors, as a centralized approach allows the government to maintain control over all aspects of socio-economic development, ensure stability, and respond promptly to emerging challenges. However, despite the evident advantages of unified strategic management, this system also gives rise to several issues, including weak municipal autonomy, limited regional capacity for independent planning and budget management, and a high degree of dependence of municipalities on central government decisions.

The territorial basis of municipalities in the Republic of Azerbaijan is defined by administrative units such as districts, cities, towns, and villages located within the country. According to the provisions of Section IV of the Constitution of the Republic of Azerbaijan, the functions of local self-government are carried out by municipalities (Constitution of the Republic of Azerbaijan, 1995). The first municipal election campaign took place on December 12, 1999, while the most recent local self-government elections were held in 2019. During these elections, 15,566 members were elected across 1,606 municipalities (Holding the first municipal elections in the Republic of Azerbaijan, 2023). To ensure their functioning, municipalities receive financial support from the state budget.

More than 25 years have passed since the establishment of municipalities in Azerbaijan. The European Charter of Local Self-Government holds a significant place in the legal framework regulating the activities of local self-government bodies (European Charter of Local Self-Government, 1985). Upon joining the Council of Europe, Azerbaijan committed to ratifying this international document. The provisions of the Charter have been legally integrated into the national legal system, holding a priority status.

The Charter ratified based on the Law of the Republic of Azerbaijan dated January 28, 2002, "On the Approval of the European Charter of Local Self-Government". (Law of the Republic of Azerbaijan on the ratification of the European Charter on Local Self-Government, 2002). However, several articles of the Charter remain unratified, including Article 4.3 (on the distribution of public responsibilities), Article 7.2 (on the reimbursement of expenses for local elected officials in the performance of their duties), Articles 9.5 and 9.6 (on financial equalization procedures and the coordination of redistributed resources with local self-government bodies), as well as Article 10.3 (on the cooperation of municipalities with counterparts from other countries) (European Charter of Local Self-Government, 1985).

This international legal instrument establishes key principles for the organization and functioning of local self-government bodies, but it allows for adapting its provisions to the national realities of the member states. In 2013, Azerbaijan ratified Article 10.3 with the condition that any international cooperation of municipalities would require prior approval from the country's state authorities (Vöhringer & Dickson, 2021).

Since gaining independence, Azerbaijan has adopted a significant body of legal acts regulating the activities of local self-government bodies. The foundations for their formation and functioning were first established in the country's Constitution, adopted in December 1995. Specifically, Articles 142, 143, 144, 145, and 146 of the ninth chapter of the Constitution are dedicated to local self-government bodies, which must be created based on democratic elections, function collegially, and possess financial and material independence (Constitution of the Republic of Azerbaijan, 1995).

The development of the legal framework for local self-government was further continued in 25 specialized laws and numerous amendments made to them. Among the key legislative acts regulating this area, the following can be highlighted: The Law "On the Rights of Elections to Municipalities" (Decree of the President of the Republic of Azerbaijan on the application of the Law of the Republic of Azerbaijan on the rules of municipal elections, 1999), the Law "On the Status of Municipalities" (Law of the Republic of Azerbaijan on the status of municipalities, 1999), the Law "On the Financial Foundations of Municipalities" (Law of the Republic of Azerbaijan on the Fundamentals of Municipal Finance, 1999), the Law "On the Status of a Municipality Member" (Law of the Republic of Azerbaijan on the status of a municipal member, 2000), the Law "On Municipal Service" (Law of the Republic of Azerbaijan on Municipal Service, 1999), the Law "On the Territories and Lands of Municipalities" (Law of the Republic of Azerbaijan on Municipal Territories and Lands, 1999), the Law "On the Water Economy of Municipalities" (Law of the Republic of Azerbaijan on Municipal Water Management, 2001), the Law "On Administrative Control over the Activities of Municipalities" (Law of the Republic of Azerbaijan on administrative control over the activities of municipalities, 2003) and others.

In addition, the norms regulating the activities of local self-government bodies have been incorporated into various codes, including the Land (Land Code of the Republic of Azerbaijan, 1999), Labor (Labor Code of the Republic of Azerbaijan, 1999), Tax (Tax Code of the Republic of Azerbaijan, 2000) and others. Decrees of the Cabinet of Ministers of the Republic of Azerbaijan and regulatory acts of central executive authorities also play an important role in regulating the activities of municipalities (Resolution of the Cabinet of Ministers of the Republic of Azerbaijan on Amendments to Some Decisions of the Cabinet of Ministers of the Republic of Azerbaijan, 2000). These measures contribute to establishing a legal foundation for the effective functioning of the local self-government system in the country.

Thus, the legal foundation for the activities of local self-government bodies includes laws on local self-government, the Constitution of the Republic of Azerbaijan, legislative and regulatory acts of executive authorities, as well as the Constitution of the Nakhchivan Autonomous Republic (Constitutional Law of the Republic of Azerbaijan on the Approval of the Constitution of the Nakhchivan Autonomous Republic, 1998) and acts regulating activities within this autonomy. Further development of legislation in this area requires reforms and constant optimization of the legal framework, aimed at aligning it with the provisions and requirements of the European Charter of Local Self-Government.

The legal foundation of municipal governance in Azerbaijan is largely formed based on the Constitution, as well as legislative acts adopted by the parliament and the president. As a result, municipalities have a lower degree of autonomy in developing regulations and procedures that take into account local specifics and community needs compared to many other countries. In Azerbaijan, regulatory legal acts are typically characterized by a high degree of detail (Analysis of Azerbaijani Legislation On Freedom Of Expression, 2017). For municipalities, which are a relatively new institution in the country's legal system, such detailing is often beneficial. Legislation stipulates that each municipality has a charter, the number of municipal council members is determined based on the population size, and officials, council committees, and city departments are created following parliamentary mandates. However, this highly detailed approach also leads to the emergence of cumbersome procedures, making it difficult to implement even minor changes that could be beneficial to a municipality at its discretion.

Current state of decentralization in Azerbaijan

The state, through legislative acts, can assign specific tasks to local self-government bodies, impose certain restrictions on them, and control their activities through state bodies with supervisory authority. Furthermore, it can apply measures of accountability based on Article 51 of the Law "On the Status of Municipalities" (Law of the Republic of Azerbaijan on the status of a municipal member, 2000). The state, possessing sovereignty over its territory and serving as the ultimate guarantor of the exercise of public authority, requires local self-government bodies to strictly adhere to the minimum set of powers established by law. Self-governing communities are not permitted to refuse the exercise of these powers, except in special cases specified in the law, primarily when the powers are transferred to the state or another level of self-government due to the inability of local self-government bodies to perform the corresponding functions.

Local self-government establishes a regime of special activities, the subject of which differs from state administration in specific matters. The advisability of independently addressing local issues without the involvement of state bodies is, on the one hand, determined by a certain freedom of action, and on the other hand, by additional responsibility to the population and dependence on it. All of this complicates the fulfillment of managerial tasks by local self-government bodies compared to state administration bodies, but at the same time, it provides the necessary impetus and opportunities for the management process to account for the diversity and differential conditions of local populations' living circumstances (Huseynov, 2023). An important condition for strengthening the self-government principles in local governance is the social integration of the municipality's population, which manifests through both external and internal factors. The external factor of integration is expressed in the organized unity of the structural elements of the local self-government system, as well as the methods and rules by which they impact the objects of governance. Internal factors of integration are determined by the common interests and needs of the municipality's population.

As previously mentioned, the Constitution of the Republic of Azerbaijan establishes that local executive authority is vested in the heads of local executive bodies. These bodies represent territorial structures of state power operating in regions, cities, and urban districts. They are led by executive heads who are appointed and dismissed by the President of the Republic of Azerbaijan, and their powers are also defined by presidential decrees.

However, the current legislation lacks clear delineation of powers between appointed local executive bodies and elected municipal councils. Legislative acts do not provide sufficient provisions for creating an effective local self-government structure or clear mandates for municipal governance.

In practice, despite the municipalities' potential for development and demonstrated interest in reforms, they face limitations due to insufficient powers, which hinders their functioning as independent entities. All municipalities encounter a range of common issues that restrict their capabilities and require a systemic solution (Local self-government in Azerbaijan: few improvements observed, limited powers and weak financial position of municipalities must be urgently addressed, 2021). Among these issues:

1. The presence of local executive bodies, which serve as parallel, and in some cases duplicative, forms of local self-government, represents the most significant problem.
2. There is insufficient public involvement in the decision-making process at the municipal level, limiting municipalities' ability to effectively set priorities and organize the delivery of relevant services.
3. Azerbaijani municipalities predominantly operate in isolation, lacking sufficient mechanisms for networking and exchanging experiences or information.
4. The competence of municipalities remains predominantly structural and more limited than what is provided by legislation. Their activities are generally confined to the maintenance of municipal roads, cemeteries, parks, and the execution of specific tasks related to social assistance not covered by the central government.

Despite some improvements in the functioning of municipalities, significant concerns remain regarding factors hindering the development of local self-government in Azerbaijan. The key problems identified include the lack of real powers for municipalities, their undefined status as state institutions, and the shortage of their financial resources. This is highlighted in the monitoring report by the Congress of Local and Regional Authorities of the Council of Europe (Local self-government in Azerbaijan: few improvements observed, limited powers, and weak financial position of municipalities must be urgently addressed, 2021). The report contains recommendations that must be implemented as a matter of urgency. The document highlights positive changes. It also welcomes the improvement in the quality and transparency of municipal bodies' work, the first delegation of functions to municipalities in 2020, and the increase in the proportion of women and youth in municipal councils following the 2019 elections (Local Government Country Profile, 2022; Statement of Preliminary Findings And Conclusions, 2020; Country Gender Profile Azerbaijan, 2021). Nevertheless, the report points out that in Azerbaijan, municipalities are not recognized as state institutions and do not belong to the overall system of public administration. Instead, they are viewed as an expression of civil society. At the same time, their powers remain limited and do not have a comprehensive or exclusive nature.

The Role of Financial Decentralization in Local Government

In Azerbaijan, the regulation of the principles for the formation and use of municipal finances, the process of local budget preparation, the powers of municipalities in these areas, as well as their interaction with the relevant executive authorities, is carried out by the Law "On the Basics of Municipal Finances" (Law of the Republic of Azerbaijan on the Fundamentals of Municipal Finance, 1999). Under this legislation, the state grants local self-government bodies certain powers, such as adopting binding acts, forming their own budget, and including local taxes and other revenues in it.

However, despite the formal financial autonomy provided, the actual situation of municipalities remains weak, as evidenced by the analysis of their financial condition (Salmanly, 2024). According to Article 12(2) of the Law "On Municipal Taxes" (Law of the Republic of Azerbaijan on local (municipal) taxes and payments, 2001) independent auditors are authorized to oversee the process of collecting and spending tax revenues that flow into the municipal budget. Additionally, Article 13 of the Law "On the Financial Foundations of Municipalities" (Law of the Republic of Azerbaijan on the Fundamentals of Municipal Finance, 1999) establishes that legislative and executive bodies have the right to monitor the use of funds allocated to municipalities by these government authorities.

However, in light of the principles of local self-government, state control over funds entering the municipal budget is undesirable. At the same time, mandatory oversight by independent auditors or audit commissions over all financial resources, regardless of their source, is an essential condition for ensuring transparency and accountability in municipal finances.

Since local executive bodies in Azerbaijan are integrated into the central government structure and do not have an autonomous status, the relationship between local and centralized revenues and expenses of the central government cannot be regarded as a reflection of the actual level of fiscal decentralization. In practice, fiscal decentralization proves to be even more limited than reflected in the budgetary data. The own revenues of municipalities remain significantly insufficient to perform the functions assigned to them by law. This limits municipalities' ability to operate in areas that are formally open to their management and intensifies their financial dependence on central authorities. Municipalities are also deprived of the right to independently set their tax rates, highlighting their limited powers in financial management (Aliyev, 2023).

In this context, an important question arises: what is the real role of municipal authorities in increasing the revenues of local budgets through their activities? What role does municipal consolidation play in this process?

An analysis of the structure of local budget revenues shows that the main sources of growth remain the property tax of individuals and transfers from the state budget, including subsidies and grants (Opinion of the Chamber of Accounts of the Republic of Azerbaijan on the draft state budget of the Republic of Azerbaijan for 2024, 2023).

According to statistical data, around 9% of local budget revenues are formed through the property tax on individuals (How to increase the financial capabilities of municipalities, 2011). Even though the legislation grants municipalities the authority to collect local taxes, including property tax on individuals, local authorities face significant challenges in implementing this function.

The main problem is the insufficient effectiveness of property tax collection, which is a key source of revenue for municipalities. Many local authorities lack sufficient experience in this area, which hinders the effective administration of taxation.

One of the most significant barriers is the lack of inventory valuation of buildings, which makes their taxation impossible. According to Article 198 of the Tax Code of the Republic of Azerbaijan, property tax on individuals is calculated based on the cadastral value of buildings located in their private ownership (Tax Code of the Republic of Azerbaijan, 2000). However, research shows that a significant portion of residential buildings subject to taxation lacks a registered inventory value.

This issue is particularly acute in rural areas, where approximately 90% of homes do not have an inventory valuation, making their taxation nearly impossible. Such a structural deficiency severely limits municipalities' ability to mobilize revenue through property taxes.

In some cases, municipalities independently assess houses without an inventory value and apply calculated tax amounts. However, this practice directly contradicts the provisions of the Tax Code. In some regions, such as the city of Baku, tax collection is carried out by other agencies. Urban municipalities enter into agreements with housing maintenance organizations (HMO) to facilitate tax collection, which contradicts the Tax Code, as it does not allow the involvement of such organizations in the tax collection process.

The greatest increase in resources directly dependent on municipal activities has been recorded in the area of fees for the use of municipal lands for sanatorium-resort, hotel, and tourist services, as well as for stationary or mobile trade, public catering, and other services. However, these sources account for only 4% of local budget revenues (Aliyev, 2024).

To reduce the financial dependence of municipalities on the central government, it is essential to strengthen their revenue bases. This requires granting municipalities the ability to independently set tax rates, as well as implementing the principle of co-financing in the case of government transfers. Such an approach will ensure the sustainable development of municipal budgets and enhance the autonomy of local self-government (Sadigova, 2021).

The Role of Citizens in Local Government

It should be acknowledged that the principles of decentralization of governance, subsidiarity, and self-organization of citizens, developed with consideration of European experience to address local issues, have not yet found a full and adequate reflection in Azerbaijan's legislative framework. Furthermore, the practice of local self-government implementation significantly differs from the perception of it as an institution of civil society. In most cases, local self-government effectively performs functions supporting state authority, leading to a distortion of its democratic nature (Salimli, 2022).

The fundamental principle of Western democracy lies in the priority of the individual, who enters into a social contract to create a government oriented toward the common good, defined by the electorate. This approach to democracy has historically developed organically, beginning with initiatives at the local level. The emergence of democratic institutions, including municipal governance, was driven by the immediate needs of citizens, who independently initiated their formation. In these societies, cultural traditions foster open discussions of public issues and active engagement with government representatives, particularly at the local level.

Azerbaijan is a state with a high degree of centralized governance. The ethos of Azerbaijani culture is often based on family and community values, where power is traditionally viewed as a hierarchically organized structure, emanating from the "patriarch" to the people. Historical and cultural features, including the influence of the Soviet period with its authoritarian governance models, contributed to the formation of a respectful attitude toward authority. While Azerbaijan has not had a fully developed tradition of municipal governance, government administrators have carried out local administrative functions for decades.

The study of the genesis and stages of development of local self-government in Azerbaijan shows that various forms of self-governance have existed in the country since ancient times. Despite similarities to analogous institutions in other countries, they had unique features that manifested in their structure, composition, and areas of activity. At the same time, the level of development of these forms of self-governance at different historical periods depended on state policy. In most cases, local self-government functions were focused on carrying out tasks set by the central authority (Alakbarov et al, 2021).

In Azerbaijan, municipalities are not considered state institutions providing public services within a unified system of public administration. Instead, they are perceived as institutions of civil society. However, the nature of the top-down reforms and the distribution of powers based on the "top-down" principle suggest that such civil society institutions are primarily formed at the initiative of the central authority. It should be noted that the principle of subsidiarity, widely applied in international local governance practices, is absent from the Law of the Republic of Azerbaijan "On the Status of Municipalities" (Law of the Republic of Azerbaijan on the status of municipalities, 1999).

Forms of direct citizen participation in local self-government are also limited. For example, according to the Laws of the Republic of Azerbaijan "On the Status of Municipalities" (Law of the Republic of Azerbaijan on the status of municipalities, 1999) and "On Local Public Opinion Surveys" (Law of the Republic of Azerbaijan on Local Opinion Poll, 1999) dated November 30, 1999, the procedure for conducting local surveys is regulated in a rather formalized manner. The Law "On the Status of Municipalities" allows for citizens' meetings in municipalities with a population of fewer than 500 people. These meetings provide residents aged 18 and over, who have the right to vote, with the opportunity to express their views on local issues, make proposals, form collective opinions, and make decisions.

Additionally, according to the Model Statute "On the Neighborhood Committees of Municipalities" (Law of the Republic of Azerbaijan on Approval of the Model Regulations on Neighborhood Committees of Municipalities, 2001) approved on May 8, 2001, neighborhood committees, elected at a general citizens' meeting with 5 to 11 members for a two-year term, are authorized to address local issues and represent opinions and proposals. However, their activities are strictly limited by legislative frameworks, imposing additional constraints on the effectiveness of self-government initiatives.

In most cases, municipalities lack organizational and personnel capacity, as well as the training and knowledge needed to perform even the limited powers granted to them by law. To strengthen social integration at the municipal level, the population must have interests and needs that can be addressed by municipal authorities. However, the low level of citizen engagement in local self-government activities is often explained by insufficient awareness of its essence and functions, a weak understanding of its role in democratic transformation processes, and the absence of a developed "social potential."

Although the Constitution grants municipalities the right to adopt binding legal acts for citizens and legal entities within their territory, they are not included in the list of regulatory instruments that constitute part of Azerbaijan's legal system. This leads to uncertainty regarding municipalities' regulatory powers, making it difficult to implement their independent legislative initiatives.

Mechanisms for Control over the Activities of Local Government Bodies

An essential prerequisite for citizens' trust in government and municipal service is the transparency of their activities and open reporting. Sufficient regulatory provisions to ensure the transparency of municipal activities are outlined in the adopted legal acts concerning municipalities. These provisions manifest in the relationships between the municipalities, the state, and the population. According to part 4 of Article 15 of the Republic of Azerbaijan's Law "On the Status of Municipalities" (Law of the Republic of Azerbaijan on the status of municipalities, 1999), a member of the municipality is required to report to the voters at least once every 6 months. According to part 5 of Article 17 of this law, standing and other committees are responsible and accountable to the municipality that elected them.

According to Article 52-2 of the aforementioned law, municipalities report to the Milli Majlis (National Assembly) of the Republic of Azerbaijan on the implementation of additional powers granted to the municipality by the legislative authority under part II of Article 144 of the Constitution (Constitution of the Republic of Azerbaijan, 1995), and the use of financial resources allocated from the state budget to local budgets in cases specified in the law. Furthermore, municipalities must submit annual reports by April 1. Every year, on the Monday of the third week of January, municipalities report to voters on the work done, including the use of financial resources and municipal property. The report is prepared in writing and approved at a municipality meeting. To inform the local population, the report is displayed on special notice boards in front of the town hall, and it is also communicated to the public through announcements, bulletins, leaflets, local media, websites, and other means.

To ensure transparency, the Republic of Azerbaijan also adopted the "Public Participation Law" (Law of the Republic of Azerbaijan on Public Participation, 2013), which provides for the involvement of citizens in the implementation of public administration. This law regulates relationships arising from the engagement of citizens in the exercise of public administration. The main objectives of public participation are to organize effective interaction between local government bodies and the public, ensure openness and transparency in the activities of local government bodies, shape and implement state policy, consider public opinion and the legitimate interests of citizens when making decisions, and protect fundamental human and citizen rights.

According to the requirements of the law, all work related to the preparation and execution of the local budget must be carried out transparently. For example, according to Article 10 of the Republic of Azerbaijan's Law "On the Basics of Municipal Finance" (Law of the Republic of Azerbaijan on the Fundamentals of Municipal Finance, 1999) the draft decision on the local budget for the next fiscal year, along with the relevant documents, must be submitted for discussion at the municipal assembly and approved no later than October 15 of the current year. The draft local budget must be published within 10 days of its submission to the municipal assembly for public awareness. According to paragraph 3 of Article 11 of this law, municipalities must submit semi-annual and annual reports on the implementation of the local budget for consideration by the municipal assembly in the manner established by their charter. Semi-annual financial reports must be submitted by the 15th day of the month following the reporting period, and annual financial reports must be submitted by January 30 of the following year. Municipalities approve the submitted financial reports within 15 days through a decision of the municipal assembly. To inform the local population, municipalities publish the annual report through announcements, bulletins, leaflets, local media, websites, and other means. According to Article 13 of the law, municipalities oversee the implementation of the local budget, including the compliance of funds spent with the approved budgetary indicators, and for this purpose, they engage independent auditors at least once a year. To inform the local population, the results of the audit must be posted on special notice boards in front of the municipal building for one month from the date they are presented to the municipality.

According to Article 12.3 of the Law of the Republic of Azerbaijan "On Local Taxes and Fees" (Tax Code of the Republic of Azerbaijan, 2000), the activities of municipalities in the collection and use of local taxes and fees must be carried out with full transparency. For this purpose, municipalities and relevant supervisory commissions regularly report to residents living in the municipality, issue bulletins, and post annual reports on special boards in front of the municipal building.

According to part 8 of Article 56 of the Land Code of the Republic of Azerbaijan (Land Code of the Republic of Azerbaijan, 1999), the relevant executive authorities and municipalities are obligated to inform the population about available land plots for sale and lease, as well as programs for involving new lands in civil turnover. Additionally, they are required to publish annual reports in the mass media.

Strengthening the human resource potential in municipalities and ensuring the legality of local government activities also depends on the transparent process of municipal service recruitment. According to Article 5-1 of the Law of the Republic of Azerbaijan "On Municipal Service" (Law of the Republic of Azerbaijan on Municipal Service, 1999), recruitment to municipal service must be conducted through a competitive process. The creation, activities, rights, and responsibilities of the competition commission are determined by this Law. To facilitate the application of the law in this area, a methodological guide titled "Transparency in Municipal Service Recruitment" (Ministry of Justice of the Republic of Azerbaijan Center for Work with Municipalities, 2019) was prepared, which has been sent to all municipalities by the municipal affairs center and posted on the Ministry of Justice's website. This document outlines the organization of municipal service, the rules for recruitment, restrictions on recruitment, the process of announcing a recruitment competition, document submission, conducting the competition, and evaluating the competition results.

According to Article 9.1.1 of the Law of the Republic of Azerbaijan "On Access to Information" (Law of the Republic of Azerbaijan on Access to Information, 2005), municipalities are considered the owners of information. According to Article 10 of this Law, information subjects must ensure the right of everyone to freely, without obstacles, and on equal terms access information from their information resources, as specified by this Law. For this purpose, the information owner must appoint a responsible person for information matters or create a structural unit that provides information services.

Municipalities should not forget that one of the important conditions for their effective operation is the trust, confidence, and support of the local population. It must be acknowledged that, at the present stage, the public's interest in participating in the activities of municipalities has significantly weakened, as evidenced by the extremely low voter turnout in local elections. For instance, there are violations in the use of municipal lands, financial and economic activities, and tax collection. The fact that municipal elections are strongly influenced by local executive authorities reduces their significance and diminishes interest in participating. This is because many municipalities are still not fully familiar with their powers, municipal chairpersons act irresponsibly, and decisions are often made unilaterally.

However, these factors should not be interpreted as a justification for abandoning the institution of local self-government, as it is at this level of government, in conditions where political will is manifested, that it is much easier for citizens to practically use their influence on the authorities and exercise control over them. The declining interest in local elections can be explained by significant mistakes made in the formation of municipalities, and as a result, unsatisfactory activities of organized municipalities, where instead of solving local issues, they are more engaged in extraneous matters. In this context, the problem of establishing local self-government under new conditions is more closely related to the difficulties in organizing and conducting elections. These difficulties are expressed, on one hand, in attempts by government officials, especially local officials, to resist the development of true people's power, and on the other hand, in the insufficient legal culture and public activity of the population.

RESEARCH RESULTS

The results of the research highlight the importance of clear legislative and institutional regulation of the interaction between state authorities and local self-government bodies. The effectiveness of local self-government directly depends on state policy aimed at supporting this institution, as well as the level of stability and clarity in their relationships. The analysis shows that while the powers of local authorities are enshrined in law, they require clarification and adaptation for more effective implementation of tasks at the local level. A significant role in this process is played by the principle of subsidiarity, which is not yet sufficiently reflected in national legislation, hindering the full-scale development of local self-government.

An important aspect of the study is the financial and personnel autonomy of local authorities in Azerbaijan. According to the Ministry of Finance of Azerbaijan's 2023 report, the state budget revenues amounted to 35 billion 574.8 million manats, which is 16 percent higher than the 2022 figures (Report on the results of the activities of the chamber of auditors of the Republic Of Azerbaijan in 2023, 2024). However, despite the overall growth in the budget, local authorities still face limited financial autonomy, which can affect their operational efficiency.

One example of successful implementation of digital technologies in local governance is the launch of the "Digital Executive Power" portal (Digital Executive Power, 2021) in 2021. Developed by the Electronic Government Development Center of the State Agency for Public Service and Social Innovations under the President of Azerbaijan (ASAN), this portal provides online services for executive authorities, improving the accessibility and transparency of government services for citizens (ASAN service, 2012).

Additionally, the "Citizens' Electronic Appeals Portal" project received international recognition, winning first place in the "E-Government" category at the WSIS Prizes 2021 competition. This portal allows citizens, especially those in rural areas, to submit online applications, track their status, and receive feedback from government bodies (Azerbaijan's digital project has received recognition from the world community, 2021).

The research revealed that the current system of interaction between state authorities and municipalities is predominantly characterized by a "top-down initiative", which limits the autonomy of local authorities and their ability to independently address local issues. At the same time, there is a need to stimulate "bottom-up initiative", where local self-government bodies take an active role in initiating changes and interacting with state structures. This requires clarifying the scope of powers of both sides, as well as clearly defining the responsibility for the implementation of specific tasks to avoid duplication of functions and inconsistencies in actions, which negatively impact both local self-government and the activities of state structures.

One of the key conclusions is the necessity of resource support for local government bodies. The transfer of additional powers to municipalities should be accompanied by the corresponding transfer of financial, material, and human resources. Without such support, the expansion of powers may lead to a decrease in their effectiveness. It is also important to consider that the limited number of qualified personnel and insufficient public awareness of the essence of local self-government hinder active citizen involvement in this process, which emphasizes the need for educational work and the promotion of social integration.

Furthermore, the research highlights the need for the development of mechanisms to protect local self-government from undue interference by state authorities. The legislative framework should serve as a guarantee of stability in their functioning and protect their independence. To achieve these goals, it is necessary to improve the legal and institutional foundation of local self-government, including the development of effective strategic planning, management, and monitoring tools.

Thus, the research results confirm that the successful functioning of local self-government bodies requires a comprehensive approach, including legislative changes, strengthening institutional independence, supporting local initiatives, and providing sufficient resources. This approach will enable municipalities to become a fully-fledged institution of civil society, capable of effectively addressing socio-economic development tasks at the local level.

SOLUTIONS AND RECOMMENDATIONS

The local self-government system in Azerbaijan is a complex mechanism that, despite having a clear legal framework, continues to face challenges such as duplication of functions, dependence on central authorities, and the need for effective governance mechanisms at the local level. One of the key issues is the insufficient autonomy of municipalities, which is reflected in limited financial and administrative capacities as well as strict oversight by state bodies. The formally established powers of local self-government often overlap with the functions of executive structures, leading to inefficient resource allocation and a lack of clear accountability for decision-making.

In the context of ongoing centralization, municipalities largely depend on state subsidies, which restricts their ability to independently generate budgets and implement long-term socio-economic development programs. This dependency affects their capacity to respond effectively to the needs of the population and adapt to local challenges. Additionally, the institutional weakness of local authorities is evident in the shortage of qualified personnel, the absence of sustainable mechanisms for interaction with civil society and the business sector, and insufficient transparency in decision-making processes.

Systemic challenges are illustrated with real-world case studies from selected Azerbaijani municipalities. For example, recent pilot programs for e-governance and local transparency mechanisms launched in Baku's suburban areas demonstrate both the potential and limitations of local digital transformation initiatives.

Several critical aspects have been explored in more detail, including the impact of urbanization on local governance, the growing need for climate-adaptive local policy frameworks, and the gender imbalance in local leadership structures. These areas are supported with data and examples from both national and international sources.

Specific objectives are defined: (1) assessing the institutional and legal framework of state-municipal cooperation in Azerbaijan; (2) identifying key obstacles to effective local self-governance, particularly regarding financial and administrative autonomy; and (3) developing recommendations for enhancing transparency, civic engagement, and policy coordination between levels of government.

FUTURE RESEARCH DIRECTIONS

Future research in the field of municipalities and local self-government should focus on exploring comprehensive approaches to optimizing their functioning and interaction with state authorities. An important direction is the study of the principle of subsidiarity and its adaptation into national legislation, which will allow for a clear delineation of powers between various levels of government. Additionally, it is necessary to develop models for the effective allocation of financial, human, and material resources to ensure the sustainability of local self-government as their functions expand.

Special attention should be given to examining mechanisms for protecting the autonomy of local self-government from undue interference by state authorities. Within this direction, it is important to analyze international practices and adapt the best ones to local conditions, focusing on ensuring the stability and independence of municipal bodies. A promising area of research is exploring strategies for increasing citizen involvement in the local self-government process, including issues of public awareness, enhancing legal literacy, and promoting social integration.

Future studies should also address the formation of the institutional capacity of local self-government, including the development of municipal staff competencies, the creation of professional training programs, and enhancing their motivation. An important aspect is researching the role of digital technologies and their integration into local governance processes, which will enhance transparency and the efficiency of decision-making.

Furthermore, it is essential to investigate the socio-economic effectiveness of transferring powers to local self-government bodies, focusing on assessing their impact on the quality of life for citizens. Research should include the analysis of interactions between municipalities and the private sector, developing mechanisms for stimulating green investments at the local level, and implementing sustainable resource management practices. Additionally, studying potential mechanisms for engaging civil initiatives and NGOs in addressing local issues is critical.

Thus, future research directions should be oriented towards creating a systemic and sustainable approach to the development of local self-government, capable of ensuring a balance between state support and the autonomy of municipalities, as well as creating effective tools for solving local and national challenges.

CONCLUSION

In conclusion, the efficiency and sustainability of municipalities and local self-government bodies largely depend on the quality of interaction with state authorities, clarity in legislative regulation, and the availability of necessary resources. State policy plays a crucial role in shaping the conditions for the development of local self-government by determining their powers, responsibilities, and autonomy levels. Despite the existing legislative frameworks, issues related to the insufficient detailing of mechanisms for power division, resource provision for municipalities, and the lack of clear accountability for delegated functions are observed in some cases.

One of the main tasks of local self-government is the implementation of the principle of subsidiarity. However, its practical realization in Azerbaijan remains in its early stages. Legislation often involves control by state authorities, which may create risks of interference in the autonomy of municipalities. At the same time, state authorities need to ensure compliance with the rule of law and the efficiency of local self-government, which requires the development of balanced regulatory mechanisms. The lack of institutional memory and weak citizen involvement in local governance processes also pose significant obstacles to the development of self-government.

In the context of transitioning to more sustainable governance models, municipalities can play a significant role in implementing the principles of green economy, sustainable development, and social integration. However, this will require both state support in the form of normative and financial guarantees, as well as the enhancement of municipal authorities' competencies. Improving the local self-government system requires a systematic approach, including legislative reforms, encouraging civic activity, developing partnerships between the state and municipalities, and utilizing modern technologies to improve transparency and operational efficiency.

Thus, the successful development of local self-government can become an important element of societal democratization and sustainable growth in the country.

REFERENCES

Alakbarov, U., Mamedov, N., Gabibova, Z., & Rahimli, R. (2021). Evolution of public administration in the post-soviet countries. Azerbaijan republic. *Civil Service*, *23*(2 (130)), 97–118. DOI: 10.22394/2070-8378-2021-23-2-97-118

Aliyev, S. (2023). False Messages to the Public About Municipalities. Baku Research Institute. https://bakuresearchinstitute.org/en/false-messages-to-the-public-about-municipalities/

Aliyev, S. (2024). Failure to Devolve: Azerbaijan Avoids Promised Devolution of Power to Municipalities by Merging Them Instead. Baku Research Institute. https://bakuresearchinstitute.org/en/failure-to-devolve-azerbaijan-avoids-promised-devolution-of-power-to-municipalities-by-merging-them-instead/

Analysis Of Azerbaijani Legislation On Freedom Of Expression. Council of Europe. (2017). https://rm.coe.int/azerbaijan-analysis-of-legislation-on-freedom-of-expression-december-2/16808ae03d

ASAN service. (2012) https://asan.gov.az/en

Atar, E., & Kirboz, Ş. (2024). Local governance reforms in post-soviet Azerbaijan: A comprehensive analysis of structural changes and reform initiatives. *Janus-NET*, *15*(2), 2. DOI: 10.26619/1647-7251.15.2.11

Azerbaijan's digital project has received recognition from the world community. (2021). https://www.trend.az/business/it/3428690.html

Constitution of the Republic of Azerbaijan [Azərbaycan Respublikasının Konstitusiyası]. (1995). https://e-qanun.az/framework/897

Constitutional Law of the Republic of Azerbaijan on the Approval of the Constitution of the Nakhchivan Autonomous Republic. (1998). [Naxçıvan Muxtar Respublikasının Konstitusiyasının təsdiq edilməsi haqqında Azərbaycan Respublikasının Konstitusiya Qanunu]. https://e-qanun.az/framework/1755

Country Gender Profile Azerbaijan. EU 4Gender Equality: Reform Help Desk. European Union. (2021). https://euneighbourseast.eu/wp-content/uploads/2022/07/eu4genderhelpdesk_azerbaijangenderprofile_v3.pdf

Digital Executive Power. (2021). https://my.gov.az/serviceCategories/52f0ccb5-059a-4589-9777-e9f5208b4d91

Huseynov, S. Z. (2023). Organisation of local self-government in the Republic of Azerbaijan. *Futurity Economics & Law, 3*(4), 239–254. DOI: 10.57125/FEL.2023.12.25.15

Huseynov, S. Z. (2023). Local Self-Government Bodies in the Republic of Azerbaijan: Legal Status, Tasks and Prospects. *Futurity Economics&Law, 3*(2), 18–40. DOI: 10.57125/FEL.2023.06.25.02

Kim, M., & Cho, M. (2019). Examining the role of sense of community: Linking local government public relationships and community-building. *Public Relations Review, 45*(2), 297–306. DOI: 10.1016/j.pubrev.2019.02.002

Klimovský, D., & Swianiewicz, P.. (2010). Territorial Consolidation Reforms. In Swianiewicz, P. (Ed.), *Europe. Edition: 1st, Publisher: OSI/LGI.*

Labor Code of the Republic of Azerbaijan. (1999). [Azərbaycan Respublikasının mək Məcəlləsi]. https://e-qanun.az/framework/46943

Land Code of the Republic of Azerbaijan. (1999). [Azərbaycan Respublikasının Torpaq Məcəlləsi]. https://e-qanun.az/framework/46942

Law of the Republic of Azerbaijan on Access to Information. (2005). [İnformasiya əldə etmək haqqında Azərbaycan Respublikasının Qanunu]. https://e-qanun.az/framework/11142

Law of the Republic of Azerbaijan on Approval of the Model Regulations on Neighborhood Committees of Municipalities. (2001). [Bələdiyyələrin məhəllə komitələri haqqında Nümunəvi sasnamənin təsdiq edilməsi barədə Azərbaycan Respublikasının Qanunu]. https://e-qanun.az/framework/3547

Law of the Republic of Azerbaijan on local (municipal) taxes and payments. (2001). [Yerli (bələdiyyə) vergilər və ödənişlər haqqında Azərbaycan Respublikasının Qanunu]. https://e-qanun.az/framework/1470

Law of the Republic of Azerbaijan on Local Opinion Poll. (1999). [Yerli rəy sorğusu haqqında Azərbaycan Respublikasının Qanunu]. https://e-qanun.az/framework/5227

Law of the Republic of Azerbaijan on Municipal Service. (1999). [Bələdiyyə qulluğu haqqında Azərbaycan Respublikasının Qanunu]. https://e-qanun.az/framework/5228

Law of the Republic of Azerbaijan on Municipal Territories and Lands. (1999). [Bələdiyyələrin əraziləri və torpaqları haqqında Azərbaycan Respublikasının Qanunu]. https://www.taxes.gov.az/az/post/195

Law of the Republic of Azerbaijan on Municipal Water Management. (2001). [Bələdiyyələrin su təsərrüfatı haqqında Azərbaycan Respublikasının Qanunu]. https://e-qanun.az/framework/2760

Law of the Republic of Azerbaijan on Public Participation. (2013). [İctimai iştirakçılıq haqqında Azərbaycan Respublikasının Qanunu]. https://e-qanun.az/framework/26879

Law of the Republic of Azerbaijan on the Fundamentals of Municipal Finance. (1999). [Bələdiyyələrin maliyyəsinin əsasları haqqında Azərbaycan Respublikasının Qanunu]. https://e-qanun.az/framework/5231

Law of the Republic of Azerbaijan on the status of a municipal member. (2000). [Bələdiyyə üzvünün statusu haqqında Azərbaycan Respublikasının Qanunu]. https://e-qanun.az/framework/507

Law of the Republic of Azerbaijan on the status of municipalities. (1999). [Bələdiyyələrin statusu haqqında Azərbaycan Respublikasının Qanunu]. https://e-qanun.az/framework/4770

Local Government Country Profile. UN Women. (2022). https://localgov.unwomen.org/country/AZE

Local self-government in Azerbaijan: few improvements observed, limited powers and weak financial position of municipalities must be urgently addressed. Congress of Local and Regional Authorities. (2021). https://www.coe.int/en/web/congress/-/local-self-government-in-azerbaijan-few-improvements-observed-limited-powers-and-weak-financial-position-of-municipalities-must-be-urgently-addressed

Ministry of Justice of the Republic of Azerbaijan Center for Work with Municipalities. (2019). Collection of methodological documents Baku. “Red N Line” LLC., 32 p.

Opinion of the Chamber of Accounts of the Republic of Azerbaijan on the draft state budget of the Republic of Azerbaijan for 2024. (2023). [Azərbaycan Respublikasının 2024-cü il dövlət büdcəsinin layihəsinə Azərbaycan Respublikası Hesablama Palatasının rəyi]. https://sai.gov.az/files/r%C9%99y%202024%20layih%C9%99-892107023.pdf

Regulations on local executive authorities. Decree of the President of the Republic of Azerbaijan, (2012). https://baku-ih.gov.az/en/legislation2.html

Report on the results of the activities of the chamber of auditors of the Republic Of Azerbaijan in 2023. (2024). [Azərbaycan Respublikası auditorlar palatasının 2023-cü ildə fəaliyyətinin yekunlarına dair hesabat]. https://www.audit.gov.az/Upload/Files/2019/HESABAT_illik-2023_son1.pdf

Resolution of the Cabinet of Ministers of the Republic of Azerbaijan on Amendments to Some Decisions of the Cabinet of Ministers of the Republic of Azerbaijan. (2000). [Azərbaycan Respublikası Nazirlər Kabinetinin bəzi qərarlarına dəyişikliklər edilməsi haqqında Azərbaycan Respublikası Nazirlər Kabinetinin Qərarı]. https://e-qanun.az/framework/212

Sadigova, Z. (2021). The Improvement of E-Municipality Systems In Azerbaijan Local Governments. *70th International Scientific Conference on Economic and Social Development.*

Salimli, N. (2022). Transparency in local self-government. The papers of the Ministry of Justice of the Republic of Azerbaijan. https://justice.gov.az/categories/1038

Salmanly, F. (2024). *Basic principles and historical stages of development of local self-government.*

Salzberger, E. M. (1993). A positive analysis of the doctrine of separation of powers, or: Why do we have an independent judiciary? *International Review of Law and Economics*, *13*(4), 349–379. DOI: 10.1016/0144-8188(93)90029-5

State Statistical Committee of the Republic of Azerbaijan. Classification of administrative territorial divisions, [Azərbaycan Respublikasının Dövlət Statistika Komitəsi. İnzibati ərazi bölgüsü təsnifatı]. (2024). stat.gov.az. 2024-02-28.

Statement Of Preliminary Findings And Conclusions/ International Election Observation Mission Republic of Azerbaijan – Early Parliamentary Elections. (2020). https://www.oscepa.org/en/documents/election-observation/election-observation-statements/azerbaijan/statements-3/3952-2020-parliamentary-1/file

Steenmans, K., Robin, E., Acuto, M., Iwaszuk, E., & Garza, L. O. (2023). Governing the informed city: Examining local government strategies for information production, consumption and knowledge sharing across ten cities. *Urban Governance*, *3*(4), 243–251. DOI: 10.1016/j.ugj.2023.09.001

Tax Code of the Republic of Azerbaijan. (2000). [Azərbaycan Respublikasının Vergi Məcəlləsi]. https://e-qanun.az/framework/46948

Vöhringer, B., & Dickson, S. (2021). Monitoring of the application of the European Charter of Local SelfGovernment in Azerbaijan. 40th SESSION Second part Report CG (2021) 40-21.

Wienen, J., & Mosler-Törnström, G. (2013). The Congress of Local and Regional Authorities. Local and regional democracy in Azerbaijan. 23rd SESSION Strasbourg. https://rm.coe.int/local-and-regional-democracy-in-azerbaijan-resolution-recommendation-m/1680719568

ADDITIONAL READING

Gustafsson, S., & Mignon, I. (2019). Municipalities as intermediaries for the design and local implementation of climate visions. *European Planning Studies*, *28*(6), 1161–1182. DOI: 10.1080/09654313.2019.1612327

Nordberg, K., & Narbutaité Aflaki, I. (2024). Public sector readiness for value co-creation: The diffusion of a governance innovation. *Public Money & Management*, *106*(1), 1–12.

Nordberg, K., Virkkala, S., & Mariussen, Å. (2023). Municipalities and communities enabling social innovations in peripheral areas – case studies from Ostrobothnia, Finland. *Geografiska Annaler. Series B, Human Geography*, *106*(1), 74–95. DOI: 10.1080/04353684.2023.2225537

Schmieder, L., Scheer, D., Gaiser, J., Jendritzki, I., & Kraus, B. (20123). Municipalities as change agents? Reconsidering roles and policies in local energy sector-coupling, *Energy Research & Social Science*, 103, 103210, .DOI: 10.1016/j.erss.2023.103210

Skill, K., Farhangi, M., & Trygg, K. (2023). Size matters: Action space for sustainability transition among planners in Swedish municipalities. *Urban Research & Practice*, *17*(3), 329–346. DOI: 10.1080/17535069.2023.2209554

Thakur, S. S., & Nel, A. (2023). Taking a back seat: The politicization of municipal environmental governance in South Africa. *The South African Geographical Journal*, *106*(2), 212–229. DOI: 10.1080/03736245.2023.2272893

KEY TERMS AND DEFINITIONS

Citizen Participation: Involving residents in decision-making processes by local self-government bodies to increase transparency, accountability, and the social significance of decisions.

Financial Sustainability of Municipalities: The ability of local self-government bodies to generate and effectively manage financial resources for performing their functions on a long-term basis.

Interaction between the State and Municipalities: A system of coordination and regulation of relations between state authorities and local self-government bodies, including the distribution of powers, provision of resources, and control of their activities.

Legislative Framework for Local Self-Government: A set of legal acts that regulate the organization, functioning, and control of local self-government bodies, ensuring the stability and predictability of their activities.

Local Self-Government: A system of organizing power at the local level, where the residents of a specific territory independently and under their responsibility address local matters within the limits set by law.

Municipalities: Local self-government bodies endowed by law with limited powers, financial resources, and responsibility for addressing local matters.

Principle of Subsidiarity: A governance principle that suggests solving issues at the lowest level of government where possible, with higher levels providing support when necessary.

Chapter 7
Local Self-Government in India:
A Critical Analysis through the Lens of Democratic Decentralization

Jipson Joseph
https://orcid.org/0009-0005-1795-5051
Christ University, Bengaluru, India

Ananya Pandey
https://orcid.org/0000-0002-2419-6314
Christ University, Bangalore, India

ABSTRACT

Local Self-Government (LSG) existed in a variety of forms throughout India. LSG was seen as an effective form of day-to-day management and administration in rural areas in India. This ensured a democratic form of administration even during the time of monarchs. Although it had a setback during the Muslim and British rulers period, it continued to exist. Gandhi raised his voice for increased decentralization and self-rule of the villages. Although the Constitution did not provide such an option, many committees opined that the local governance should be entrusted to the local people. Accordingly, LSG got constitutional recognition through the 73rd and 74th Amendments in 1992. It provided a three-tier system of governance at the regional level as well. Using analytical and critical lenses, this chapter examines the functioning of the constitutionally established LSG model through the lens of democratic decentralization to expose how far it has achieved its objective.

DOI: 10.4018/979-8-3373-5576-4.ch007

1 INTRODUCTION

Local Self-Government (LSG) stands for democratic governance at the grassroots level. Democracy refers to people's independent power in governance (Awasthi, 2024). Although democracy originated in the Ancient Greek Polis, Athens, around BCE 508, it became a vibrant and globally preferred political and governance system only in the 20th century, especially after the Second World War (Olorunlana, 2023). Democracy has various forms: direct, representative, presidential, parliamentary, and participatory. It also functions in centralized and decentralized forms. The contemporary democratic system favors a decentralized government (Arends et al., 2023). However, decentralization is not limited to democracies, as other forms of government also follow this model (Faguet, 2014; Smith, 2023). However, in this article, the authors focus on decentralized governance in a democratic system. Democratic decentralization refers to the system of governance in which more and more people are actively involved in governance at the national, regional, and local levels (Uddin, 2018). It is very effective for the proper and systematic governance of large countries like India. LSG is an erudite example of democratic decentralization. It affirms that people at local levels have a right to decide and run their projects for the well-being of local society and operate them autonomously with the support of regional and national governments (Campbell, 2001). It functions based on the principle that people at local levels have more awareness of their issues and interests than the central or regional policymakers. Accordingly, local policy-making and decision-making processes will be more effective for the welfare of the local community.

India's focus on LSG existed even before the pre-British period. However, the present understanding and tradition of LSG started with Mahatma Gandhi's idea of Gram Swaraj. It revolved around a self-reliant village of reconstruction (Johnson, 2003). For Gandhi, India lives in villages, and its growth depends on the self-sufficiency of its villages. He called for revitalizing the conventional Panchayat Raj System to empower villages. Although there were some reservations, the post-independent period took up the Gandhian initiative and highlighted the Community Development Program, affirming the importance of local self-governance. The government of India constituted various committees to examine the scope of decentralization, which called for the institution of the Panchayati Raj System. Based on their suggestions, the 73rd and 74th Amendments of the Constitution were made, which guaranteed the institution of LSG. Thereafter, the three-tier system of governance was established, which provided options for decision-making and developmental projects at the local, state, and central levels. The local level of governance consists of Panchayats (village, block, and district levels) and municipalities

(Municipal council and municipal corporation). Such a system provided the option for effective governance at the local level.

The enactment of the Panchayati Raj Act and the Constitutional Amendments widened India's governance scope. It emphasizes the increased role of women and the active engagement of local bodies in ensuring the region's education, healthcare, and public utility maintenance. The governments in each period prioritized the development of local bodies by giving them more power and decision-making roles. However, their financial resources are minimal, and they still need to depend on the central and state governments to ensure the availability of financial support (Joseph & Thomas, 2023). It creates confusion and various challenges at certain times. Besides, the politicization of LSG has demotivated the true spirit of constitutional amendment despite it being an effective form of governance. Political parties, unfortunately, take the governance of local bodies as a means to increase their vote bank for the elections to the State Assembly and Central Parliament. LSG sometimes lacks transparency and accountability, causing serious repercussions to societal welfare. The benefits and advantages at certain times are limited to a few people and do not reach the majority (Bhardwaj, 2023). However, the most complicated issue is its dependency on superior forms of governance.

In this perspective, this chapter critically analyzes the present state of LSG in India through the lens of decentralization. When we examine the governance of India, it affirms that decentralization exists in theory and is actively propagated, but in practice, it fails to make any substantial changes in the system. The laws and policies are to be implemented efficiently to realize a genuine decentralized form of governance that benefits people. The LSG system became a constitutional provision in India almost three decades ago, and hence, the chapter attempts to evaluate how far the objective of decentralization has been achieved. It also will try to suggest some guidelines and policy frameworks for LSG's effective functioning.

2 DECENTRALIZED DEMOCRACY: A MODEL FOR COOPERATIVE FEDERALISM

Decentralization, a political or governance process, is a contribution of the past generation (Johnson, 2003). Towards the end of the 20th century, almost 80% of countries followed this principle of governance, now visible in nearly all parts of the globe (Faguet, 2014). Rodden (2006) claims decentralization and federalism are the most successful governance trends over the last 50 years. Rodden's claim is still valid, even after two more decades. The debate on centralization and decentralization revolves around "the locus of decision-making authority." When one or relatively few individuals make decisions, it is an example of centralized governance, whereas if lower-level members share the decision-making authority, it becomes decentralized (Altamimi et al., 2023, p. 170). Decentralized democracy refers to the democratic system of government in which power is decentralized to address local people's needs effectively. Decentralization focuses on people's participatory governance instead of the top-down hierarchical model. The globe prioritized decentralization, believing it could improve the quality of governance (Faguet, 2014).

Scholars and institutions define decentralization in various ways. Center for Democracy and Governance (CDG, 2000, p. 6) describes it as "a process of transferring power to popularly elected local governments." The transfer of power is the fundamental characteristic feature of decentralization. The local officials' presence cannot be considered decentralized LSG as these officials are ultimately responsible to their higher authorities, not the people. Decentralization calls for the elected people's governing power in local governance. Decentralization is also defined as "the administrative reform to division and dissemination of central government authorities, activities, rights, and responsibilities to the distant grassroots administrative units" (Uddin, 2018, p. 1). Decentralization, accordingly, is an effective mechanism for checking the concentration of power in the hands of a few at the center. It implies that by dividing power into different levels of government, the nature of administration can be transformed into people-friendly and beneficial. The more centralization there is, the greater the chance of becoming autocratic (Altamimi et al., 2023). Decentralization calls for transferring administrative authority, public resources, and responsibilities from the central and state levels to the local level to make governance and policies beneficial to the public (Johnson, 2003). Decentralizing fiscal powers is also essential to its efficient functioning (Meenakshisundaram, 1999). If power is decentralized, it helps the governance system to become competitive in responding to people's demands. The Indian scenario affirms that administrative and fiscal decentralization are unevenly implemented in the States. When these essentialities are uneven, it adversely affects the local democratic system (UGLC, 2008).

Decentralization depends on three essential conditions: a strong political commitment of the higher-level government authorities towards local bodies, the relative autonomy of the local bodies towards the decision-making and implementation process, and the availability of resources at the local level (Meenakshisundaram, 1999). Both higher and lower levels of bodies are not separate entities but essential complementary parts that work together for the well-being of society. It demands cooperation and mutual support for their effective functioning. The higher levels of government should provide the required resources, autonomy, and support to the lower bodies so that they can function together for the welfare of the people. Decentralization is beneficial as it supports people's active participation in local affairs by identifying community priorities, giving practical experience to all sections of people in the practice of democratic principles, encouraging pluralistic thoughts at the local level policy debates, and empowering marginalized communities with more powers (CDG, 2000; Johnson, 2003). It provides easy access to people in the policy-making and decision-making process. It is also beneficial to societal well-being and economic growth. However, the outcome depends on the design of decentralization (OECD, 2019).

Decentralization also should be analyzed through the lens of cooperative federalism. Compared to classical federalism, which stands for coordination and independence, cooperative federalism demands cooperation and interdependence among the Centre, States, and local bodies. It emphasizes collaboration for addressing various issues of people at different levels of society and governance (Tariq et al., 2018). Decentralization calls for transferring power from the popularly elected central or state governments to the popularly elected local governments. The people elect both systems of governance for their governance. The elected bodies' ultimate objective is to ensure their people's security and welfare. The transfer of powers should be understood from this perspective. It is a mechanism to empower local governments with more political authority, greater financial resources, and increased administrative responsibilities to effectively function and coordinate welfare programs (Sheikh, 2014). Such a decentralized system of governance can become more efficient as it is closely linked to democracy, development, and good governance.

Although Gandhi had an energetic vision of decentralized governance for India, neither Nehru nor the Constitutional Fathers effectively supported or propagated this ideal setting (Manor, 1999). It might be due to the circumstances immediately after the independence, such as the separation of India and Pakistan, tensions at the borders, and internal issues concerning the choices of kings and the like (Kannan, 1993). These circumstances forced India to prioritize centralized governance, which they changed almost 45 years after the independence with the 73rd and 74th constitutional amendments. Decentralization became a constitutional mandate with this historic step, which should be strictly followed throughout India for effective governance as the country is comparatively larger and diverse.

3 LOCAL SELF-GOVERNMENT IN INDIA: A HISTORICAL SKETCH

Local Self-Government became the central idea of Indian political ideology and governance within the ambit of a worldwide reformative decentralization movement. The whole globe sincerely responded to the inspirational project of LSG due to many factors, such as dispersing power among smaller units to overcome its past reminiscence of dictatorship, reducing the size of central government for transforming towards a more efficient economy, increasing the involvement of the public in governance and decision-making, addressing the poor performance of central governments, and responding positively to the public demand for a substantial reform (CDG, 2000). The demand for decentralization and LSG originated not only from social and political movements or from the larger public but also from policymakers and political elites, who thought it would provide a better governance framework. Many believe that decentralizing powers, functions, and responsibilities can solve the asymmetry of power (DeSouza, 2003). Local self-rule is essential for countries like India, with large sizes and enormous populations (Johnson, 2003). From the period of independence, India focused on some forms of decentralization to address issues like poverty and the empowerment of marginalized sections of society (Drèze & Sen, 1996). It became an official form of governance with the 73rd and 74th Constitutional Amendments. India's two-tier system of governance thereafter became a three-tier system. However, in federal states like India, the autonomy of the LSG varies depending on each state's policies. In India, it depends on the specific devolution schemes of each state (OECD, 2019).

LSG consists of three words: local, self, and government. A specific definition that includes all the nuances of LSG is rarely seen. Although there is no precise definition, it refers to the self-rule of people in a local area, such as a village or a municipality. The idea is very progressive as it insists that the needs and aspirations of people in a particular area are unique to them, and only they can better address their issues with appropriate solutions. They know the possibility of efficiently tackling their natural resources by making appropriate taxation and administration facilities for that area if proper governing power is given without any external interference. That is, it refers to the governance of local people without any external interference in their local area of a village or a municipality (Srivastava, 2002). This section examines how the system of LSG evolved in India until the institution of various committees.

3.1 Pre-British Period

Sydney Web considered LSG "as old as the hills." This is specifically true with the Indian system of governance. India's panchayat system of governance is as old as the hills. Panchayati Raj Institutions (PRIs) can be traced back to the Vedic period. The original terms used to refer to PRIs were *sabhas* and *samiti*. Panchayat literally refers to the governance of a local society by an assembly of five members elected by the villagers. 'Panch' also denotes five gods or essential materials (Kumar, 2015). They believed the elected members represented gods or *panchabhutas* (five fundamental elements, such as earth, water, air, fire, and space) to the community. This assembly of five had great administrative and judicial powers over the village. Even the kings sought the approval of panchayats to make certain decisions and other vital matters in that village (Bhardwaj, 2023). There is evidence of its active presence during the Gupta and Maura kingdoms. It existed even during the Muslim rule, but the rulers did not strongly support it as they preferred centralization. The Muslim rulers recognized Zamindars and local chiefs but excluded people's authority (Kumar, 2015). The pre-British period affirms that the LSG has a long history, starting from the Vedic period and passing through various stages, where it received support and setbacks.

3.2 British Period

During British governance, from the period of the East India Company onwards, the PRIs had a hard time as they never prioritized decentralization or local governance. They tried to destroy the village governance system to foster their centralized interests. Some attempts were made to revitalize the PRIs after the first war of independence in 1857 (Bhardwaj, 2023). Decentralization became a policy initiative with Lord Ripon's Resolution of 1882. The liberal-minded Ripon established local bodies with this Resolution. Even without defining the term, Ripon used 'local self-government' to refer to local bodies in villages and municipalities (Srivastava, 2002). He is thus called the Father of LSG in India. According to the 1882 Resolution, district and local boards were formed, and non-officials were started to be included through election. However, only tax-payers were allowed to take part in the election. This Resolution aimed to make Indians capable of managing their affairs. However, it also was beneficial to the Britishers. The Indians were intensely demanding a participatory role in the decision-making process. Lord Ripon acknowledged this demand but insisted that the participation be reserved for tax-payers. If the Indians prefer to manage their affairs, they should be tax-payers. Thereafter, the 1907 Royal Commission on Decentralization affirmed the significance of PRIs at the village level. A slow process towards more independence and functions of PRIs was visible in the coming years. Eight provinces and six native states promoted PRIs during 1925-26. More decentralization was suggested with the 1935 Government of India Act. Although local bodies had some powers, everything remained under the supervision of the British government (Bhardwaj, 2023). The British period was a period of severe setbacks concerning PRIs and LSG, as the British authorities preferred a centralized system of governance. Some changes occurred due to the pressure tactics of the Indian leaders, but they cannot be considered significant except for the contributions of Lord Ripon.

3.3 Gandhi's Gram Swaraj

India's most significant example of decentralization can be seen in Gandhi's unique vision of the village system, which was called Gram Swaraj. The word Gram stands for village, and Swaraj refers to self-rule. Gandhi insisted that instead of caste, untouchability, and various other forms of exploitation, Gram Swaraj should revolve around universal education, economic self-sufficiency, and democratic governance at the village level (Johnson, 2003). Swaraj does not stand for acquiring authority for a few but refers to the progressive vision of empowering people with the capacity to regulate or control those in authority (Garg & Raut, 2015). He initiated the Gram Swaraj concept by reconstructing villages like Champaran in 1917, Sevagram in 1920, and Wardha in 1938. He prioritized the physical, mental, economic, political, and moral development of each individual in the village. An all-inclusive development of the individual was the motto of Gandhian Gram Swaraj. It is called an independent village republic, and the idea was that the village would be sufficient for various wants like food, clothes, water, and shelter. Besides, it upheld principles like 100% literacy, no untouchability, and harmonious living with all denominations. His idea was that every village should be transformed into a model village through the inspirational concept of Gram Swaraj. While the village was designed to be independent regarding various wants, it depended on many other things with other villages promoting harmonious living (Joshi, 2002; Garg & Raut, 2015). His Gram Swaraj is a 'self-rule village,' where people need not depend on higher forms of government for economic, political, and moral support, as it is genuinely independent (Vaddiraju, 2017). However, no village exists in isolation without cooperating with the neighboring villages. Although the Nehruvian idea of centralized state policies for development disagreed with the Gandhian self-governing ideal village concept, Gram Swaraj had a tolerable existence immediately after independence (Manor, 1999).

3.4 Community Development Program

The post-independent scenario of poverty, unemployment, and lack of development, especially in the rural areas, pressurized the Central government to initiate the Community Development Program (CDP). Although its remote origin can be traced back to 1946, it became a policy agenda with the First Five-Year Plan (1951-1956). CDP was launched in 1952 with 55 projects in different parts of the country. The project area was comparatively huge, consisting of three developmental blocks. Each block covered approximately 100 villages and a population of 60000-70000. The project had to be completed within 36 months (3 years), which was divided into 3 months for the planning stage, 6 months for the initiation stage, 18 months for the operation stage, 6 months for the consolidation stage, and 3 months for the finalization stage (Dayal, 1960). It was estimated that during the first five-year plan, CDP became beneficial to 14000 villages covering 77.5 million people (Bansal, 2016). CDP originated from the Nehruvian ideology of centralized rapid development. It devised a systematic strategy for realizing the self-governing of the local communities in partnership with the centralized policies for effective development (Manor, 1999). Just one year after the launching of CDP, the planning commission launched another program called the National Extension Services (NES). Unlike CDP, NES was a permanent program covering the whole country (Bansal, 2016). Both CDP and NES have contributed to ensuring progress and welfare for people immediately after the independence. They helped the central government address and solve a tough time's complexities.

4 AN EVALUATION OF VARIOUS COMMITTEES: PROPOSAL FOR LSG

Although the Second Five-Year Plan (1956-1961) had devised a plan for decentralized governance through the increased implementation of NES, which was designed to work by employing Block Development Officers, Assistant Development Officers, and village-level workers, it did not become effective as the initiative to transfer power to the local bodies was not adequately carried out (Kumar, 2015). During this period, the Central government instituted various committees to study and evaluate the need for the PRIs and their roles and functions. The section below analyzes some crucial committees to understand this progression clearly.

4.1 Balwant Rai Mehta Committee

During the Second Five-Year Plan period, the government of India appointed a committee under the chairmanship of Balwant Rai Mehta to study and evaluate the working of CDP and NES for improving the economic and social conditions of rural areas through utilizing local initiatives and resources. The committee reported that the CDP would be effective only when the local community is given increased power in its planning, decision-making, and implementation stages. It suggested the establishment of elected bodies with appropriate devolution of powers. However, it said that the basic unit of LSG should be at the block level as it cannot be too small or too big. It suggested that the body should be elected for five years with less governmental interference. It demanded that the LSG should be given powers concerning agriculture, small-scale industries, road building, drinking water, and sanitation. Zilla panchayat's role should be advisory (Kumar, 2015).

4.2 Ashok Mehta Committee

In 1978, the Janatha Party-led central government instituted a high-level committee under Ashok Mehta's chairmanship to recommend ways to strengthen PRIs. It submitted the report with 132 recommendations within one year. It suggested a two-tier system at panchayats: district and mandal levels. It reserved constituencies for scheduled castes and scheduled tribes and two seats for women. It further insisted that the PRIs should be formed by direct election conducted by the State Election Commission and demanded that taxation powers be provided to PRIs (Bhardwaj, 2023). The term for the elected members was four years. The Zilla Parishad should be the primary unit, not the Panchayat Samiti, as it has better leadership and resources. Political parties can be involved in the election. Based on the recommendations of this committee, States like Karnataka, Andra Pradesh, and West Bengal passed legislation in favor of PRIs (Kumar, 2015).

4.3 G. V. K. Rao Committee

The National Planning Commission appointed the Rao Committee in 1985 to study the various aspects of PRIs. The committee suggested that the PRIs have a significant role in addressing people's problems at the grassroots level. It insisted that the PRIs should be activated with all necessary support to transform them into effective organizations. It argued that the block development office should be the center of rural development programs (Kumar, 2015).

4.4 L. M. Sanghvi Committee

The Sanghvi committee of 1986, after a thorough analysis of PRIs, suggested that the local bodies of self-governance would increase people's participation in the planning and development of rural areas. It suggested that a provision for LSG should be included with an Amendment of the Constitution for recognizing, protecting, and promoting people's local self-governance. It considered Grama Sabha to be the base unit of LSG. Surprisingly, it argued that political parties should not be involved in the panchayat elections (Kumar, 2015). It wanted PRIs to be separate bodies without political interference to ensure effective governance. If politics enters the election process of local bodies, it may influence the choices and preferences of the higher levels of government, complicating the governance of the local bodies.

4.5 Gadgill Committee

In 1988, the Gadgill committee was formed to propose ideas about transforming the PRIs into more effective organs. This committee's report became the foundation for drafting the Amendment bill. In agreement with the previous committees, it also suggested giving constitutional status to the PRIs. It preferred the three-tier system of governance at village, block, and district levels. Besides preferring a five-year term for LSG and a direct election for its members, it insisted on reserving a certain number of seats for women and backward classes. PRIs must prepare and implement socio-economic development plans in light of people's well-being and society's welfare. It suggested transferring a list of subjects in the constitution to the law-making capacity of the PRIs so that effective functioning can be ensured. They should also be given power to levy, collect, and appropriately use taxes and duties to benefit the local community. Besides, it called for establishing a State Finance Commission to coordinate and oversee the distribution of funds to the PRIs and a State Election Commission to coordinate its election process (Kumar, 2015).

5 73rd AND 74th CONSTITUTIONAL AMENDMENTS: AN ANALYSIS

Very few countries in the world mention LSG or contain rules of local governance in their Constitutions (Srivastava, 2002). However, the last decade of the 20th century witnessed enormous growth in India's decentralization policies and progressive constitutional changes concerning local governance. It was evident with the 73rd and 74th Constitutional Amendments in 1992. Most of the above-analyzed committees affirmed the importance of constitutional protection to LSGs. In 1989, Rajiv Gandhi introduced the 64th Constitutional Amendment bill for empowering the PRIs with a constitutional mandate, but it was defeated in the Rajya Sabha. V. P. Singh introduced another bill with the same intention in the Lok Sabha in 1990, but it did not pass through. However, the P. V. Narasimha Rao government modified the 1990 bill and introduced it in 1992, which was passed by both houses of the Parliament (Bhardwaj, 2023). Both Amendments were enacted in 1993, and all states enacted legislation to implement LSG by April 1994. LSG became a constitutional body with these Amendments, which was previously a mere part of the Directive Principles of State Policy (Kumar, 2015). Even before the 1992 constitutional Amendments, many States had designed LSG based on various committee suggestions, but it lacked constitutional protection. This lacuna was solved by the historic constitutional Amendments of 1992. Besides, the Constitution identified Panchayats and Municipalities as "Self" governments enlarging their scope, powers, and functions (Srivastava, 2002). While incorporating LSG into the Constitution, the liberal constitutionalists affirm that it is part of a larger political system. With the Amendments, they argue that strengthening local democracy became effective (Vaddiraju, 2017). It is true that with the constitutional mandates, the scope of LSG has been enlarged and strengthened. However, it undermined the Gandhian idea of independent self-rule of the local bodies.

5.1 73rd Constitutional Amendment

The 73rd Constitutional Amendment gave sufficient opportunities to interpret and implement the mind of the Constitutional Fathers concerning decentralization and recognition of the third-tier system of governance at the sub-state level. It formally provided legal recognition to the inspirational agenda of Panchayati Raj u/A 243 of the Constitution of India (Johnson, 2003). However, the Amendment insisted that due to the special circumstances of the Indian federation, the States needed to pass their conformity legislation for enlisting the powers, functions, and responsibilities of LSG in each state (World Bank, 2000). So, the characteristic features of LSG vary according to the State policies and delegation. The Act provided the constitutional recognition for political decentralization and PRIs, but the administrative and fiscal decentralization policies depend on each state's legislation.

The 73rd Amendment added part IX with the title "The Panchayats," consisting of 16 clauses (u/A 243 to 243(O)) and the eleventh Schedule to the Constitution. Among these 16 articles, Article 243 (G) gives a detailed list of functions to be performed by PRIs, and the eleventh Schedule enlists the subjects that are given to the law-making power of the PRIs. It brought in the concept of participative democracy in place of representative democracy. This Act also underlined two types of provisions: mandatory, which the states should adopt, and voluntary, which the states may or may not adopt. The State has the freedom to implement the voluntary provisions of the act, taking into account the local geographical and politico-administrative factors (Bhardwaj, 2023). However, States should implement the mandatory provisions for an ordered system in the country.

According to the Act, Gram Sabha is the foundation of the Panchayati Raj system. It established a three-tier system of PRIs, with elected bodies at the village, block, and district level. However, if a state's population is below 2 million, it is not required to introduce a block-level Panchayat. It provided direct elections for choosing the representatives to all three levels for 5 years and reserved 1/3 of the seats for women and backward classes. The Act thus wanted a stable government at the local level and preferred an active role to the traditionally marginalized sections of society in the PRIs. It also established the possibilities for a state election commission to supervise, organize, and oversee Panchayat elections at all levels and a state finance commission for reviewing and revising the financial position of Panchayats on five-year intervals and making recommendations to the State Governments about the distribution of panchayath funds (Sheikh, 2014).

Concerning Article 243, the Supreme Court of India in State of UP v. Pradhan Sangh Kehettra Samity held that while organizing the village panchayat, it should be kept in mind that they are to be the self-governing body at the lowest end of the democratic polity with an effective say in the conduct of their affairs including its plans, policies, and programs and their execution and not merely a satisfaction of participation but also an authentic experience in the governance of their affairs. The 73rd Amendment thus tried to ensure people's active role in the governance of their PRIs. However, it also has certain drawbacks like the absence of enough funds and resources, the unnecessary intervention of local MPs and MLAs, complexity caused by the discretionary power given to the State legislature to delegate powers, responsibilities, and finance, and lack of secretarial support and technical competence causing troubles for bottom-up planning and decision-making.

5.2 74th Constitutional Amendment

Together with the 73rd Amendment, the parliament also passed the 74th Amendment of the Constitution. It added part IX A with the title "The Municipalities," consisting of 18 clauses, and inserted the 12th Schedule enlisting the subjects transferrable to the power of municipalities. The 74th Amendment mainly focuses on Urban Local Government. It provided a three-tier structure in urban governance consisting of a Nagar Panchayat for a transitional area, a Municipal Council for a smaller urban area, and a Municipal Corporation for a large urban area depending on factors like population, density of population, percentage of employment in non-agricultural activities, generation of revenue, and economic importance. Most of the characteristics of the 73rd Amendment, including terms, elections, administration, state legislation, and financial support, also apply to the 74th Amendment. Besides, it also has more or less the same types of drawbacks as the PRIs (Bhardwaj, 2023). Hence, this chapter does not delve separately into all the details of the 74th Amendment.

6 FUNCTIONS OF THE LSG

India's rural areas were primarily influenced by three axes: caste system, patriarchy, and land complexities. It marginalized certain sections of people, like the lower caste, women, and landless, without enough chances to raise their voices in the public sphere (DeSouza, 2003). All these insecurities increased the country's poverty rate and income inequality as well. It led to the enormous concentration of income and wealth in a few hands. The origin of LSG reshaped this rural system with the possibilities of their active participation in decision-making and economic growth. People's needs and aspirations will be fulfilled through their effective participation in LSG only when there is genuine redistribution of land, increased awareness of the importance of education and healthcare, creation of more employment opportunities, and improved transportation and communication facilities (Johnson, 2003). LSG, being an efficient tool of decentralized governance, can enhance the true spirit of governance with a positive approach towards local needs. A centralized governance system cannot address every need of the local community. But when the government becomes more decentralized, people's needs and demands at the bottom line will be more easily addressed (Arends et al., 2023). While analyzing the subjects in the 11th and 12th Schedules of the Constitution, we understand that they mainly address the people's grassroots-level needs. The 11th Schedule comprises 29 subjects, and the 12th includes 18 items. It shows that compared to urban local governance, the Constitution emphasized the importance of the PRIs, affirming the tradition of Gandhian Gram Swaraj and CDP. All the subjects included in the two schedules mentioned above are equally important. However, this chapter limits our focus to three main areas: education, healthcare, and public utility management.

6.1 Education

The Universal Declaration of Human Rights (UDHR) demanded all countries ensure basic education as a significant element of developmental policies. Almost all the countries, including India, followed this demand. After including LSG systems in the constitution with defined areas of concern, primary education became an essential field of LSGs. With the 1992 Amendment Act, the local administration became accountable for the provisions provided for education at the local level (Rajput, 2002). With various programs like Sarva Shiksha Abhiyan and the Right of Children to Free and Compulsory Education Act, 2009, and its Amendment in 2012, the government of India enlarged the scope of the project of universal elementary education. Its implementation is mainly done through local administrative bodies. They oversee the day-to-day administration of the primary schools in their administration area. They monitor the quality of education with enhanced teacher training programs and other supporting mechanisms. Quality of education also depends on the quality of buildings, infrastructure facilities, availability of nutritious food, and continuous interaction with the parents and students. The elected representatives should ensure that no children miss the opportunity of primary education for whatever reason. However, mere assignment of responsibilities without proper allotment of funds and other resources will not do justice to the assigned duties. Besides, elements like bureaucratization and corruption also undermine the appropriate implementation process (Baby & Subhash, 2023). However, if the local administration is provided with organized functions, relevant human resources, substantial authority, and required funds, it can effectively perform its functions in the field of education (Praveen, 2018).

6.2 Healthcare

Article 25 of the UDHR affirms every person's right to health. The State parties thus become duty-bound to guarantee this right to every individual. Public health facilities were not adequate in India for a good period. However, significant progress has occurred since the last decade of the 20th century. The evolution of PRIs and other local government bodies with the constitutional mandate energized this process (Suman & Sthitapragyan, 2024). Healthcare is a vital area of concern of the LSG under the 11th and 12th Schedules of the Constitution. Since healthcare is one of people's immediate concerns, they often approach the nearest authorities. As part of administrative decentralization, primary and secondary healthcare institutions were transferred to LSGs in most States. For instance, in the State of Kerala, both primary health centers and family welfare centers were transferred to Gram Panchayat, community health centers were transferred to the supervision of block panchayats, taluk hospitals to municipalities or corporations, and district hospitals were entrusted to the supervision of district panchayats (Thomas & Rajesh, 2011). LSGs are given power in the healthcare sector depending on the size of its area. This allowed for improving the quality of healthcare services through better coordination and management by the local administrative bodies. However, rural healthcare faces a lack of infrastructure, a shortage of registered practitioners, and a lack of required funds. To support LSG's initiatives for strengthening the healthcare mission in rural areas, the government of India launched the National Rural Health Mission in 2005, which functions along with the PRIs. LSG's proper and effective supervision of the healthcare service centers in the local areas can improve the value of healthcare services and their benefits to the larger public. Efficient coordination among the LSG authorities and healthcare workers can ensure better services (Bhardwaj, 2023).

6.3 Public Utility Management

Each locality has its unique needs and demands. A centralized project and policy may not do justice to the local demands. The advantage of LSG is that it can efficiently analyze people's real situations and interests and devise plans accordingly. Proper management and allocation of resources at the local level can significantly address issues like poverty, malnutrition, lack of basic infrastructure facilities, and unemployment. Besides, LSG can better coordinate public resources, local supporters, civil societies, and NGOs to uplift the vulnerable sections of society (Johnson, 2003). Public utility services include those essential for people's day-to-day lives. This consists of many things like drinking water supply, sanitation, waste management, electricity, transport facilities, road construction, streetlights, and healthcare. In a study on the urban water supply system, Nyathikala et al. (2023) affirm that there is a significant advantage for the people with the coordination of LSG bodies concerning water supply. However, issues like quality management, water loss, collection of charges, and proper implementation of policies need to be addressed. A lack of coordination adversely affects people, as happened in Bangalore during the 2024 summer season. In some regions of Bangalore, people only had a water supply once a week, causing enormous tensions. The lack of summer rainfall was the primary reason for this scarcity. However, the issue became worse, along with poor management. For waste management, each state has its unique methods that are implemented through the LSGs. The state of Kerala has formed a group called Haritha Karma Sena and provided infrastructure facilities to collect waste depending on its nature. It devises strategies for its effective management (LSG Dept., 2021). Certain LSGs, like the Corporation of Indore, are highly acclaimed for their effective system and implementation strategies for waste management. Like this, the LSGs devise policies and programs about other areas of public utility services. However, many policies are not adequately implemented due to a lack of funds and human resources, affecting human security.

7 LSG AND FINANCE: AN EVALUATION

Analyzing the role of the local government system in Latin America, Campbell (2001, p. 2) states that about 10-50% of the central government revenues are being spent by the local bodies, and he terms it "the quiet revolution." But coming to India, Jha (2000) states that one of the weaknesses of LSG is the problem of revenue generation. They are assigned a plethora of responsibilities, but concerning finance, they face severe discrimination from the higher levels of government. Fiscal decentralization should be prioritized to enable the LSG to function more effectively. Financial autonomy is the essential prerequisite for any system of governance. When the local bodies do not have enough funds and resources, their involvement and functioning are affected. How can the LSG satisfy the interests of people without appropriate financial autonomy?

Fiscal decentralization is a species of decentralization (Raghunathan, 2012), which refers to transferring power to levy and collect taxes, duties, tolls, and fees and spending of public funds. With the support of financial decentralization, LSG can achieve financial autonomy and effective governance. Fairer and equitable devolution of funds helps local governments to address people's needs and requirements significantly. Both central and state finance commissions need to address the concerns of LSGs to provide enough budgetary allocation to satisfy people's interests through local bodies. If enough funds are provided to the LSGs, they can better engage in their welfare policies and projects without pleading for financial support from the higher levels of government (Joseph & Thomas, 2023). Central and State governments do not favor the concerns of local bodies if different political parties govern them. They allocate funds to the local bodies depending on the party that governs them. This political bias and favoritism is one of the serious threats to India's fiscal decentralization and local governance.

The devolution of funds from the higher levels to the lower level of governance is not charity but a matter of right. However, Issac (2001) argues that the financial devolution of funds to the local bodies happens only on paper. This is the biggest drawback of decentralization in India. The LSGs are practically forced to plead for funds and get approval from the State government for their projects, even those that also fall under their purview. This adversely affects the efficiency of local governance. Although LSGs are given the power to levy and collect taxes and other fees and duties, the phrase "subject to such limits" added to this provision weakens the autonomy of the LSGs. They also need to address the possibilities to increase the revenue, including own source revenue for effective functioning. However, they mostly lack proper plans and policies for this objective. The increased staff costs are another concern that challenges their welfare policies and programs. Besides, LSGs are criticized for lack of transparency and accountability and non-maintenance of accounts (Joseph & Thomas, 2023).

LSG's financial autonomy is an essential element for its effective functioning. Both central and state governments should show positivity towards the needs of local bodies to make them capable of administering their welfare policies. Besides, they also need to devise strategies and plans for increasing their revenue. At the same time, they should address various challenges that can endanger their financial accountability and transparency. The government at different levels of the country should collaboratively function for the welfare of its people. It should not restrict its welfare policies to the biased political interests of its parties. The interests of the political party are not superior to the genuine concerns of the people.

8 LSG AND DECENTRALIZATION: A CRITICAL ANALYSIS

LSG is a form of democratic decentralization. With the support of decentralization, LSG's functioning and the country's governance are supposed to become more democratic. Democratic local governance thus stands for the most decentralized form of government. It implies that local governance is carried out in a "responsive, participatory, accountable, and increasingly effective (i.e., democratic) fashion" (CDG, 2000, p. 7). LSG's decentralized nature helps to advance people's participation, enhance accountability and transparency of the governing persons, and control the autocracy and supremacy of the higher power-holders (Uddin, 2018). A higher level of government (Central or State) is evaluated from the performance perspective. In contrast, citizens expect accountability and higher chances of participation from the local governments (Arends et al., 2023). While increasing the involvement of people in the LSG, States can enhance people's trust as their increased participation will make them more accountable. The right to hold local elected representatives and officials responsible for their actions and policies should be the essential feature of decentralized LSG (Johnson, 2003). However, this accountability principle can be undermined through the seizure of local governance by certain elites like landlords, employers, or political leaders (Faguet, 2014). Although there are reservations for women and backward classes, there is a tendency to hold power behind the curtain. This is a confusing scenario throughout the world. The elected representatives should have the conviction that they are elected by the people to whom they are supposed to be responsible. The interests of local people will be prioritized in local governance only when there is a lack of external interference and special emphasis on their participatory role with the prerogative of making them accountable to society. Accountability to superior authorities and accountability to people have different outcomes in satisfying local people's needs (OECD, 2019). To become efficient, LSG should adhere to accountability towards people. But in today's Indian society, the over-influence of politics in local governance forces elected representatives to show accountability to their political parties and governments at higher levels instead of showing their allegiance towards real power-holders, i.e., people.

Gandhiji had envisioned that the concentration of economic and political powers into the hands of a few would cause troubles in participatory democracy. However, decentralization can promote efficiency and performance and eradicate unnecessary pressures from the central government (Uddin, 2018). Without devolution, the power imbalance between the governed and the governing always caused insecurities (Faguet, 2014). While Gandhi emphasized decentralization as an end in itself, and the World Bank and other international institutions considered it a means to an end, liberal constitutionalists considered it both an end and a means (Vaddiraju, 2017). The real spirit of decentralization and LSG is to increase the participation of people in governance. Still, the present Indian scenario exposes that this objective is not fully achieved as the power is concentrated in the political parties' hands. It further troubles the balance between the governed and the governing and reduces decentralization as a means for the political parties to gain power at the State and Central levels.

World Bank's (2000) study on Indian decentralization affirms that India is among the best performers in political decentralization but among the poor in administrative decentralization. Although there are some progressive changes regarding administrative decentralization, this observation is still valid even after 25 years. In the present scenario, fiscal decentralization causes more trouble than administrative decentralization. The local bodies are given more responsibilities without enough financial resources and support. Besides, the overlapping of powers and responsibilities is another complex situation. Sometimes, the higher levels of government get involved in the internal matters or governance system of the LSG, causing them trouble. Due to the pressure of the political parties, LSG prioritizes the interests of higher government levels instead of the people's concerns (UGLC, 2008). Political, administrative, and fiscal decentralization should effectively happen without reservation for a systematic and welfare-oriented governance.

The most crucial drawback of the LSG system in India is the lack of uniformity regarding the nature, functions, responsibilities, and other essential characteristics of LSG throughout the country. It all varies according to the State legislation. The nature of election to the local bodies varies from state to state. The Constitutional Amendments also give powers to the state government to dissolve local bodies. This creates enormous dependency issues. The functioning of Grama Sabha is another convoluted eroteme. Grama Sabha includes all the voting members of a panchayat, which is an essential feature of enhancing people's participatory role. But how far it is effectively working is a serious concern. Some elected representatives call just their preferred people and wind up the meeting without any active discussion and decision-making. Some people attend the Grama Sabha to ensure they get some benefits from the local bodies. Without sincere debate, planning, decision-making, and strategies for implementation, the option for Grama Sabha becomes useless. At the same time, urban local government has no such assembly of registered voters to make their stance in the decision-making process (UGLC, 2008).

9 CONCLUSION

From the Vedic period onwards, India has a long history of decentralization and local self-rule. It existed throughout history with many ups and downs. Both Muslim and British rulers did not promote it and suffered enormous setbacks during the British period. In the post-independence period, Gandhian Gram Swaraj and CDP highlighted the importance of rural development with decentralized and centralized policies, respectively. Both decentralization and LSG became a Constitutional mandate with the 73rd and 74th Constitutional Amendments of 1992. Decentralized LSGs have many advantages, including people's increased contribution to governance, systematic utilization of local natural resources, systematic expansion of public utilities, meaningful efforts for addressing regional imbalances, effective control of the unsystematic regulatory barriers, and substantial communication with the remote areas and their needs (Uddin, 2018). Democratic decentralization, if properly employed, can become a more advantageous form of government because it has the characteristic features of local election, lobbying, campaigning, collective responsibility, and free press. Besides, it can also address political instabilities to promote effective governance. India's LSG system must effectively work to ensure people's interests, as India is vast and diverse. The Central and State governments have limitations in reaching the grassroots levels of Indian society. Although there is a constitutional provision for LSGs, their working highly depends on the provisions of funds, responsibilities, and functions allotted to them by the central and state governments. To achieve the Gandhian dream of an ideal independent village, policymakers should provide more powers and appropriate circumstances for implementing the LSGs.

REFERENCES

Altamimi, H., Liu, Q., & Jimenez, B. (2023). Not Too Much, Not Too Little: Centralization, Decentralization, and Organizational Change. *Journal of Public Administration: Research and Theory*, *33*(1), 170–185. https://academic.oup.com/jpart/article/33/1/170/6549741. DOI: 10.1093/jopart/muac016

Awasthi, A. (2024). The Evolution of Democracy: Historical Perspectives and Modern Challenges. *International Journal of Scientific Research, 13*(9), 465–470. https://www.ijsr.net/getabstract.php?paperid=SR24908134052

Baby, D. M., & Subhash, P. D. (2023). Role of Local Authorities in Development of Primary Schools. *Research Review International Journal of Multidisciplinary* 8(3), 106-113. https://rrjournals.com/index.php/rrijm/article/view/537

Bansal, S. (2016). An Evolution of Community Development in India. *IJRESS* 6(9), 57-69. https://www.indianjournals.com/ijor.aspx?target=ijor:ijress&volume=6&issue=9&article=006

Bhardwaj, S. (2023). *Local Self-Government in India: A Comprehensive Approach.* MPP House.

Campbell, T. (2001). *The Quiet Revolution: The Rise of Political Participation and Leading Cities with Decentralization in Latin America and the Caribbean.* University of Pittsburgh Press.

CDG. (Center for Democracy and Governance). (2000). *Decentralization and Democratic Local Governance Programming Handbook.* CDG Bureau for Global Programs.

Dayal, R. (1960). *Community Development Program in India.* Kitab Mahal.

DeSouza, P. R. (2003). The Struggle for Local Government: Indian Democracy's New Phase. *Publius*, *33*(4), 99–118. https://www.jstor.org/stable/3331198. DOI: 10.1093/oxfordjournals.pubjof.a005015

Drèze, J., & Sen, A. (1996). *India: Economic Development and Social Opportunity.* Oxford University Press. DOI: 10.1093/oso/9780198290124.001.0001

Faguet, J.-P. (2014). Decentralization and Governance. *World Development*, *53*, 2–13. https://www.sciencedirect.com/science/article/abs/pii/S0305750X13000089. DOI: 10.1016/j.worlddev.2013.01.002

Garg, B. S., & Raut, A. V. (2015). Adarsh Gram: A Gandhian Dream of Gram Swaraj. *Indian Journal of Community Medicine : Official Publication of Indian Association of Preventive & Social Medicine, 40*(1), 1–4. https://pmc.ncbi.nlm.nih.gov/articles/PMC4317974/. DOI: 10.4103/0970-0218.149260 PMID: 25657504

Jha, S. (2000). Fiscal Decentralization in India: Strengths, Limitations and Prospects for Panchayati Raj Institutions. *Background Paper No. 2*. World Bank. DOI:DOI: 10.13140/RG.2.1.3813.2884

Johnson, C. (2003). Decentralization in India: Poverty, Politics and Panchayati Raj. *Working Paper 199*. ODI. https://assets.publishing.service.gov.uk/media/57a08cf240f0b6497400154e/wp199_print.pdf

Joseph, J., & Thomas, A. K. (2023). A Critical Analysis of the Distribution of Finance to the Municipalities and Control and Supervision of State. In Bhardwaj, S. (Ed.), *Local Self-Government in India: A Comprehensive Approach* (pp. 261–291). MPP Press.

Joshi, D. (2002). *Gandhiji on Villages*. Mani Bhavan Gandhi Sangrahalaya.

Kannan, K. P. (1993). Local Self-Government and Decentralized Development. *EPW* 28(49), 2644-2646. https://www.epw.in/journal/1993/49/commentary/panchayat-raj-act-local-self-government-and-decentralised-development

Kumar, R. (2015). Historical Development of Panchayati Raj in India. *IJMSS, 3*(8), 523–530.

Manor, J. (1999). *The Political Economy of Democratic Decentralization*. The World Bank. DOI: 10.1596/0-8213-4470-6

Meenakshisundaram, S. S. (1999). Decentralization in Developing Countries. In S. N. Jha & P. C.

Nyathikala, S. A., Jamasb, T., Llorca, M., & Kulshrestha, M. (2023). Utility Governance, Incentives, and Performance: Evidence from India's Urban Water Sector. *Utilities Policy, 82*, 101534. DOI: 10.1016/j.jup.2023.101534

OECD. (2019). *Making Decentralization Work: A Handbook for Policymakers*. OECD.

Olorunlana, T. J. (2023). The History of Democracy: From Ancient Athens to Present-Day. *ReseachGate*. DOI:DOI: 10.13140/RG.2.2.36785.15209

Praveen, R. (2018). Implementation of RTE Act: A Case Study of Two Gram Panchayats in Karnataka. *IJISSH, 3*(2), 29–36.

Raghunathan, T. R. (2012). *Decentralization and Local Governments: The Indian Experience*. Orient Black Swan.

Rajput, J. S. (2002). Education. In Gupta, S. P. (Ed.), *Indian Vision* (pp. 42–47). Planning Commission. (Original work published 2020)

Rodden, J. A. (2006). *Hamilton's Paradox: The Promise and Peril of Fiscal Federalism*. Cambridge University Press.

Sheikh, Y. A. (2014). Democratic Decentralization in India: An Overview. *IJSSIR* 3(7), 196-203. https://www.researchgate.net/publication/329415345_DEMOCRATIC_DECENTRALISATION_IN_INDIA_AN_OVERVIEW

Smith, B. C. (2023). *Decentralization: The Territorial Dimension of the State*. Routledge. DOI: 10.4324/9781003404927

Srivastava, T. N. (2002). Local 'Self' Government and the Constitution. *EPW* 37(30), 3190-3198. https://www.epw.in/journal/2002/30/special-articles/local-self-government-and-constitution.html

Suman, D., & Sthitapragyan, R. (2024). Rural Local Government and Healthcare Delivery in an Eastern Indian State. *Asian Journal of Social Science*, *52*(3), 121–127. https://www.sciencedirect.com/science/article/abs/pii/S1568484924000248. DOI: 10.1016/j.ajss.2024.06.006

Tariq, M., Khan, A., & Rizwan, M. (2018). An Analysis of the Major Theories of Federalism. *Global Social Sciences Review* 3(4), 400-412. https://www.gssrjournal.com/article/An-Analysis-of-the-Major-Theories-of-Federalism

Thomas, M. B., & Rajesh, K. (2011). Decentralization and Interventions in Health Sector: A Critical Inquiry into the Experience of Local Self Governments in Kerala. *Working Paper 271*. Institute for Social and Economic Change. https://www.isec.ac.in/wp-content/uploads/2023/07/WP-271-Benson-Thomas-and-Rajesh.pdf

Uddin, K. (2018). Decentralization and Governance. In Ali Farazmand (Ed.), *Global Encyclopedia of Public Administration, Public Policy and Governance* (pp. 1-7). Springer.

UGLC. (2008). *Decentralization and Local Democracy in the World*. The World Bank.

Vaddiraju, A. K. (2017). *Federalism and Local Government in India*. Studium Press.

World Bank. (2000). *Overview of Rural Decentralization in India*. World Bank.

Chapter 8
Reinforcing Local Governance in India:
The Impact of Judicial Oversight on Panchayati Raj Institutions

Souvik Dhar
https://orcid.org/0000-0002-5472-9193
Brainware University, Kolkata, India

Meenu Gupta
https://orcid.org/0000-0002-0396-0993
Amity University, Noida, India

Kaushik Banerjee
https://orcid.org/0000-0002-3276-2048
Brainware University, Kolkata, India

ABSTRACT

Judicial decisions of the Indian Judiciary on elections of Panchayat (local governance) reflect that the Indian Judiciary is one of the main authorities to be consulted in cases concerning democratic processes of local governance. This chapter dealt with some landmark judgments in matters concerning interference with candidacy, manipulation of voter lists, ballot secrecy, procedural adherence, and candidacy eligibility. It has shown devotion to the integrity and accountability of local governance. Indian Constitution made administration accountable to the people for any malpractices. Malpractices, as evidenced by many judicial pronouncements, often subverted this model. The intervention of the judiciary is needed to secure the integrity of elections. This chapter has advocated for a robust and transparent electoral system. Judicial intervention has highlighted systemic failures. Indian

DOI: 10.4018/979-8-3373-5576-4.ch008

Courts have enthused the formulation of policies to reduce electoral malpractices. The policy innovations can deepen democracy by empowering local self-governments in a strong and decisive manner.

INTRODUCTION

"Panchayat" elections, i.e., local self-government elections, form the cornerstone of democracy in India. They enable individuals in rural communities to select their local leaders and be involved in decision-making processes. These elections are frequently impacted by issues like: corruption, caste-driven politics, and the abuse of authority. Such problems can diminish the value of democratic process and public confidence in local government. To tackle these issues, the Indian judiciary has intervened to guarantee that "Panchayat" elections are held in a free and equitable way. The judicial system in India is crucial for safeguarding democracy. This is truer at the level of local self-government. A major domain where the judiciary has influenced significantly is in "Panchayat" (local self-government in India) elections. The function of "Panchayat" as local self-governance entities in rural regions is so important that the elections play a vital role in village-level democracy. These elections frequently encounter difficulties such as: interference in candidacies, issues with voter lists, absence of ballot confidentiality, and concerns regarding candidate eligibility. The Indian judiciary has tackled these issues through several landmark rulings. Indian Judiciary have tried to conduct "Panchayat" elections fairly and transparently. This chapter examines the involvement of Indian Judiciary in "Panchayat" elections. This chapter has also reviewed significant court rulings, and offers suggestions to enhance the electoral system.

Background: Role of Indian Judiciary in Election of Local Self-Governance

The Indian judiciary has issued numerous significant rulings to tackle issues in "Panchayat" elections. These rulings have centred on matters like:

- Interference in Candidacy: Influential individuals or groups attempt to sway who is eligible to run in "Panchayat" elections. This weakens the democratic process. The courts have stepped in to guarantee that every qualified candidate has a fair chance to take part in elections. For instance, in the matter of '*State of Uttar Pradesh versus Pradhan Sangh Kshetra Samiti, (1995)AIR 1995 SC 1512*', the Apex Court of India determined that no outside authority can interfere in the candidacy process. The Apex Court affirmed that only the Election Commission has the authority to make decisions on these issues (Ministry of Panchayati Raj, 2020).

- Irregularities in Voter Lists: In numerous "Panchayat" elections, it is seen that, the voter lists remain outdated. Compact and error-free voter lists are crucial for fair and transparent elections. Such voter list resulted in the omission of qualified voters. The judiciary has imposed stringent measures to guarantee that voter lists are updated and precise (Ministry of Panchayati Raj, 2020).
- Ballot Confidentiality: The confidentiality of the ballot is a core tenet of democracy. It guarantees that voters can cast their votes without the fear of being intimidated. In '*Kuldip Nayar versus Union of India, AIR 2006 SC 3127*', the Supreme Court reinforced the significance of ballot confidentiality. The Supreme Court declared that any breach of this principle would pose a grave danger to democracy (Ministry of Panchayati Raj, 2020).
- Procedural Compliance: "Panchayat" elections should adhere to established protocols to guarantee impartiality. The judiciary has stepped in when election protocols were not adhered to.
- Candidacy Qualifications: The qualifications of candidates represent another important concern in "Panchayat" elections. In numerous instances, individuals with criminal histories or those lacking the necessary qualifications attempt to run for office. The courts have adopted a firm position against these practices.

INTERFERENCE IN CANDIDACY: JUDICIAL DECISIONS

- **Surinder Kaur *versus* State of Punjab & Ors., 1996**

The appellant contested the legitimacy of the elections for the role of 'Sarpanch' (Chief) (Ministry of Panchayati Raj, 2020). The appellant claimed that she was filing her nomination papers because, one of the respondents, grabbed and ripped her nomination papers (*Surinder Kaur versus State of Punjab*, 1996). Moreover, her spouse was arrested by law enforcement, and no measures were implemented in response to her grievances. The High Court issued a stay on the case, but concerning respondent was recognized as the elected 'Sarpanch' (Chief). The respondent stated that the appellant did not try to submit her nomination papers. Feeling wronged, the appellant submitted a writ petition to the High Court. Such appeal being rejected, prompting her to seek the Supreme Court's intervention.

The Supreme Court struggled to accept that the appellant had not submitted her nomination papers, particularly considering she had served as the 'Sarpanch' (Chief) for the last fifteen years. The Court deduced that she aimed to run in the elections and had taken measures to submit her nomination papers promptly. As a result, the Court determined that the elections lacked legal validity, invalidated the respondent's election, and instructed the authorities to arrange for re-elections within one month. The Court noted that illegally hindering a candidate from participating in elections constitutes a clear breach of the law. Based on this reason alone, the election may be annulled.

- **Raghvendra Kumar *versus* Prabal Kumar & Ors., 2013**

The respondent submitted nomination papers to run for the position of 'Pradhan' (Chief) of 'Gram Panchayat' (Ministry of Panchayati Raj, 2020). Even though it was initially approved, his nomination was subsequently revoked by the 'Returning Officer' because of his conviction under Section 307 of the Indian Penal Code, 1860 (*Raghvendra Kumar versus PrabalKumar*, 2013). The petitioner submitted a writ petition to the Allahabad High Court, asserting that, he was granted bail and that his conviction did not entail moral turpitude. The High Court suspended the annulment of his nomination, permitting him to run in the election. The respondent eventually won the election.

The appellant brought their case to the Supreme Court. The Apex Court recognized that although the respondent had been granted bail, their conviction remained intact, and an appeal was still ongoing in the High Court. The Court stressed that being granted bail is not the same as being acquitted. Consequently, the Supreme Court granted the appeal. The Apex Court ordered the respondent to leave the position of the "Pradhan" (Chief). The Court made it clear that being released on bail does not allow an individual to run for the "Gram Pradhan' (Head of the Village)' elections, since it does not overturn the conviction (*Raghvendra Kumar versus PrabalKumar*, 2013).

VOTER LIST IRREGULARITIES: JUDICIAL DECISIONS

- **Boddula Krishnaiah & Anr. *versus* State Election Commissioner, A.P. & Ors., 1996**

The respondents were unable to cast their votes in the Gram "Panchayat" elections because their names had been removed from the electoral rolls (Ministry of Panchayati Raj, 2020). They went to the High Court. The High Court gave an interim order to refrain the authority from announcing the election results and instructed the respondents to cast their votes once the polls had concluded (*Boddula Krishnaiah versus State Election Commissioner*, 1996). The appellants contested this ruling in the Supreme Court.

The Supreme Court reaffirmed the remarks expressed in earlier cases, noting that (*Boddula Krishnaiah versus State Election Commissioner,* 1996),

> *'...irregularities damaging the election must be presented to the election tribunal, and the High Court, while exercising its writ jurisdiction, should refrain from issuing any orders that disrupt or delay the election proceedings.'*

The Court determined that the order from the High Court was not legally valid, and the petition submitted to the High Court was permissible. The decision to permit the respondents to cast their votes after the polls was deemed incorrect, as it would hinder the election process. The Court ruled that the losing candidate could submit an election petition regarding this issue.

BALLOT SECRECY AND PROCEDURAL ADHERENCE: JUDICIAL DECISIONS

- **M.V. Venkataramana Bhat *versus* Returning Officer, 1993**

The appellant was defeated in the election for 'Gram Pradhan' (Village Head) by the winner by a single vote (Ministry of Panchayati Raj, 2020). The appellant contested the election through a writ petition, asserting that two nominated members wished to vote for him but were intentionally obstructed from casting their votes by the respondents. The High Court rejected the petition, prompting the appellant to seek an appeal in the Supreme Court (*M.V. Venkataramana Bhat versus Returning Officer,* 1993).

The Apex Court upheld the High Court's view that the person, who secured a temporary injunction against the voting by the two appointed members, did not behave in a bona fide way. The Court observed that such person was not a participant in the election. Rather, he had submitted the petition at the suggestion of the winning candidate, helping the winning candidate to secure the election through misuse of the judicial process. The Court concurred with the appellant that the respondent's actions had significantly impacted the election. As there was no clause in the relevant laws to dispute the legitimacy of elections, the Supreme Court deemed it suitable to declare the elections invalid and mandated re-elections.

- **Jaenendra Kumar Phoolchand Daftari *versus* Rajendra Ramsukh Mishra, 1993**

In the case of *Jaenendra Kumar Phoolchand Daftari versus Rajendra Ramsukh Mishra*, elections for the position of 'Sarpanch' (Chief) were conducted using a secret ballot method, resulting in the respondent losing to the appellant by a single vote (Ministry of Panchayati Raj, 2020). The respondent submitted an election petition to the Collector. He contended that the conducting elections via secret ballot without a demand has breached Rule 10 of the "Bombay Village 'Panchayats' Sarpanch' and Upa-'Sarpanch' Election Rules', 1964" (*Jaenendra Kumar Phoolchand Daftari versus Rajendra Ramsukh Mishra,* 1993). One of the "Panchayat" members was an uneducated woman who had voted using a ballot featuring the names of the candidates, not icons. The Election Commissioner and the Collector annulled the election, and the High Court decided in favor of the respondent, mandating new elections. The appellant brought their case to the Supreme Court, asserting that the secret ballot elections took place following a request from a member of the "Panchayat." The presiding officer saw no necessity to assign symbols to the candidates since he was unaware of one member's illiteracy. The Supreme Court noted that *(Jaenendra Kumar Phoolchand Daftari versus Rajendra Ramsukh Mishra,* 1993),

> *'Rules 10 and 13 required the presiding officer to carry out the elections through a show of hands unless any member requested a ballot.'*

The Court determined that no request was made for voting via ballot. It was also stated that assigning election symbols was not essential, but a unique method could be created by the presiding officer to help any illiterate voter cast their ballot. Therefore, the appeal was rejected, and the decisions of the lower authorities and the High Court were confirmed by the Supreme Court.

CANDIDATE ELIGIBILITY AND DISQUALIFICATION

- **Som Lal *versus* Vijay Laxmi, 2008**

The appellant secured victory in the elections for the position of 'Sarpanch' (Chief) of the Gram "Panchayat" (Ministry of Panchayati Raj, 2020). The respondent submitted an election petition, claiming that the appellant was employed as a Fireman with the "Haryana State Agricultural Marketing Board" and was disqualified from running for elections due to holding a position of profit. The appellant contested this, referencing legal provisions which disqualified individuals holding office of profit under any "Panchayat," Municipality, Union, or State government, but excluded those under local authorities or Marketing Boards.

The election tribunal and the High Court annulled the appellant's election as 'Sarpanch' (Chief), asserting that disqualification under any of the statutes was an adequate impediment. The appellant brought the case to the Supreme Court, which observed that the 'Punjab State Election Commission Act, 1994', was implemented after the "Punjab Panchayati Raj Act, 1994", and its provisions took precedence. The Court decided that (*Som Lal versus Vijay Laxmi,* 2008),

> *'...The disqualifications specified in the Punjab State Election Commission Act, 1994, will take precedence over those in the Punjab Panchayati Raj Act, 1994.'*

Therefore, the appellant was not barred from running in the elections. The ruling of the High Court was overturned, and the appeal was granted.

- **Zelia M. Xavier Fernandes E. Gonsalves *versus* Joana Rodrigues & Ors., 2012**

The appellant served as a member of the certain "Panchayat". (Ministry of Panchayati Raj, 2020). The "Panchayat" called for bids to gather market fees for 2008-09, and the bids received included those from the appellant's spouse, and the respondent. Appellant's spouse's offer was the greatest and approved. The respondent submitted applications to the Deputy Director of "Panchayat" and the Goa State Election Commission, claiming that the appellant ought to be disqualified from the "Panchayat" under 'Section 10(f) of the Goa "Panchayat" Raj Act, 1994', because of her husband's contract. The Commission reached a consensus and disqualified the appellant from serving as a "Panchayat" member.

The High Court dismissed the appellant's later writ petition, prompting her to take her case to the Supreme Court. The appellant argued that simply being married did not create a financial interest according to Section 10. Nevertheless, the Supreme Court examined the statutes in Goa, especially Section 10(f) of the Goa "Panchayat" Raj Act, 1994, along with pertinent judicial precedents. The Court determined that (*Zelia M. Xavier Fernandes E. Gonsalves versus Joana Rodrigues*, 2012),

> *'...The financial benefits from the contract given to the appellant's spouse were community assets. In Goa's community property system, the law ensures that both spouses equally share the profits. Consequently, the appellant held an indirect stake in her husband's agreement.'*

As a result, the appellant was barred from the "Panchayat" membership.

RECOUNTING OF VOTES: JUDICIAL DECISIONS

- **Baldev Singh *versus* Shinder Pal Singh, 2006**

The appellant and the respondent garnered an identical number of votes in the elections for the position of 'Sarpanch' (Chief) (Ministry of Panchayati Raj, 2020). In accordance with Rule 35 of the "Punjab "Panchayat" Election Rules, 1994", a lottery was conducted among them, resulting in the appellant being named the 'Sarpanch' (Chief). The respondent submitted an election petition, claiming that merely 821 votes were cast, with the appellant obtaining just 397 votes, while he had received 412 votes. The Election Tribunal mandated a vote recount, subsequently declaring the respondent as the 'Sarpanch' (Chief).

The High Court affirmed the Tribunal's decision concerning the vote recount. The Supreme Court observed that (*Baldev Singh versus Shinder PalSingh*, 2006).

'...the witnesses had not undergone cross-examination regarding the assertions about whether the respondent had previously asked for a vote recount and if any irregularities had occurred during the election process.'

The Court considered the fax message dispatched by the presiding officer to the District Collector, which detailed the circumstances of vote parity, the lottery selection, and the respondent's action of tearing the chits. The Court noted that (*Baldev Singh versus Shinder PalSingh*, 2006),

'...the formal action should be assumed to have occurred as part of the regular business procedure. A recount should not typically be ordered to occur.'

Therefore, the rulings of the Tribunal and the High Court were annulled, and the appeal was granted.

- **Udey Chand *versus Surat Singh*, 2009**

The appellant defeated the respondent by a margin of four votes in the elections for the position of 'Sarpanch' (Chief) (Ministry of Panchayati Raj, 2020). The respondent submitted an election petition, requesting a vote recount and claiming that the Returning Officer improperly recorded the vote tally due to political influence and in collusion with the appellant. The Election Tribunal mandated a recount, which the High Court upheld. The appellant brought the case to the Supreme Court, claiming that there was no evidence on record to substantiate a case for recounting.

The Supreme Court emphasized the election law principle that a request for inspecting and recounting ballot papers impacts the confidentiality of the vote and should not be granted automatically. The esteemed Supreme Court noted,

'...Since an order for inspecting and recounting the ballot papers impacts the confidentiality of the votes, such an order cannot be issued automatically.'

On further examination of Section 176(4)(a) and 176(4)(b) of the "Haryana Panchayati Raj Act, 1994", the Court expressed its opinion in the case of *Udey Chand versus Surat Singh*, 2009 (Ministry of Panchayati Raj, 2020),

> *'...simple claims of irregularities in the election procedure would not warrant a recount.'*

Moreover, upon examining the facts, the Court determined that the election petition included ambiguous claims. No substantial facts justifying a recount of the elections were presented. The documentation of evidence was also inadequate. It was suggested that a slim margin of 4 votes alone did not indicate that there had been any irregularity or illegality in the vote counting process. The appeal was granted, and the recount orders issued by the Election Tribunal and upheld by the High Court were annulled. The court noted that an order for recounting must be validated by checking that (*Udey Chand versus Surat Singh*, 2009),

> *'...two fundamental conditions are met. Firstly, the election petition requesting a re-count of the ballots must include a comprehensive account of all relevant facts that support the claims of irregularity or illegality in the counting process.'*

The Court further held that,

> *'... Secondly, based on the evidence presented in support of the claims, the Tribunal must be prima facie convinced that to resolve the dispute and ensure thorough and effective justice between the parties, issuing such an order is absolutely essential.'*

The Court determined that the election petition included unclear claims and lacked any substantial facts justifying a recount of the elections. Evidence was also inadequately documented. The Court stated that a narrow margin of four votes did not in itself suggest that there was any irregularity or illegality in the vote counting process. The appeal was granted. Thus, the recount orders issued by the Election Tribunal and confirmed by the High Court, were eventually annulled..

- **Harnek Singh *versus* Charanjit Singh, 2005**

In *Harnek Singh versus Charanjit Singh* and Ors., the appellant and the respondent competed in elections for the Chairman position of the Gram "Panchayat" (Ministry of Panchayati Raj, 2020). Both candidates attained the same number of votes, causing a breakdown in law and order, which necessitated the suspension of the election process. The polls were rescheduled by the Returning Officer, and the appellant was declared victorious. The respondent contested the election, asserting that the Returning Officer lacked the authority to set a new date for the polls, since only the Election Commission had that power. Following the rejection of his application by the lower authorities, the respondent submitted a writ petition to the High

Court. The High Court decided in favour of the respondent, nullifying the election. The appellant subsequently took the case to the Supreme Court.

The Supreme Court determined that the main issue raised by the respondent in the writ petition was the dismissal of a legitimate vote cast for him and his assertion to be recognized as the chairman. The Court determined that these complaints ought to have been addressed via an election petition instead of a writ petition. Citing relevant legal provision, which empowers the Election Tribunal in electoral issues, the Court determined that the High Court's ruling to annul the election was unwarranted. The Supreme Court overturned the High Court's decision and granted the appeal. The Court emphasized that (*Harnek Singh versus CharanjitSingh*, 2005),

> *'...Article 243O of the Constitution mandates that election disputes must be resolved through election petitions.'*

The Court observed that,

> *'...While this does not entirely bar judicial review, which is part of the basic structure of the Constitution, such jurisdiction is not ordinarily exercised when an effective alternative remedy is available.'*

The Apex Court of India further noted that (*Harnek Singh versus CharanjitSingh*, 2005),

> *'...High Court's plenary jurisdiction under Article 226 is discretionary and should not be exercised when an alternative remedy exists.'*

- **Kattinokkula Murali Krishna *versus* Veeramalla Koteswara Rao and Others**

In this case, the primary concern was discrepancies in the vote counting process during the election for the position of 'Sarpanch' (Chief) (Ministry of Panchayati Raj, 2020). The respondent was defeated by the appellant by a slim margin of two votes. The petitioner submitted an election petition, claiming abnormalities in the vote counting procedure. He asserted that certain votes for him were dismissed, while others were inaccurately tallied for a different candidate. Even though the respondent was unable to present concrete evidence for his assertions, the Election Tribunal observed multiple corrections in the vote tally documentation. As the Election Officer was unable to clarify these overwritings, the Tribunal mandated a recount for the sake of transparency. The High Court supported this ruling, leading the appellant to take the case to the Supreme Court.

The Supreme Court noted that the claims in the election petition were unclear and inadequate to demonstrate a prima facie case for a recount. The Court determined that the Tribunal was right in disregarding these allegations. Nonetheless, the Court decided that a recount could not be mandated solely on the grounds that it would not harm either party or due to the close margin of victory. The Court highlighted that the responsibility to demonstrate the irregularities fell on the respondent, and concerns related to overwriting were not mentioned in the election petition. The appeal was granted, and the directive for a recount was annulled. In this case, the Supreme Court clarified that,

'...a recount order should be granted only if the election petition includes all necessary facts, backed by evidence, indicating irregularities in the counting procedure.'

The Court further observed that,

'...the confidentiality of the ballot is a core tenet of democracy, and requests for recounts should not be issued without careful consideration.'

It is also observed by the Apex Court that,

'...The principle of prejudice has no bearing on the decision to mandate a recount. Every case needs to be resolved according to its unique facts and circumstances.'

No-Confidence Motions and Amendments to "Panchayati Raj' Laws: Judicial Decisions

- **Bhanumati *versus* State of Uttar Pradesh**

In this case, the main concern was the 'constitutional legality of Sections 9, 15, and 28 of the U.P. Amendment Act of 2007 for Panchayat Laws' (Ministry of Panchayati Raj, 2020). These changes eliminated the positions of *"Up-Pramukh," "Senior Up-Pramukh," "Junior Up-Pramukh,"* and *"Upadhyaksha."* They likewise presented the idea of a no-confidence motion concerning the "Panchayat". It had further shortened the time frame for introducing such a motion from two years to one and decreased the requirement from a special majority to a simple majority. The appellants contended that these amendments weakened the 'Panchayati' principles and facilitated executive intrusion. The Supreme Court noted that (*Bhanumati versus State of Uttar Pradesh*, 2010),

'...Article 243C(5) of the Constitution explicitly permitted the State Legislature to outline the election process for the Chairperson.'

The Court dismissed the claim that the statute could not encompass a no-confidence motion against the Chairman solely due to its absence in the Constitution. The Court likewise rejected the claim that the amendment threatened the stability and dignity of the "Panchayati Raj' Institution. They observed that although a chairperson might be removed owing to a no-confidence vote, they would still retain their membership, maintaining the continuity of "Panchayat" as an institution. As a result, the Court affirmed the constitutional legitimacy of the 'U.P. "Panchayat" Laws (Amendment) Act, 2007', and rejected the appeals.

RESERVATION POLICY: JUDICIAL DECISIONS

- **Dr. K. Krishna Murthy and Others *versus* Union of India (UOI) and Another**

In this matter, three writ petitions contesting the reservation policies implemented by certain states in 'Panchayats' and Municipalities were considered collectively (Ministry of Panchayati Raj, 2020). The petitioners contested the idea of reserving the chairperson position in elected local bodies. They also challenged the 'constitutional legitimacy of Articles 243D(4), 243D(6), 243T(4), and 243T(6) of the Constitution', along with 'comparable provisions in the statutes of Karnataka and Uttar Pradesh (India)'. The petitioners contended that these provisions infringed upon the principles of democracy and equality, integral to the "basic structure" of the Constitution. They also asserted that,

'...Karnataka Panchayati Raj Act established reservations surpassing the 50% limit, contravening judicial precedents.'

The Apex Court of India ruled that (*Dr. K. Krishna Murthy versus Union of India*, 2010),

'...Articles 243D(6) and 243T(6), which allow for reservation for Other Backward Classes (OBCs), were simply facilitative measures and did not infringe upon Article 14 of the Constitution.'

The Court decided that overly restrictive reservations imposed by state laws for OBCs could not serve as a reason to invalidate these constitutional provisions. Nonetheless, the Court warned that (*Dr. K. Krishna Murthy versus Union of India*, 2010),

'...maximum limit of 50% for vertical reservations benefiting Scheduled Castes (SCs), Scheduled Tribes (STs), and OBCs must be maintained.'

The Court additionally specified that (*Dr. K. Krishna Murthy versus Union of India*, 2010),

'...horizontal reservations for women are to be excluded when determining the 50% threshold.'

The petitioners additionally contested the reservation for the chairperson position, claiming it breached the principle of equality (Ministry of Panchayati Raj, 2020). The Court dismissed this argument, clarifying that the chairperson role was not an individual position but rather part of a broader set of such roles allocated on a rotational basis. The Court determined that although reserving chairperson positions limited the political involvement of unreserved groups to a degree, it satisfied the criteria for reasonable classification. The aim of guaranteeing proper representation and empowerment of marginalized groups in local self-governance bodies was considered a valid governmental objective.

The Court highlighted that the characteristics and objectives of reservations in local self-governance differ from those in higher education and public sector jobs. The Supreme Court noted that (*Dr. K. Krishna Murthy versus Union of India*, 2010),

> *'...Articles 243D and 243T offer a unique constitutional foundation for affirmative action, and the principles developed under Articles 15(4) and 16(4) are not directly applicable to local self-governance.'*

The Court affirmed the 'constitutional legitimacy of Articles 243D(6) and 243T(6) of Indian Constitution'. The Apex Court right observed that, they simply allow state legislatures to allocate seats and chairperson positions for backward classes. The Court held that issues regarding excessive reservations ought to be tackled via targeted challenges to state laws.

SCOPE AND POWER OF AN AUTHORITY: JUDICIAL DECISIONS

- **Shobhabai Narayan Shinde *versus* The Divisional Commissioner, Nashik Division, Nashik & Ors.**

In this case, the main question was if an appeal could be submitted to the 'Divisional Commissioner' regarding an order issued by the 'Collector' (Ministry of Panchayati Raj, 2020). The Collector, as per 'Section 14B(1) of the Maharashtra Village "Panchayats" Act, 1959', refused to disqualify a 'Sarpanch' (Chief)/Member of the "Panchayat", for not submitting an account of election expenses in the required time and form. The High Court permitted the appeal, but the Supreme Court reversed this ruling.

The Apex Court ruled that,

> *'...there was no option for appeal against a decision made by the 'State Election Commission or its representative (the Collector) as per Section 14B(1).'*

Such an order becomes irreversible, and even the State Election Commission is unable to re-evaluate it. The Court decided that the Divisional Commissioner lacked the authority to review an appeal concerning the Collector's decision. As the High Court had delved into the substance of the matter, the Supreme Court chose not to review the validity of the Collector's ruling. Reinstating the Collector's decisions, the contested ruling was annulled, and the writ petitions submitted by the appellants were granted,

- **Secretary, Sarvodaya Educational Society *versus* Ginjala Panasaiah and Ors.**

In this matter, the Supreme Court examined if a "Gram Panchayat" was permitted to auction its property as instructed by the High Court (Ministry of Panchayati Raj, 2020). The *"Vakalapudi Gram Panchayat"* in Andhra Pradesh, India, first agreed to utilize a plot of land for a public park but subsequently chose to hand it over to the appellant for constructing a school. The High Court invalidated the resolutions, determining that any transfer must take place solely via a public auction. The Supreme Court determined that the regulations did not allow the sale of "Panchayat"-owned land via public auction for profit. The main factor should be the public's interest. The Apex Court granted the appeal and annulled the High Court's ruling, stressing that the sale of "Panchayat" property should favor public interest rather than profit.

- **Gram Panchayat, Patiala *versus* State of Punjab and Others**

In this case, the "Panchayat" adopted a resolution in accordance with 'Section 26 of the Punjab Gram Panchayats Act, 1952', prohibiting the sale of intoxicating liquor at a liquor vend situated near a school and a health center (Ministry of Panchayati Raj, 2020). The 'Excise and Taxation Commissioner' rejected the resolution, referencing three FIRs concerning illegal liquor distillation in the village. The "Gram Panchayat" contested this ruling in the High Court, which rejected the petition. The Supreme Court acknowledged the validity of the "Gram Panchayat's" claims but pointed out that the license duration had lapsed, making the petition ineffective. The Court determined that the Commissioner needs to weigh social welfare alongside revenue factors when making these decisions.

- **Radhakisan Rathi *versus* Additional Collector, Durg**

In this case, the question was if a *"Janapada Panchayat"* had the authority to impose a theatre tax on cinema halls that had already been taxed by municipal authorities (Ministry of Panchayati Raj, 2020). The appellants contended that after municipalities had imposed cinema taxes, the "Panchayat" was not permitted to impose an extra tax. The Supreme Court dismissed this claim, stating that the "Panchayat" possessed the power to impose taxes in its region, despite the area also being under municipal governance. The Court decided that various legislative bodies are permitted to levy taxes on the same entity for different reasons.

- **R.N.A. Britto *versus* Chief Executive Officer and Others**

In this legal matter, the question was whether a Secretary of the "Panchayat," a state employee, could appeal to the Administrative Tribunal to contest his dismissal (Ministry of Panchayati Raj, 2020). The Supreme Court ruled that "Panchayat"

Secretaries are employees of the state government and can seek remedies for service-related issues at the Tribunal. The Court determined that the Karnataka Administrative Tribunal had authority over the issue.

FINDINGS

The Apex Court's rulings regarding "Panchayat" elections in India highlight the judiciary's critical function in protecting democratic practices at the local level. Through a series of significant rulings, the courts have tackled essential matters such as candidate interference, irregularities in voter lists, secrecy of ballots, adherence to procedures, and eligibility of candidates. These actions emphasize the need for a strong and clear electoral system to avert conflicts and misconduct. Such actions will guarantee that the people's desires are faithfully represented in election results. The cases analyzed in this paper highlight common themes and offer important insights into the difficulties encountered in local governance. The cases also present a guide for enhancing the electoral process.

A major contribution of the judiciary has been its involvement in tackling interference in candidacy. Cases like, 'Surinder Kaur *versus* State of Punjab & Ors.' and 'Raghvendra Kumar *versus* Prabal Kumar & Ors.' illustrate the courts' attempt to ensure that candidates are not unfairly barred from contesting in elections. The judiciary has maintained in aforementioned cases that any illegal hindrance to candidacy is a clear breach of the law. These decisions highlight the necessity of establishing a system in which all qualified candidates can engage freely and equitably in the election process.

The judiciary has significantly contributed to tackling irregularities in voter lists, as demonstrated in case of 'Boddula Krishnaiah & Anr. *versus* State Election Commissioner, A.P. & Ors.' The courts have emphasized that election conflicts need to be settled by election tribunals without interfering with the current electoral process. This method guarantees the preservation of the integrity of electoral process. Simultaneously, the method will help to handle complaints. The judiciary has repeatedly warned against excessive intervention by upper courts. This has highlighted the importance of a balanced method that honors the independence of election tribunals.

The judiciary has also concentrated on ballot confidentiality and compliance with procedures. Cases such as 'M.V. Venkataramana Bhat *versus* Returning Officer and Tahsildar & Ors.' and 'Jaenendra Kumar Phoolchand Daftari *versus* Rajendra Ramsukh Mishra' are prrof of that. The cases emphasize the courts' dedication to ensure that elections are carried out in a way that maintains the ideals of fairness and transparency. The judiciary has consistently determined that any departure from set procedures can jeopardize the integrity of the electoral process. The Courts have given huge importance to confidentiality in election process. These decisions highlight the significance of following procedural standards. The process can guarantee that every voter, including those who are illiterate, can cast their vote without obstruction. As reflected in 'Som Lal *versus* Vijay Laxmi & Ors.' and 'Zelia M. Xavier Fernandes E. Gonsalves *versus* Joana Rodrigues & Ors.', the judiciary has also tackled matters concerning candidate eligibility and disqualification. These instances emphasize the judiciary's function in interpreting and enforcing laws pertinent to disqualification. The Judiciary has tried to ensure, again and again, that candidates are not unjustly prevented from running in elections. The judiciary has highlighted the importance of clear and consistent application of disqualification standards. This is to ensure that the electoral process stays inclusive and representative.

In instances where votes are recounted, like 'Baldev Singh *versus* Shinder Pal Singh & Anr.' and 'Udey Chand *versus* Surat Singh & Ors.', the courts have highlighted the significance of preserving ballot secrecy. The Judiciary has repeatedly observed that recounts should only be initiated if there is solid proof of irregularities. These decisions emphasize the necessity for a careful method to recounts. These steps are taken to ensure that the integrity of the election process remains intact. Ultimately, the judiciary has tackled matters concerning no-confidence motions and changes to 'Panchayati Raj' laws, as demonstrated in 'Bhanumati *versus* State of Uttar Pradesh'. The judiciary has affirmed the constitutional legitimacy of modifications that enhance accountability and transparency in local administration. While allowing such modifications, the Judiciary has also tried to ensure that such alterations do not jeopardize the stability and dignity of "Panchayati Raj' institutions in India. The Supreme Court has repeatedly affirmed the constitutional legitimacy of reservation policies in local governance. The Court has further defined the jurisdiction and authority of different bodies under local self-government. The Judiciary has attempted to ensure in aforementioned cases that local governance operates openly and serves the public good. These rulings strengthen the tenets of democracy, equality, and justice. The Judiciary has tried to establish a strong foundation for local self-governance in India.

CHALLENGES IN LOCAL GOVERNANCE

"Panchayat" elections still have many hurdles despite the efforts of the judiciary against the same. Voter ignorance, corruption, and caste-based politics are some of these. It is in fact a challenging situation to maintain the laws and rules to do with voting. Thus, continuous intervention of judiciary and reforms in the electoral process is a must. In the rural setting, "panchayat" elections—ground-level politics are inevitable in ensuring real decentralization and true participation of the people. Through the regular elections and the seats of the least represented groups, such as women, SCs, and STs, the 73rd Constitutional Amendment Act of 1992, granted “Panchayati Raj” institutions, a justified position in the constitution. The free and impartial treatment in election processes become a topic of concern due to the various drawbacks associated with the same. Differences might involve social and political aspects but also some technical and structural details. This is why the voting procedures and systems in local self-government in India is always under judicial scanner.

CONCLUSION

The role of the judiciary in “Panchayat” elections has been essential towards embedding the democratic processes in the citizens at the very basic level. These initiatives bring to light the requirement for deeper structural transformations to mitigate the issues that lead to election disputes. To make the system better and more transparent, enforcing election regulations, setting up independent election observation bodies, and properly educating the voters are important steps. By such measures, India could strengthen the democratic engagement from the bottom up. This will make certain that elections are held in a trustworthy, open, and orderly manner. The circumstances concerning local elections in India are examples of how complex the process of ensuring fairness in elections is as well as maintaining law and order. The judiciary's involvement in these situations is of great importance, but it also demonstrates overly reactive approaches to individual grievances, which should never occur if strong internal controls elections exist. The discussed legal proceedings illustrate the following problems: restrictive criteria for filing candidatures, alterations of electoral rolls, breaches of ballot secrecy, procedural breaches, and criteria of contesting candidates. All of them resulted in important legal rulings that have influenced the local electoral system. The legal determinations are in line with the ideals of democracy and justice. The “Panchayat” elections are central to democracy in India. It helps rural people in self-governance. These types of elections have different sets of problems such as systemic and operational, social and political, as well as administrative and logistical. There is a need to use various strategies to solve these problems. The electoral body, the judiciary, and relevant stakeholders need to collaborate in solving these problems. India can guarantee that “Panchayat” elections are done freely, fairly, and without any corruption by strengthening the electoral framework, increasing civic education, and enforcing laws on elections. This will definitely foster democracy at the local levels.

RECOMMENDATION

In order to encourage the development of the right electoral laws and procedures, it is also essential to adopt the provision of the appropriate and timely penalties to those who would seek to subvert the democratic system. Indeed, this is vital for deterring undesirable behaviour and for promoting a smooth electoral process. The formation of the local electoral monitoring systems can be a solution that may allow for better efforts in the conductance of the elections and quicker and better conflict resolution in case of need. Thereby it will decrease the number of cases that are submitted to the courts of law for decisions. The implementation of these systems will aid in making sure that all people, specifically those that live in the remote and rural areas fully comprehend what they are entitled to and how they can make their voting exercise a success. If we make the Election Commission more well-resourced and independent, it will surely be a good contribution to the government's effort on the matter.

The Election Commission should be given more authority to monitor the "Panchayat" elections and to ensure their fair conduct. These include the ability to penalize the violators of the electoral laws. Voters' interest also should be a key target. Voters should be familiar with their rights and the importance of their participation in the elections. We can easily do this via awareness campaigns, seminars, and the use of mass media. Greater voter awareness will result in a more democratic electoral process. The enforcement of strict electoral norms is vital to avoid irregularities. The legislation relating to the election process should be stringently enforced. Only then, we can ensure an honest and just election.

Strict action towards the corrupt electoral practices is indispensable. The technological optimization of the electoral process is the most important matter. The technology is the tool that can be also used for the voters' registration, the election itself, and counteracting unjust behaviour. Nevertheless, judicial review will be the mechanism whereby adversarial policies at the election will be considered and resolved. The judiciary is obligated to guarantee the efficiency of the Indian electoral system by resolving such difficulties as personal interference with the voting process, the absence of a clear system in voter registration, and the restriction of the number of candidates. In this way, the judiciary will be capable not only of protecting democratic values but also of making the process "Panchayat" elections run properly in a fair and open manner. Besides, the expected effects of the proposals which will be made the strongest after implementation would be diminished. The larger number of enforcement and supervision units is sure to minimize election disputes because it will be prophecy which processes that are just will be followed by both the candidates as well as voters. An independent monitoring body will make sure speedy resolutions of the complaints. As a result, the election will be corruption-free and at the same time, the judiciary will have lesser burdens. As a result, more educated citizens will have a better understanding of politically important issues and will show more trust in the electoral system. Through the implementation of these measures, it would be possible to improve the democratic process in the local self-government.

REFERENCES

Bhanumati *versus* State of Uttar Pradesh, through its Principal Secretary and Ors., AIR 2010 SUPREME COURT 3796 (2010).

Boddula Krishnaiah and another *versus* State Election Commissioner, A.P. & Ors., 1996 AIR 1595 (1996).

R.N.A. Britto *versus* Chief Executive Officer and Others, Civil Appeal No. 718 of 1993 (1993).

Udey Chand *versus* Surat Singh and Anr., 2009 AIR SCW 6688 (2009).

Dr. K. Krishna Murthy and Ors. *versus* Union of India (UOI) and Anr., 2010 AIR SCW 3368 (2010).

Jaenendra Kumar Phoolchand Daftari *versus* Rajendra Ramsukh Mishra, Civil Appeal No. 1303 of 1993 (1993).

Surinder Kaur *versus* State of Punjab & Ors., 1996 AIR 1507 (1996).

Kattinokkula Murali Krishna *versus* Veeramalla Koteswara Rao and Ors., AIR 2010 SUPREME COURT 24 (2010).

Raghvendra Kumar *versus* Prabal Kumar and Ors., 2013 AIR SCW 6208 (2013).

Som Lal *versus* Vijay Laxmi and Ors., AIR 2008 SUPREME COURT 2088 (2008).

Ministry of Panchayati Raj, Government of India. (2020). Panchayat Elections in India: A Review. Retrieved from https://panchayat.gov.in

Gram Panchayat, Patiala *versus* State of Punjab and Others, SLP No. 5322 of 1990 (1990).

Radhakisan Rathi *versus* Additional Collector, AIR 1995 SUPREME COURT 1540 (1995).

Secretary, Sarvodaya Educational Society *versus* Ginjala Panasaiah and Ors., C.A. No. 2078 of 2000 (2000).

Shinde, S. N. *versus* The Divisional Commissioner, Nashik Division, Nashik & Ors., CIVIL APPEAL NO. 56 OF 2022 (2022).

Baldev Singh *versus* Shinder Pal Singh and Anr., AIRONLINE 2006 SC 303 (2006).

Harnek Singh *versus* Charanjit Singh and Ors., 10 SC CK 0085 (2005).

Venkataramana Bhat, M. V. *versus* Returning Officer and Tahsildar & Ors., 1993 LawSuit(SC) 567 (1993).

Zelia M. Xavier Fernandes E. Gonsalves *versus* Joana Rodrigues and Ors., AIR 2012 SUPREME COURT 988 (2012).

Chapter 9
Mental Health Support in Education: The Power of Policy in Knowledge Mobilization Efforts

Dellannia Segreti
https://orcid.org/0009-0007-7320-9808
University of Toronto, Canada

ABSTRACT

This paper will contextualize the current state of the education system using a future-oriented lens to analyze mental health and the education system. Situated within the Canadian context (namely the province of Ontario), it calls on various scholarly dialogues to highlight the importance of knowledge mobilization. The function of policy in addressing mental health and the role of educators is emphasized, given the effectiveness of policy in making large-scale change. It is suggested that a policy-based approach be taken within teacher education programs, to ensure that educators will be supported and equipped with future-oriented skills and competencies. Future studies should aim to collect qualitative and quantitative understandings of the impact of teacher education programs and the efficacy of courses aimed at bridging the gap between traditional teacher education programs and programs that include aspects of mental health training.

THE ROLE OF TEACHERS

Historically, the role of teachers in society has not been stagnant and has changed with the times. In the 1700s, teachers were strictly male career schoolmasters, who would need to be "capable of teaching READING, WRITING, ARITHMETICK, and

DOI: 10.4018/979-8-3373-5576-4.ch009

the Latin TONGUE…" (PBS, n.d.). The roles of teachers have ultimately changed, because of the interactions between education and society at large (Goble & Porter, 1977). This shift is evident in Holt-Reynolds' (1999) discussion on Constructivist pedagogies, where the role of a teacher is defined to be powerful and to help "our students learn to think".

The ever-changing role of a teacher was historically a larger part of the movement toward freedom in education. In 1918, John Dewey questioned, "How can the child learn to be a free and responsible citizen when the teacher is bound?" (PBS, n.d.). Therefore, as Dewey suggested, teachers have moved beyond a restrictive model to education, where the teachers were told what, when and how to teach, with each student receiving the same teachings (Lanier, 1997). The movement towards freedom in education is evidenced by Lanier's (1997) work that takes a closer look at what it means to be an educator. Lanier (1997) begins to define teaching as a multifaceted profession, allowing teaching to move away from a restrictive "show-and-tell", to a model where students are at the centre of their learning. Teaching is no longer "information-dispensing, custodial childcare and sorting out academically inclined students from other [students]" (Lanier, 1997).

Anadi, Mulla and Jadhav (2018) outline that the role of a 21st-century teacher is to "know students and their mindsets, [know] about today's technology, to develop meaningful professional relationships with students, facilitate and inspire student learning and creativity so that all the students achieve in the global society".

CURRENT YOUTH MENTAL HEALTH CRISIS

In keeping in mind, the ever-changing role of a teacher, as Goble and Porter (1977) pointed out, the relationship between society, the community, and the teaching profession continues to be strengthened. Professionals have recorded that youth mental health should be a top priority for health care in Canada (Malla et. al., 2018). Malla and colleagues (2018) highlight the early onset of most mental disorders and substance abuse, and how the long delays and lack of access to quality care, can impact students. Butler and Pang (2014) provide statistics to represent the severity of the above-mentioned: one in six people under 19 are adequately diagnosed and only one in five people under 12 receive the needed treatment. To further emphasize the growing risk youth face, from 2011 to 2018, the prevalence of poor perceived mental health, diagnosed mood and anxiety disorders, and suicide in youth, increased (Wiens et. al., 2020). Time and time again, it has been noted that mental health, wellness, and illness affect the health and well-being of an individual across their lifetime (Butler & Pang, 2014). Canada's Chief Public Health Officer included in their 2011 report that mental health is correlated with student school dropout and completion rates (Butler & Pang, 2014), which is where research on mental health concerns for Canadian youth has direct implications for the field of Education[1]. In further emphasizing the importance of support for youth, Wiens et. al. (2020) state that the mental health of youth is continually changing and requires reliable monitoring to ensure that adequate social and economic resources are allocated. It is imperative, that when discussing mental health, the impact of the COVID-19 pandemic and the resulting stressors, is included. Craig et. al. (2022) found a "higher than expected clinically concerning number of symptoms of mental health…in Canadian adolescents". Notably, when looking at the current crisis, we must reserve making conclusions on the reasons for the observed increases in mental health concerns, as they are less apparent from the studies conducted to date (Wiens et. al., 2020).

MENTAL HEALTH SUPPORT

Teachers and Mental Health Support

In acknowledging that youth around the world are experiencing an increased need for support with their mental health, teachers' mental health is also something that has come to the fore. The Ontario College of Teachers (OCT) (n.d.), a professional regulatory college for the teaching profession in the province of Ontario, Canada, highlights that it is important that Ontario Certified Teachers model for others by maintaining their wellness. A practicing teacher, who writes online as The Secret Teacher (2017), published an anonymous article in The Guardian and highlighted that self-care is a vital component of being an effective therapeutic teacher. Agarwal (2022) highlights that teachers often ignore their stress and anxiety levels due to their unconditional love for education and teaching children. However, experts have highlighted that stress consequently gets passed on from teachers to their students (Agarwal, 2022). Accordingly, mental health in the realm of the education system is twofold; teachers need support and undoubtedly students need support, as mental health is important for teachers and students alike (TwoSigmas, 2019). While acknowledging that teachers' mental health and well-being are important, this paper aims to look at the role of policy and the subsequent role of the teacher in providing students with some of the needed support within the classroom.

Students and Mental Health Support

Schools may currently be working to respond to their student's needs, but many teachers feel like they are caught in the middle of an "impossible situation" (Korbey, 2022). In 2010 the Ontario College of Teachers published a piece by Melodie

McCullough (2010), which highlighted that in a class of 30 students, six of them may be struggling with a mental health disorder, with only one of those six students receiving treatment. In the article, this stark fact is followed by the question of "What's a teacher to do?" (McCullough, 2010). This article can be used to deduce that this concern is not new to the field of education, however, no sizable changes have been implemented to directly support teachers or students. Here a resource gap is evident and policy reform is needed to address this systematic experience within the school system. In looking at a global stage, Behrani (2016) outlined that teachers technically do not need to have the skills needed for them to act as school counsellors or psychologists. This is in contrast with reality, which is that not every school will have access to counsellors, leaving many teachers being the adult figures that students may approach for assistance or advice (Behrani, 2016).

The province of Ontario released a Policy/Program Memorandum 169 in late 2023, to be put into effect in 2024 (King's Printer for Ontario, 2023). This memorandum demonstrates that both the Ministry of Education and the Ministry of Health are working together to build a continuum of care for students in the province of Ontario (King's Printer for Ontario, 2023). The memorandum was put into place to outline requirements for school boards and school authorities to provide students with "culturally responsive, evidence-informed student mental health promotion, prevention and early intervention services that respect students as complex individuals and provide appropriate supports for their diverse needs" (King's Printer for Ontario, 2023). The 7th requirement, which is targeted at school boards, reads "Enhanced Educator and Staff Mental Health Literacy" (King's Printer for Ontario, 2023). The memorandum clearly outlines that educators are "well-positioned to teach all students about mental health....and notice students about whom they may have a concern and know how to respond to those observations" (King's Printer for Ontario, 2023). This is an example of a formal acknowledgement of the importance of mental health and well-being for students and its interconnection with the education system. Within this requirement, the memorandum includes teacher training, given that teachers are recognized to play a pivotal role (King's Printer for Ontario, 2023). Incorporating teacher training on the topic of mental health within teacher education programs will ensure that the efforts mentioned above are sustained for the long term, providing teachers with the knowledge and confidence needed to successfully play their part.

Importantly, it has been documented that across North America, mental health and counselling resources are stretched so thin at schools, that teachers are having to step in and be the first and last resort for many students (Korbey, 2022). One Colorado teacher stated, "Every adult in the building has acted as a mental health provider whether we have performed it well, or willingly, or not" (Korbey, 2022). This sentiment is seemingly shared across the profession, as Dahlke (2021) wrote that “Teachers are not mental health professionals, and I desperately want to stay in my lane” while highlighting that “children won’t thrive academically until their physiological and safety needs are met”.

The British Columbia Ministry of Education (2001) created various guides that touched upon mental health disorders that students may be struggling with, which are offered as a resource for teachers. The volume on Depression provides a few suggestions that have proven to be successful. Two of the practices are: “effective collaboration and consultation with other service providers and taking action to support students in an informed way” (The British Columbia Ministry of Education, 2001). Connecting it to an Ontario context, the Ontario College of Teachers (OCT) (n.d.) published a Professional Advisory that discusses how teachers ought to support students’ mental health. It opens with the following statement “Ontario Certified Teachers (OCTs) support students’ mental health.” (OCT, n.d.), demonstrating that supporting students’ mental health is the classroom teacher's responsibility. Further, OCT (n.d.) highlights that Ontario Certified Teachers are recognized to support the service of students’ mental health, by working to “promote positive mental health, destigmatize conditions, and help to identify and report students at risk”. It then becomes clear that there is a disconnect between what formal training is provided and what they are recognized to do by the College. Teachers are expected to learn to recognize behaviours of concern and intervene appropriately (OCT, n.d.).

The gap between teacher training and the need within the classroom is ever-growing, leaving a gap between realities and the necessary future skills and competencies. The Secret Teacher (2017) stated, “It often falls to teachers to support families in crisis, but we don’t always have the skills. We should be given the tools to make a real difference” and “I held many meetings with parents where I felt more like a counsellor or social worker than social leader…didn’t have the skills or training to give this level of support”, demonstrating a teachers’ call to action. Michael Salvatori (2019), OCT CEO and Registrar, shared “Teachers are often first to recognize changes in student behaviour…Well-informed Ontario Certified Teachers can help to ensure that students with mental health concerns get the help they need”. While there are websites that have a variety of links to resources for teachers to read through and learn from, this is not enough to provide new teachers with the confidence and knowledge needed. Teacher education programs are great opportunities to train and educate new cohorts of teachers on what they will need to know in their classroom, similar to how the curriculum is mandated to be taught and unpacked within all teacher education programs.

ACTION ORIENTED FUTURE POLICIES

In acknowledging that teachers are responsible for, and expected to, perform certain duties, and have various responsibilities regarding student mental health, ultimately, there is a gap between what teachers are taught in their teacher education programs, and what is required of them in practice. As included within the Education Act, "all partners in the education sector have a role to play" and it "authorizes the Minister to establish policies and guidelines respecting student mental health" (King's Printer for Ontario, 2023). Ball et. al. (2019), outlines the impact that teacher readiness has on facilitating positive mental health in Inclusive Classrooms. Ball et. al.'s (2019) work, highlighted Hussein and Vostanis (2013), explored various teachers' perceptions of mental health problems. It was shared that teachers "feel burdened, lack confidence supporting mental health needs, experience difficulty identifying mental health problems, [and] are uncomfortable discussing mental health problems or emotional health" (Hussein & Vostanis, 2013).

Teacher Education Programs

A proposed next step is to look at the inclusion of counselling education within teacher education programs. Diaz (2020) acknowledges that our youth's mental health is requiring schools to rethink their traditional role. Grossman, Hammerness, and McDonald (2009) identified that as we redefine teaching, we must also re-imagine teacher education. In doing so, knowledge mobilization efforts within teacher education programs are responsive for future skills and competencies needed within the classrooms.

Despite the role of teachers drastically changing in practice, formal support and training seem to have not caught up. Climie and Altomare (n.d.) provided a Canadian perspective on mental health in schools and shared recommendations to best support students in the classroom. One of the suggested recommendations that Climie and Altomare (n.d.) put forward was "the role of teacher training programs in training pre-service teachers to understand and identify students with mental health concerns". The Secret Teacher (2017) echoes this idea by sharing that within their counselling education course, "every theory and new approach I learned about had lightbulbs popping in my head. There were so many parallels with teaching and so much potential for applying this in the classroom".

Koller and Bertel (2006) discussed the limited amount of training in mental health received by pre-service teachers, followed by a lack of competency-based training in identifying mental health issues. This is connected to the Ontario context, as the OCT (n.d.) expects teachers to "help to identify and report students at risk". This gap is highlighted by John Dabell (2019) who shared "Counselling is a huge part of being a teacher, but no one teaches us how to be counsellors. Teaching training institutions certainly fall flat on their faces here". Climie and Altomare (n.d.) thus make a strong argument that mental health awareness and education, in this paper linked to counselling education specifically, should be included within teacher training programs, in response to the demand from the field.

Further, scholars have discussed the implications of including various pieces of training and courses within teacher education programs, to enhance the readiness and abilities of new teachers. Lai-Yeung (2014) acknowledges that teachers have multiple roles to perform and must be competent in their responsibilities towards their students. It was highlighted that teachers are responsible for providing guidance and counselling to students; thus, they must receive proper training to be successful (Lai-Yeung, 2014). In a published study, a training model was used with pre-service teachers in an undergraduate preparation program, which found that students indeed have various training needs (Lai-Yeung, 2014). It was highlighted that future studies will need to be conducted to provide recommendations for future teacher training (Lai-Yeung, 2014). In connecting the above to practice, The Secret Teacher (2017) shared how a counselling course revolutionized their teaching. In a similar light, Chang et al. (2021) tangibly outlined the importance of training courses, as educational neuroscience concepts effectively influenced lesson design (from 51% before the course to 90% after completion) when teachers participated in the training.

While programs to that extent have not been implemented fully in teacher education programs, the possible benefits have been highlighted in a small-scale study conducted by Doikou and Diamandidou (2011). Doikou and Diamandidou (2011) investigated the outcomes of a brief teacher education program that aimed to enhance teachers' counselling skills, and their competence to apply social and emotional learning program intervention activities in the classroom. According to student teachers' reflections, the program was able to provide them with new knowledge surrounding communication and counselling that they felt would be useful in teaching practice (Doikou & Diamandidou, 2011). This finding was echoed by Eastmon (2009), who ran workshops aimed to help secondary teachers look at counselling skills in their classroom and build up the skills needed, in direct response to teachers acknowledging the importance of counselling skills in the classroom. This provides promising data for institutions to adopt similar models.

In terms of a possible model that institutions can adopt, Walz and Bleuer (n.d.) suggest the Counseling Curriculum for Teachers (CCT) Model, as it aims to provide teachers with the opportunity to "acquire knowledge about the main counselling approaches, strategies, and techniques, which will enable them to work successfully with culturally and linguistically diverse and exceptional students and families". Ultimately the CCT model will equip teachers with the necessary counselling skills needed to be effective educators (Walz and Bleuer, n.d.).

The inclusion of counselling education courses into the existing teacher education programs will indeed take some time, aligned with the province of Ontario's current memorandum (King's Printer for Ontario, 2023),which aims to address the teacher knowledge gap through its targeted approaches. Importantly, teachers should not feel obligated, like The Secret Teacher (2017), to "enroll in a full counselling qualification course and then return to teaching". Fazel and colleagues' (2023) study found that when a School Mental Health Toolbox (SMHT) training program was utilized, the tools acquired were relevant to practice by the majority of teacher attendees. This emphasizes the possibilities associated with a partnership within the fields of education and mental health (Fazel et al., 2023) and how this work can begin to be included within various levels of the system through policy efforts.

Collaboration between Psychologists and Teachers

The interdisciplinary nature of education calls for there to be collaborations between mental health professionals and teachers. The synergies between the fields are indeed innately connected. With students limited access to ongoing support, and the parallel limited communication between professionals in their respective fields, it is imperative that the stream of communication be strengthened to reflect the abundant time they spend at school. This is reflected in the Policy/Program Memorandum 169 mentioned previously (King's Printer for Ontario, 2023). Here the importance of collaboration to build "a continuum of mental health and addictions care across schools, community-based child and youth mental health providers, and hospitals that is coordinated, comprehensive and responsive to the needs of every student" is mentioned (King's Printer for Ontario, 2023).

Similarly, this concept has been discussed by various scholars, including Fazel and colleagues (2023) who have outlined that partnerships between school staff and mental health professionals have the potential to improve access to mental health support for students. As mentioned above, any amount of additional teacher training in mental health and counselling education cannot replace psychologists and other professionals who are integral to the field. An important distinction made by the Secret Teacher (2017), is that the goal is not to train teachers as counsellors but to provide them with the basic training in this area of expertise, to positively impact students. This is echoed through the importance of interprofessional education which highlights that training in isolation from other professionals is not a beneficial approach (Curran, Ungar & Pauze, 2006). At the core is the importance of interprofessional collaboration to benefit students and assist teachers in fulfilling their multi-faceted roles on a day-to-day basis. To highlight this important synergy and call for further collaboration, Curran, Ungar and Pauze (2006), from The Canadian Collaborative Mental Health Initiative, have curated a resource for collaborative mental health care educators, helping them to work towards improving the mental health and well-being of Canadians by enhancing relationships and improving collaboration. Curran, Ungar and Pauze (2006) emphasize the importance of a collaborative practice approach, where interprofessional teams work together to make a difference. An example of such is the implementation of interprofessional education sessions, where interdisciplinary professionals can learn together to improve their respective practices and fields (Curran, Ungar, & Pauze, 2006). In this light, the Policy/Program Memorandum 169 aims to include this idea within their multi-tiered system of supports that will aim to deliver school-based mental health services, which are part of community-based mental health as well (King's Printer for Ontario, 2023). This demonstrates that the education system is taking steps to move forward in the right direction for improving knowledge mobilization within schools on the topic of student mental health.

However, as Ekornes (2015) highlights, interprofessional collaboration is not without its barriers. Ekornes's (2015) study found that barriers related to interprofessional collaboration with the goal of mental health promotion included the following: communication and confidentiality, time constraints, contextual presence and understanding, cross-systems contact, school leadership, and teacher competence in mental health. If future education policies took into consideration the importance of interprofessional collaboration across various disciplines, and in this context, beyond mental health promotion, teacher education becomes a prominent piece of the larger puzzle. As Ekornes (2015) outlined, teacher competence in mental health is a current barrier, however, it does not systematically need to be. In taking a holistic approach to future policy directions, teachers are better equipped to do their jobs, which comes at great benefits to their students.

FUTURE DIRECTIONS AND CONCLUSIONS

To better understand the changing roles of teachers and the current climate of the educational system, research that looks at the effectiveness of the inclusion of counselling education within teacher education programs is the next step. The findings from future research can be used to create a strong proposal for regulatory colleges of teachers, to consider including counselling education as a required branch that certified teacher education programs must include in their programs. A variation of the CCT Model should be adopted (Walz & Bleuer, n.d.), with the inclusion of Indigenous perspectives on mental health and counselling. The CCT Model could include "(1) contemporary therapeutic systems for working with diverse student populations and their families, (2) basic counselling strategies and techniques, (3) multicultural counselling concepts, issues, and practices, (4) philosophical, ethical and legal issues, and (5) counselling learning activities" (Walz & Bleuer, n.d.). This approach can demonstrate how regulatory bodies can update their policies to better respond to the increasing mental health crisis students and teachers are faced with. Future research in this area will extend the current literature and be part of the tangible evidence needed to make informed policy decisions going forward.

Overall, this paper demonstrates how policy can play a large role in advancing the current state of the education system. The power of knowledge mobilization is at the fore and carries much importance to ensure that all needs are met within the system. Policy is an effective and efficient way to mobilize large-scale change. Therefore, to ensure that students are supported within schools, a policy-based approach should be taken within teacher education programs, to ensure that educators are supported and equipped with future-oriented skills and competencies.

REFERENCES

Agarwal, S. (2022). *Why is Mental Health Important for Teachers?* Suraasa. https://www.suraasa.com/blog/why-is-mental-health-important-for-teachers

Ball, J., Penney, S., Young, G., Harris, G., & Joy, R. (2019). *Teacher Readiness: Teacher attitudes, opinions, and perspectives toward facilitating positive mental health in the classroom.* https://www.researchgate.net/publication/338777674_Teacher_readiness_Teacher_attitudes_opinions_and_perspectives_towards_facilitating_positive_mental_health_in_the_classroom

Behrani, P. (2016). Importance Of Teaching Counselling Skills To Teachers. *MIER Journal of Educational Studies, Trends & Practices, 6*(1), 17-25. https://www.mierjs.in/index.php/mjestp/article/view/1452/1077

British Columbia Ministry of Education. (2001). *Teaching Students with Mental Health Disorders: Resources for Teachers.* British Columbia Ministry of Education: Special Programs Branch. https://cemh.lbpsb.qc.ca/Portals/cemh/Mood/Teaching-Students-Mental-Health-Disorders.pdf

Butler, M., & Pang, M. (2014). *Current Issues in Mental Health in Canada: Child and Youth Mental Health.* Library of Parliament. https://epe.lac-bac.gc.ca/100/201/301/weekly_checklist/2014/internet/w14-18-U-E.html/collections/collection_2014/bdp-lop/eb/2014-13-eng.pdf

Chang, Z., Schwartz, M. C., Hinesley, V., & Dubinsky, J. M. (2021). Neuroscience Concepts Changed Teachers' Views of Pedagogy and Students. *Frontiers in Psychology, 12*, 685856. Advance online publication. DOI: 10.3389/fpsyg.2021.685856 PMID: 34456800

Climie, E., & Altomare, A. (n.d.). *Supporting Children with Mental Health Concerns in Classrooms.* https://files.eric.ed.gov/fulltext/EJ1033189.pdf

Craig, S. G., Bondi, B., Ames, M., & Pepler, D. (2022). Canadian adolescents' mental health and substance use during the COVID-19 pandemic: Associations with COVID-19 stressors. *Canadian Journal of Behavioural Science.* Advance online publication. DOI: 10.1037/cbs0000305

Curran, V., Ungar, T., & Pauze, E. (2006). *Strengthening Collaboration through Interprofessional Education: A Resource for Collaborative Mental Health Care Educators.* Canadian Collaborative Mental Health Initiative. https://www.shared-care.ca/files/EN_Strengtheningcollaborationthroughinterprofessionaleducation.pdf

Dabell, J. (2019). *Teacher Training Gap: Counselling*. John Dabell: Every Day Is A School Day. https://johndabell.com/2019/09/21/teacher-training-fail-counselling/

Dahlke, E. (2021). *I'm a Teacher, and I Can't Live Like This*. Medium. https://medium.com/educate-pub/im-a-teacher-and-i-can-t-live-like-this-95052a0e38ec

Diaz, C. N. (2020). Students' Mental Health: The Importance of the Teacher's Role and Training. *Revista Educacion las Americas, 10*(2), 277–287. Advance online publication. DOI: 10.35811/rea.v10i2.125

Doikou, M., & Diamandidou, K. (2011). Enhancing teachers' counselling skills: Student teachers' views on a teachers' education programme. *European Journal of Teacher Education, 34*(1), 61–79. DOI: 10.1080/02619768.2010.534979

Eastmon, S. (2009). Counselling Skills for Teachers in Secondary Schools: Observations from One-day Workshops. *Pastoral Care in Education: An International Journal of Personal. Pastoral Care in Education, 13*(2), 25–28. DOI: 10.1080/02643949509470919

Ekornes, S. (2015). Teacher Perspectives on Their Role and the Challenges of Interprofessional Collaboration in Mental Health Promotion. *School Mental Health, 7*(3), 193–211. Advance online publication. DOI: 10.1007/s12310-015-9147-y

Fazel, M., Soneson, E., Sellars, E., Butler, G., & Stein, A. (2023). Partnerships at the Interface of Education and Mental Health Services: The Utilization and Acceptability of the Provision of Specialist Liaison and Teacher Skills Training. *International Journal of Environmental Research and Public Health, 20*(5), 4066. Advance online publication. DOI: 10.3390/ijerph20054066 PMID: 36901077

Goble, N. M., & Porter, J. F. (1977). *The*. UNESCO. https://eric.ed.gov/?id=ED167485

Grossman, P., Hammerness, K., & McDonald, M. (2009). Redefining teaching, re-imagining teacher education. *Teachers and Teaching, 15*(2), 273–289. DOI: 10.1080/13540600902875340

Holt-Reynolds. (1999). What does the teacher do? Constructivist pedagogies and prospective teachers' beliefs about the role of a teacher. *Teaching and Teacher Education, 16*(2000), 21-32. https://citeseerx.ist.psu.edu/document?repid=rep1&type=pdf&doi=32dde0b9ac17f08b78cd078c1150862c18ff3b43

Hussein, S. A., & Vostanis, P. (2013). Teacher training intervention for early identification of common child mental health problems in Pakistan. *Emotional & Behavioural Difficulties, 18*(3), 284–296. DOI: 10.1080/13632752.2013.819254

King's Printer for Ontario. (2023). *Policy/Program Memorandum 169.*https://www.ontario.ca/document/education-ontario-policy-and-program-direction/policyprogram-memorandum-169#section-5

Koller, J. R., & Bertel, J. M. (2006). Responding to today's mental health needs of children, families and schools: Revisiting the preservice training and preparation of school-based personnel. *Education & Treatment of Children*, *29*(2), 197.

Korbey, H. (2022). *What's the Role of Teachers in Supporting Student Mental Health?* Edutopia. https://www.edutopia.org/article/the-doctor-is-in-your-classroom/

Lai-Yeung, S. W. C. (2014). The Need for Guidance and Counselling Training for Teachers. *Procedia: Social and Behavioral Sciences*, *113*, 36–43. DOI: 10.1016/j.sbspro.2014.01.008

Lanier, J. T. (1997). *Redefining the Role of the Teacher: It's a Multifaceted Profession*. Edutopia. https://www.edutopia.org/redefining-role-teacher

Malla, A., Shah, J., Iyer, S., Boksa, P., Risha, J., Andersson, N., Lal, S., & Fuhrer, R. (2018). Youth Mental Health Should Be a Top Priority for Health Care in Canada. *Canadian Journal of Psychiatry*, *63*(4), 216–222. DOI: 10.1177/0706743718758968 PMID: 29528719

McCullough, M. (2010). *Support for Health Minds.* Professionally Speaking: The Magazine of the Ontario College of Teachers. https://professionallyspeaking.oct.ca/december_2010/features/healthy_minds.aspx

Ontario College of Teachers. (n.d.). *Mental Health.* Ontario College of Teachers: Ontario's Teaching Regulator. https://www.oct.ca/members/research/mental-health

PBS. (n.d.). *Only A Teacher: Teaching Timeline*. PBS Online. https://www.pbs.org/onlyateacher/timeline.html

The Secret Teacher. (2017). *Secret Teacher: a counselling course revolutionized my teaching*. The Guardian. https://www.theguardian.com/teacher-network/2017/apr/01/secret-teacher-counselling-training-revolutionised-teaching

TwoSigmas. (2019). *Mental Health – Why it's Important for Teachers and Students Alike.* Medium. https://medium.com/@twosigmas/mental-health-why-its-important-for-teachers-and-students-alike-cc7ce39a7914

Walz, G. R., & Bleuer, J. C. (n.d.). *ACA Knowledge Center*. https://www.counseling.org/docs/default-source/vistas/improving-teaching-and-learning-a-counseling-curriculum-model-for-teachers.pdf?sfvrsn=6

Wiens, K., Bhattarai, A., Pedram, P., Dores, A., Williams, J., Bulloch, A., & Patten, S. (2020). A growing need for youth mental health services in Canada: Examining trends in youth mental health from 2011 to 2018. *Epidemiology and Psychiatric Sciences, 29*(115), 1–9. DOI: 10.1017/S2045796020000281 PMID: 32299531

ADDITIONAL READINGS

Allman, K. L., & Slate, J. R. (2013). DISCIPLINARY CONSEQUENCES ASSIGNED TO STUDENTS WITH EMOTIONAL DISORDER, LEARNING DISABILITY, OR OTHER HEALTH IMPAIRMENT: EFFECTS ON THEIR ACADEMIC ACHIEVEMENT. *The Journal of Educational Research, 7*(1).

Arslan, G., & Allen, K. A. (2022). Complete mental health in elementary school children: Understanding youth school functioning and adjustment. *Current Psychology (New Brunswick, N.J.), 41*(3), 1174–1183. DOI: 10.1007/s12144-020-00628-0

Brown, J. S. (2018). Student mental health: Some answers and more questions. *Journal of Mental Health (Abingdon, England), 27*(3), 193–196. DOI: 10.1080/09638237.2018.1470319 PMID: 29768071

Cappella, E., Hamre, B. K., Kim, H. Y., Henry, D. B., Frazier, S. L., Atkins, M. S., & Schoenwald, S. K. (2012). Teacher consultation and coaching within mental health practice: Classroom and child effects in urban elementary schools. *Journal of Consulting and Clinical Psychology, 80*(4), 597–610. DOI: 10.1037/a0027725 PMID: 22428941

Evensen, M. (2019). Adolescent mental health problems, behaviour penalties, and distributional variation in educational achievement. *European Sociological Review, 35*(4), 474–490. DOI: 10.1093/esr/jcz015

Halladay, J., Bennett, K., Weist, M., Boyle, M., Manion, I., Campo, M., & Georgiades, K. (2020). Teacher-student relationships and mental health help seeking behaviors among elementary and secondary students in Ontario Canada. *Journal of School Psychology, 81*, 1–10. DOI: 10.1016/j.jsp.2020.05.003 PMID: 32711720

Henriksen, D., & Gruber, N. (2024, March). System-wide school mindfulness: Addressing elementary students' social-emotional learning and wellbeing. []. Frontiers Media SA.]. *Frontiers in Education, 9*, 1272545. DOI: 10.3389/feduc.2024.1272545

Istiqomah, W. N., Ahmad, A., Suryadi, E., & Jannah, S. R. (2024). The Islamic Religious Education Teacher Program on Students' Mental Health of Elementary School. *International Journal on Advanced Science, Education, and Religion*, *7*(2), 177–185.

Jeffries, V., & Salzer, M. S. (2022). Mental health symptoms and academic achievement factors. *Journal of American College Health*, *70*(8), 2262–2265. DOI: 10.1080/07448481.2020.1865377 PMID: 33513071

Liu, S., Jie, S., & Yu, X. (2024). The use of digital teaching resources in teaching mental health in elementary school. *International Journal of New Developments in Education*, *6*(4).

MacLeod, S. (2017). Elementary Teachers' Perspectives on Student Mental Health.

Muller, R., Morabito, M. S., & Green, J. G. (2021). Police and mental health in elementary and secondary schools: A systematic review of the literature and implications for nursing. *Journal of Psychiatric and Mental Health Nursing*, *28*(1), 72–82. DOI: 10.1111/jpm.12704 PMID: 33073464

Murphy, J. M., Guzmán, J., McCarthy, A. E., Squicciarini, A. M., George, M., Canenguez, K. M., Dunn, E. C., Baer, L., Simonsohn, A., Smoller, J. W., & Jellinek, M. S. (2015). Mental health predicts better academic outcomes: A longitudinal study of elementary school students in Chile. *Child Psychiatry and Human Development*, *46*(2), 245–256. DOI: 10.1007/s10578-014-0464-4 PMID: 24771270

O'Connor, M., Cloney, D., Kvalsvig, A., & Goldfeld, S. (2019). Positive mental health and academic achievement in elementary school: New evidence from a matching analysis. *Educational Researcher*, *48*(4), 205–216. DOI: 10.3102/0013189X19848724

Raffaele Mendez, L. M., Drymond-Cundy, M. J., Suldo, S. M., & Dedrick, R. F. (2024). Are Elementary Educators Prepared to Address Student Mental Health in Title 1 Schools? An Examination of Role Breadth, Self-Efficacy, and Attitudes Toward Trauma-Informed Care. *School Mental Health*, *16*(4), 1–15. DOI: 10.1007/s12310-024-09680-8

Sanchez, A. L., Cornacchio, D., Poznanski, B., Golik, A. M., Chou, T., & Comer, J. S. (2018). The effectiveness of school-based mental health services for elementary-aged children: A meta-analysis. *Journal of the American Academy of Child and Adolescent Psychiatry*, *57*(3), 153–165. DOI: 10.1016/j.jaac.2017.11.022 PMID: 29496124

Stone, G. L., Hinds, W. C., & Schmidt, G. W. (1975). Teaching mental health behaviors to elementary school children. *Professional Psychology*, *6*(1), 34–40. DOI: 10.1037/h0076603

Vang, S. J. (2024). *A GRANT PROPOSAL TO PROMOTE MENTAL HEALTH THROUGH A MINDFULNESS IMPLEMENTATION FOR AN UNDER-RESOURCED RURAL SCHOOL DISTRICT* (Doctoral dissertation, California State University, Stanislaus).

Walter, H. J., Gouze, K., & Lim, K. G. (2006). Teachers' beliefs about mental health needs in inner city elementary schools. *Journal of the American Academy of Child and Adolescent Psychiatry*, *45*(1), 61–68. DOI: 10.1097/01.chi.0000187243.17824.6c PMID: 16327582

Wegmann, K. M., Powers, J. D., Swick, D. C., & Watkins, C. S. (2017). Supporting academic achievement through school-based mental health services: A multisite evaluation of reading outcomes across one academic year. *School Social Work Journal*, *41*(2), 1–22.

ENDNOTES

1 See listed Additional Readings to learn more about student mental health and its connections with the education system around the world.

Chapter 10
Mapping Research Trends Digital Communication on Public Policy:
A Systematic Literature Review

Ayu Evita Sari
https://orcid.org/0009-0002-8527-3819
Universitas Muhammadiyah Malang, Indonesia

Ali Roziqin
https://orcid.org/0000-0001-8336-3103
Universitas Muhammadiyah Malang, Indonesia

Salahudin Salahudin
https://orcid.org/0000-0001-5687-0812
Universitas Muhammadiyah Malang, Indonesia

Susenohaji Susenohaji
https://orcid.org/0009-0002-0363-4124
University of Brawijaya, Malang, Indonesia

ABSTRACT

This study aims to examine the trend of scientific research related to digital communication on public policy. The research method used a systematic literature review based from 94 scientific articles from the Scopus. Data were collected from Scopus database and data analysis using the VOSviewer Application. The study revealed that with 94 scientific articles on Digital Communication on Public Policy that had gone through the review including data by year, by author, by country or territory, by subject area, issue clustering data and grouping. The chapter contribute to the

DOI: 10.4018/979-8-3373-5576-4.ch010

development of driving forces for further research on Digital Communication on Public Policy. This article has limitations that only review articles sourced from the Scopus database. This study aids in the process of formulating and creating future policies.

INTRODUCTION

Public policy has become a crucial point to communicate for society. Public policy communication has the consequence that every party involved in the policy, both the subject and the policy object, really knows and understands the meaning and purpose of the policy (König, 2021). Policy communication has more than just socialization in mind. The policy has been communicated to the various stakeholders, including the community, who are expected to provide information and education, influence public opinion through movement, attract or mobilize support for the policy's existence, and help people become more mature in their understanding, particularly in terms of understanding the purpose, the implementation process, and the impact that will result from such a policy (Roziqin et al, 2021). Therefore, policy communication is not only necessary in the planning and implementation process, but also essential as an evaluation material and feedback. Therefore, the local government continues to synergize in ensuring that the policy can be communicated to all parties with one of its strategies, namely through digital. This digitalization also emerged as a form of government dynamism in the era and the continuously growing ICT sophistication as well as the demands of the public related to access facility as form of transparency and also government accountability (Roziqin et al., 2024; Stone et al., 2022).

There should be mentioned that a large body of prior research has examined digital-based public policy communications. According to Vega-Ramírez, Castro-Duarte, and Quintana-Figueroa (2023) in his research at the Institute of Education in Chile, effective public policy communication can be a driving force for success and compliance in policy implementation, through the dissemination of digital-based information. While according to Dai, Cheng, and Liu (2023), Digital-based public policy communication will be a landscape of policy dissemination and public opinion formation, which can foster networking and also emotional value interaction through policy communication contacts that have been carried out. Another inquiry by Vlad et al. (2023) also suggests that through digital policy communication, communication between people and government can be intertwined with a cellular component, which at the same time changes the way local governments think, plan, and implement policies. This must be a new strategy in policy communication to the public to the rural institutions.

This study was carried out using a systematic and meta-analysis approach (PRISMA) to reveal relevant documents related to the topic, namely "digital era public policy". Previously, similar topics have been studied through a narrative review approach to interpret the application of BDA (Big Data Analysis) in public policy (Hossin et al., 2023). This narrative review explains data in the form of processed scientific article documents related to topics related to the use of certain applications. Further, studied by Aditya et al. (2023), the study explains the digital divide in Smart City policy. This research shows that there is a digital gap in the implementation of Smart City in local government. Through quantitative data collected from the results of questionnaires in sub-districts in Tangerang City with 400 participants which were then processed using the SEM-PLS (Structural Equation Modeling- Partial Least Square), it was found that there was a digital gap regarding policy Smart City.

There is also previous research with studies regarding the usefulness of digital technology which is expected to create a positive impact on government administration and also the country's democracy. However, this actually gave rise to a negative impact which ultimately encouraged the latest contributions between relevant actors in making Platform Regulatory Policies. This article is a pioneer that shows 3 approaches in regulating social media platforms, the advantages and disadvantages of content modernization, process-based co-regulation, and alternative regulation (Stockmann, 2023). Structural radicalism in information and communication systems is of greater concern, especially through policy exploration to ensure the creation of ambitious policies that can be communicated and implemented to the public so that the models offered can truly serve the information and communication needs of society through digital systems. Focusing within a broader framework is also very important with the provision that policies must always pay attention to aspects of politics, economics, technology platforms, even journalism (Pickard, 2023).

Although there has been a lot of previous research that has studied Digital Communication Public Policy, there are still few articles that have been created using the method of Systematic Literature Review or SLR with Scopus database. Through scopus database, new articles will be limited and selected according to context and topic. The research is focused on 94 selected scientific articles which are subsequently analyzed and reviewed using Scopus and the Viosvewer Application to obtain relevant data related to the articles. Given that the SLR method is a scientific method that has the strength and advantage in understanding research issues based on previous research (Mu & Wang, 2022). Therefore, this method can evaluate various trends and the existence of a topic discussed in the global scope (Wahyudin & Rahayu, 2020). The more or more often the topic is discussed, the greater the global attention to such research issues that one of them is about Digital Communication Public Policy (Albuainain, 2022). That's why, this research is concentrated on reviewing and generating trend data on issues that are loaded in scientific articles. Data range of years, scale of productivity of authors, country of origin, as well as subject area will be matched with the power of data and descriptive analysis. Even the topics or fields of study most dominant or most existing in the writing of Digital Communication Public Policy will be presented with a database.

This research has a focus of research among them to answer and analyze related developments in research on Digital Communication Public Policy in the world. Given this, it would be very useful to see to what extent a study topic or issue has been placed as a research focus. This activity may also be characterized as a means of observing how digital-based public policy communication is still being examined at the rate of development as a trend of study.Besides, this research is aimed at generating evidence of how strong and how dominant a subject is in a scientific article. In the process, this research uses qualitative methods through the content analysis process with the approach of Systematic Literature Review or SLR. The scientific articles analyzed are obtained from the Scopus Database which is subsequently processed to obtain certain data. the document processed uses the Vosviewer Application to get a trend data from the scientific articles that have been reviewed. Thus, this research will of course contribute to the development of science, especially for public administration related to future policy development, what action should be taken in the near future, what kind of planning should be drawn up for the future mainly focused on public policy communication strategies through digital platforms.

METHOD

The research was conducted using the SLR or Systematic Literature Review method and studied using a qualitative approach. The SLR method is chosen in view of the lack of research focused on reviewing scientific articles on Digital Communication Public Policy. SLR itself can be used to see the trends in writing as well as the existence of research on a topic or related issue in the world. SLR method can be a reference for identifying, interpreting, analyzing, and evaluating all available research in a particular field of topic which is also necessary in determining the research agenda (Triandini et al., 2019). Next, a qualitative approach is chosen in the presentation of data results through analysis studies that are descriptive. It is worth noting that research with a qualitative approach is focused on understanding a condition in a context by guiding through detailed and in-depth descriptions. The description is in a natural or natural portrait setting and also what really happens in the study data . Using this method, you can answer questions related to the development of the study Digital Communication Public Policy, including sub questions:

RQ1: How are the trends of scientific publications in the topic of Digital Communication Public Policy based on year, author, region, and also subject?
RQ2: How is the spread of research topics based on the cluster of scientific publications in the topic of Digital Communication Public Policy in the last 1 year, namely 2023-2024?
RQ3: How is the trend of scientific publication topics in the topic of Digital Communication Public Policy in the last year 2023-2024?

Research is conducted in accordance with the PRISMA protocol or Prefereed Reporting Items of Systematic Reviews and Meta-Analyses. The stages performed according to the protocol are Identification, Screening, and Included from the Scopus database(Rethlesfsen et al., 2021). The identification phase begins with the initial phase of article search, registration process, login, and entering keywords in the Scopus search column. The next stage or screening phase is the stage of determining the number of articles recorded from the Scopus Database. Ensure that articles are relevant to selected topics, scientific criteria, English-language articles, journal types, and also easy access in full paper form. Furthermore, there is a process to identify articles that have strong links to digital-based public policy communication topics and are accessible in the form of RIS. Ensure the number of articles selected and set as future references is valid on the basis of certain provisions in order to narrow the scope of the language and ensure that new articles appear relevant to the topic being studied. The last is the establishment of an article that has been rigorously verified and validated in the Scopus system.

Initially the document search was done by entering the keyword "Communication" AND "Public Policy" as well as adding keywords in the second column with details of the steps as follows:

Figure 1. Stages of the SLR method

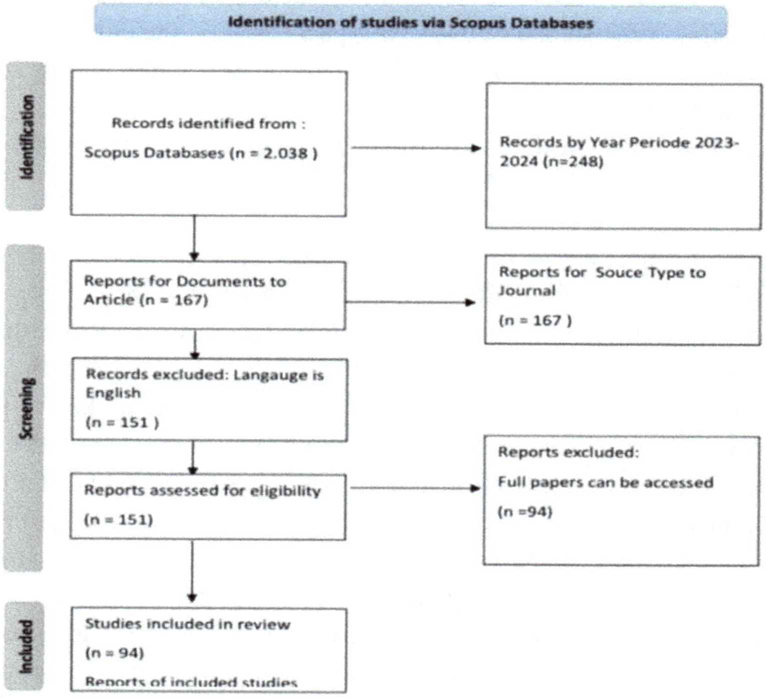

Source: processed by author

The articles that have been filtered will then be processed using Scopus Analysis and subsequently in the Review using the VOSviewer Application to obtain the required data.

RESULTS AND DISCUSSION

The results of data analysis from the Scopus Database based on the annual trend of articles can be visualized through the graph in Figure 2. The results of classification by year were carried out on 94 selected scientific articles in the Scopus Database that were relevant to the study of the topic of Digital Communication on Public Policy. In this context, the analysis is limited to the last 1 year period, namely 2023 to 2024. Please note that this research was conducted in April 2024. Referring to the graph below, in 2023 there were 45 scientific publications with the topic Digital Communication on Public Policy included in the Scopus Database. While in 2024, starting from January to July, there are 49 scientific articles that have been published and included in the Scopus Database.

Annual Trends

Reflecting on the data on the number of publications of articles on Digital Communication on Public Policy in the Scopus Database, it can be shown that every year the topic always attracts the attention of many researchers around the world. This is based on the reality that the rapid development of the times cannot be separated from the utilization of new platforms, one of which is as a medium for policy communication. This topic has very broad derivatives and research clusters. Given that it is based on digital, public policy communication can generate interactions between actors ranging from government, public, private sector, and academics. In addition, every year updates and updates are made to ensure that the steps taken by the government are in accordance with the demands and needs of the community. Research on the topic can also be aimed at providing solutive recommendations regarding the implementation of digital communication in public policy.

Figure 2. Publication trends by year

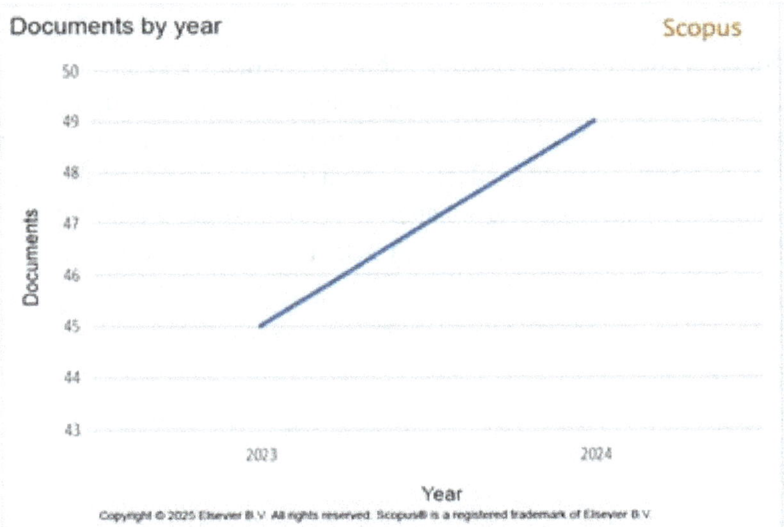

Source: Scopus Analysis Data on 29 July 2024

There is a relevant article published in 2023 entitled "Digital News and Political Tweets in the Lower Austrian Municipal Elections: A Case Study on Digital Journalism and political Communication" written by Lampoltshammer, De Luc & Thurnay (2023). This research correlates with the use of digital systems as a transformation towards digital governance in particular in every public policy step, one of which is public policy communication. Then this scientific article becomes a comprehensive study that identifies nonlinear interactions between news organizations, politicians, and the general public especially during the elections in Austria, where such interactions can form a dynamic evolution of a public discourse concerning politics in which there is a high sensitivity. Then there is an article by Xie, (2024) entitled "The Platformation and Transformation of the Digital Public Sphere: An Introduction". The study of this article seeks to introduce the complex landscape of social media and its development of integration both in the social and political world. Relevant to public policy communications, this analysis focuses on the emergence and growth of new platforms, localized mobile communication trends, technology structures in various dimensions. It also implies a presentation of diverse perspectives through the presentation of six editions of papers that will contribute to the understanding of digital communication, citizen participation, the existentialism of democracy, and also the transformation of public spaces. In this context, digital media and changing public policy communication strategies will always be dynamic.

Trend Mapping Based on Author

The identification results in Figure 3 above show data that there are authors who have done previous research on relevant topics related to a digital public policy communication. From the Scopus Database analysis results on Figure 3, there is a top 10 ranking of authors whose identified each has 1 scientific article related to the topic in the Scops Database. The ten authors include Abdul Malik, Achillas, Adha, Adi, Aditya, Anggarwal, Agley, Agrawal, Aldonis, and Alcarria.

Figure 3. Publication trends by author

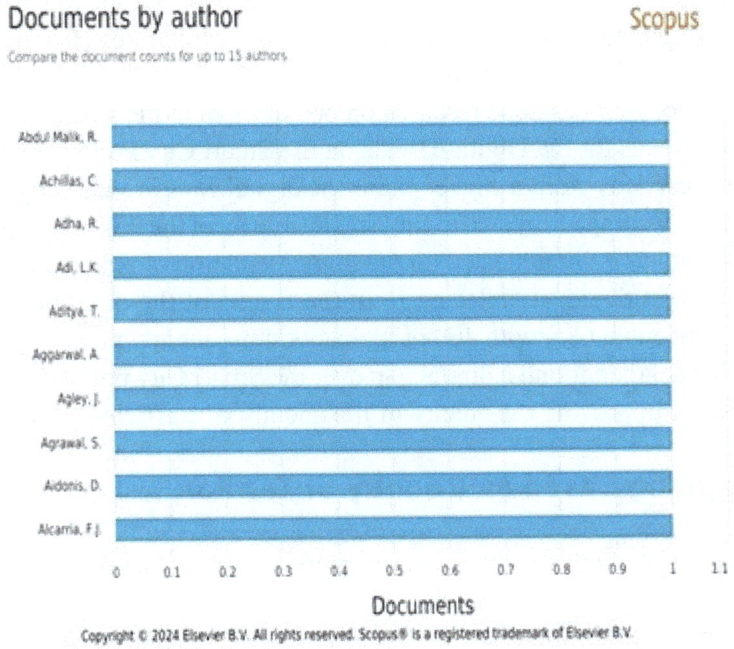

Source: Scopus Analysis Data

The second-ranked author is Charisios Achillas, C with his work entitled "Auditing Accessibility of Pavements and Points of Interest in Urban Areas: The 'Seek & Go' Tool †". The study examines the development of accessibility through increasing digital systems on a global scale, one in the policy sector. Therefore, this essay Achillas et al., (2023) presents the latest digital tool called 'Seek and Go' which is specifically designed for people with disabilities. The outcome is expected to be a state-of-the-art alternative for disabled people as well as a new recommendation for the government to formulate its future policy strategy. Given that disabled people should get more attention from the local government. Whatever policy the local government makes, it must take into account the existence of people with disabilities who always require special measures, so a study of this kind of renewal article will be necessary.

In the study Saefudin et al., (2023) the author in the fourth series of work Adi L.K entitled "Regulating Fake News and Hoaxes: A Comparative Analysis of Indonesia and Malaysia" then examined a policy of prohibition of the dissemination of fake news or hoax. The work tried to explain the Hoax News Policy which has been implemented through research from two countries namely Indonesia and also Malaysia. The exhibition of the results in the study comprehensively shows that both Indonesia and Malaysia are both synergistic in the issue of the spread of hoax news. Indonesia's step through the ratification of the KUHP Act and Malaysia's move through the Implementation of Communication and Multimedia Content Forum. The policy is also aimed at building co-operation with various parties. The author with the fifth position has done research on one of them in the next article entitled "Community Needs for the Digital Divide on the Smart City Policy" by the fourth position author Toddy Aditya who explains the digital gaps in smart city policy. So the study of this writing is directed to find out the impact of the Smart City policy that the government has communicated on the implementation of Aditya et al., (2023). Through the cognitive data collected from the results of the questionnaire on 13 districts in Tangerang City with 400 participants subsequently processed using the SEM-PLS Model then found a digital gap over the Smart City policy. While Smart City is aimed at improving the quality of life and also the efficiency of services.

Trend Mapping Based on Country or Territory

Based on the study of the results in the chart, it is clear that there are countries with the top 10 in the number of publications that are most relevant to related topics. First there are the United States with 19 articles, the United Kingdom with 13 articles, Brazil, Germanny, and Spain with 10 articles, Australia and Italy with 7 articles, China with 6 articles, India with 5 articles, and finally Canada with 4 articles relevant to the research topic of Digital Communication Public Policy.

Figure 4. Publication trends by country or territory

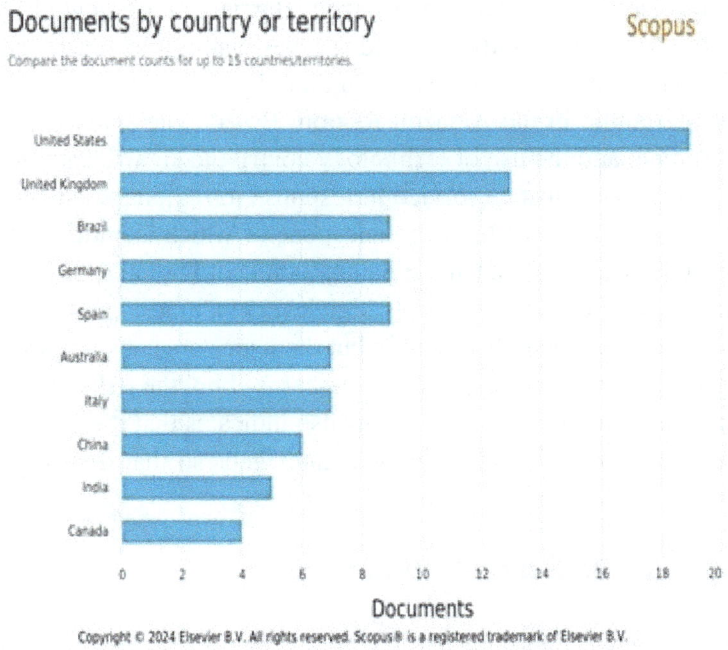

Source: Scopus Analysis Data

The first in the United States is a scientific paper entitled "Impact, Utilization and Applications of Digital Media for Government in Rural Settings. A Comparative US-Romania Research" **by** Vlad et al. First, the study seeks to examine how mature rural institutions in the U.S. and Romania are in using digital media as a communication and information channel between governments and their citizens. Then it is supplemented by a comparative study on rural government communication strategies to assess the extent to which the use of digital media and other media in the context of effectiveness. Then a relevant article published in the United Kingdom is the work of Onyango & Ondiek, (2023) entitled "Digitalising Analogue Policy Targets! 'Digital Capabilities' of Older Persons and Policy Digitalisation of Social Safety Net Programs in a Developing Country Context". It initially highlighted the innovation-related digitization policy that has been expanding rapidly in most policy sectors. The exhibition of this writing is then directed to focus on the issue of the digital capabilities and abilities of the elderly in Kenya that affect the availability of technology and implementation of use. Especially in the implementation of digital policy through health and e-payment platforms.

Further in the State of Brazil there is a relevant article entitled "Digital Access to Judicial Services in the Brazilian Amazon: Barriers and Potential" by writers Moraes et al., (2024). The study is aimed at investigating the advantages of technology, information, and communication in digital governance in access to justice services for the public in the Amazon Region, Brazil. The study concludes that digital government and the use of technology contribute significantly to simplifying public access to the justice service in response to regional adjustments. Then there is Germany with nine relevant articles, one of which is entitled "ICT-Based Environmental Participation in China: Same, Same but Digital?" by Bondes et al., (2024). This article tries to show a fairly high level of Chinese public participation in digital-based environmental protection but there are some obstacles such as confidence in government agencies as well as concerns about the risks of taking action online. In addition, the study in the writing also indicates that there are limitations of ICT in the context of its use which generates gaps so that it is imperative for advanced policy relevant to the issue.

Trend Mapping Based on Subject Area

Referring to Figure 4 with the display of data documents by subject are as the result of the processing of scientific article documents through Scopus, obtained data subject area with each amount of a percentage of at least a scientific article with the choice of the subjects. Starting with social sciences at 27.7%, medicine at 16.3%, other at 12.0%, computer science at 10.2%, environmental at 9.6%, engineering at 5.4%, business and management at 4.8%, arts and humanism at 4.2%, economics at 4.2, energy at 3.0%, and finally multidisciplinary at 2.4%. It seems that Social Science is the most comprehensible subject in the topic of Digital Communication Public Policy, the social field is very often used in previous research studies. The study and extensive scope of the social sphere is misleading the cause of the dominance of the subject. Not to mention, policy communication is really focused on suppressing all kinds of misunderstandings about decision-making and policy implementation processes. The study of social sciences is said to be very broad because it covers a wide range of forms and patterns of interaction carried out by individuals, groups, and societies.

Figure 5. Publication trends by subject area

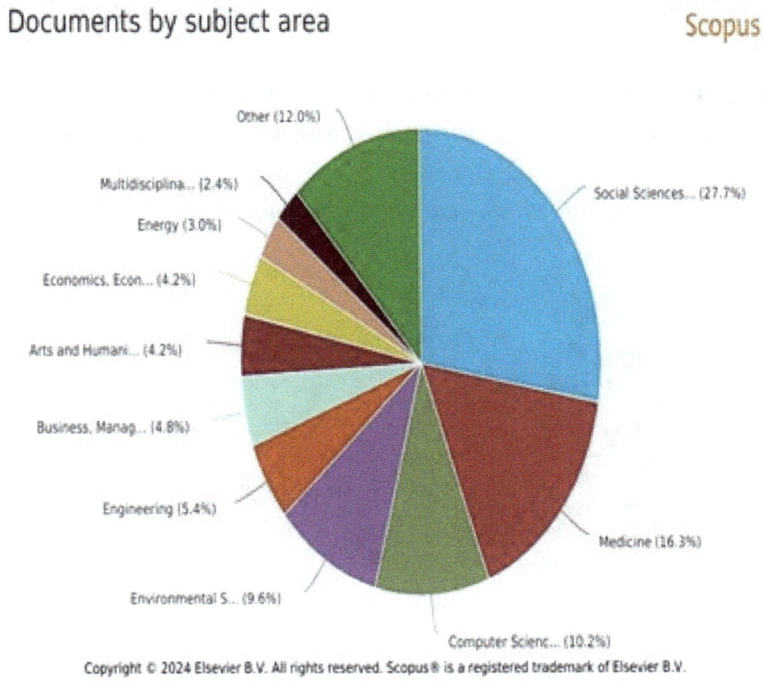

Source: Scopus Analysis Data

As for scientific articles that are relevant to the subject of social science, on of then is entitled "The Role of Public Administration and Social Media Educational Socialization in Influencing Public Satisfaction on Population Service: the Mediating role of Population Literacy Awareness" is an article by Junaidi et al., (2024). The article examines the relationship between public administration, socialization of education in social media, population literacy awareness, and public satisfaction in the context of population service. Then an article on computer science as one of the digital potential was written by Kong & Liu, (2023) entitled "The Relationship between ICT Use and Perceived Life Satisfaction among Older People in Korea: The Mediating Effect of Social Capital". The study focuses on the impact of ICT use on the life satisfaction of elderly people during pandemics, and examines the role of social capital mediation. Furthermore, this article implies to formulate public policy, facilitating an understanding of the consequences of the use of digital information among older people, which not only complements previous studies but also provides a theoretical basis for systematic research on digital literacy and the well-being of older people. The last example is the subject of the Other article with one of the relevant articles entitled "Open Science and Policy Interface: The Tanzania Perspective" by Muneja, (2023). The article examines the policy interface and framework that supports the practice of open science in Tanzania in research efforts.

Trend Mapping Based On Vosviewer Networking Visualization Related To Previous Research Keywords

Figure 6. Networking visualization realted to previous research keywords

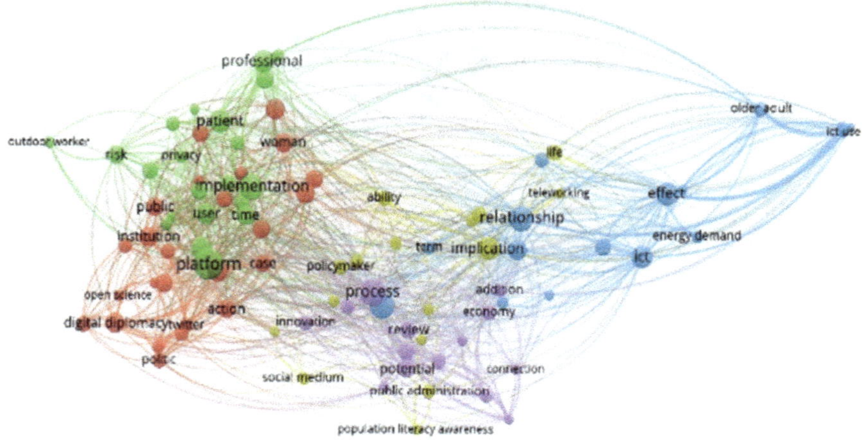

Source: VOSviewer Review Result

Referring to the visualization of the above image then each circle represents the keyword that has been taken from each article title and also abstract. The colour of the cluster indicates the existence of a relationship and the smallness of the number of publications shown in circles. The more articles that are relevant to the keyword, the larger the circle size. From the visualization results like the picture above, there are 5 clusters consisting of 94 articles. Each of these clusters is presented in different colors to see the outstanding and more dominant concepts or topics in each cluster. Or it can be understood that every cluster has a different colour and is used to see a list of concepts that are outstanding or dominant in each of the cluster. This data can of course be used as a reference for further research through the identification of topics that have been discussed in previous research. Cluster 1 is blue on the left, cluster 2 is purple on the bottom, claster 3 is yellow on the middle, clister 4 is green on the top, and cluster 5 is red on the right. The keyword on the sticker type can be seen more detailedly in the table below.

Table 1. VOSviewer network visualization data realted to previous research keywords

Cluster	Concept Name	Total
Cluster 1	ICT use, older adult, effect, energy demand, ICT, relationship, term	7
Cluster 2	addition, economy, connection, review, potential, process, innovation	7
Cluster 3	life, teleworking, implication, ability, public administration, social medium, policy maker	7
Cluster 4	professional, patient, privacy, implementation, user, time, platform, outdoor worker	9
Cluster 5	woman, public, institution, case, action, open science, digital, diplomacy, twitter, politic	10

Source: Researcher Prpcessed Data

In cluster 1, there are seven concepts that relate to ICT and ICT use. It is relevant to one of the scientific articles entitled "ICT-Based Environmental Participation in China: Same, Same but Digital?" written by Bondes et al., (2024). The article shows that the level of participation of Chinese citizens in digital-based environmental protection is quite high but generates a gaps in usage. So it's imperative that we have an advanced policy that is relevant to the issue. Then a scientific article related to the effect or impact in cluster 1 is entitled "Tech companies and the public interest: the role of the state in governing social media platforms" which is the result of research by Stockmann, (2023). The article highlights the usefulness of digital technology which is expected to have a positive impact on the maintenance of government and also the democracy of the country. In order to cope with the negative impact, it is necessary to make the latest contribution between the actors involved in the formulation of the Platform Regulatory Policy

Achilan article entitled "Auditing Accessibility of Pavements and Points of Interest in Urban Areas: The 'Seek & Go' Tool †". The study, written by Achillas et al., (2023) focused on the latest digital tool innovation called "Seek and Go" designed specifically for people with disabilities. The outcome is expected to be a state-of-the-art alternative for disabled people as well as a new recommendation for the government to formulate its future policy strategy. Referring to cluster three, it's known there are nine keywords, one of them is public administration. The term is relevant to one of the scientific papers written by Junaidi et al., (2024) entitled "The Role of Public Administration and Social Media Educational Socialization in Influencing Public Satisfaction on Population Services: The Mediating Rule of Population Literacy Awareness". The article highlights a relationship between public administration, socialization of education in social media, population literacy awareness, and public satisfaction in the context of population services.

There is a scientific article relevant to cluster 4 through the use of the word implementation entitled "EU Digital Communication Strategy During the Covid-19 Vaccination Campaign: Framing, Contents and Attributed Roles at Stake" written by Alcarria & Navarro, (2023). The study highlights the protection efforts undertaken by the government during the COVID-19 period, including through digital-based policy communication strategies in the vaccine campaign process. Then referring to the 5th cluster, there's the keyword one of them is open science. There is an article relevant to the context entitled "Open Science and Policy Interface: The Tanzania Perspective" by Muneja, (2023).The article examines the policy interface and framework that supports the practice of open science in Tanzania in research efforts.

Trend Mapping Based On Density Visualization

On the result of the data using the Vosviewer application, the topic density or the dominant topic data of the entire article has been obtained through the Scopus Database as described at the beginning. This data is very important in order to contain topics or issues that are very often researched related to Digital Transformation Public Policy. Before conducting research it is important to understand the topic taken and also the instructions related to the topic. It can be seen in Figure 6 in the context of the main language then previous research with the theme of Digital Communication Public Policy "there are some words that dominate found among them (1) Implementation, (2) Platform, (3) Process. Other topics such as (4) process, (5) patient, (6) professional, and also (7) Relationship does seem a little concentrated but not as close as the previous 3 topics that conclude that the topic is studied but is not as often as the main topic before. It can be seen that the dominance of the words above is seen from the concentration of the color. The more concentrated the yellow colour is on a particular topic, the more dominant it is. Three keywords found indicate a topic of discourse that was frequently used in previous research. The words are linked in such a way that they are relevant to the discussion of digital public policy communications.

Figure 7. Trend mapping based on density visualization

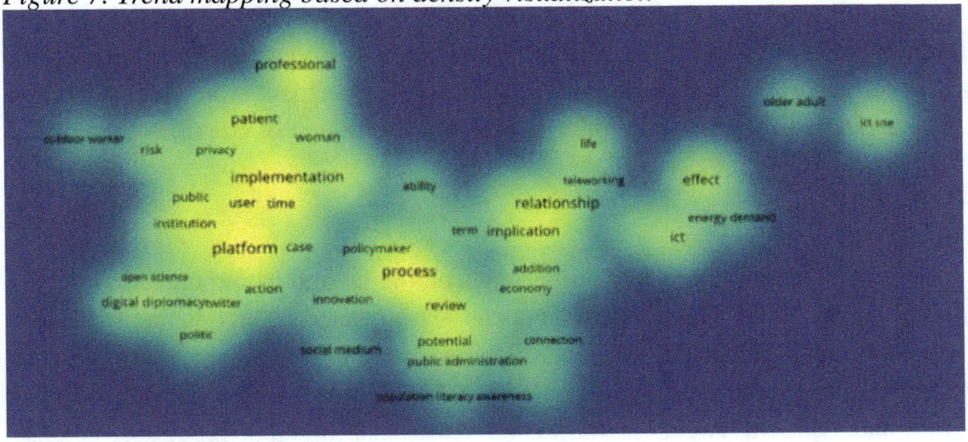

Source: VOSviewer Review Result

Referring to the image, it can be identified that public policy communication is indeed a trend study discussed from a variety of perspectives. It is triggered by several factors such as:

1. Digital base can be a reinforcer in the public policy communication strategy as one of the instruments supporting the implementation of policy
2. Policy communication is more important than just the socialization of policy
3. Policy communication can be the way 'clicktivism' in facilitating public rejection of a policy
4. Dynamization of public policy strategy based on the penetration of the Internet and ICT development
5. A public communication plan must be able to satisfy the needs of the public, gauge public reaction, create a favorable impression of the organization, give updates on what has been, is, and will be done, and benefit the community (Dong et al., 2023).

Referring to this context, an analytical study can be done among others in the work relevant to the dominant word Implementation (1) entitled "EU Digital Communication Strategy During the Covid-19 Vaccination Campaign: Framing, Contents and Attributed Roles at Stake" written by Alcarria & Navarro, (2023). The scientific paper is largely focused on the implementation of a digital-based Covid-19 vaccination policy communication in the EU based on the highest strategy carried out. In Then there is a written work relevant to the word Platform (2) in the scientific article entitled "The Platformation and Transformation of the Digital Public Sphere: An Introduction" by Xie, (2024) which discusses the development and integration of social media platforms in the political field. Next article relevant to the dominant word Process (3) is entitled "Digital Access to Judicial Services in the Brazilian Amazon: Barriers and Potential" a work written by Moraes et al., (2024) which in essence focuses on the process of implementation of digital-based civil justice policy for communities in the Amozon region of Brazil.

Discussion

This research produced mapping studies on the Digital Communication Public Policy theme which has gone through the review stage by Scopus and also the Vosviewer application. The result was 94 previous articles that were relevant to the topic. This can be proven by example in 2023 through research entitled "Digital News and Political Tweets in the Lower Austrian Municipal Elections: A Case Study on Digital Journalism and Political Communication" by Lampoltshammer et al., (2023) which relates to The use of digital systems as a transformation towards digital governance, one of which is in public policy communication. It is true that this study comprehensively identifies interactions between news organizations, politicians and the general public, especially during the Austrian elections. Then in 2024 an article by Xie, (2024) entitled "The Platformation and Transformation of the Digital Public Sphere: An Introduction". attempted to introduce the complex landscape of social media and also the development of its integration in both the social and political worlds. This is considered relevant to the new public policy communication strategy using digital media due to the emergence of new platforms in the communication system

Furthermore, the results of the author's data-based study and analysis show the author's productivity and activeness in publishing. Likewise, the results of studies and data analysis based on regions or countries have identified previous scientific articles with productive authors as well as the order of countries that have published the most on related topics. Referring to author-based data, the work entitled "Auditing Accessibility of Pavements and Points of Interest in Urban Areas: The 'Seek & Go' Tool †" written by Achillas et al. (2023) conducted a study on the latest digital tool, namely 'Seek and Go', which is specifically designed for people with disabilities. This presentation tries to show attention to the disabled side that they as special creatures also need the offer of digital tools and facilities that can make life easier. Furthermore, based on country data, United Stade succeeded in occupying the top position of the country most productive in publishing based on related topics. The work of Tudor Vlad et al. (2023) entitled "Impact, Utilization and Applications of Digital Media for Government in Rural Settings. A Comparative US-Romania Research" seeks to convey the digital maturity of rural institutions in the US and Romania. Digital maturity itself can be seen through the use of digital media as a means of communication between the government and its citizens, the use of digital media in administering government, as well as providing public services, especially in the context of effectiveness and efficiency.

Previous literature studies, for example, as mentioned above, used studies in the social field, namely in life, interactions and dynamics of community life. The results of subject-based analysis of course show that the field of social sciences is the subject of choice for most research. This field is discussed very often considering that social science itself is a broad and very deep study. The article entitled "The Relationship between ICT Use and Perceived Life Satisfaction among Older People in Korea: The Mediating Effect of Social Capital" written by Kong & Liu, (2023) shows that there is life satisfaction among the elderly during the pandemic. The results of the analysis study further explain the clustering of issues and also the grouping of data based on dominant topics in articles relevant to the topic of Digital Communication Public Policy. In the context of the Networking Visualization Related to Previous Research Keywords data, it shows 5 clusters from the 94 articles identified. The image visualization presented shows that each cluster has a different color and is used to see a list of concepts that stand out or are more dominant in each cluster. The article entitled "The Role of Public Administration and Social Media Educational Socialization in Influencing Public Satisfaction on Population Services: The Mediating Role of Population Literacy Awareness" by researchers Junaidi et al., (2024) is included in cluster 3 where the emphasis is on the relationship between administration public, educational outreach on social media, population literacy awareness, and public satisfaction in the context of population services. Bearing in mind that implementing digital facilities requires a lot of synergy and also contributions from various parties because administering government and providing access to services cannot be done personally.

Each keyword had a purpose that matched the color's thickness, according to the density-based analysis's findings, suggesting that it was the most commonly used keyword in earlier research. The subject is one that has bold or deep colors. Data based on Density Visualization shows several dominant words found, namely (1) Implementation, (2) Platform, (3) Process. Previous research entitled "Digital Access to Judicial Services in the Brazilian Amazon: Barriers and Potential" by Moraes et al., (2024) represents the dominant word, namely 'Process'. This research study highlights a process of implementing digital-based justice policies for communities in the Amozon region, Brazil. This is motivated by the condition of the people who live around the Amazon River and are quite far from the justice table. The concept of digital-based justice policy is a solution and alternative to extending the government's hand in fulfilling public service.

CONCLUSION

In conclusion, this research aims to examine trend of scientific publications on the topic of digital communication in public policy identified based on the Scopus Database and VOSViewer application. These data include trends based on year, author, country, subject, topic classification, and dominant topic trend data. Referring to annual trend data with a period of one year, 85 scientific articles were produced in 2023 and 10 scientific articles in 2024 when the research was conducted. Meanwhile, trend data by author shows that the top 10 authors were identified as each having 1 scientific article in the Scopus Database related to the topic. Then referring to trend data based on country of origin, the United States ranks first with a total of 19 articles published on Scopus for 1 year. In addition, there is also data based on trends in the field of study, which shows Social Sciences as the largest field of study in publications on digital communication in a public policy. The percentage of the number of Social Sciences even reached 27.7%, in contrast to the number of the last subject, multi-disciplinary, which was only 2.4%. Next there is trend data based on clusters, showing that there are 5 clusters with several keywords that have a large number of publications. Finally, through the Density visual data, there are several dominating words found including (1) Implementation, (2) Platform, (3) Process, (4) Relationship. The density of color in the visual data in these 4 keywords shows that this topic has often been studied in previous research.

This paper can make a real contribution to the development of further research that is relevant to the topic raised. The results of the analysis on 94 Scopus indexed scientific papers have provided an overview of publication trends for 2023 to 2024 which shows trend data based on year, author, country, and also the field of study raised. The use of the Vosviewer Application also produces additional data that shows publication trends based on related topics through cluster division and also trends in topics that are dominantly published by researchers in various countries during that period. However, this research is still limited because the scientific articles analyzed are still sourced from the Scopus database only. Not to mention the time period chosen in this paper is only focused on related articles published in 2023-2024. Restrictions on the use of English-language articles were also made in this study.

Recommendations that can be given for further research are to strengthen data through the use of scientific articles sourced from other international databases such as Web of Science and Dimensionds Scholars. The time period can also be extended to the last 5 years. Given that this research only uses articles published in 2023 and 2024. So further research needs to expand the time span and also articles that are multilingual so that the data obtained is also stronger. Then referring to the data that has been processed and presented through 6 types of trends, it can be concluded that writing articles about digital literacy awareness, old age digital users, open science, policy makers, and abilities associated with the digital communication process in public policy can be done in the future. Given that these topics are still rarely raised by researchers from various countries in recent years. More varied research contexts will certainly support the results of new research that is more contributive. For example, those related to digital literacy awareness among the public. This research contribute to help the process of making and developing policies in the future

REFERENCES

Achillas, C., Aidonis, D., Tsolakis, N., Tsampoulatidis, I., Mourouzis, A., Bialas, C., & Koritsoglou, K. (2023). Auditing Accessibility of Pavements and Points of Interest in Urban Areas: The 'Seek & Go' Tool †. *Signals*, *4*(3), 604–616. DOI: 10.3390/signals4030032

Aditya, T., Ningrum, S., Nurasa, H., & Irawati, I. (2023). Community needs for the digital divide on the smart city policy. *Heliyon*, *9*(8). Advance online publication. DOI: 10.1016/j.heliyon.2023.e18932

Albuainain, M. A. (2022). How digital communication provides better government services: Assessing the Tawasul System in Bahrain. *Cities (London, England)*, *128*, 103790. DOI: 10.1016/j.cities.2022.103790

Alcarria, F. J., & Navarro, J. T. (2023). EU digital communication strategy during the COVID-19 vaccination campaign: Framing, contents and attributed roles at stake. *Communicatio Socialis*, *36*(3), 153–174. DOI: 10.15581/003.36.3.153-174

Bondes, M., Kostka, G., & Rabe, W. (2024). ICT-based environmental participation in China: Same, same but digital? *Environmental Science & Policy*, *154*, 103688. DOI: 10.1016/j.envsci.2024.103688

Dai, Y., Cheng, X., & Liu, Y. (2023). Information Alienation and Circle Fracture: Policy Communication and Opinion-Generating Networks on Social Media in China from the Perspective of COVID-19 Policy. *Systems*, *11*(7), 340. Advance online publication. DOI: 10.3390/systems11070340

Dong, C., Zheng, Q., & Morehouse, J. (2023). What do we know about government public relations (GPR)? A systematic review of GPR in public relations literature. *Public Relations Review*, *49*(1), 102284. DOI: 10.1016/j.pubrev.2022.102284

Hossin, M. A., Du, J., Mu, L., & Asante, I. O. (2023). Big Data-Driven Public Policy Decisions: Transformation Toward Smart Governance. *SAGE Open*, *13*(4), 1–19. DOI: 10.1177/21582440231215123

Junaidi, A., Basrowi, B., Sabtohadi, J., Wibowo, A. M., Wibowo, S. S., Asgar, A., Pramono, E. P., & Yenti, E. (2024). The role of public administration and social media educational socialization in influencing public satisfaction on population services: The mediating role of population literacy awareness. *International Journal of Data and Network Science*, *8*(1), 345–356. DOI: 10.5267/j.ijdns.2023.9.019

Kong, H., & Liu, H. (2023). The Relationship between ICT Use and Perceived Life Satisfaction among Older People in Korea: The Mediating Effect of Social Capital. *Sustainability (Basel), 15*(12), 9353. Advance online publication. DOI: 10.3390/su15129353

König, P. D. (2021). A magic bullet in policy communication? On the ambiguous use of framing in policy research. *Policy Studies, 42*(1), 60–79. DOI: 10.1080/01442872.2019.1581153

Lampoltshammer, T. J., De Luca, G., & Thurnay, L. (2023). Digital News and Political Tweets in the Lower Austrian Municipal Elections: A Case Study on Digital Journalism and Political Communication. *Social Sciences (Basel, Switzerland), 12*(1), 18. Advance online publication. DOI: 10.3390/socsci12010018

Mu, R., & Wang, H. (2022). A systematic literature review of open innovation in the public sector: Comparing barriers and governance strategies of digital and non-digital open innovation. *Public Management Review, 24*(4), 489–511. DOI: 10.1080/14719037.2020.1838787

Muneja, P. (2023). Open Science and Policy Interface: The Tanzania Perspective. *East African Journal of Science, Technology and Innovation, 4*(Special Issue 2). DOI: 10.37425/eajsti.v4i3.771

Onyango, G., & Ondiek, J. O. (2023). Digitalising analogue policy targets! 'Digital capabilities' of older persons and policy digitalisation of social safety net programs in a developing country context. *Journal of Technology in Human Services, 41*(4), 348–375. DOI: 10.1080/15228835.2023.2263494

Pickard, V. (2023). Another Media System is Possible: Ripping Open the Overton Window, from Platforms to Public Broadcasting. *Javnost (Ljubljana), 30*(2), 284–297. DOI: 10.1080/13183222.2023.2201804

Rethlesfsen, M., Kirtley, S., Waffenschmidt, S., Ayala, A., Moher, D., Page, M., Jonathan, K., & Group, P.-S. (2021). *PRISMA-S: an extension to the PRISMA Statement for Reporting Literature Searches in Systematic Reviews.*

Roziqin, A., Kamil, M., Romadhan, A. A., & Zakaria, I. (2024). The dark side of local public sector innovation: insights from SAMPADE innovation. *Journal of Science and Technology Policy Management*. DOI: 10.1108/JSTPM-01-2024-0001

Roziqin, A., Mas'udi, S. Y. F., & Sihidi, I. T. (2021). An analysis of Indonesian government policies against COVID-19. *Public Administration and Policy, 24*(1), 92–107. DOI: 10.1108/PAP-08-2020-0039

Saefudin, Y., Ismail, N., Susanti, R., & Adi, L. K. (2023). Regulating Fake News and Hoaxes: A Comparative Analysis of Indonesia and Malaysia. *Journal of Human Rights. Culture and Legal System*, *3*(3), 656–677. DOI: 10.53955/jhcls.v3i3.113

Stockmann, D. (2023). Tech companies and the public interest: The role of the state in governing social media platforms. *Information Communication and Society*, *26*(1), 1–15. DOI: 10.1080/1369118X.2022.2032796

Vega-Ramírez, J., Castro-Duarte, P., & Quintana-Figueroa, C. (2023). Communication of Results of Educational Policies: Impact Levels of Educational Policies in the Digital Society. *Societies (Basel, Switzerland)*, *13*(2), 34. Advance online publication. DOI: 10.3390/soc13020034

Vlad, T., Hin ea, C., Neam u, B., & Stănică, V. (2023). Impact, Utilization and Applications of Digital Media for Government in Rural Settings. A Comparative US-Romania Research. *Transylvanian Review of Administrative Sciences*, *2023*(70), 128–155. DOI: 10.24193/tras.70E.7

Wahyudin, Y., & Rahayu, D. N. (2020). Analisis Metode Pengembangan Sistem Informasi Berbasis Website: A Literatur Review. *Jurnal Interkom: Jurnal Publikasi Ilmiah Bidang Teknologi Informasi Dan Komunikasi*, *15*(3), 26–40. DOI: 10.35969/interkom.v15i3.74

Xie, M. (2024). *The platformation and transformation of the digital public sphere: An introduction*. Communication and the Public., DOI: 10.1177/20570473241228627

Chapter 11

Collective Capabilities and Local Democratic Governance to Transform Public Education: A Case Study on The Brazilian State of Ceará

Pınar Çuhadar
https://orcid.org/0000-0001-6302-7735
Mardin Artuklu Üniversitesi, Artuklu, Turkey

ABSTRACT

Amartya Sen's Capability Approach (CA) provides an alternative understanding of development, welfare, and democracy. Amartya Sen focuses on the non-material roots of welfare, such as agency freedom, and the material roots of economic development. However, his approach's liberal roots, which put individuals at the center of analysis, have been criticized in various aspects. The literature on collective capabilities provides arguments for filling these criticized gaps in the CA. This study aims to discuss the role of social movements in transforming the power relations created by the neoliberal economic and political system, along with its relationship between education and deliberative democracy through collective capabilities, using the solid example of the Brazilian state of Ceará. By examining Ceará, it is expected to see how collective capabilities can transform public education into a more inclusive direction in the long term.

DOI: 10.4018/979-8-3373-5576-4.ch011

INTRODUCTION

The global education crisis is one of the essential subject areas discussed by the international development agenda. Three hundred million students do not have a sufficient level of basic numeracy and literacy skills necessary for further levels of education. Moreover, 84 million children and young people will leave school by 2030 (Imchen & Ndem, 2020). Discussions on access to and quality of education,[1] subjects such as appropriate skills development, gender equality, better school infrastructure, equipment, educational materials and resources, scholarships, or teaching practices should be questioned, along with how resources are distributed among different income groups (Imchen & Ndem, 2020). Children living in poverty in urban and rural areas with various ethnic and religious affiliations, exposed to gender discrimination, are excluded from the education system, which is an urgent problem for national and international development agendas (Imchen & Ndem, 2020). Therefore, access to quality education is not only an economic but also a political discussion topic with its mutual relation with social justice, development, and poverty alleviation, as well as the production system and the unequal power relations created by the international division of labor (Tikly, 2017).

Amartya Sen's pioneering work, 'Development as Freedom,' considerably impacts the rethinking of social and economic development. His ideas also substantially impacted the Millennium Development Goals and Sustainable Development Goals, which place education at the center of fighting poverty and development (Stewart, 2019). Along with education and social policy, democratic participation and negotiations also have a prominent place in the Capability Approach (CA) for removing barriers to freedom and improving quality of life beyond the mere aspect of improving the productivity of labor and human capital (Kjeldsen & Bowin, 2012; Sen, 1999). However, the liberal tradition and individualistic roots of CA, which lead to an incomplete understanding of social ties and collective action, are also questioned for their role in formalizing democratic institutions for deliberative democracies (Gasper, 2023; Feldman & Gellert, 2006; İbrahim, 2006; Rosignoli, 2018; Tully, 2013).

This study aims to discuss the role of social movements as collective action in democratic local governance for transforming the power relations created by the neoliberal economic and political system (Tarlau, 2014) and their relationship with education and deliberative democracy through collective capabilities (Olssen et al., 2004) using the experience of the Brazilian state of Ceará. Latin America, where education is central to political debates and strong social movements (O'Cadiz et al., 1998), and the Brazilian State of Ceará (Tarlau, 2014) will offer an essential contribution in analyzing the reflections of theoretical debates in practice.

Ceará, as a Northeastern state, which is one of the least developed parts of Brazil, had the lowest success in national assessments in primary education indicators until 2007. However, in recent years, the state ranked third in early elementary school and first in late elementary school in Brazil's basic education index (Brazilian Report, 2023). The assessments in Brazil also measure the levels of equal opportunities provided by the local governments and the state. The Brazilian Education Opportunities Index (*Índice de Oportunidades da Educação Brasileira-IOEB*) compares regions' achievements supporting Brazilian education inclusivity. Based on IOEB results, Ceará's scores have improved in the last ten years. While the Brazilian average IOEB score is 5.2, Ceará's score has reached 5.5. for 2023 (IOEB, 2024). Oliveira, Justo, and De Lucena (2024) also mention that Ceará was second after San Paulo in inclusive and quality education. Although Ceará has been the subject of many reports, dissertations, and articles as an example of best practices for remedying learning poverty, efficient allocation of resources, transparency, accountability, education governance, and political capacity (UNESCO, 2017; Loureiro et al., 2020; Yan et al., 2022), it has not been discussed in terms of critical theory, CA and collective capabilities.

This study was designed as an explanatory case study to examine the experience of a progressive social movement initiated by poor groups to initiate democratic negotiation and transform the system through education within the framework of collective capabilities. The case study used various reports, scientific articles, documentaries, and doctoral dissertations on Ceará and in-depth interviews with key international experts on Brazil and Latin America's education as data resources. The study also aims to show step by step how democratic governance and social transformation succeed through education and social movements. Glette and Wiig (2022) mention that case studies provide detailed information about complex social phenomena. However, they also say the drawbacks, such as generalizability and bias from the author's interpretation, cause bias (Glette & Wiig, 2022). The primary constraint of this study is the language barrier in Portuguese, so only resources in English can be revised for the case. However, it provides an insight into how essential it is to design context-specific education policies for development.

SEN'S CAPABILITY APPROACH AND EDUCATION

Using Western and non-western deep philosophical heritage, Amartya Sen, with his criticisms of the welfare and social justice concept offered by utilitarianism (Nussbaum, 2020), started economic discussions on the need to see, interpret, and measure development as human development and expanded his perspective on the subject by saying that welfare cannot be limited to only material assets (Sen, 1999).

CA is defined as an approach or theory that gained depth with the contribution of many thinkers, especially Martha Nussbaum (Robeyns, 2017; Nussbaum, 2020). This study focuses on Sen's capability approach for a conceptual framework and public policy evaluation.

Amartya Sen provides an alternative perspective to development as a 'process of expanding real freedoms that people enjoy' (Sen, 1999, p. 3) beyond indicators such as per capita income. According to Sen, development is achieved through free agency, which evaluates its achievements according to its value world and can create change. For people to live the life they want, it requires considering both process freedom, in terms of not restricting their actions, and opportunity freedom, in terms of their ability to make choices (Sen, 1999).

CA presents a perspective on the standard of living and well-being beyond the utilitarian approach, which focuses on commodities, consumption bundle preferences, and maximization behaviors. The key and integrated concepts of capability, functioning, conversion factors, and informational bases for judgment and justice are at the center of the conceptual framework of this approach. (Kjeldsen & Bonvin, 2012). While functioning indicates what has been achieved or has been done, capability refers to having the freedom to live the life you want (Kjeldsen & Bonvin, 2012). The informational base of judgment indicates the role of public reasoning on a person's valuable beings and doings. Sen rejects the rationality-reduced instrumental rationality, which analyzes human behavior as utilitarian interest-seeking ground and defends the constructive role of democracy and public reasoning for collective decisions (Kjeldsen & Bonvin, 2012). He argues that freedoms are more important measures of well-being than rights and functioning. He recommends that the purpose of public policies should focus on creating opportunities for people to live the good life they reason to value (Bonvin & Laruffa, 2018).

Conversion factors explain how personal, social, and environmental factors affect how commodities transform into functions (Robeyns, 2017). When the conversion is associated with education, it considers the differences in access to resources or the transformation of resources into prosperity through education according to class, ethnicity, and gender differences between individuals (Hart, 2012). Agency and freedom can potentially convert a person's value to education and aspirations to reach the life she or he wants. The CA and public debate promote the publicization of information and awareness of the practices and challenges that limit one's aspirations (Unterhalter, 2003).

Besides education, Sen (1999) also included social protection, the role of local peace-building institutions, the importance of removing freedom-limiting conditions of economic, social, and political participation, and civil and political rights. In this regard, Sen (1999) has identified five areas: political freedoms, economic freedoms, social opportunities, transparency, and protective security, which he considers instrumental and which indirectly and directly affect other areas of freedom for the individual to reach the life she or he chooses to live (Sen, 1999).

LITERATURE REVIEW

CA is criticized for contributing to the depoliticization of poverty; however, social movements (as a collective action) are politicizing poverty and need to be examined in poverty analysis (Deveaux, 2021, cited from Kolers, 2023). Collective action aims to change the status of a particular group, not just the participants in the action, and it ranges from demonstrations to individual voting behavior or other organizations that encourage collective action (Van Zomeren & Iyer, 2009). Social movements can be seen as long-term collective actions in which individuals excluded by the political and social structure come together or try to solve social problems in different geographical contexts, from local to global, by working together against inequalities, exclusion, and subordination (Anyon, 2009).

Instead of Sen's CA's individualist perspective, literature on collective capabilities examines the society-individual relationship within the scope of collective action and capabilities (Ibrahim, 2006; Ibrahim, 2017). Robeyns (2017: p.116) defines collective capabilities as 'a group or collective is needed to engage in collective action to reach the capability that the members of that group find valuable'. Although much research has discussed collective action and capabilities (Evans, 2002; İbrahim, 2006; İbrahim, 2017; Murphy, 2014; Rosignoli, 2019; Stewart, 2005), it is accepted that collective capabilities must be improved in capability approach-based studies.

The number of studies that take capability from individuality and expand it to include collective action is rapidly increasing. By examining self-help initiatives, İbrahim (2006) explains three pillars of extending collective capabilities: economic endowments and assets of people experiencing poverty, individual capabilities covering functioning sets, and social capital supporting mutual trust and solidarity. She defends that collective action achieved through coordination among formal and informal institutions is also necessary for enabling low-income people to realize their well-being achievement and well-being freedom. However, the role of collective capabilities in institutional transformation in a neoliberal state is not questioned. İbrahim (2017) provides a much deeper understanding by improving a model formed for understanding the grassroots of social innovations by reframing and reconceptualizing the process to understand how context impacts social innovations. İbrahim (2017) argues that social innovations can be successful, scalable, and sustainable when they promote individual-level positive behavioral change, support collective agency for the community, and encourage reforms at the institutional level based on her conceptual framework in which she explains conscientization, conciliation, collaboration (3C) model (İbrahim, 2017).

Evans (2002) mentions that growth strategies require a strong democratic understanding and functioning in that people determine economic priorities rather than a weak sense of democracy, such as a democracy reduced merely to elections. Despite Sen's insistence on individualism, building the life people reason to value requires collective action. It needs to be questioned how culture and economic power relations restrict capabilities (Evans, 2002). Although Sen firmly accepts individualism, Evans (2002) argues that realizing the reason to value the capabilities he deals with requires more than individual efforts, so he posits that capability expansion is beyond individuals' challenge and needs collective action (Evans, 2002). Stewart (2005) also defends that social structures construct group identities and that people form group identities to provide political power and authority and preserve economic resources. According to her, while Nussbaum's terminology gives way to the explanation of group behaviors, Sen's CA needs to examine collective action more explicitly.

Murphy (2014) examines collective capability linked to indigenous people's self-determination. He mentions the importance of well-organized collective action for colonized political communities like Indigenous people to shape laws and rights that directly impact their future. Murphy (2014) argues that CA mainly focuses on the role of political participation in individual self-determination, which causes a very restricted understanding of the political environment of disadvantaged groups. Deveaux (2021), on the other hand, by expanding the concept of collective capability as political collective capability, has put forward a conceptualization separate from the mainstream individualist capabilities approach and the mainstream collective capability approach (cited from Kolers, 2023). This approach deems poverty as a problem of the political system and the relationship between the people living in poor conditions and those living in good conditions. It attributes value to social movements because they allow the politicized poor to transform the system (cited from Kolers, 2023).

These arguments aim to extend the CA perspective to collective action. However, conceptually, they do not seek to deepen the discussion on education, deliberative democracy, and social movements and their role in development and capability expansion. This study aims to fill this research gap.

CRITIQUES OF THE CAPABILITY APPROACH: DEMOCRACY, DELIBERATION, POWER, AND NEOLIBERALISM

Neoliberalism is seen as an economic system and the final stage of international corporations' efforts to establish and redesign relations within all social institutions with market values by infiltrating the state's political power, and public education is no exception to the neoliberal transformation process (Brown, 2003; Harvey, 2015; Glassman & Patton, 2015). However, these power relations and inequalities also present a dilemma with an expectation from education, which also argues itself to be the cement of a robust civil society required by a democratic system (Olssen, Codd & O'Neil 2004).

Considering these areas of freedom, in Amartya Sen's CA, democracy is also seen as essential in terms of making the voices of disadvantaged groups heard and determining the policies to be set to improve their welfare levels, as well as not suppressing and recognizing their voices (Bonvin & Laruffa, 2018). In this respect, democracy has both instrumental and intrinsic value in CA. Its instrumental value comes from both the informational basis, that is, it allows politicians to be pressured to identify the problems that are the source of poverty and to produce solutions, and it contributes to the creation of collective consciousness (Bonvin & Laruffa, 2018). According to Bonvin & Laruffa (2018), Sen's understanding of democracy overlaps with deliberative rather than liberal representative democracy.

Deliberative democracy is a theory of normative democracy developed by the German thinker Habermas that provides criteria for assessing the legitimacy of liberal democracy. The achievements of democracy and its rational results depend on the egalitarian communication established to allow the information to flow from the periphery to the center to hear the voice of the surrounding civil society (Biebricher, 2007). In this sense, systems that make room for discussion and negotiation in the public sphere gain legitimacy. In this respect, the goal of negotiation is harmony and consensus rather than systemwide change (Biebricher, 2007). This process should not be understood with isolated individuals but with dialogues aimed at developing solidarity in a mutually interacting community (Susen, 2017). However, deliberative democracy may not be the best solution unconditionally for disadvantaged groups who are pressured into democratic deliberation (Dryzek, 2002). There is also the danger of encouraging oppressive self-control, preserving political hierarchies, and masking unequal participation in democratic deliberation (Dryzek, 2002).

According to Habermas, institutions and procedures in the public sphere are collectively more important than common values (Englund, 2010). His deliberative democracy in education is a pragmatic necessity ensuring modernity's continuity. Thus, educational institutions can be interpreted as the most important institution that facilitates the formation of democratic deliberation. This idea is why qualities like pluralism and tolerance for cultural differences are expected to be instilled in public schools (Englund, 2010). Glassman and Patton (2014) argue that Sen leaves the relationship between democracy and education ambiguous since there is always a danger in improving and protecting democracy in conditions where state administrators limit their sources of information. Sen intuitively makes sense of the impact of sociopolitical conditions on information sources but does not deepen the debate (Glassman & Patton, 2014).

Power, defined as 'a way in which specific actions may structure the field of other possible actions' (Foucault, 1982, p. 791), has ways and methods to disseminate the information it produces throughout every layer of society via social networks, which are the means of creating and disseminating information, and to define freedom and democracy according to its purposes (Foucault, 1978; Foucault, 1982). This idea provides a perspective that explains how neoliberalism, through education and other social policies, designs social institutions according to the market's needs (Cotoi, 2011; Hastings, 2019; Olssen et al., 2004).

Foucault's theoretical and conceptual framework on information bases and the relationship between education and power can deepen the debate on knowledge, education, and democracy in CA at this point (Olssen et al., 2004). Like Sen, Foucault considers individual agency, agency freedom, and well-being agency as having a limited effect on one's circumstances (Tobias, 2005). According to Foucault, power can be defined as power relations, processes, and systems embedded in social relations from the lowest layers to the top of the social structure pyramid, which use different tools and techniques and resist change (Lynch, 2014). These relationships manifest in the 'discourse' in every aspect of daily life, so evaluating the individual in complex power relations is necessary rather than being an independent agent in daily life (Lynch, 2014). Foucault also critically examines political reasoning with his analysis of the strategic state and questions how the state has shaped all the apparatuses, rationality, and mentality in the historical flow. The term "governmentality" is used by Foucault, which explains the state's effect on the management tools it uses in conjunction with the rationality of management (Biebricher, 2007). According to Foucault, power is interrelated in producing and disseminating knowledge. Sovereign power can be represented in schools as one-way, top-down disciplinary power (Felten et al., 2004). This sovereign can transform education and training processes into tools of surveillance, classification, and exclusion (Ball, 2019).

Sen, on the other hand, intuitively made sense of the influence of socio-political conditions on information sources but did not deepen the discussion (Glassman & Patton, 2014). The Brazilian educator and philosopher Paulo Freire provides insight into these arguments. He not only argues that poor, marginalized groups, in particular, can move away from the socioeconomic and sociocultural sources of information they are surrounded by but also supports his argument with practical applications (Glassman & Patton, 2014). For Freire (1998), education is a process of emancipation, and this cultural action should remove people from sociocultural conditioning of thinking. This is because human dependency is the essence of a silent and closed society. Human emancipation and cultural action require dialogue and the separation of science and ideology (Freire, 1998). 'Science and philosophy together provide the principles of action for conscientization. Conscientization refers to the process in which men, not as recipients but as knowing subjects, achieve a deepening awareness both of the sociocultural reality that shapes their lives and of their capacity to transform that reality' (Freire, 1970, p. 452).

Despite coming from different social backgrounds, Freire and Habermas's ideas converge about authoritarian systems and educational policies by emphasizing the neglect of basic human needs as part of the human capital theory of the capitalist educational process (Morrow & Torres, 2002). While Freire focuses on postcolonial and oppressed communities, Habermas aims to foster mutual dialogue with a universal language. Habermas has not established a system as transparent as Freire's critical pedagogy in enabling the marginalized 'others' to establish mutual dialogue and develop moral consciousness and related pedagogy. Thus, Habermas developed a communication theory based on idealized dialogues rather than social realities, central to Freire's theoretical arguments (Morrow & Torres, 2002).

Freire values the role of education in democracy by considering the role of conscious citizens in a democratic society (Torres & Morrow, 1998). He transforms the educational process into mutual dialogues, taking into account the working and marginalized urban poor formed by the urbanization process of Brazil, as well as gender, race, and ethnic differences (Torres & Morrow, 1998). These dialogues aim to transform the social structure shaped by domination and oppression, which is embodied in everyday life and reflected in the unequal social relations between the educator and the educated. For this reason, his critical pedagogy questions the relationship between knowledge and power, while dialogue prefers the use of language (Torres & Morrow, 1998). This perspective offers an alternative viewpoint that differs from neoliberal educational practices and emphasizes collective action, which complements CA education perspectives (Glassman & Patton, 2014).

Table 1. The General Ideas of Sen, Habermas, Foucault, and Freire

	Sen	Habermas	Foucault	Freire
Theoretical Arguments	Capability Approach	Critical Theory	Critical Theory	Critical Pedagogy
Interpretation of freedom	Process and opportunity freedom / Agency freedom	Communicative freedom/ Public sphere	Freedom shaped by power, Critical to state, Negative freedom / Agency freedom	Human emancipation/ Collective agency
Informational Base	Public debate and democracy	Deliberative democracy, Egalitarian communication	Governmentality power's impact on knowledge	Conscientization
Education	Basic capability/ functioning	Necessary for mutual tolerance	Tool of state for governmentality	Tool for transforming society

Resource: Prepared by the author based on a literature review.

Why should we extend arguments about democracy, education, and collective action in CA? This discussion is essential for analyzing how the neoliberal discourse, as Foucault pointed out, has taken deeper root in society through schools and how it reproduces society according to its needs. However, such an analysis will help understand how the historical and institutional conditions of neoliberal discourse and power transformation are formed. Otherwise, the line between neoliberal governance and democratic governance will become invisible in discussions within the field of education.

NEOLIBERALISM, DEMOCRACY, AND EDUCATION

Neoliberalism should be seen as an ideal economic system with market values and an effort to embed these values into the state's political power and relations within all social institutions (Brown, 2003). These arguments also undermine liberalism's claim to transform capitalism through democracy because of the gap between liberal democratic ideals and neoliberal reality. Although liberalism guarantees the individual's economic, political, and social rights with equal opportunity while minimizing the state's role in the economy, neoliberalism is a candidate for dismantling the whole system with its rationality and its cost-benefit calculations made in all social relations (Brown, 2003).

The role of democracy in the discourse of neoliberal governance should also be scrutinized. The concept of governance can be limited by a public administration understanding that applies the neoliberal market and efficiency-focused modernist-rationalist-economist perspective to the state-citizen relationship, often used interchangeably with democratic governance practices in a broad sense (Bevir, 2014). At its core, democratic governance is a concept that prioritizes partnerships and networks, sees the inclusivity and fairness of institutions as the primary source of their legitimacy, and defines accountable policymaking processes as essential conditions alongside civil society and media freedom, with active oversight of other stakeholders (Bevir, 2014).

The devastation caused by strict pro-market policies implemented in many developing countries in the 1980s and 90s is the fundamental reason for the evolution into a period where political institutions and actors are re-empowered, and searches in the realm of democracy arise (Peters & Pierre, 2006). CA is not indifferent to the search for a new definition of citizenship, as it explains people's welfare through their capabilities, meaning their freedoms. However, the individualism in Amartya Sen's CA may fall short of understanding the definition of citizenship as a product of historical processes and social interaction (Pfister, 2012). This situation also complicates understanding power relations' effects on agency, choices, and environment if political economy is excluded from the picture (Pfister, 2012).

These practices have also spread the view that social movements can be a means of social transformation without the state and that civil society, as a symbol of democracy and participation, can represent a stateless solution for social policies in all areas (Boden, 2011). This perspective ensures that many social movements have a limited impact on local development and their regions and that neoliberalism continues to exist without undergoing any transformation through collective action (Boden, 2011). As Harvey (2015) emphasizes, neoliberal expansionism, which supports freedoms with arguments of economic entrepreneurship and individual freedoms, also creates tension between old social movements that adopt class struggle as a principle and individualist, consumerist, or identity-based social movements, making it difficult for them to unite to rebuild the sense of social justice distorted by neoliberalism.

The neoliberal discourse and the view that the poverty of the entrepreneur and the individual is the cause of their poverty has created a delusion in the working class that individual effort can improve their living conditions (Accioly, 2020). This individualism is an obstacle to social transformation. The standardized school curriculum prioritizes individuality and competition in adapting students to the labor market; meanwhile, essential attitudes such as anger, objection, claim, and questioning are prevented from pursuing social transformation (Accioly, 2020).

Political relations, which are considered like market relations, reduce democracy to voting and underestimate the potential of collective behavior to create change and deliberation (Mintrom, 2001). The market-based perspective sees education as human capital and views it as a skill that prepares a person for competitive market exchanges (Mintrom, 2001). This is a process in which social movements must initiate the change of the capitalist state, and this process requires people to redefine themselves within a collective logic and to support their existing living conditions with solidarity (Tarlau, 2014).

EDUCATION IN BRAZIL AS A MEANS TO MAINTAIN CLASS DISPARITIES

Brazil was a colony of the Portuguese kingdom from the 16th to 19th century. Official schools in Brazil began to spread in the 1500s through the missionary activities of the Christian Catholic Church (Society of Jesus), supporting the influence of Portuguese colonialism in the region (Vidal & de Faria Filho, 2008). These activities aimed to have locals set aside their own cultures to learn and understand the new world presented by the colonizers. However, the indigenous children did not adopt the new culture, while missionaries focused on educating the children of Portuguese white elites (Vidal & de Faria Filho, 2008).

The unequal power relations created by Brazil's economic and political structure have excluded people experiencing poverty from economic wealth and political decision-making processes. Brazil was the last African slave trader to abandon slavery in 1888. In the country, economic and political power is concentrated in the hands of landowners, and the elites in power have prevented the participation of people with low incomes in political life by linking the right to vote with the right to education (Accioly, 2020).

In 1827, legal regulations regarding education were made, expanding the 1824 Constitution in 1834 through the Additional Act, which granted the Provincial Assemblies the authority to regulate primary education at the first and second levels, while the Imperial State was responsible for higher education. However, due to insufficient financial resources in the provinces, adequate funding for primary education was not allocated, although attention was paid to the education of the elites. As a result, throughout the 19th century, Brazilian education was characterized as elitist and exclusive for people with low incomes and enslaved people (Accioly, 2020). The legal arrangements made in 1881 linked the right to vote with income, property, and literacy, arguing that illiterate people would not have the competence to determine the nation's fate. This situation gave only 1.8 percent of the population the right to be educated and participate in politics. The 1891 Constitution also brought about fiscal decentralization, further depriving poor regions of the right to education. When the Republic was declared in 1889, 90% of the population was illiterate. (Vidal & de Faria Filho, 2008; Accioly, 2020).

The educational reforms in Brazil are closely related to slowing migration between rural and urban areas and increasing agricultural productivity with more educated farmers. While the 1934 Constitution reinforced the public role in education, it also legalized allocating at least 10% of the budgets of the Union, States, and Municipalities, mandating a 25% quota for supporting rural education from the Union. However, since the rural modernization efforts targeted only wealthy landowners, this period also opened the door to the land struggles of peasants (Vidal & de Faria Filho, 2008).

Import substitution, introduced after the First World War, was instrumental in Brazil's rapid growth of the urban middle class and working class. The educational needs of this new urban population have been the determinant of the country's education strategy (Accioly, 2020). Although the 1934 Constitution enacted under Getúlio Dornelles Vargas (1930-1945 and 1951-1954) took steps to make education universal, the 1937 Constitution considered basic and vocational education sufficient for people experiencing poverty. The same constitution has put secondary education and its continuation at the service of privileged classes. Conservative right-wing governments have been effective in prioritizing religious education in public schools and monopolizing the right to education in public schools for privileged classes, thereby paving the way for private education (Accioly, 2020).

Despite the enthusiasm of the colonial period to revive the relations of production, nationalist movements grew as the broader masses of people with low incomes joined the emancipation efforts of nationalist intellectuals (Motta & Nilsen, 2011). This has also led to articulating the demand for social justice in anti-colonialist national movements. However, this has also been a period during which a development rhetoric based on economic accumulation and requiring strict state intervention has gained validity (Motta & Nilsen, 2011). It has been observed that the living conditions of the lower-income groups within the coalition formed by landowners, industrialists, the elites in the state bureaucracy, and the middle class have become complex in every way, exacerbated by racial and ethnic discrimination (Motta & Nilsen, 2011).

SEEKING DEMOCRACY AND ITS LINK WITH EDUCATION: THE PERIOD OF COLLECTIVE AGENCY FORMATION IN BRAZIL

In Brazil, the opposing left-wing public education proponents adopted the principle of opening public schools to all segments (Maria del Pilar et al., 1998). In the 1960s, Freire's pedagogy significantly impacted public education in Latin America. During this period, the Movement for Popular Culture gained strength as a movement that embraced Freire's vision of education. This movement took steps to awaken critical consciousness among large sections of the long-oppressed population, such as the enslaved Africans and European-disposed individuals, and to equip them with the knowledge to transform the elite structures in society (Maria del Pilar et al., 1998). This process is a significant turning point in transforming dominant discourse and developing negotiation skills among low-income people. This transformation has occurred through applying critical pedagogy, which can be seen as an extension of critical theory (Gadotti & Torres, 2009).

Freire linked Brazil's lack of democratization to its colonial legacy, incorporating colonialism into his analysis of the exploitation of the country's material and human resources, the role of the elite in maintaining the existing structure, and the silencing of the oppressed low-income people (Gadotti & Torres, 2009). He also argued that liberalism offered an education system that enabled the maintenance of dominant power relations. He suggested that unqualified education also perpetuated the poor and wealthy dependent relationship. The expansion of adult education during the 1950s and the 1960s effectively challenged the existing situation of local elites in the eyes of people with low incomes (Accioly, 2020; Gadotti & Torres, 2009). From this perspective, the primary goal was to foster a collective awareness of the living conditions of low-income people and the economic and political causes of poverty (Maria del Pilar et al.,1998). This process did not limit education to basic literacy skills. People experiencing poverty were also given qualities such as a dignified life and self-confidence through group work. Local community empowerment was at the heart of this movement, and the goal was to create a new governance system along with social movements. Freire is also considered to be the father of the educational policies of the Workers' Party, PT (*Partido dos Trabalhadores*) (Maria del Pilar et al.,1998).

In the 1980s, the PT emerged as a political vehicle for social movements, opening space for the representation of the poor sections and for their demands to be included in politics (Levy, 2012). This laid the foundation for critical pedagogy, incorporating the lives of communities into the curriculum and restructuring the educational bureaucratic functioning by considering participation. It involved a complex process of providing quality education for the working class, transforming people experiencing poverty, changing teacher attitudes, revising curriculum content and instructional strategies, and democratizing regional administrations (Maria del Pilar et al., 1998).

Freire's ideas were implemented when PT won the mayorship in Sao Paulo. During this period, initiatives such as improving teacher salaries, expanding access to education widely, and promoting participatory school management and planning were also included among the goals (Maria del Pilar et al., 1998). The impact of Freire's approach, the influence of leftist movements, and the role of the PT government in Sao Paulo's current education system cannot be denied. The PT became an umbrella under which grassroots movements such as feminist groups and neighborhood associations were gathered, and this diversity impacted the PT's education policy. The PT and Freire made decentralization, autonomy, and participation the fundamental principles of education (Maria del Pilar et al., 1998).

NEOLIBERAL COUNTERATTACK ON BRAZIL'S EDUCATION

In the period between 1980 and 1990 and the subsequent years, the high-interest payments caused by the debt crisis experienced by Brazil led to a preference for reducing social expenditure, including education (Borges, 2008). These cuts increased the income gap between the industrialized South and the impoverished North. During this period, the significant lack of coordination between the central authority and the states and municipalities resulted in the central government losing its power over local education policies, leading to a decline in the quality of education across the country (Borges, 2008). However, during the same period, new political actors emerged in subnational administrations that devised innovative solutions to eliminate educational patronage relations (Borges, 2008).

Before the Federal Constitution of 1988, issues such as weak coordination between states and municipalities, inequality in the distribution of public resources, and differences in institutionalization levels were significant challenges in providing educational services. This constitution left the education of children aged seven to fourteen to the states and municipalities (Segatto & Abrucio, 2018). Before decentralization, expenditures were determined according to the power dynamics between local governments and the central government, affecting the implementation of long-term projects or public borrowing (Zarur, 1993). The financial structure that changed with decentralization necessitated transferring resources from central to local governments. The Municipal Participation Fund (FPM) was created, and the transfer of tax revenues was tied to this fund. The unrestricted resource flow also ensured service delivery continuity (Zarur, 1993).

From the 1990s to the early 2000s, under the presidencies of Fernando Collor de Melo (1990–92), Itamar Franco (1992–03), and Fernando Henrique Cardoso (1995–98 and 1999–2002), neoliberalism also affected the Brazilian education system, with the primary goal of educating people according to the needs of the market (Maria, Carvalho & Mendes, 2011). During this period, several educational reforms were implemented. In 1990, the National System of Evaluation of Basic Schooling (*SAEB - Sistema Nacional de Avaliação da Educação Básica)* introduced a monitoring system to reveal inequalities in education (Yan et al., 2023). The increase in regional income disparities caused the educational achievement gap to widen, which led to the development of mechanisms to regulate the flow of funds between the central government and municipalities. The Fund for the Development of Primary and Lower Secondary Education (FUNDEF) was launched in 1996 as a system that distributed taxes among municipal and state governments based on student enrollment rates (Yan et al., 2023). 2007, this system was included in early childhood education and was renewed as FUNDEB. The constitutional amendment of 1999 extended compulsory education from ages 7-14 to 4-17 (Yan et al., 2023). Federal, state, and municipal governments must allocate a certain proportion of their educational budgets. The law set 25% of tax revenues for state and municipal governments, while the federal government must allocate at least 18% of the public budget (Boekle-Giuffrida, 2013). Furthermore, voluntary contributions encouraged to be used in education are also noteworthy. However, it should also be noted that the relationship between the state and municipalities in Brazil is intertwined with the imperatives created by historical conditions (Boekle-Giuffrida, 2013).

Although Freire's influence was excluded from formal education during this period, informal education channels did not prevent people with low incomes from developing collective consciousness, continuing the organized struggle for their rights, and transforming formal education. This influence is most evident in the Landless Workers Movement (*Movimento dos Trabalhadores Rurais Sem Terra*, or MST) (Maria del Pilar et al., 1998).

THE EFFORT OF COLLECTIVE CAPABILITIES FOR DEMOCRATIC GOVERNANCE TO TRANSFER PUBLIC EDUCATION THROUGH SOCIAL MOVEMENTS: THE LANDLESS WORKER MOVEMENT EXAMPLE

Brazil's income inequality has long been linked to the unequal distribution of productive lands. There has been an expectation for land reforms for more than three decades. Landowners and landless peasants represent two sides of land reform (Martins, 2004). The conflict between these two groups can also be discussed in terms of opposition to and support for neoliberal agricultural policies. These conflicts have sparked collective struggles within social movements. The MST is one of the prominent examples of a social movement that opposes neoliberalism and mobilizes mass actions through the occupation of non-productive lands (Martins, 2004). The MST first took action in 1979 in Encruzilhada Natalino, Rio Grande do Sul (South). The basis for the movement's actions is the 1964 Brazilian land law, which stipulates that "private property may be expropriated in cases where it is not cultivated or where contradictions arise between the owner and the workers, or where environmental damage is caused" (Martins, 2004, p. 19). Officially founded in 1984, the MST initiated the occupation movement, which affected approximately 1.5 million families and organized them to participate in collective production (Tarlau, 2015; Mariano & Tarlau, 2019).

What sets this movement apart is that it can transform public education and play an effective role in the reforms implemented by public authorities regarding the education system (Tarlau, 2015). The fact that Freire's ideas could be combined with the liberation movement of the Catholic Church was a compelling factor in the formation of the MST. When the period between 1960 and 1980 is examined, it is seen that the Catholic clergy, who had an essential place in solidarity networks, took part in political activities using the theology of liberation against social injustice and poverty. This process was a necessary source of inspiration for establishing the MST (Tarlau, 2015; Mariano & Tarlau, 2019).

In 1987, the MST began to focus on transforming public education rather than popular education, a movement that also demonstrated the need to convert the public education system for broader economic and political reforms (Tarlau, 2015). The MST has incorporated this pedagogical approach into its activities to improve cultural literacy levels, the perceptions about social justice, and the agricultural production practices among its members. In MST schools (Education for and by the Countryside - *Educação do Campo*), students were encouraged to be leaders and activists actively working for social justice rather than merely being members of the MST (Tarlau, 2014; Tarlau, 2015; Mariano & Tarlau, 2019). The training provided by this movement was able to bolster their emancipation efforts by explaining the political identity of the landless peasants and the deprivation stemming from lack of capital and property (Barbosa, 2016).

CEARÁ'S EDUCATIONAL REFORMS, DEMOCRATIC GOVERNANCE, AND THEIR RELATIONSHIP WITH SOCIAL MOVEMENTS

Ceará is characterized by prevalent poverty and has been known for nepotism and oligarchic practices perpetuated by landowners and the military elite following the military coup known as *Pacto dos Coronéis* (Colonels' Agreement) (Zientarski, Menezes & Silva, 2019). These practices are regarded as the causes of poverty in the region, which has prompted discussions on the power dynamics within the state in a series of CIC (Ceará Industrial do Ceará)-funded forums, which included representatives of the left parties. In the 1980s, with broad support from social movements, the leftist sections, which were opposed to neopatrimonialist practices in Ceará, were able to elect Maria Luiza Fontenele, the Workers' Party (PT) candidate, as the president of the City of Fortaleza (1985) (Zientarski, Menezes & Silva, 2019). Similarly, in the quest for electing government representatives (*Partido*

Popular Socialista - PPST), Tasso Jereissati emerged as an alternative candidate for state government in 1986. Jereissati's candidacy, backed by young entrepreneurs, presented an alternative against clientelism and the corruption of the colonels (Borges, 2008). This alternative strengthened the tendency to engage in solidarity with civil society to diminish old elites' influence on public policy. Although local administrators were in close contact with the World Bank and other international institutions during this period, no evidence suggests that external influences drove educational reforms (Borges, 2008).

In the unique political landscape of Brazil and Ceará, politics, social movements, and educational reforms appear to be interconnected parts of a whole. Zarur's 1993 study provides a comprehensive explanation of how education was transformed after the decentralization of municipalities. The study examines and compares the practices of three municipalities in Ceará that achieved success in educational advancements and improvements in academic quality after the constitutional change in 1988. These municipalities are Icapul, Croate, and Horizonte. To better understand the role of municipal initiatives in Ceará's educational success, it is helpful to elaborate on the scope of the past policies implemented by these municipalities. When the activities of these municipalities are examined, it is possible to see the relationship between the selection of teachers and administrators and the nepotism prevalent in the region. For this reason, efforts were initially made to combat corruption and nepotism, followed by implementing practices that improve living conditions, such as free transportation, to bring qualified teachers into the system. School hours were reorganized according to the needs of the local people and the production system, and a dialogue system was established that considered families' opinions (Zarur, 1993). In Icapul, the representatives of neighborhood associations and other unions are also allowed to negotiate with municipal councilors and secretaries regarding the municipal budget and be directly involved in income and expenditure audits (Zarur, 1993).

The second initiative taken for education was the dissemination of literacy education. To achieve this, the Education Department of Icapul adopted Freire's Culture Circles and Constructivism methods, integrating cultural elements into education within the child's environment (Zarur, 1993).

The key lesson here is how participation is defined by the state (Lima, 2019). Understanding who participates in democratic deliberation is pivotal. Therefore, the question of how the state is transformed becomes quite essential. As education reaches more significant segments of society, it also increases the representation of low-income people within various administrative units of public institutions (Lima, 2019). In this regard, the potential for the representatives of social movements to enter the state holds considerable importance. Only then will it be possible to open up elite structures to the representation of different groups. Decentralization and governance alone do not guarantee such participation in policymaking and discourse (Lima, 2019). This transformation has created an effective change through a conscientization process that allows oppressed groups to recognize their realities rather than through Habermas's universally idealized dialogue language. When viewed from a Foucault perspective, instead of the dominant discourse and power relations being reproduced by schools, understanding these power relations through an alternative discourse has brought about a significant transformation process.

CEARÁ'S CURRENT SUCCESS

In Ceará, many municipalities, especially the municipality of Sobral, draw attention to their increasing success graph in the Basic Education Development Index *(IDEB)* prepared by Brazil's Ministry of Education *(MEC)* between 2005 and 2017, which aims to evaluate student achievement (Loureiro et al., 2020).

It is above the Brazilian average (5.7 in 2019) and above Ceará's average (6.3 in 2019) (Yan et al., 2023). In their study on behalf of the World Bank, Loureiro et al. (2020) state that Ceará has achieved success in 'just over a decade.' They summarize the secret of Ceará's success as follows:

> *Concretely, the formula for the education success of Ceará has five main ingredients, which are supported by international evidence on what works in education. The first three ingredients involve sound financing and pedagogical policies, namely: (i) incentives, both financial and non-financial, for municipalities to achieve better education outcomes; (ii) technical support to the municipal school networks struggling to improve learning goals, with a strong focus on enhancing teacher effectiveness and achieving universal literacy at the right age; and (iii) the use of a robust and reliable monitoring and assessment system, which continuously assesses key results of education, chiefly student learning. These three ingredients emphasize instructional coherence in terms of the alignment of the curriculum (what students are expected to learn), teachers' pedagogical approaches (how students are taught), and learning assessment (how the system checks whether students are learning). They also show consistent implementation over time, building on earlier preparatory reforms. (Loureiro et al., 2020)*

In Ceará, educational success in primary and secondary education is as crucial as pacifying the socioeconomic conditions of families and placing the responsibility of children's education on schools, focusing on the development of basic skills, and applying to the *Bolsa Família*, a conditional support program, to remove barriers in children's access to education (Expert interview 1). However, it should also be acknowledged that with the popular education movements of Latin America, an alternative understanding of development and production has become widespread, even in rural areas. This alternative understanding deviates from neoliberal policies and carries education beyond the ideas of the neoliberal market and its material welfare criteria. (Expert interview 2).

Based on the examples represented, the combination of political equality and equal access to education has led to the development of an alternative approach to the individualistic educational practices advocated by the neoliberal understanding of education. This approach aims to develop collective agency instead of individual agency. In this way, the individual who establishes a connection between himself/herself and his/her social class has developed collective agency, transforming the unequal system in which he/she lives and redefining the sets or clusters of capabilities.

Indeed, in Brazil and other Latin American countries, the unfair distribution of economic and political power is not defined Independently of the development of leftist parties and their access to governing power within democratic governance, which is the primary variable that leads to the redistribution of income and the proper functioning of dysfunctional institutions (Huber & Stephens, 2014). In Ceará, right-wing governments stayed in power between 2002-2007, and after 2007, left-wing governments came to power (Tarlau, 2023). However, the education policies in basic education have remained independent of ideological differences (Louise et al., 2020). In Ceará, where left-wing governments were at the forefront during the reign of national right-wing governments in Brazil, the cooperation between the state and the MST and other social movements also ensured that rural education reforms remained in place (Tarlau, 2022).

This situation needs to be evaluated in terms of politicized social movements' ability (such as the MST's ability) to be influential in the policies of political parties and their ability to act independently of government and state power (Tarlau, 2014). There is a belief that the PT government deviated from its socialist ideology after taking office and entered into cooperation with the neoliberal state apparatus. According to proponents of this view, the PT has transformed many of the NGOs it co-operated with within the neoliberal state, causing them to deviate from the ideals they advocated. However, the MTS was not affected by this negative transformation by remaining outside the power relations of the neoliberal state and preserving its autonomy (Lima, 2019; Maria, Carvalho & Mendes, 2011; Tarlau, 2014). In this case, collective agency development and popular education movements, which remove neoliberal discourse from educational practices, can also transform power through collective capabilities.

The Lula administration was torn between receiving social support without severing ties with social movements and not entirely ignoring the interests of large corporations. Demands for land reform also effectively shaped MST's ties with universities, academics, and students, making universities a counter-hegemonic force in Ceará (Maria, Carvalho & Mendes, 2011).

CONCLUSION

When we examine the general situation regarding educational policy changes in Brazil and Ceará, we see that it is essential not only for the country to develop collective agencies to address political and economic inequalities arising from education but also for poor people to live lives they reason to value. Collective capabilities both create and expand the ability of social movements to achieve political representation and power. The successes in educational policies show pathway dependency through the displacement of economic and political elites created by unique circumstances. This factor should be considered when disseminating education policies as best practices. Although education produces equality and is dependent on providing agency freedom away from competitive pressure, it is impossible to think of agency freedom independently of the social context. It is seen that conscientization being a part of the educational processes can reinforce both the teacher's and the student's sense of responsibility for themselves and society. Thus, the experience of Brazil teaches lessons about the role of democracy and social movements in creating equal conditions, as well as the need for public administration to provide consensus and for democratic participation to spread to all layers of society. In addition, it is noteworthy that in determining education policies, the concrete realities of society should be taken into account, the public administrative and financial system should be examined, and the coordination established between local governments and the central state authority has gained importance.

Neoliberal educational policies tend to survive by limiting democratic participation, which the existing models of capital accumulation place within social institutions, and by preserving the power of economic and political elites. Only the collective capabilities of progressive social movements can persuade the ruling powers to take a third path through democratic deliberation because social movements can transform the dominant discourse to enable negotiations in the public sphere. In this way, building democratic governance is also vital for producing lasting solutions to inequalities beyond the discourse of neoliberal governance. Sen's CA extends the discussions on collective capabilities. Future research can explore this topic further through field research in Brazil's various regions and other Latin American countries and their educational experiences.

Funding Statement

This book chapter is one of the outputs of the project entitled 'Rethinking the Relationship between Regional Development, Education and Social Policy with Capabilities Approach'(Project number: 10599B19201483) supported by TUBITAK BIDEB.

REFERENCES

Accioly, I. (2020). The Attacks on the Legacy of Paulo Freire in Brazil: Why He Still Disturbs so Many? In Macrine, S. (Ed.), *Critical Pedagogy in Uncertain Times*. Education, Politics and Public Life. Palgrave Macmillan., DOI: 10.1007/978-3-030-39808-8_8

Anyon, J. (2009). Progressive Social Movements and Educational Equity. *Educational Policy*, *23*(1), 194–215. DOI: 10.1177/0895904808328523

Ball, S. J. (2019). A Horizon of Freedom: Using Foucault to Think Differently about Education and Learning. *Power and Education*, *11*(2), 132–144. DOI: 10.1177/1757743819838289

Barbosa, L. P. (2016). Educação do Campo [Education for and by the countryside] as a Political Project in the Context of The Struggle for Land in Brazil. *The Journal of Peasant Studies*. Advance online publication. DOI: 10.1080/03066150.2015.111912

Bevir, M. (2014). Democratic Governance: A Genealogy. *Observatoire de la société Britannique,* (16), 19-36. DOI: 10.4000/osb.1695

Biebricher, T. (2007). Habermas and Foucault: Deliberative Democracy and Strategic State Analysis. *Contemporary Political Theory*, *6*(2), 218–245. DOI: 10.1057/palgrave.cpt.9300280

Boden, M. (2011). Neoliberalism and Counter-Hegemony in the Global South: Reimagining the State. In Social Movements in the Global South: Dispossession, Development, and Resistance (pp. 83–103). London: Palgrave Macmillan UK DOI: 10.1057/9780230302044_4

Boekle-Giuffrida, B. (2013). Brazilian Federalism as Polity, Politics, and Beyond: Examining Primary Education with Case Studies in Ceará and Pernambuco.Doctoral dissertation. Freie Universitat, Berlin.

Bonvin, J., & Laruffa, F. (2018). Deliberative Democracy in the Real World, The Contribution of the CA. *International Review of Sociology*, *28*(2), 216–233. DOI: 10.1080/03906701.2018.1477101

Borges, A. (2008). State Government, Political Competition, and Education Reform: Comparative Lessons from Brazil. *Bulletin of Latin American Research*, *27*(2), 235–254. DOI: 10.1111/j.1470-9856.2008.00265.x

Brazilian Report (2023). The Education Model Lula Wants to Replicate throughout Brazil. Retrieved from https://www.wilsoncenter.org/blog-post/education-model-lula-wants-replicate-throughout-brazil (07.08.2024).

Brown, W. (2003). Neoliberalism and the End of Liberal Democracy. *Theory & Event*, *7*(1), 15–18. DOI: 10.1353/tae.2003.0020

Cotoi, C. (2011). Neoliberalism: A Foucauldian Perspective. *International Review of Social Research*, *1*(2), 109–124. DOI: 10.1515/irsr-2011-0014

Dryzek, J. S. (2002). Difference democracy: The consciousness-raising group against the gentlemen's club. Deliberative Democracy and Beyond: Liberals, Critics, Contestations, 57-80.

Englund, T. (2010). Educational Implications of the Idea of Deliberative Democracy. In Habermas, Critical theory and Education Eds M. Murphy, T. Fleming (pp. 27–40). Routledge.

Evans, P. (2002). Collective Capabilities, Culture, and Amartya Sen's Development as Freedom. *Studies in Comparative International Development*, *37*(2), 54–60. DOI: 10.1007/BF02686261

Expert Interview 1. Education expert from Ceará. Interview Date: 06.06.2023

Expert Interview 2. Education expert from the UK. Interview Date: 27.07.2023

Feldman, S., & Gellert, P. (2006). The Seductive Quality of Central Human Capabilities: Sociological Insights Into Nussbaum And Sen's Disagreement. *Economy and Society*, *35*(3), 423–452. DOI: 10.1080/03085140600845008

Felten, P., Little, D., & Pingree, A. (2004). 11: Foucault and the Practice of Educational Development: Power and Surveillance in Individual Consultations. *To Improve the Academy: A Journal of Educational Development*. 540.173-188.

Foucault, M. (1978). *Security, Territory, Population, Lectures at College de France 1977-1978*. Palgrave.

Foucault, M. (1982). The Subject and Power. *Critical Inquiry*, *8*(4), 777–795. DOI: 10.1086/448181

Freire, P. (1970). Cultural Action and Conscientization. *Harvard Educational Review*, *40*(3), 452–477. DOI: 10.17763/haer.40.3.h76250x720j43175

Freire, P. (1998). Cultural Action and Conscientization. *Harvard Educational Review*, *68*(4), 499.

Gadotti, M., & Torres, C. A. (2009). Paulo Freire: Education for development. *Development and Change*, *40*(6), 1255–1267. DOI: 10.1111/j.1467-7660.2009.01606.x

Gasper, D. (2023). Amartya Sen as a Social and Political Theorist – on Personhood, Democracy, and 'Description as a Choice.'. *Journal of Global Ethics*, *19*(3), 386–409. DOI: 10.1080/17449626.2023.2255600

Glassman, M., & Patton, R. (2014). Capability through participatory democracy: Sen, Freire, and Dewey. *Educational Philosophy and Theory*, *46*(12), 1353–1365. DOI: 10.1080/00131857.2013.828582

Glette, M. K., & Wiig, S. (2022). The Headaches of Case Study Research: A Discussion of Emerging Challenges and Possible Ways out of the Pain. *The Qualitative Report*, *27*(5), 1377–1392. DOI: 10.46743/2160-3715/2022.5246

Hart, C. S. (2012). The Capability Approach and Education. *Cambridge Journal of Education*, *42*(3), 275–282. DOI: 10.1080/0305764X.2012.706393

Harvey, D. (2015). *Neoliberalizmin Kısa Tarihi*. İstanbul Sel Yayıncılık.

Hastings, M. (2019). Neoliberalism and Education. *Oxford Research Encyclopedia of Education*. Retrieved 10 Apr. 2025, from https://oxfordre.com/education/view/10.1093/acrefore/9780190264093.001.0001/acrefore-9780190264093-e-404

Huber, E., & Stephens, J. D. (2014). *Democracy and the Left: Social Policy and Inequality in Latin America*. University of Chicago Press.

Ibrahim, S. (2017). How to Build Collective Capabilities: The 3C-model for Grassroots-led Development. *Journal of Human Development and Capabilities*, *18*(2), 197–222. DOI: 10.1080/19452829.2016.1270918

Ibrahim, S. S. (2006). From Individual to Collective Capabilities: The Capability Approach as a Conceptual Framework for Self-help. *Journal of Human Development*, *7*(3), 397–416. DOI: 10.1080/14649880600815982

Imchen, A., & Ndem, F. (2020). *Addressing the Learning Crisis: An Urgent Need to Better Finance Education for the Poorest Children*. UNICEF.

IOEB. (2024). Dados e análise. Retrieved from: https://ioeb.org.br/dados-e-analise/ (04.04.2025)

Kjeldsen, C. C., & Bonvin, J. M. (2015). The Capability Approach, Education and the Labour Market. In Otto, H. U. (Eds.), *Facing Trajectories from School to Work. Technical and Vocational Education and Training: Issues, Concerns and Prospects, 20*. Springer., DOI: 10.1007/978-3-319-11436-1_2

Kolers, A. (2023). Collective Political Capabilities. *Ethics & Global Politics, 16*(2), 46–54. DOI: 10.1080/16544951.2023.2216110

Levy, C. (2012). Social Movements and Political Parties in Brazil: Expanding Democracy, the 'Struggle for the Possible' and the Reproduction of Power Structures. *Globalizations*, *9*(6), 783–798. DOI: 10.1080/14747731.2012.739340

Lima, V. (2019). The Limits of Participatory Democracy and the Inclusion of Social Movements in Local Government. *Social Movement Studies*, *18*(6), 667–681. DOI: 10.1080/14742837.2019.1629277

Loureiro, A., Gropella, E., & Arias, O. (2020). There is No Magic: The Formula for Brazil's Ceará and Sobral Success to Reduce Learning Poverty. Retrieved from https://blogs.worldbank.org/education/there-no-magic-formula-brazils-ceara-and-sobral-success-reduce-learning-poverty

Lynch, R. A. (2014). Foucault's Theory of Power. In Michel Foucault (pp. 13–26). Routledge.

Maria, S., Carvalho, G., & Mendes, J. E. (2011). The University and the Landless Movement in Brazil: The Experience of Collective Knowledge Construction through Educational Projects in Rural Areas. In Motta, S. C., & Nilsen, A. G. (Eds.), *Social Movements in the Global South.* Rethinking International Development Series. Palgrave Macmillan., DOI: 10.1057/9780230302044_6

Mariano, A., & Tarlau, R. (2019). The Landless Workers Movement's itinerant schools: Occupying and transforming public education in Brazil. *British Journal of Sociology of Education*, *40*(4), 538–559. DOI: 10.1080/01425692.2019.1565989

Martins, D. (2004). *M. (2000) Neo-Liberalizme Karşı MST'nin Kafa Tutuşu. İçinde Topraksızlar*. İletişim Yayınları.

Mintrom, M. (2001). Educational Governance and Democratic Practice. *Educational Policy*, *15*(5), 615–643. DOI: 10.1177/0895904801015005001

Morrow, R. A., & Torres, C. A. (2002). *Reading Freire and Habermas: Critical Pedagogy and Transformative Social Change*. Teachers College Press.

Motta, S., & Nilsen, A. G. (2011). Social Movements and/in the Postcolonial: Dispossession, Development, and Resistance in the Global South Motta, S., & Nilsen, A. G. (Eds.). (2011). Social Movements in the Global South: Dispossession, development and resistance. Springer.

Murphy, M. (2014). Self-determination as a Collective Capability: The Case of Indigenous Peoples. *Journal of Human Development and Capabilities*, *15*(4), 320–334. DOI: 10.1080/19452829.2013.878320

Nussbaum, M. (2020). The Capabilities Approach and the History of Philosophy. In E. Chiappero-Martinetti, S. Osmani, & M. Qizilbash (Eds.), *The Cambridge Handbook of the Capability Approach* (pp. 13–39). chapter, Cambridge: Cambridge University Press. DOI: 10.1017/9781316335741.003

O'Cadiz del Pilar, M. Wong, P. L., & Torres, C. A. (1998). Creating the Popular Public School: Theoretical Foundations and Policy Initiatives. In Education and Democracy (pp. 71-105). Routledge.

Oliveira, E. S., Justo, W. R., & De Lucena, M. A. (2024). The Dynamics of Public High School Student Performance in Ceará: A Study of the Case of Sobral in Brazil. *Journal of the Humanities and Social Sciences*, *29*(3), 12–24. DOI: 10.9790/0837-2903011224

Olssen, M., Codd, J. A., & O'Neill, A. (2004). *Education Policy: Globalization, Citizenship, and Democracy*. Sage. DOI: 10.4135/9781446221501

Peters, B. G., & Pierre, J. (2006). Governance, Government, and the State. Theories and Issues, 209-222.

Pfister, T. (2012). Citizenship and Capability? Amartya Sen's Capabilities Approach from a Citizenship Perspective. *Citizenship Studies*, *16*(2), 241–254. DOI: 10.1080/13621025.2012.667615

Robeyns, I. (2017). *Wellbeing, Freedom, and Social Justice: The Capability Approach Re-examined*. Open Book Publishers. DOI: 10.11647/OBP.0130

Rosignoli, F. (2019). Categorizing Collective Capabilities. *Partecipazione e Conflitto*, 11(3), 813-837. DOI: 10.1285/i20356609v11i3p813

Segatto, C. I., & Abrucio, F. L. (2018). Multiple Roles of State Governments in the Brazilian Education Policy: the cases of Ceará, Mato Grosso do Sul, São Paulo and Pará. Reviste de Administração Pública, 52, 1179-1193. http://dx.doi.org/DOI: 10.1590/0034-761220170047

Sen, A. (1999). *Development as Freedom*. Alfred Knop Publishing.

Stewart, F. (2005). Groups and Capabilities. *Journal of Human Development*, *6*(2), 185–204. DOI: 10.1080/14649880500120517

Stewart, F. (2019). Human Development Approach: An Overview. *Oxford Development Studies*, *47*(2), 135–153. DOI: 10.1080/13600818.2019.1585793

Susen, S. (2017). Jürgen Habermas. The Routledge Handbook of Language and Politics, 43.

Tarlau, R. (2014).Occupying Land, Occupying Schools: Transforming Education in the Brazilian Countryside UC Berkeley Electronic Theses and Dissertations

Tarlau, R. (2015). How Do New Critical Pedagogies Develop? Educational Innovation, Social Change, and Landless Workers in Brazil. *Teachers College Record, 117*(11), 1–36. DOI: 10.1177/016146811511701103

Tarlau, R. (2022). *Collaboration and Contestation: State Actors and MST Activists Reforming Rural Education.* Accountability Research Center.

Tikly, L. (2017). The Future of Education for All as a Global Regime of Educational Governance. *Comparative Education Review*, 61(1), 000–000. https://doi.org/DOI: 10.1086/689700

Tobias, S. (2005). Foucault on Freedom and Capabilities. *Theory, Culture & Society, 22*(4), 65–85. DOI: 10.1177/0263276405053721

Torres, C. A., & Morrow, R. A. (1998). Paulo Freire, Jürgen Habermas, and Critical Pedagogy: Implications for Comparative Education. *Critical Studies in Education, 39*(2), 1–20.

Tully, J. (2013). Two Ways of Realizing Justice and Democracy: Linking Amartya Sen and Elinor Ostrom. *Critical Review of International Social and Political Philosophy, 16*(2), 220–232. DOI: 10.1080/13698230.2012.757914

UNESCO. (2017).Brazil Country Case Study. Retrieved from https://unesdoc.unesco.org/ark:/48223/pf0000259531

Unterhalter, E. (2003). Education, Capabilities, and Social Justice. In UNESCO EFA Monitoring Report, 4.

Van Zomeren, M., & Iyer, A. (2009). Introduction to the Social and Psychological Dynamics of Collective Action. *The Journal of Social Issues, 65*(4), 645–660. DOI: 10.1111/j.1540-4560.2009.01618.x

Vidal, D. G., & de Faria Filho, L. M. (2008). Schooling in Brazil. In Going to School in Latin America, 55. Bloomsbury Publishing, Vieira, S. L., Plank, D. N., & Vidal, E. M. (2019). Educational Policy in Ceará: Strategic processes. Educação & Realidade, 44.

Yan, Y., Sano, H., & Sumiya, L. A. (2023). Policy Capacity Matters for Education System Reforms: A Comparative Study of Two Brazilian States. *Journal of Comparative Policy Analysis, 25*(2), 253–281. DOI: 10.1080/13876988.2022.2110472

Zarur, S. B. (1993). From Bad to Good Government: The Case of Three Local Governments in Ceará, Brazil (Doctoral dissertation, Massachusetts Institute of Technology).

Zientarski, C., Menezes, H. C. M., & Silva, S. D. O. D. (2019). Democratic Management in Public Education: A Paradox of the Brazilian Neopatrimonialist State?-The Case of Ceará. *Educação em Revista*, 35.

ENDNOTE

1 https://en.unesco.org/themes/education/sdgs/materiail/04

Compilation of References

Accioly, I. (2020). The Attacks on the Legacy of Paulo Freire in Brazil: Why He Still Disturbs so Many? In Macrine, S. (Ed.), *Critical Pedagogy in Uncertain Times*. Education, Politics and Public Life. Palgrave Macmillan., DOI: 10.1007/978-3-030-39808-8_8

Achillas, C., Aidonis, D., Tsolakis, N., Tsampoulatidis, I., Mourouzis, A., Bialas, C., & Koritsoglou, K. (2023). Auditing Accessibility of Pavements and Points of Interest in Urban Areas: The 'Seek & Go' Tool †. *Signals*, *4*(3), 604–616. DOI: 10.3390/signals4030032

Adger, W. N. (2000). Institutional adaptation to environmental risk under the transition in Vietnam. *Annals of the Association of American Geographers*, *90*(4), 738–758. DOI: 10.1111/0004-5608.00220

Aditya, T., Ningrum, S., Nurasa, H., & Irawati, I. (2023). Community needs for the digital divide on the smart city policy. *Heliyon*, *9*(8). Advance online publication. DOI: 10.1016/j.heliyon.2023.e18932

Ağaoğulları, M. Ali. (2007). *Toplumsal-Siyasal Çatışmanın Erdemi: Machiavelli ile Montesquieu'den Alınacak Dersler*, "Mete Tunçay'a Armağan" içinde, (Derleyenler: Mehmet Ö. Alkan, Tanıl Bora, Murat Koraltürk), İletişim Yayınları, İstanbul.

Agarwal, S. (2022). *Why is Mental Health Important for Teachers?* Suraasa. https://www.suraasa.com/blog/why-is-mental-health-important-for-teachers

Akça, G. (2007). *Osmanlı Millet Sisteminin Dönüşümü*. Doğu Anadolu Bölgesi Araştırmaları.

Akıllı, H., & Akıllı, H. S. (2014). Decentralization and Recentralization of Local Governments in Turkey. *Transylvanian Review of Administrative Sciences*, *42E*, 5–24.

Aksu, D., & Akman, Ç. (2023). Mısır Arap Cumhuriyeti'nin Yerel Yönetim Yapısı: Karşılaştırmalı Bir Analiz. *Karadeniz Sosyal Bilimler Dergisi, 15*(28), 57–76. DOI: 10.38155/ksbd.1246159

Alakbarov, U., Mamedov, N., Gabibova, Z., & Rahimli, R. (2021). Evolution of public administration in the post-soviet countries. Azerbaijan republic. *Civil Service, 23*(2 (130)), 97–118. DOI: 10.22394/2070-8378-2021-23-2-97-118

AlAshry, M. S. (2022). A critical assessment of the impact of Egyptian laws on information access and dissemination by journalists. *Cogent Arts & Humanities, 9*(1), 2115243. DOI: 10.1080/23311983.2022.2115243

Albuainain, M. A. (2022). How digital communication provides better government services: Assessing the Tawasul System in Bahrain. *Cities (London, England), 128*, 103790. DOI: 10.1016/j.cities.2022.103790

Alcarria, F. J., & Navarro, J. T. (2023). EU digital communication strategy during the COVID-19 vaccination campaign: Framing, contents and attributed roles at stake. *Communicatio Socialis, 36*(3), 153–174. DOI: 10.15581/003.36.3.153-174

Aliyev, S. (2023). False Messages to the Public About Municipalities. Baku Research Institute. https://bakuresearchinstitute.org/en/false-messages-to-the-public-about-municipalities/

Aliyev, S. (2024). Failure to Devolve: Azerbaijan Avoids Promised Devolution of Power to Municipalities by Merging Them Instead. Baku Research Institute. https://bakuresearchinstitute.org/en/failure-to-devolve-azerbaijan-avoids-promised-devolution-of-power-to-municipalities-by-merging-them-instead/

Alm, J., Buschman, R. D., & Sjoquist, D. L. (2011). Rethinking local government reliance on the property tax. *Regional Science and Urban Economics, 41*(4), 320–331. DOI: 10.1016/j.regsciurbeco.2011.03.006

Altamimi, H., Liu, Q., & Jimenez, B. (2023). Not Too Much, Not Too Little: Centralization, Decentralization, and Organizational Change. *Journal of Public Administration: Research and Theory, 33*(1), 170–185. https://academic.oup.com/jpart/article/33/1/170/6549741. DOI: 10.1093/jopart/muac016

Amoatey, C., & Hayibor, M. V. K. (2017). Critical success factors for local government project stakeholder management. *Built Environment Project and Asset Management, 7*(2), 143–156. DOI: 10.1108/BEPAM-07-2016-0030

Analysis Of Azerbaijani Legislation On Freedom Of Expression. Council of Europe. (2017). https://rm.coe.int/azerbaijan-analysis-of-legislation-on-freedom-of-expression-december-2/16808ae03d

An, D. T. (2023). The Role of Local Government in Private Investment Intentions: A Case Study in Vietnam. *International Journal of Sustainable Development and Planning*, *18*(2), 439–446. DOI: 10.18280/ijsdp.180212

Andrew, S. (2022). *This town of 170,000 replaced some cops with medics and mental health workers. It's worked for over 30 years*. CNN.

Anyon, J. (2009). Progressive Social Movements and Educational Equity. *Educational Policy*, *23*(1), 194–215. DOI: 10.1177/0895904808328523

Arıkboğa, Ü. (2004), Yönetimler Arası Mali İlişkiler: Türkiye'de Merkezi Yönetim ile Büyükşehir Belediyeleri Arasındaki Mali İlişkilerin Niteliği Üzerine Bir Araştırma, İstanbul, Yaylacık Matbaası, s:1-284

Arıkboğa. (2021), Dünyada Yerel Yönetimler ve Mali Yapıları "İtalya'da Yerel Yönetimlerin İdari ve Mali Yapısı", Nobel Yayınevi, s: 503-535

ASAN service. (2012) https://asan.gov.az/en

Atar, E., & Kirboz, Ş. (2024). Local governance reforms in post-soviet Azerbaijan: A comprehensive analysis of structural changes and reform initiatives. *Janus-NET*, *15*(2), 2. DOI: 10.26619/1647-7251.15.2.11

Awad, H. (2022). *Centralised and Decentralised: The Authoritarian Upgrading of the Egyptian System of Local Governance*. Academic.

Awasthi, A. (2024). The Evolution of Democracy: Historical Perspectives and Modern Challenges. *International Journal of Scientific Research*, *13*(9), 465–470. https://www.ijsr.net/getabstract.php?paperid=SR24908134052

Azerbaijan's digital project has received recognition from the world community. (2021). https://www.trend.az/business/it/3428690.html

Baby, D. M., & Subhash, P. D. (2023). Role of Local Authorities in Development of Primary Schools. *Research Review International Journal of Multidisciplinary* 8(3), 106-113. https://rrjournals.com/index.php/rrijm/article/view/537

Bahl, R. W., Sethi, G., & Wallace, S. (2010). Fiscal decentralization to rural local governments in India: A case study of west Bengal state. *Publius*, *40*(2). https://scholarworks.gsu.edu/cgi/viewcontent.cgi?article=1320&context=econ_facpub

Baldev Singh *versus* Shinder Pal Singh and Anr., AIRONLINE 2006 SC 303 (2006).

Baldini, G.& Baldi, B. (2014), Decentralization in Italy and the Troubles of Federalization, Regional and Federal Studies,24(1), s:87-108.

Ball, J., Penney, S., Young, G., Harris, G., & Joy, R. (2019). *Teacher Readiness: Teacher attitudes, opinions, and perspectives toward facilitating positive mental health in the classroom.* https://www.researchgate.net/publication/338777674_Teacher_readiness_Teacher_attitudes_opinions_and_perspectives_towards_facilitating_positive_mental_health_in_the_classroom

Ball, S. J. (2019). A Horizon of Freedom: Using Foucault to Think Differently about Education and Learning. *Power and Education*, *11*(2), 132–144. DOI: 10.1177/1757743819838289

Bansal, S. (2016). An Evolution of Community Development in India. *IJRESS* 6(9), 57-69. https://www.indianjournals.com/ijor.aspx?target=ijor:ijress&volume=6&issue=9&article=006

Barbosa, L. P. (2016). Educação do Campo [Education for and by the countryside] as a Political Project in the Context of The Struggle for Land in Brazil. *The Journal of Peasant Studies*. Advance online publication. DOI: 10.1080/03066150.2015.111912

Bardhan, P., & Mookherjee, D. (2006). *Decentralization and Local Governance in Developing Countries: A Comparative Perspective*. The MIT Press. DOI: 10.7551/mitpress/2297.001.0001

Bardhan, P., & Mookherjee, D. (2006). *Decentralization, corruption, and government accountability: An overview. Handbook of Economic Corruption*. Edward Elgar Publishing. DOI: 10.4337/9781847203106.00013

Bayraktar, S. (2007). *Türk kamu yönetiminde adem-i merkeziyetin sınırları: Yerel yönetimler ve reformlar*. TODAİE Yayınları.

Beer, C. (2025). Judicial Federalism and Abortion in Mexico and the United States. *PS, Political Science & Politics*, *58*(1), 52–55.

Behrani, P. (2016). Importance Of Teaching Counselling Skills To Teachers. *MIER Journal of Educational Studies, Trends & Practices, 6*(1), 17-25. https://www.mierjs.in/index.php/mjestp/article/view/1452/1077

Bellamy, F. D. (2023). *U.S. data privacy laws to enter new era in 2023*. Reuters.

Besley, T., & Burgess, R. (2002). The political economy of government responsiveness: Theory and evidence from India. *The Quarterly Journal of Economics*, *117*(4), 1415–1451. DOI: 10.1162/003355302320935061

Betsill, M. M., & Bulkeley, H. (2021). Cities and the multilevel governance of global climate change. In *Understanding Global Cooperation* (pp. 219–236). Brill. DOI: 10.1163/9789004462601_014

Bevir, M. (2014). Democratic Governance: A Genealogy. *Observatoire de la société Britannique,* (16), 19-36. DOI: 10.4000/osb.1695

Bhanumati *versus* State of Uttar Pradesh, through its Principal Secretary and Ors., AIR 2010 SUPREME COURT 3796 (2010).

Bhardwaj, S. (2023). *Local Self-Government in India: A Comprehensive Approach.* MPP House.

Bhawalkar, J., Saraf, A., & Malik, M. M. (2024). The opioid crisis, preventing and managing substance abuse in India: A systematic review. *Cureus, 16*(10), e70600. DOI: 10.7759/cureus.70600

Biebricher, T. (2007). Habermas and Foucault: Deliberative Democracy and Strategic State Analysis. *Contemporary Political Theory*, *6*(2), 218–245. DOI: 10.1057/palgrave.cpt.9300280

Binh, N. T., & Giai, N. Q. (2021). Study on Citizen participation in local governance in Vietnam. *NISPAcee Journal of Public Administration and Policy*, *14*(2), 87–109. DOI: 10.2478/nispa-2021-0016

Birkmann, J., Garschagen, M., Kraas, F., & Quang, N. (2010). Adaptive urban governance: New challenges for the second generation of urban adaptation strategies to climate change. *Sustainability Science*, *5*(2), 185–206. DOI: 10.1007/s11625-010-0111-3

Boddula Krishnaiah and another *versus* State Election Commissioner, A.P. & Ors., 1996 AIR 1595 (1996).

Boden, M. (2011). Neoliberalism and Counter-Hegemony in the Global South: Reimagining the State. In Social Movements in the Global South: Dispossession, Development, and Resistance (pp. 83–103). London: Palgrave Macmillan UK DOI: 10.1057/9780230302044_4

Boekle-Giuffrida, B. (2013). Brazilian Federalism as Polity, Politics, and Beyond: Examining Primary Education with Case Studies in Ceará and Pernambuco.Doctoral dissertation. Freie Universitat, Berlin.

Boex, J., & Yilmaz, S. (2010). An analytical framework for assessing decentralized local governance and the local public sector. *Urban Institute Working Paper.*

Boggero, G. (2016), "The Establishment of Metropolitan Cities in Italy: An Advance or a Setback for Italian Regionalism?", Perspectives on Federalism, S.8(3), ss.1-22.

Bohlooli Zamani, M. A. H. S. A., & Dessì, S. (2017). Local governments' approach towards green bond. An opportunity for Italian municipalities to finance green projects in the public real estate sector.

Bondes, M., Kostka, G., & Rabe, W. (2024). ICT-based environmental participation in China: Same, same but digital? *Environmental Science & Policy*, *154*, 103688. DOI: 10.1016/j.envsci.2024.103688

Bonsón, E., Royo, S., & Ratkai, M. (2015). Citizens' engagement on local governments' Facebook sites. An empirical analysis: The impact of different media and content types in Western Europe. *Government Information Quarterly*, *32*(1), 52–62. DOI: 10.1016/j.giq.2014.11.001

Bonvin, J., & Laruffa, F. (2018). Deliberative Democracy in the Real World, The Contribution of the CA. *International Review of Sociology*, *28*(2), 216–233. DOI: 10.1080/03906701.2018.1477101

Borges, A. (2008). State Government, Political Competition, and Education Reform: Comparative Lessons from Brazil. *Bulletin of Latin American Research*, *27*(2), 235–254. DOI: 10.1111/j.1470-9856.2008.00265.x

Brazilian Report (2023). The Education Model Lula Wants to Replicate throughout Brazil. Retrieved from https://www.wilsoncenter.org/blog-post/education-model-lula-wants-replicate-throughout-brazil (07.08.2024).

Briffault, R. (1996). Public finance in the american federal system: basic patterns and current issues. Colum. J. Eur. L., 2, 533. https://scholarship.law.columbia.edu/faculty_scholarship/3575

British Columbia Ministry of Education. (2001). *Teaching Students with Mental Health Disorders: Resources for Teachers.* British Columbia Ministry of Education: Special Programs Branch. https://cemh.lbpsb.qc.ca/Portals/cemh/Mood/Teaching-Students-Mental-Health-Disorders.pdf

Brown, W. (2003). Neoliberalism and the End of Liberal Democracy. *Theory & Event*, *7*(1), 15–18. DOI: 10.1353/tae.2003.0020

Butler, M., & Pang, M. (2014). *Current Issues in Mental Health in Canada: Child and Youth Mental Health.* Library of Parliament. https://epe.lac-bac.gc.ca/100/201/301/weekly_checklist/2014/internet/w14-18-U-E.html/collections/collection_2014/bdp-lop/eb/2014-13-eng.pdf

Callanan, M. (2005). Institutionalizing participation and governance? New participative structures in local government in Ireland. *Public Administration*, *83*(4), 909–929. DOI: 10.1111/j.0033-3298.2005.00483.x

Campbell, T. (2001). *The Quiet Revolution: The Rise of Political Participation and Leading Cities with Decentralization in Latin America and the Caribbean*. University of Pittsburgh Press.

Çarkoğlu, A., & Kalaycıoğlu, E. (2009). *The rising tide of conservatism in Turkey*. Palgrave Macmillan. DOI: 10.1057/9780230621534

CDG. (Center for Democracy and Governance). (2000). *Decentralization and Democratic Local Governance Programming Handbook*. CDG Bureau for Global Programs.

Çetin, H. (2007). *Çağdaş siyasal Akımlar*. Orion Kitabevi.

Chang, Z., Schwartz, M. C., Hinesley, V., & Dubinsky, J. M. (2021). Neuroscience Concepts Changed Teachers' Views of Pedagogy and Students. *Frontiers in Psychology, 12*, 685856. Advance online publication. DOI: 10.3389/fpsyg.2021.685856 PMID: 34456800

Cheema, G. S., & Rondinelli, D. A. (2007). *Decentralizing Governance*. Brookings Institution Press.

Cheema, G. S., & Rondinelli, D. A. (Eds.). (2007). *Decentralizing governance: Emerging concepts and practices*. Brookings Institution Press.

Choi, Y. S., Cho, C. L., & Wright, D. S. (2004). Administrative autonomy among american state agencies: An empirical analysis of fragmentation and functionalism. *International Journal of Public Administration, 27*(6), 373–398.

Choutagunta, A. (2025, April 19). G. P. Manish, and Shruti Rajagopalan. 2021. "Battling COVID-19 with dysfunctional federalism: Lessons from India.". *Southern Economic Journal, 87*(4), 1267–1299. https://www.jstor.org/stable/27189159

Çınar, M. (2011). The Justice and Development Party and the Kemalist Establishment. *Turkish Studies, 12*(1), 1–16. DOI: 10.1080/14683849.2011.563181

Citizens Foundation. (2022). *Better Reykjavik Annual Report*. https://citizens.is

Climie, E., & Altomare, A. (n.d.). *Supporting Children with Mental Health Concerns in Classrooms*.https://files.eric.ed.gov/fulltext/EJ1033189.pdf

Constitution of the Republic of Azerbaijan [Azərbaycan Respublikasının Konstitusiyası]. (1995). https://e-qanun.az/framework/897

Constitutional Law of the Republic of Azerbaijan on the Approval of the Constitution of the Nakhchivan Autonomous Republic. (1998). [Naxçıvan Muxtar Respublikasının Konstitusiyasının təsdiq edilməsi haqqında Azərbaycan Respublikasının Konstitusiya Qanunu]. https://e-qanun.az/framework/1755

Cotoi, C. (2011). Neoliberalism: A Foucauldian Perspective. *International Review of Social Research, 1*(2), 109–124. DOI: 10.1515/irsr-2011-0014

Council of Europe. (2017), Local and Regional Democracy in Italy, https://www.coe.int/en/web/congress/-/local-and-regional-democracy-in-italy, (Erişim Tarihi: 03.02.2025)

Council of Europe. (2017). *European Charter of Local Self-Government.* Strasbourg: Council of Europe Publishing. https://www.coe.int/en/web/conventions/full-list/-/conventions/treaty/122

Country Gender Profile Azerbaijan. EU 4Gender Equality: Reform Help Desk. European Union. (2021). https://euneighbourseast.eu/wp-content/uploads/2022/07/eu4genderhelpdesk_azerbaijangenderprofile_v3.pdf

Craig, S. G., Bondi, B., Ames, M., & Pepler, D. (2022). Canadian adolescents' mental health and substance use during the COVID-19 pandemic: Associations with COVID-19 stressors. *Canadian Journal of Behavioural Science.* Advance online publication. DOI: 10.1037/cbs0000305

Cuadrado-Ballesteros, B. (2014). The impact of functional decentralization and externalization on local government transparency. *Government Information Quarterly, 31*(2), 265–277. DOI: 10.1016/j.giq.2013.10.012

Çukurçayır, M. A. & Eroğlu, H. (2011). "Belediye Meclisleri Üzerine Bir Değerlendirme." *Yerel Yönetim Araştırmaları Dergisi*, 1(2), ss. 56–75.

Curran, V., Ungar, T., & Pauze, E. (2006). *Strengthening Collaboration through Interprofessional Education: A Resource for Collaborative Mental Health Care Educators.* Canadian Collaborative Mental Health Initiative. https://www.shared-care.ca/files/EN_Strengtheningcollaborationthroughinterprofessionaleducation.pdf

Dabell, J. (2019). *Teacher Training Gap: Counselling.* John Dabell: Every Day Is A School Day. https://johndabell.com/2019/09/21/teacher-training-fail-counselling/

Dahlke, E. (2021). *I'm a Teacher, and I Can't Live Like This.* Medium. https://medium.com/educate-pub/im-a-teacher-and-i-can-t-live-like-this-95052a0e38ec

Dai, Y., Cheng, X., & Liu, Y. (2023). Information Alienation and Circle Fracture: Policy Communication and Opinion-Generating Networks on Social Media in China from the Perspective of COVID-19 Policy. *Systems*, *11*(7), 340. Advance online publication. DOI: 10.3390/systems11070340

Dao, T. H. M., & Nguyen, T. A. T. (2015). Citizen-centered local governance in Vietnam: The participation at local level. *Citizen Participation in Selected Local Governance of Asia Pacific Countries*, 111-128.

Dayal, R. (1960). *Community Development Program in India*. Kitab Mahal.

de Tocqueville, A. (2017). *Amerika'da Demokrasi* (M. Tüzel, Çev.). İstanbul: Türkiye İş Bankası Kültür Yayınları. (Orijinal eser 1835'te yayımlanmıştır.)

Dekker, R., Emilsson, H., Krieger, B., & Scholten, P. (2015). A local dimension of integration policies? A comparative study of Berlin, Malmö, and Rotterdam. *The International Migration Review*, *49*(3), 633–658. DOI: 10.1111/imre.12133

DeSouza, P. R. (2003). The Struggle for Local Government: Indian Democracy's New Phase. *Publius*, *33*(4), 99–118. https://www.jstor.org/stable/3331198. DOI: 10.1093/oxfordjournals.pubjof.a005015

Diaz, C. N. (2020). Students' Mental Health: The Importance of the Teacher's Role and Training. *Revista Educacion las Americas*, *10*(2), 277–287. Advance online publication. DOI: 10.35811/rea.v10i2.125

Dick-Sagoe, C. (2020). Decentralization for improving the provision of public services in developing countries: A critical review. *Cogent Economics & Finance*, *8*(1), 1804036. DOI: 10.1080/23322039.2020.1804036

Digital Executive Power. (2021). https://my.gov.az/serviceCategories/52f0ccb5-059a-4589-9777-e9f5208b4d91

Doikou, M., & Diamandidou, K. (2011). Enhancing teachers' counselling skills: Student teachers' views on a teachers' education programme. *European Journal of Teacher Education*, *34*(1), 61–79. DOI: 10.1080/02619768.2010.534979

Dong, C., Zheng, Q., & Morehouse, J. (2023). What do we know about government public relations (GPR)? A systematic review of GPR in public relations literature. *Public Relations Review*, *49*(1), 102284. DOI: 10.1016/j.pubrev.2022.102284

Dr. K. Krishna Murthy and Ors. *versus* Union of India (UOI) and Anr., 2010 AIR SCW 3368 (2010).

Drèze, J., & Sen, A. (1996). *India: Economic Development and Social Opportunity*. Oxford University Press. DOI: 10.1093/oso/9780198290124.001.0001

Dryzek, J. S. (2002). Difference democracy: The consciousness-raising group against the gentlemen's club. Deliberative Democracy and Beyond: Liberals, Critics, Contestations, 57-80.

Eastmon, S. (2009). Counselling Skills for Teachers in Secondary Schools: Observations from One-day Workshops. *Pastoral Care in Education: An International Journal of Personal. Pastoral Care in Education, 13*(2), 25–28. DOI: 10.1080/02643949509470919

Ebenstein, W. (2003). *Siyasi Felsefenin Büyük Düşünürleri*. (Çeviren: İsmet Özel), Şule Yayınları, İstanbul

Ekornes, S. (2015). Teacher Perspectives on Their Role and the Challenges of Interprofessional Collaboration in Mental Health Promotion. *School Mental Health, 7*(3), 193–211. Advance online publication. DOI: 10.1007/s12310-015-9147-y

Elazar, D. J. (1987). *Exploring Federalism*. University of Alabama Press.

El-Gamal, A. A., Ismail, M. M., & El Bagoury, A. A. (2025). The Role of Coordination Mechanisms Between the central Government and Local Administration Units. In *Improving the Performance of the Local Administration Bodies in Egypt* (pp. 325–330). Arab Journal of Administration.

Elsharkawy, S. (2022). *Decentralization in Egypt: More than 10 years of a stumbling path*. Arab Forum for Alternatıves.

Englund, T. (2010). Educational Implications of the Idea of Deliberative Democracy. In Habermas, Critical theory and Education Eds M. Murphy, T. Fleming (pp. 27–40). Routledge.

Erbay, Y. & Akgün, H. (2017), Türkiye'de ve Avrupa'da Yerel Yönetimler, Yayımevi: Uluslararası İlişkiler Kütüphanesi, 2. Basım, s:832

Evans, P. (2002). Collective Capabilities, Culture, and Amartya Sen's Development as Freedom. *Studies in Comparative International Development, 37*(2), 54–60. DOI: 10.1007/BF02686261

Expert Interview 1. Education expert from Ceará. Interview Date: 06.06.2023

Expert Interview 2. Education expert from the UK. Interview Date: 27.07.2023

Faguet, J. P. (2014). Decentralization and governance. *World Development, 53*, 2–13. DOI: 10.1016/j.worlddev.2013.01.002

Faguet, J. P., & Shami, M. (2008). Fiscal decentralization and local government performance. *World Development, 36*(9), 1653–1679.

Fan, X., Qiu, S., & Sun, Y. (2020). Land finance dependence and urban land marketization in China: The perspective of strategic choice of local governments on land transfer. *Land Use Policy*, *99*, 105023. DOI: 10.1016/j.landusepol.2020.105023

Fazel, M., Soneson, E., Sellars, E., Butler, G., & Stein, A. (2023). Partnerships at the Interface of Education and Mental Health Services: The Utilization and Acceptability of the Provision of Specialist Liaison and Teacher Skills Training. *International Journal of Environmental Research and Public Health*, *20*(5), 4066. Advance online publication. DOI: 10.3390/ijerph20054066 PMID: 36901077

Feldman, S., & Gellert, P. (2006). The Seductive Quality of Central Human Capabilities: Sociological Insights Into Nussbaum And Sen's Disagreement. *Economy and Society*, *35*(3), 423–452. DOI: 10.1080/03085140600845008

Felten, P., Little, D., & Pingree, A. (2004). 11: Foucault and the Practice of Educational Development: Power and Surveillance in Individual Consultations. *To Improve the Academy: A Journal of Educational Development*. 540.173-188.

Fisher, R. C. (2022). *State and local public finance*. Routledge. DOI: 10.4324/9781003030645

Foucault, M. (1978). *Security, Territory, Population, Lectures at College de France 1977-1978*. Palgrave.

Foucault, M. (1982). The Subject and Power. *Critical Inquiry*, *8*(4), 777–795. DOI: 10.1086/448181

Freire, P. (1970). Cultural Action and Conscientization. *Harvard Educational Review*, *40*(3), 452–477. DOI: 10.17763/haer.40.3.h76250x720j43175

Fritzen, S. A. (2006). Probing system limits: Decentralisation and local political accountability in Vietnam. *Asia Pacific Journal of Public Administration*, *28*(1), 1–23. DOI: 10.1080/23276665.2006.10779312

Fukuyama, F. (2013). What is governance? *Governance: An International Journal of Policy, Administration and Institutions*, *26*(3), 347–368. DOI: 10.1111/gove.12035

Gadotti, M., & Torres, C. A. (2009). Paulo Freire: Education for development. *Development and Change*, *40*(6), 1255–1267. DOI: 10.1111/j.1467-7660.2009.01606.x

Gainsborough, M. (2003). *Changing political economy of Vietnam: the case of Ho Chi Minh City*. Routledge. DOI: 10.4324/9780203222317

Garg, B. S., & Raut, A. V. (2015). Adarsh Gram: A Gandhian Dream of Gram Swaraj. *Indian Journal of Community Medicine : Official Publication of Indian Association of Preventive & Social Medicine*, *40*(1), 1–4. https://pmc.ncbi.nlm.nih .gov/articles/PMC4317974/. DOI: 10.4103/0970-0218.149260 PMID: 25657504

Gasper, D. (2023). Amartya Sen as a Social and Political Theorist – on Personhood, Democracy, and 'Description as a Choice.'. *Journal of Global Ethics*, *19*(3), 386–409. DOI: 10.1080/17449626.2023.2255600

Gaventa, J. (2004). Participatory development or participatory democracy? Linking participatory approaches to policy and governance. *IDS Bulletin*, *35*(2), 1–11. DOI: 10.1111/j.1759-5436.2002.tb00020.x

Geray, C. (1997), Ülke Ülke Yerel Yönetimler(İtalya), Çağdaş Yerel Yönetimler Dergisi,Cilt6, sayı:1, s: 53-76.

Glassman, M., & Patton, R. (2014). Capability through participatory democracy: Sen, Freire, and Dewey. *Educational Philosophy and Theory*, *46*(12), 1353–1365. DOI: 10.1080/00131857.2013.828582

Glette, M. K., & Wiig, S. (2022). The Headaches of Case Study Research: A Discussion of Emerging Challenges and Possible Ways out of the Pain. *The Qualitative Report*, *27*(5), 1377–1392. DOI: 10.46743/2160-3715/2022.5246

Gluck, A. (2022). MDL nationalism, federalism, and the opioid epidemic. *De Paul Law Review*, *70*(2), 321. https://via.library.depaul.edu/law-review/vol70/iss2/5

Goble, N. M., & Porter, J. F. (1977). *The*. UNESCO. https://eric.ed.gov/?id= ED167485

Goelzhauser, G., & Konisky, D. M. (2020). The state of American federalism 2019–2020: Polarized and punitive intergovernmental relations. *Publius*, *50*(3), 311–343. DOI: 10.1093/publius/pjaa021

Göze, A. (2007). *Siyasal Düşünceler ve Yönetimler*. Beta Basım Yayın.

Gram Panchayat, Patiala *versus* State of Punjab and Others, SLP No. 5322 of 1990 (1990).

Grogan, C. M. (2025). Medicaid's Political Development since 1965: How a Fragmented and Unequal Program Has Expanded. *Journal of Health Politics, Policy and Law*, *50*(2), 137–164.

Grossman, P., Hammerness, K., & McDonald, M. (2009). Redefining teaching, re-imagining teacher education. *Teachers and Teaching*, *15*(2), 273–289. DOI: 10.1080/13540600902875340

Gupta, S. (2025). Developing India's Food Processing Sector: Farm Politics, Federalism, and State-Directed Development. *Studies in Comparative International Development*, •••, 1–26.

Hanna, N. (2016). *The State and its Servants: Administration in Egypt from Ottoman Times to the Present.* American University in Cairo.

Harb, M., & Atallah, S. (2020). *Local Governments and Public Goods: Assessing Decentralization in the Arab World.* London College of Professional Studies.

Harnek Singh *versus* Charanjit Singh and Ors., 10 SC CK 0085 (2005).

Hart, C. S. (2012). The Capability Approach and Education. *Cambridge Journal of Education, 42*(3), 275–282. DOI: 10.1080/0305764X.2012.706393

Harvey, D. (2015). *Neoliberalizmin Kısa Tarihi.* İstanbul Sel Yayıncılık.

Hastings, M. (2019). Neoliberalism and Education. *Oxford Research Encyclopedia of Education.* Retrieved 10 Apr. 2025, from https://oxfordre.com/education/view/10.1093/acrefore/9780190264093.001.0001/acrefore-9780190264093-e-404

Heitzman, J., & Worden, R. L. (1996, January). India: a country study. < bound method Organization. get_name_with_acronym of< Organization: Library of Congress>>.

Helbawy, H. E. (2024). *Decentralization as a Tool for Service Delivery and Development The Egyptian and Dutch Experience.* Urban Library.

Helsinki City Executive Office. (2021). *OmaStadi Evaluation Report.* https://omastadi.hel.fi

Henry, N. (2015). *Public administration and public affairs.* Routledge.

Hill, D. M. (2024). *Democratic theory and local government.* Taylor & Francis. DOI: 10.4324/9781003583561

Ho, A. T. K. (2002). Reinventing local governments and the e-government initiative. *Public Administration Review, 62*(4), 434–444. DOI: 10.1111/0033-3352.00197

Holt-Reynolds. (1999). What does the teacher do? Constructivist pedagogies and prospective teachers' beliefs about the role of a teacher. *Teaching and Teacher Education, 16*(2000), 21-32. https://citeseerx.ist.psu.edu/document?repid=rep1&type=pdf&doi=32dde0b9ac17f08b78cd078c1150862c18ff3b43

Hope, K. R. (2001). The new public management: Context and practice in Africa. *International Public Management Journal, 4*(2), 119–134. DOI: 10.1016/S1096-7494(01)00053-8

Hossin, M. A., Du, J., Mu, L., & Asante, I. O. (2023). Big Data-Driven Public Policy Decisions: Transformation Toward Smart Governance. *SAGE Open*, *13*(4), 1–19. DOI: 10.1177/21582440231215123

Huber, E., & Stephens, J. D. (2014). *Democracy and the Left: Social Policy and Inequality in Latin America*. University of Chicago Press.

Hue, T. H. H., & Tung-Wen Sun, M. (2022). Democratic governance: Examining the Influence of citizen participation on local government performance in Vietnam. *International Journal of Public Administration*, *45*(1), 4–22. DOI: 10.1080/01900692.2021.1939713

Huseynov, S. Z. (2023). Local Self-Government Bodies in the Republic of Azerbaijan: Legal Status, Tasks and Prospects. *Futurity Economics&Law*, *3*(2), 18–40. DOI: 10.57125/FEL.2023.06.25.02

Huseynov, S. Z. (2023). Organisation of local self-government in the Republic of Azerbaijan. *Futurity Economics & Law*, *3*(4), 239–254. DOI: 10.57125/FEL.2023.12.25.15

Hussein, S. A., & Vostanis, P. (2013). Teacher training intervention for early identification of common child mental health problems in Pakistan. *Emotional & Behavioural Difficulties*, *18*(3), 284–296. DOI: 10.1080/13632752.2013.819254

Iannello, C. (2002) Italian Republic, United Cities and Local Governments- Co untry Public: Italy, University of Naples, https://www.gold.uclg.org/sites/default/files/Italy_0.pdf, (Erişim Tarihi: 07.01.2005)

Ibrahim, A. H. (2024). *Decentralization and its Impact on Improving Public Services*. University of North Maluku. DOI: 10.21744/ijss.v7n2.2278

Ibrahim, S. (2017). How to Build Collective Capabilities: The 3C-model for Grassroots-led Development. *Journal of Human Development and Capabilities*, *18*(2), 197–222. DOI: 10.1080/19452829.2016.1270918

Ibrahim, S. S. (2006). From Individual to Collective Capabilities: The Capability Approach as a Conceptual Framework for Self-help. *Journal of Human Development*, *7*(3), 397–416. DOI: 10.1080/14649880600815982

Imchen, A., & Ndem, F. (2020). *Addressing the Learning Crisis: An Urgent Need to Better Finance Education for the Poorest Children*. UNICEF.

IOEB. (2024). Dados e análise. Retrieved from: https://ioeb.org.br/dados-e-analise/ (04.04.2025)

Italiano, G. (2025), https://www.governo.it/it/costituzione-italiana/parte-seconda-ordinamen to-della-repubblica/titolo-v-le-regionile-province-e-i.Erişim Tarihi: 02.02.2025

Jaenendra Kumar Phoolchand Daftari *versus* Rajendra Ramsukh Mishra, Civil Appeal No. 1303 of 1993 (1993).

Jalali, M. S., Botticelli, M., Hwang, R. C., Koh, H. K., & McHugh, R. K. (2020). The opioid crisis: A contextual, social-ecological framework. *Health Research Policy and Systems*, *18*(1), 87. DOI: 10.1186/s12961-020-00596-8

Jha, S. (2000). Fiscal Decentralization in India: Strengths, Limitations and Prospects for Panchayati Raj Institutions. *Background Paper No. 2*. World Bank. DOI:DOI: 10.13140/RG.2.1.3813.2884

Johnson, C. (2003). Decentralization in India: Poverty, Politics and Panchayati Raj. *Working Paper 199*. ODI. https://assets.publishing.service.gov.uk/media/57a08cf240f0b6497400154e/wp199_print.pdf

Joshi, D. (2002). *Gandhiji on Villages*. Mani Bhavan Gandhi Sangrahalaya.

Junaidi, A., Basrowi, B., Sabtohadi, J., Wibowo, A. M., Wibowo, S. S., Asgar, A., Pramono, E. P., & Yenti, E. (2024). The role of public administration and social media educational socialization in influencing public satisfaction on population services: The mediating role of population literacy awareness. *International Journal of Data and Network Science*, *8*(1), 345–356. DOI: 10.5267/j.ijdns.2023.9.019

Jutting, J., Corsi, E., & Stockmayer, A. (2005). Decentralization and poverty reduction. *OECD Development Centre Working Paper*, 236.

Kadarpeta, R. S. R., Anand, J. S., & Achungura, G. (2024). Strengthening Public Financing of Primary Healthcare in India: A Perspective. *Health Services Insights*, *17*, 11786329241249289.

Kadıoğlu, A. (2005). Denationalization of citizenship? The Turkish experience. *Citizenship Studies*, *9*(3), 357–377.

Kannan, K. P. (1993). Local Self-Government and Decentralized Development. *EPW* 28(49), 2644-2646. https://www.epw.in/journal/1993/49/commentary/panchayat-raj-act-local-self-government-and-decentralised-development

Karapin, R. (2020). Federalism as a double-edged sword: The slow energy transition in the United States. *Journal of Environment & Development*, *29*(1), 26–50.

Karpat, K. H. (1985). *Ottoman population, 1830–1914: Demographic and social characteristics*. University of Wisconsin Press.

Kattinokkula Murali Krishna *versus* Veeramalla Koteswara Rao and Ors., AIR 2010 SUPREME COURT 24 (2010).

Kavruk, H. (2021), Yerel ve Bölgesel Yönetimler-Yerel Yönetimler, Birlikler, Ajanslar, Özel Alan Yönetimleri, Ankara, Nobel Yayınevi, s:457

Keating, M. (2009). *The Independence of Scotland: Self-government and the shifting politics of union*. Oxford University Press. DOI: 10.1093/acprof:o-so/9780199545957.001.0001

Keleş, R. (2016). *Yerinden Yönetim ve Siyaset* (9. Baskı). İstanbul: Cem Yayınları.

Kelly, M. J. (1998). Political Downsizing: The Re-Emergence Of Self Determination, and The Movement Toward Smaller, Ethnically Homoge nous States, HeinOnline. *Drake Law Review*, *49*, 209–397.

Kerkvliet, B. J. T. (2004). Surveying local government and authority in contemporary Vietnam. *Beyond Hanoi: local government in Vietnam*, 1-27.

Kessy, A. (2013). Decentralization and Citizens' Participation: Some Theoretical and Conceptual Perspectives: 219. Brill. kohli, A. (2004). State-Directed Development: Political Power and Industrialization in the Global Periphery p143-180. Cambridge.

Keyman, E. F., & Koyuncu, B. (2005). Globalization, alternative modernities and the political economy of Turkey. *Review of International Political Economy*, *12*(1), 105–128. DOI: 10.1080/09692290500049896

Keyman, F. (2010). *Modernleşme, Ulus-Devlet ve Demokrasi: Türkiye Üzerine Tezler*. İstanbul Bilgi Üniversitesi Yayınları.

Kim, M., & Cho, M. (2019). Examining the role of sense of community: Linking local government public relationships and community-building. *Public Relations Review*, *45*(2), 297–306. DOI: 10.1016/j.pubrev.2019.02.002

King's Printer for Ontario. (2023). *Policy/Program Memorandum 169*.https://www.ontario.ca/document/education-ontario-policy-and-program-direction/policyprogram-memorandum-169#section-5

Kjeldsen, C. C., & Bonvin, J. M. (2015). The Capability Approach, Education and the Labour Market. In Otto, H. U. (Eds.), *Facing Trajectories from School to Work. Technical and Vocational Education and Training: Issues, Concerns and Prospects, 20*. Springer., DOI: 10.1007/978-3-319-11436-1_2

Klimovský, D., & Swianiewicz, P.. (2010). Territorial Consolidation Reforms. In Swianiewicz, P. (Ed.), *Europe. Edition: 1st, Publisher: OSI/LGI*.

Koçak, H. (1996), "Ülke Ülke Yerel Yönetimler- İtalya'da Yerel Yönetimler" Çağdaş Yerel Yönetimler, cilt 5, sayı 4, Temmuz 1996, s:57-66

Kolers, A. (2023). Collective Political Capabilities. *Ethics & Global Politics*, *16*(2), 46–54. DOI: 10.1080/16544951.2023.2216110

Koller, J. R., & Bertel, J. M. (2006). Responding to today's mental health needs of children, families and schools: Revisiting the preservice training and preparation of school-based personnel. *Education & Treatment of Children*, *29*(2), 197.

Kong, H., & Liu, H. (2023). The Relationship between ICT Use and Perceived Life Satisfaction among Older People in Korea: The Mediating Effect of Social Capital. *Sustainability (Basel)*, *15*(12), 9353. Advance online publication. DOI: 10.3390/su15129353

König, P. D. (2021). A magic bullet in policy communication? On the ambiguous use of framing in policy research. *Policy Studies*, *42*(1), 60–79. DOI: 10.1080/01442872.2019.1581153

Korbey, H. (2022). *What's the Role of Teachers in Supporting Student Mental Health?* Edutopia. https://www.edutopia.org/article/the-doctor-is-in-your-classroom/

Koşar, N. (2013), "İtalya'da Yerel Yönetimler ve Merkezi Yönetim– Yerel Yönetimler Arası Mali İlişkiler", Uluslararası Yönetim İktisat ve İşletme Dergisi, Cilt 9, Sayı 18, s: 327-348

Küçük, H. (2019), 'Merkez-Çevre Teorisi Ve Yerelleşmeye Etkisi: İtalya Örneği', Journal of Political Administrative and Local Studies, cilt 2, sayı, s:1-26

Kumar, R. (2015). Historical Development of Panchayati Raj in India. *IJMSS*, *3*(8), 523–530.

Kurun, İ. (2015). *Democratisation in Egypt From A Historical Perspective: Problems, Pitfalls and Prospects.* Yönetim ve Ekonomi.

Labor Code of the Republic of Azerbaijan. (1999). [Azərbaycan Respublikasının mək Məcəlləsi]. https://e-qanun.az/framework/46943

Lai-Yeung, S. W. C. (2014). The Need for Guidance and Counselling Training for Teachers. *Procedia: Social and Behavioral Sciences*, *113*, 36–43. DOI: 10.1016/j.sbspro.2014.01.008

Lampoltshammer, T. J., De Luca, G., & Thurnay, L. (2023). Digital News and Political Tweets in the Lower Austrian Municipal Elections: A Case Study on Digital Journalism and Political Communication. *Social Sciences (Basel, Switzerland)*, *12*(1), 18. Advance online publication. DOI: 10.3390/socsci12010018

Land Code of the Republic of Azerbaijan. (1999). [Azərbaycan Respublikasının Torpaq Məcəlləsi]. https://e-qanun.az/framework/46942

Lanier, J. T. (1997). *Redefining the Role of the Teacher: It's a Multifaceted Profession*. Edutopia. https://www.edutopia.org/redefining-role-teacher

Larousse, M. (1981), Meydan Gazetecilik ve Neşriyat, İstanbul, s:5970

Law of the Republic of Azerbaijan on Access to Information. (2005). [İnformasiya əldə etmək haqqında Azərbaycan Respublikasının Qanunu]. https://e-qanun.az/framework/11142

Law of the Republic of Azerbaijan on Approval of the Model Regulations on Neighborhood Committees of Municipalities. (2001). [Bələdiyyələrin məhəllə komitələri haqqında Nümunəvi sasnamənin təsdiq edilməsi barədə Azərbaycan Respublikasının Qanunu]. https://e-qanun.az/framework/3547

Law of the Republic of Azerbaijan on local (municipal) taxes and payments. (2001). [Yerli (bələdiyyə) vergilər və ödənişlər haqqında Azərbaycan Respublikasının Qanunu]. https://e-qanun.az/framework/1470

Law of the Republic of Azerbaijan on Local Opinion Poll. (1999). [Yerli rəy sorğusu haqqında Azərbaycan Respublikasının Qanunu]. https://e-qanun.az/framework/5227

Law of the Republic of Azerbaijan on Municipal Service. (1999). [Bələdiyyə qulluğu haqqında Azərbaycan Respublikasının Qanunu]. https://e-qanun.az/framework/5228

Law of the Republic of Azerbaijan on Municipal Territories and Lands. (1999). [Bələdiyyələrin əraziləri və torpaqları haqqında Azərbaycan Respublikasının Qanunu]. https://www.taxes.gov.az/az/post/195

Law of the Republic of Azerbaijan on Municipal Water Management. (2001). [Bələdiyyələrin su təsərrüfatı haqqında Azərbaycan Respublikasının Qanunu]. https://e-qanun.az/framework/2760

Law of the Republic of Azerbaijan on Public Participation. (2013). [İctimai iştirakçılıq haqqında Azərbaycan Respublikasının Qanunu]. https://e-qanun.az/framework/26879

Law of the Republic of Azerbaijan on the Fundamentals of Municipal Finance. (1999). [Bələdiyyələrin maliyyəsinin əsasları haqqında Azərbaycan Respublikasının Qanunu]. https://e-qanun.az/framework/5231

Law of the Republic of Azerbaijan on the status of a municipal member. (2000). [Bələdiyyə üzvünün statusu haqqında Azərbaycan Respublikasının Qanunu]. https://e-qanun.az/framework/507

Law of the Republic of Azerbaijan on the status of municipalities. (1999). [Bələdiyyələrin statusu haqqında Azərbaycan Respublikasının Qanunu]. https://e-qanun.az/framework/4770

Lawrence, J., Sullivan, F., Lash, A., Ide, G., Cameron, C., & McGlinchey, L. (2015). Adapting to changing climate risk by local government in New Zealand: Institutional practice barriers and enablers. *Local Environment*, *20*(3), 298–320. DOI: 10.1080/13549839.2013.839643

Leonardsson, H., & Rudd, G. (2015). The 'local turn' in peacebuilding: A literature review of effective and emancipatory local peacebuilding. *Third World Quarterly*, *36*(5), 825–839. DOI: 10.1080/01436597.2015.1029905

Levy, C. (2012). Social Movements and Political Parties in Brazil: Expanding Democracy, the 'Struggle for the Possible' and the Reproduction of Power Structures. *Globalizations*, *9*(6), 783–798. DOI: 10.1080/14747731.2012.739340

Lewis, N. (2024). A new city is rising in Egypt. But is it what the country needs? CNN world .

Lima, V. (2019). The Limits of Participatory Democracy and the Inclusion of Social Movements in Local Government. *Social Movement Studies*, *18*(6), 667–681. DOI: 10.1080/14742837.2019.1629277

Local Government Country Profile. UN Women. (2022). https://localgov.unwomen.org/country/AZE

Local self-government in Azerbaijan: few improvements observed, limited powers and weak financial position of municipalities must be urgently addressed. Congress of Local and Regional Authorities. (2021). https://www.coe.int/en/web/congress/-/local-self-government-in-azerbaijan-few-improvements-observed-limited-powers-and-weak-financial-position-of-municipalities-must-be-urgently-addressed

Loughlin, J., Hendriks, F., & Lidström, A. (2011). *The Oxford Handbook of Local and Regional Democracy in Europe*. Oxford University Press.

Loureiro, A., Gropella, E., & Arias, O. (2020). There is No Magic: The Formula for Brazil's Ceará and Sobral Success to Reduce Learning Poverty. Retrieved from https://blogs.worldbank.org/education/there-no-magic-formula-brazils-ceara-and-sobral-success-reduce-learning-poverty

Lynch, R. A. (2014). Foucault's Theory of Power. In Michel Foucault (pp. 13–26). Routledge.

Malla, A., Shah, J., Iyer, S., Boksa, P., Risha, J., Andersson, N., Lal, S., & Fuhrer, R. (2018). Youth Mental Health Should Be a Top Priority for Health Care in Canada. *Canadian Journal of Psychiatry*, *63*(4), 216–222. DOI: 10.1177/0706743718758968 PMID: 29528719

Manor, J. (1999). *The Political Economy of Democratic Decentralization*. The World Bank. DOI: 10.1596/0-8213-4470-6

Mariano, A., & Tarlau, R. (2019). The Landless Workers Movement's itinerant schools: Occupying and transforming public education in Brazil. *British Journal of Sociology of Education*, *40*(4), 538–559. DOI: 10.1080/01425692.2019.1565989

Maria, S., Carvalho, G., & Mendes, J. E. (2011). The University and the Landless Movement in Brazil: The Experience of Collective Knowledge Construction through Educational Projects in Rural Areas. In Motta, S. C., & Nilsen, A. G. (Eds.), *Social Movements in the Global South*. Rethinking International Development Series. Palgrave Macmillan., DOI: 10.1057/9780230302044_6

Marr, D. G. (2004). A brief history of local government in Vietnam. *Beyond Hanoi: local government in Vietnam*, 28-53.

Martinez, J., & Timofeev, A. (2010). *Decentralizing Egypt: Not Just Another Economic Reform: 7-8*. International Center for Public Policy.

Martins, D. (2004). *M. (2000) Neo-Liberalizme Karşı MST'nin Kafa Tutuşu. İçinde Topraksızlar*. İletişim Yayınları.

McCarty, A. (2001, March). Governance institutions and incentive structures in Vietnam. In *Conference on Building Institutional Capacity in Asia: Public Sector Challenges and Government Reforms in South East Asia;* 12 March; Jakarta.

McCullough, M. (2010). *Support for Health Minds*. Professionally Speaking: The Magazine of the Ontario College of Teachers. https://professionallyspeaking.oct.ca/december_2010/features/healthy_minds.aspx

Meekel, T. (2008). Local government finance in Serbia. In *Local public finance in Central and Eastern Europe* (pp. 364–390). Edward Elgar Publishing. DOI: 10.4337/9781035305124.00022

Meenakshisundaram, S. S. (1999). Decentralization in Developing Countries. In S. N. Jha & P. C.

Mete, H. (2020). Kürt Sorunu, Yerel Yönetimler ve Kayyum Politikaları: Eleştirel Bir Değerlendirme. *Toplum ve Demokrasi*, *14*(2), 67–92.

Miller, D. (2002). *The Regional Governing Of Metropolitan America*. Routledge.

Ministry of Justice of the Republic of Azerbaijan Center for Work with Municipalities. (2019). Collection of methodological documents Baku. “Red N Line” LLC., 32 p.

Ministry of Panchayati Raj, Government of India. (2020). Panchayat Elections in India: A Review. Retrieved from https://panchayat.gov.in

Mintrom, M. (2001). Educational Governance and Democratic Practice. *Educational Policy, 15*(5), 615–643. DOI: 10.1177/0895904801015005001

Monks, K. (2017). Egypt plans new controls on social media. CNN world.

Montesquieu, C. (1998). *Kanunların Ruhu Üzerine I*, (Çeviren: Fehmi Baldaş), Toplumsal Dönüşüm Yayınları, İstanbul

Montesquieu, C. (2017), *Kanunların Ruhu Üzerine*, (Çev. Berna Günen), Türkiye İş Bankası Kültür Yayınları, Kitap I, Bölüm 3.

Montesquieu, C. (2016). *Kanunların Ruhu Üzerine*. (Çev. Mehmet Ali Ağaoğulları). İstanbul: Türkiye İş Bankası Kültür Yayınları. Kitap XI. *Bölüm, 4*, 6.

Morgan, P. J., & Trinh, L. Q. (2017). Fiscal decentralization and local budget deficits in Viet Nam: An empirical analysis. In *Central and Local Government Relations in Asia* (pp. 333–368). Edward Elgar Publishing. DOI: 10.4337/9781786436870.00019

Morrow, R. A., & Torres, C. A. (2002). *Reading Freire and Habermas: Critical Pedagogy and Transformative Social Change*. Teachers College Press.

Morsy, A. (2015). *A Delayed Transition: Egypt's Suspended Elections*. Middle East Institute.

Motta, S., & Nilsen, A. G. (2011). Social Movements and/in the Postcolonial: Dispossession, Development, and Resistance in the Global South Motta, S., & Nilsen, A. G. (Eds.). (2011). Social Movements in the Global South: Dispossession, development and resistance. Springer.

Mulder, F. (2023). The paradox of externally driven localisation: A case study on how local actors manage the contradictory legitimacy requirements of top-down bottom-up aid. *Journal of International Humanitarian Action, 8*(1), 5–7. DOI: 10.1186/s41018-023-00139-0

Muneja, P. (2023). Open Science and Policy Interface: The Tanzania Perspective. *East African Journal of Science, Technology and Innovation, 4*(Special Issue 2). DOI: 10.37425/eajsti.v4i3.771

Mu, R., & Wang, H. (2022). A systematic literature review of open innovation in the public sector: Comparing barriers and governance strategies of digital and non-digital open innovation. *Public Management Review*, *24*(4), 489–511. DOI: 10.1080/14719037.2020.1838787

Murphy, M. (2014). Self-determination as a Collective Capability: The Case of Indigenous Peoples. *Journal of Human Development and Capabilities*, *15*(4), 320–334. DOI: 10.1080/19452829.2013.878320

Ngo, H. V., Edelenbos, J., & Gianoli, A. (2019). Community participation and local government capacity in Vietnam: Conditions for coproduction. *Public Administration and Development*, *39*(2), 104–118. DOI: 10.1002/pad.1844

Nguyen, T. B., & Nguyen, Q. G. (2022). Transparency in Local Government in Vietnam. *Scientific Papers of the University of Pardubice. Series D. Faculty of Economics and Administration, 30*(2).

Nguyen, B., Mickiewicz, T., & Du, J. (2018). Local governance and business performance in Vietnam: The transaction costs' perspective. *Regional Studies*, *52*(4), 542–557. DOI: 10.1080/00343404.2017.1341625

Nguyen, T. V., Bach, T. N., Le, T. Q., & Le, C. Q. (2017). Local governance, corruption, and public service quality: Evidence from a national survey in Vietnam. *International Journal of Public Sector Management*, *30*(2), 137–153. DOI: 10.1108/IJPSM-08-2016-0128

Nussbaum, M. (2020). The Capabilities Approach and the History of Philosophy. In E. Chiappero-Martinetti, S. Osmani, & M. Qizilbash (Eds.), *The Cambridge Handbook of the Capability Approach* (pp. 13–39). chapter, Cambridge: Cambridge University Press. DOI: 10.1017/9781316335741.003

Nyathikala, S. A., Jamasb, T., Llorca, M., & Kulshrestha, M. (2023). Utility Governance, Incentives, and Performance: Evidence from India's Urban Water Sector. *Utilities Policy*, *82*, 101534. DOI: 10.1016/j.jup.2023.101534

O'Cadiz del Pilar, M. Wong, P. L., & Torres, C. A. (1998). Creating the Popular Public School: Theoretical Foundations and Policy Initiatives. In Education and Democracy (pp. 71-105). Routledge.

OECD. (2019). *Making Decentralization Work: A Handbook for Policymakers*. OECD.

OECD. (2020). *Decentralisation and Local Public Finance in Europe*. OECD Publications.

OECD. (2022). *Enhancing Public Participation in Local Governance: Comparative Country Studies*. OECD Publishing. ss.

Ola, R. O. (2021). *Local administration in Nigeria.* Routledge. DOI: 10.4324/9781003209546

Oliveira, E. S., Justo, W. R., & De Lucena, M. A. (2024). The Dynamics of Public High School Student Performance in Ceará: A Study of the Case of Sobral in Brazil. *Journal of the Humanities and Social Sciences, 29*(3), 12–24. DOI: 10.9790/0837-2903011224

Olivetti, M. (2014), ''Centralization vs. Decentralization: The Current Trends in Italy'', Korel Göymen ve Onur Sazlak (Ed.), Centralization Decentrali zation Debate Revisited, Sabancı Üniversitesi,İstanbul, s: 1-423

Olorunlana, T. J. (2023). The History of Democracy: From Ancient Athens to Present-Day. *ReseachGate*. DOI:DOI: 10.13140/RG.2.2.36785.15209

Olssen, M., Codd, J. A., & O'Neill, A. (2004). *Education Policy: Globalization, Citizenship, and Democracy*. Sage. DOI: 10.4135/9781446221501

Ontario College of Teachers. (n.d.). *Mental Health.* Ontario College of Teachers: Ontario's Teaching Regulator. https://www.oct.ca/members/research/mental-health

Onyango, G., & Ondiek, J. O. (2023). Digitalising analogue policy targets! 'Digital capabilities' of older persons and policy digitalisation of social safety net programs in a developing country context. *Journal of Technology in Human Services, 41*(4), 348–375. DOI: 10.1080/15228835.2023.2263494

Oommen, M. A. (2015). Local governments in the fiscal space of Indian federalism: towards more rational arrangements, RULSG Occasional Paper, https://cds.edu/wp-content/uploads/RULSG2_MAOommen.pdf

Opinion of the Chamber of Accounts of the Republic of Azerbaijan on the draft state budget of the Republic of Azerbaijan for 2024. (2023). [Azərbaycan Respublikasının 2024-cü il dövlət büdcəsinin layihəsinə Azərbaycan Respublikası Hesablama Palatasının rəyi]. https://sai.gov.az/files/r%C9%99y%202024%20layih%C9%99-892107023.pdf

Oran, B. (2001). *Türk Dış Politikası: Kurtuluş Savaşından Bugüne Olgular, Belgeler, Yorumlar (Cilt 1)*. İletişim Yayınları.

Organization for Economic Co-operation and Development. (2025). Consumer price indices (CPIs, HICPs), COICOP 1999: Consumer Price Index: Health for India [INDCP060000GYM], retrieved from FRED, Federal Reserve Bank of St. Louis; https://fred.stlouisfed.org/series/INDCP060000GYM

Ortaylı, İ. (2000). İmparatorluğun. In *Uzun Yüzyılı*. İletişim Yayınları.

Ostrom, E. (1990). *Governing the commons: The evolution of institutions for collective action*. Cambridge university press. DOI: 10.1017/CBO9780511807763

Ostrom, E. (2010). Beyond markets and states: Polycentric governance of complex economic systems. *The American Economic Review*, *100*(3), 641–672. DOI: 10.1257/aer.100.3.641

Özbudun, E. (2000). *Contemporary Turkish Politics: Challenges to Democratic Consolidation*. Lynne Rienner Publishers. DOI: 10.1515/9781626373174

Özbudun, E. (2009). *Türk Anayasa Hukuku*. Yetkin Yayınları.

Painter, M. (2003). Public administration reform in Vietnam: Problems and prospects. *Public Administration and Development*, *23*(3), 259–271. DOI: 10.1002/pad.249

PBS. (n.d.). *Only A Teacher: Teaching Timeline*. PBS Online. https://www.pbs.org/onlyateacher/timeline.html

Peters, B. G., & Pierre, J. (2006). Governance, Government, and the State. Theories and Issues, 209-222.

Pfister, T. (2012). Citizenship and Capability? Amartya Sen's Capabilities Approach from a Citizenship Perspective. *Citizenship Studies*, *16*(2), 241–254. DOI: 10.1080/13621025.2012.667615

Pham, T. H., Hoang, T. T. H., Thalassinos, E. I., & Le, H. A. (2022). The impact of quality of public administration on local economic growth in Vietnam. *Journal of Risk and Financial Management*, *15*(4), 158. DOI: 10.3390/jrfm15040158

Pickard, V. (2023). Another Media System is Possible: Ripping Open the Overton Window, from Platforms to Public Broadcasting. *Javnost (Ljubljana)*, *30*(2), 284–297. DOI: 10.1080/13183222.2023.2201804

Posner, P. W. (2011). *Democratization in Egypt: The Potential Role of Decentralization: 2-3*. The Urban Institute.

Praveen, R. (2018). Implementation of RTE Act: A Case Study of Two Gram Panchayats in Karnataka. *IJISSH*, *3*(2), 29–36.

Putnam, R. D. (1993). *Making Democracy Work: Civic Traditions in Modern Italy.* Princeton University Press.

R.N.A. Britto *versus* Chief Executive Officer and Others, Civil Appeal No. 718 of 1993 (1993).

Radhakisan Rathi *versus* Additional Collector, AIR 1995 SUPREME COURT 1540 (1995).

Raffer C.& Padovani,E.(2019), Local Public Finance in Europe:Country Reports, Gütersloh: Hertie School and Bartelsmann Stiftung, Italy, ss:141-153

Raghunathan, T. R. (2012). *Decentralization and Local Governments: The Indian Experience.* Orient Black Swan.

Raghvendra Kumar *versus* Prabal Kumar and Ors., 2013 AIR SCW 6208 (2013).

Rajput, J. S. (2002). Education. In Gupta, S. P. (Ed.), *Indian Vision* (pp. 42–47). Planning Commission. (Original work published 2020)

Rao, M. G., & Singh, N. (2001). Federalism in India: political economy and reform. Stanford Center for International Development, 1-30. https://kingcenter.stanford .edu/sites/g/files/sbiybj16611/files/media/file/108wp_0.pdf

Raynaud, P., & Rials, S. (2003). Siyaset Felsefesi Sözlüğü, (Çeviren.İsmail Yarguz, Necmettin Kamil Sevin, Emel ergun, Hüsnü Dilli), İletişim Yayınları, İstanbul

Regulations on local executive authorities. Decree of the President of the Republic of Azerbaijan, (2012). https://baku-ih.gov.az/en/legislation2.html

Report on the results of the activities of the chamber of auditors of the Republic Of Azerbaijan in 2023. (2024). [Azərbaycan Respublikası auditorlar palatasının 2023-cü ildə fəaliyyətinin yekunlarına dair hesabat]. https://www.audit.gov.az/Upload/Files/2019/HESABAT_illik-2023_son1.pdf

Resolution of the Cabinet of Ministers of the Republic of Azerbaijan on Amendments to Some Decisions of the Cabinet of Ministers of the Republic of Azerbaijan. (2000). [Azərbaycan Respublikası Nazirlər Kabinetinin bəzi qərarlarına dəyişikliklər edilməsi haqqında Azərbaycan Respublikası Nazirlər Kabinetinin Qərarı]. https://e-qanun.az/framework/212

Rethlesfsen, M., Kirtley, S., Waffenschmidt, S., Ayala, A., Moher, D., Page, M., Jonathan, K., & Group, P.-S. (2021). *PRISMA-S: an extension to the PRISMA Statement for Reporting Literature Searches in Systematic Reviews.*

Reuters. (2024). Egypt PM says Saudi's planned $5 bln investment independent of cenbank deposit. Reuters.

Rhodes, R. A. W. (2018). *Control and power in central-local government relations*. Routledge. DOI: 10.4324/9780429463518

Robeyns, I. (2017). *Wellbeing, Freedom, and Social Justice: The Capability Approach Re-examined*. Open Book Publishers. DOI: 10.11647/OBP.0130

Robinson, R. I. (2015). *Postwar Market for State and Local Government Securities*. Princeton University Press.

Rodden, J. A. (2006). *Hamilton's Paradox: The Promise and Peril of Fiscal Federalism*. Cambridge University Press.

Rodríguez-Pose, A., & Ezcurra, R. (2010). Does decentralization matter for regional disparities? *Journal of Economic Geography*, *10*(5), 619–644. DOI: 10.1093/jeg/lbp049

Rodríguez-Pose, A., & Kroijer, A. (2009). Fiscal decentralization and economic growth in Central and Eastern Europe. *Growth and Change*, *40*(3), 387–417. DOI: 10.1111/j.1468-2257.2009.00488.x

Rondinelli, D. A., & Nellis, J. (1986). Assessing Decentralization Policies in Developing Countries: The Case for Cautious Optimism p3-23. Development policy review- Oxford.

Rosignoli, F. (2019). Categorizing Collective Capabilities. *Partecipazione e Conflitto*, 11(3), 813-837. DOI: 10.1285/i20356609v11i3p813

Roziqin, A., Kamil, M., Romadhan, A. A., & Zakaria, I. (2024). The dark side of local public sector innovation: insights from SAMPADE innovation. J*ournal of Science and Technology Policy Management*. DOI: 10.1108/JSTPM-01-2024-0001

Roziqin, A., Mas'udi, S. Y. F., & Sihidi, I. T. (2021). An analysis of Indonesian government policies against COVID-19. *Public Administration and Policy*, *24*(1), 92–107. DOI: 10.1108/PAP-08-2020-0039

Rutherford, B. K. (2013). *Egypt after Mubarak: Liberalism, Islam, and Democracy in the Arab World*. Princeton University Press.

Sadigova, Z. (2021). The Improvement of E-Municipality Systems In Azerbaijan Local Governments. *70th International Scientific Conference on Economic and Social Development*.

Saefudin, Y., Ismail, N., Susanti, R., & Adi, L. K. (2023). Regulating Fake News and Hoaxes: A Comparative Analysis of Indonesia and Malaysia. *Journal of Human Rights. Culture and Legal System, 3*(3), 656–677. DOI: 10.53955/jhcls.v3i3.113

Saito, F. (2008). *Foundations for local governance: Decentralization in comparative perspective*. Springer. DOI: 10.1007/978-3-7908-2006-5

Saleh, A. (2018). Local Councils in Egypt: Decentralization and the Dream of Political Action. The legal agenda .

Salimli, N. (2022). Transparency in local self-government. The papers of the Ministry of Justice of the Republic of Azerbaijan. https://justice.gov.az/categories/1038

Salmanly, F. (2024). *Basic principles and historical stages of development of local self-government.*

Salzberger, E. M. (1993). A positive analysis of the doctrine of separation of powers, or: Why do we have an independent judiciary? *International Review of Law and Economics, 13*(4), 349–379. DOI: 10.1016/0144-8188(93)90029-5

Sayigh, Y. (2019). *Behind the Veil: Managing the Finances: 15*. Carnegie Middle East Center.

Schmidt, M. G. (2002). *Demokrasi Kuramlarına Giriş*. Vadi Yayınları.

Scholtz, C., & Munteanu, A. (2023). How cooperative is "cooperative federalism"? The political limits to intergovernmental cooperation under a de facto concurrency rule. *Constitutional Political Economy, 34*(1), 111–134.

Secretary, Sarvodaya Educational Society *versus* Ginjala Panasaiah and Ors., C.A. No. 2078 of 2000 (2000).

Segatto, C. I., & Abrucio, F. L. (2018). Multiple Roles of State Governments in the Brazilian Education Policy: the cases of Ceará, Mato Grosso do Sul, São Paulo and Pará. Reviste de Administração Pública, 52, 1179-1193. http://dx.doi.org/DOI: 10.1590/0034-761220170047

Sen, A. (1999). *Development as Freedom*. Alfred Knop Publishing.

Shah, A. (Ed.). (2006). *Local governance in developing countries*. World Bank Publications.

Shah, A., & Thompson, T. (2004). Implementing decentralized local governance: A treacherous road with potholes, detours, and road closures. *World Bank Policy Research Working Paper, 3353*, 1–27.

Shantir, M. A. (2022). Decentralization and Geographical Inequality in Egypt. Arab reform initiative .

Sheikh, Y. A. (2014). Democratic Decentralization in India: An Overview. *IJSSIR* 3(7), 196-203. https://www.researchgate.net/publication/329415345_DEMOCRATIC_DECENTRALISATION_IN_INDIA_AN_OVERVIEW

Shinde, S. N. *versus* The Divisional Commissioner, Nashik Division, Nashik & Ors., CIVIL APPEAL NO. 56 OF 2022 (2022).

Sims, D. (2012). *Understanding Cairo: the logic of a city out of control*. The American University in Cairo.

Singh, B., & Rao, R. (2021). Is there an opioid epidemic in India? *Journal of Public Health*, *43*(Supplement_2), ii43–ii50. DOI: 10.1093/pubmed/fdab322

Singh, M. P. (2001). Towards a more federalized parliamentary system in India: Explaining functional change. *Pacific Affairs*, *74*(4), 553–568. DOI: 10.2307/3557806

Smith, B. C. (2023). *Decentralization: The Territorial Dimension of the State*. Routledge. DOI: 10.4324/9781003404927

Smoke, P. (2015). Rethinking decentralization: Assessing challenges to a popular public sector reform. *Public Administration and Development*, *35*(2), 97–112. DOI: 10.1002/pad.1703

Som Lal *versus* Vijay Laxmi and Ors., AIR 2008 SUPREME COURT 2088 (2008).

Srivastava, T. N. (2002). Local 'Self' Government and the Constitution. *EPW* 37(30), 3190-3198. https://www.epw.in/journal/2002/30/special-articles/local-self-government-and-constitution.html

State Statistical Committee of the Republic of Azerbaijan. Classification of administrative territorial divisions, [Azərbaycan Respublikasının Dövlət Statistika Komitəsi. İnzibati ərazi bölgüsü təsnifatı]. (2024). stat.gov.az. 2024-02-28.

Statement Of Preliminary Findings And Conclusions/ International Election Observation Mission Republic of Azerbaijan – Early Parliamentary Elections. (2020). https://www.oscepa.org/en/documents/election-observation/election-observation-statements/azerbaijan/statements-3/3952-2020-parliamentary-1/file

Steenmans, K., Robin, E., Acuto, M., Iwaszuk, E., & Garza, L. O. (2023). Governing the informed city: Examining local government strategies for information production, consumption and knowledge sharing across ten cities. *Urban Governance*, *3*(4), 243–251. DOI: 10.1016/j.ugj.2023.09.001

Stewart, F. (2005). Groups and Capabilities. *Journal of Human Development*, *6*(2), 185–204. DOI: 10.1080/14649880500120517

Stewart, F. (2019). Human Development Approach: An Overview. *Oxford Development Studies*, *47*(2), 135–153. DOI: 10.1080/13600818.2019.1585793

Stockmann, D. (2023). Tech companies and the public interest: The role of the state in governing social media platforms. *Information Communication and Society*, *26*(1), 1–15. DOI: 10.1080/1369118X.2022.2032796

Stoker, G. (2017). *Transforming local governance: from Thatcherism to New Labour*. Bloomsbury Publishing.

Suman, D., & Sthitapragyan, R. (2024). Rural Local Government and Healthcare Delivery in an Eastern Indian State. *Asian Journal of Social Science*, *52*(3), 121–127. https://www.sciencedirect.com/science/article/abs/pii/S1568484924000248. DOI: 10.1016/j.ajss.2024.06.006

Surinder Kaur *versus* State of Punjab & Ors., 1996 AIR 1507 (1996).

Susen, S. (2017). Jürgen Habermas. The Routledge Handbook of Language and Politics, 43.

Tariq, M., Khan, A., & Rizwan, M. (2018). An Analysis of the Major Theories of Federalism. *Global Social Sciences Review* 3(4), 400-412. https://www.gssrjournal.com/article/An-Analysis-of-the-Major-Theories-of-Federalism

Tarlau, R. (2014).Occupying Land, Occupying Schools: Transforming Education in the Brazilian Countryside UC Berkeley Electronic Theses and Dissertations

Tarlau, R. (2015). How Do New Critical Pedagogies Develop? Educational Innovation, Social Change, and Landless Workers in Brazil. *Teachers College Record*, *117*(11), 1–36. DOI: 10.1177/016146811511701103

Tarlau, R. (2022). *Collaboration and Contestation: State Actors and MST Activists Reforming Rural Education*. Accountability Research Center.

Tax Code of the Republic of Azerbaijan. (2000). [Azərbaycan Respublikasının Vergi Məcəlləsi]. https://e-qanun.az/framework/46948

Thanh, S. D., & Canh, N. P. (2019). Local governance: Impacts of fiscal decentralization on government size and spending composition in Vietnam. *Asian Economic Journal*, *33*(4), 311–340. DOI: 10.1111/asej.12189

The Secret Teacher. (2017). *Secret Teacher: a counselling course revolutionized my teaching*. The Guardian. https://www.theguardian.com/teacher-network/2017/apr/01/secret-teacher-counselling-training-revolutionised-teaching

Thomas, M. B., & Rajesh, K. (2011). Decentralization and Interventions in Health Sector: A Critical Inquiry into the Experience of Local Self Governments in Kerala. *Working Paper 271*. Institute for Social and Economic Change. https://www.isec.ac.in/wp-content/uploads/2023/07/WP-271-Benson-Thomas-and-Rajesh.pdf

Tikly, L. (2017). The Future of Education for All as a Global Regime of Educational Governance. *Comparative Education Review*, 61(1), 000–000. https://doi.org/DOI: 10.1086/689700

Tobias, S. (2005). Foucault on Freedom and Capabilities. *Theory, Culture & Society*, *22*(4), 65–85. DOI: 10.1177/0263276405053721

Tocqueville, A. (1962). Amerika'da Demokrasi, (Çeviren: Taner Timur), Yenilik Basımevi, İstanbul.

Tocqueville, A. (2017). *Demokrasi Amerika'da*. (Çev. Gökhan Özcan). İstanbul: Türkiye İş Bankası Kültür Yayınları. ss. 78–81, 127, 133, 148.

Toksöz. (2009), Yerel Yönetim Sistemleri, TESEV Yayınları, İstanbul, s:1-148

Torres, C. A., & Morrow, R. A. (1998). Paulo Freire, Jürgen Habermas, and Critical Pedagogy: Implications for Comparative Education. *Critical Studies in Education*, *39*(2), 1–20.

Tortop, N. (1996), "İtalya'da Yerel Yönetimlerin Yapısı ve Son Düzenlemeler", Çağdaş Yerel Yönetimler Dergisi, Cilt:5, Sayı: 3, s: 63-70. Şan, G. (2011), "İtalya'da Yerel Yönetimler". http://www.yerelsiyaset.com/pdf, (Erişim Tarihi 05.01.2025): s.92.

Tracking Federal Funding to Combat the Opioid Crisis (March 2019). Bipartisan Policy Center. Tracking Federal Funding to Combat the Opioid Crisis.

Transparency International. (2022). *Türkiye Yolsuzluk Raporu*. Uluslararası Şeffaflık Derneği.

Tripathi, P. K., & Grigoriadis, T. N. (2023). State capacity & the soft budget constraint: Fiscal federalism, Indian style. *Asia and the Global Economy*, *3*(2), 100058. DOI: 10.1016/j.aglobe.2023.100058

Trivedi, N. (2022). Federalism in India v USA: a comparative study. Jus Corpus Law Journal, 972-979. https://www.juscorpus.com/wp-content/uploads/2022/11/191.-Niyati-Trivedi.pdf

Trung, N. S., Phuong, D. T., Thanh, B. T., & Dien, B. X. (2023). The organization of local government in Vietnam. *Russian Law Journal, 11*(3), 1010–1017.

TÜİK. (2021). *Belediye Hizmetleri ve Katılım İstatistikleri*. Türkiye İstatistik Kurumu.

Tully, J. (2013). Two Ways of Realizing Justice and Democracy: Linking Amartya Sen and Elinor Ostrom. *Critical Review of International Social and Political Philosophy, 16*(2), 220–232. DOI: 10.1080/13698230.2012.757914

TwoSigmas. (2019). *Mental Health – Why it's Important for Teachers and Students Alike*. Medium. https://medium.com/@twosigmas/mental-health-why-its-important-for-teachers-and-students-alike-cc7ce39a7914

Uddin, K. (2018). Decentralization and Governance. In Ali Farazmand (Ed.), *Global Encyclopedia of Public Administration, Public Policy and Governance* (pp. 1-7). Springer.

Udey Chand *versus* Surat Singh and Anr., 2009 AIR SCW 6688 (2009).

UGLC. (2008). *Decentralization and Local Democracy in the World*. The World Bank.

Ulusoy, A., Akdemir, T. (2006). Mahalli idareler (teori/ uygulama/maliye), Seçkin Yayınları, Ankara, s: 528

UNDP. (2020). *Local Governance in Fragile Contexts*. UNDP Publications.

UNESCO. (2017).Brazil Country Case Study. Retrieved from https://unesdoc.unesco.org/ark:/48223/pf0000259531

Unterhalter, E. (2003). Education, Capabilities, and Social Justice. In UNESCO EFA Monitoring Report, 4.

Usta, S. (2021), Dünyada Yerel Yönetimler ve Mali Yapıları (Almanya'da Yerel Yönetimlerin İdari ve Mali Yapısı), Ankara, Nobel Yayınevi, s: 17-52

Vaddiraju, A. K. (2017). *Federalism and Local Government in India*. Studium Press.

Van Zomeren, M., & Iyer, A. (2009). Introduction to the Social and Psychological Dynamics of Collective Action. *The Journal of Social Issues, 65*(4), 645–660. DOI: 10.1111/j.1540-4560.2009.01618.x

Vega-Ramírez, J., Castro-Duarte, P., & Quintana-Figueroa, C. (2023). Communication of Results of Educational Policies: Impact Levels of Educational Policies in the Digital Society. *Societies (Basel, Switzerland), 13*(2), 34. Advance online publication. DOI: 10.3390/soc13020034

Venkataramana Bhat, M. V. *versus* Returning Officer and Tahsildar & Ors., 1993 LawSuit(SC) 567 (1993).

Vesperini, G. (2011) "Regional and Local Government in Italy: An Overview",Universita Degli Studi Della Tuscia, Viterbo- Italy, Università degli studi della Tuscia, Viterbo – Italy, ss:1-24 https://images.irpa.eu/wp-content/uploads/2011/06/vesperinig .pdf, (Erişim Tarihi: 01.02.2025)

Vickers, J. (2010). A two-way street: Federalism and women's politics in Canada and the United States. *Publius*, *40*(3), 412–435.

Vidal, D. G., & de Faria Filho, L. M. (2008). Schooling in Brazil. In Going to School in Latin America, 55. Bloomsbury Publishing, Vieira, S. L., Plank, D. N., & Vidal, E. M. (2019). Educational Policy in Ceará: Strategic processes. Educação & Realidade, 44.

Vlad, T., Hin ea, C., Neam u, B., & Stănică, V. (2023). Impact, Utilization and Applications of Digital Media for Government in Rural Settings. A Comparative US-Romania Research. *Transylvanian Review of Administrative Sciences*, *2023*(70), 128–155. DOI: 10.24193/tras.70E.7

Vöhringer, B., & Dickson, S. (2021). Monitoring of the application of the European Charter of Local SelfGovernment in Azerbaijan. 40th SESSION Second part Report CG (2021) 40-21.

Vu, M. T. T., & McIntyre-Mills, J. J. (2008). Towards local government strategic planning in Vietnam: Systemic governance interventions for sustainability. *Asian Social Science*, *4*(2), 91–105.

Wahyudin, Y., & Rahayu, D. N. (2020). Analisis Metode Pengembangan Sistem Informasi Berbasis Website: A Literatur Review. *Jurnal Interkom: Jurnal Publikasi Ilmiah Bidang Teknologi Informasi Dan Komunikasi*, *15*(3), 26–40. DOI: 10.35969/interkom.v15i3.74

Walz, G. R., & Bleuer, J. C. (n.d.). *ACA Knowledge Center*. https://www.counseling .org/docs/default-source/vistas/improving-teaching-and-learning-a-counseling -curriculum-model-for-teachers.pdf?sfvrsn=6

Werr, P., & Lewis, A. (2023). *Egypt asset sales face obstacles as state maintains grip*. Reuters.

Wescott, C. G. (2003). Hierarchies, networks and local government in Viet Nam. *International Public Management Review*, *4*(2), 20–40.

Wienen, J., & Mosler-Törnström, G. (2013). The Congress of Local and Regional Authorities. Local and regional democracy in Azerbaijan. 23rd SESSION Strasbourg. https://rm.coe.int/local-and-regional-democracy-in-azerbaijan-resolution-recommendation-m/1680719568

Wiens, K., Bhattarai, A., Pedram, P., Dores, A., Williams, J., Bulloch, A., & Patten, S. (2020). A growing need for youth mental health services in Canada: Examining trends in youth mental health from 2011 to 2018. *Epidemiology and Psychiatric Sciences*, *29*(115), 1–9. DOI: 10.1017/S2045796020000281 PMID: 32299531

Woodside, A. B. (2020). *Vietnam and the Chinese model: A comparative study of Vietnamese and Chinese government in the first half of the nineteenth century* (Vol. 140). BRILL.

World Bank. (2000). *Overview of Rural Decentralization in India*. World Bank.

Xie, M. (2024). *The platformation and transformation of the digital public sphere: An introduction*. Communication and the Public., DOI: 10.1177/20570473241228627

Yan, Y., Sano, H., & Sumiya, L. A. (2023). Policy Capacity Matters for Education System Reforms: A Comparative Study of Two Brazilian States. *Journal of Comparative Policy Analysis*, *25*(2), 253–281. DOI: 10.1080/13876988.2022.2110472

Yıldız, A. (2012). *Ne Mutlu Türküm Diyebilene: Türk Ulusal Kimliğinin Etno-Seküler Sınırları (1919–1938)*. İletişim Yayınları.

Yilmaz, S., & Venugopal, V. (2013). Local government discretion and accountability in Philippines. *Journal of International Development*, *25*(2), 227–250. DOI: 10.1002/jid.1687

Zambrano, P. A. (2020). Sports betting in Indiana: The proposed legislation after Murphy V. NCAA. *Indiana Law Review*, *53*, 743.

Zarur, S. B. (1993). From Bad to Good Government: The Case of Three Local Governments in Ceará, Brazil (Doctoral dissertation, Massachusetts Institute of Technology).

Zelia M. Xavier Fernandes E. Gonsalves *versus* Joana Rodrigues and Ors., AIR 2012 SUPREME COURT 988 (2012).

Zientarski, C., Menezes, H. C. M., & Silva, S. D. O. D. (2019). Democratic Management in Public Education: A Paradox of the Brazilian Neopatrimonialist State?-The Case of Ceará. *Educação em Revista*, 35.

Zimmerman, J. F. (2001). National-state relations: Cooperative federalism in the twentieth century. *Publius*, *31*(2), 15–30.

About the Contributors

Çiğdem Akman graduated from Suleyman Demirel University, Department of Public Administration. She completed her master's degree at Sakarya University at the Institute of Social Sciences, Program of Public Administration. She completed her doctorate education at Suleyman Demirel University Institute of Social Sciences Program of Public Finance in 2015. She worked as a Lecturer at the Egirdir Vocational School between 2010-2015. In 2016, she has been appointed as an assistant professor at the Department of Public Administration at Suleyman Demirel University. Since 2020, she is working at Suleyman Demirel University, Department of Political Science and Public Administration as an associate professor. The author has books, many book chapters, and articles on Local Governments, Local Government Finance, E-government, Artificial Intelligence, Government Systems, Policy Boards, Twinning City, and Cittaslow.

Onur Kulaç is an Associate Professor in the Department of Political Science and Public Administration at Pamukkale University in Denizli, Turkey. He earned his Ph.D. in Politics and Public Administration from Pamukkale University in December 2016. He also holds a Master of Public Administration (MPA) from the University of York, UK, completed in 2011, and a bachelor's degree in International Relations from Ege University, Turkey. Currently serving as the Vice Dean of the Faculty of Economics and Administrative Sciences and the Director of the Social, Economic, and Political Research and Application Center at Pamukkale University, Dr. Kulaç has a significant role in the university's administrative and international relations efforts. His academic contributions are marked by postdoctoral research at prestigious institutions such as the University of Southern California and Pardubice University. Dr. Kulaç has made substantial contributions to public policy, higher education policy, and public administration education through numerous peer-reviewed publications and conference presentations. His research spans areas such as decision-making processes, climate change policy, and the role of think tanks in policy-making. Additionally, he has been involved in various international research projects, including studies on the impact of COVID-19 on public administration.

***

Kaushik Banerjee With over 18 years of academic experience, Prof. Kaushik Banerjee is currently HOD and Professor in the Department of Law at Brainware University, Kolkata. Previously, he served as HOD of the Department of Management. He has publications in Scopus, Web of Science, UGC CARE-listed, and other reputable journals. He supervises more than six research scholars pursuing doctorates, contributing significantly to research and academia.

Tanzer Çeliktürk is currently serving at Pamukkale University in Turkey, where he is recognized for his academic expertise and research in the field of public administration. His scholarly interests and professional work primarily focus on public policy analysis, the structure and functioning of local governments, and financial regulations within the public sector. Dr. Çeliktürk has contributed to a deeper understanding of how public institutions operate and how policy decisions are shaped and implemented, particularly within the context of local governance and fiscal accountability. His work plays a significant role in bridging the gap between theoretical frameworks and practical applications in the management of public resources and governance systems.

Hasibe Ceyhan (Dr. Lecturer) was born in Karaman in 1976. She graduated from Erciyes University, Faculty of Economics and Administrative Sciences, Department of Economics in 2004. While working as an expert and manager at state levels, she completed her master's and doctorate in Public Administration. In 2017, he was appointed to Karamanoğlu Mehmetbey University. He is currently working as a faculty member at Karamanoğlu Mehmetbey University SBMYO. Management Culture, Governance and Participation, Digitalisation, Local Governments are among the topics he has been working with interest recently.

Nguyen Chi Hai Dr. Political Science Lecturer, An Giang University, Vietnam National University Ho Chi Minh City. He teaches and conducts research at An Giang University, Vietnam National University, Ho Chi Minh City, Vietnam. His research interests and areas of research include Education, Indigenous Culture, Public Policy, Public Management, Social Sciences, and Humanities. Address: No 18, Ung Van Khiem street, Dong Xuyen ward, Long Xuyen city, An Giang province. Phone +(84) 965 118 318. Email: nchai@agu.edu.vn

Pınar Çuhadar is an Associate Professor at Mardin Artuklu University. She earned a PhD in Economics from the Çukurova University, Turkey. During her PhD, she visited İstanbul University as an academic visitor and Bologna University as an exchange student. Previously, she earned an MA in Economics at Çukurova University, focusing on fiscal policy. Her works focus on institutional economics and political economy. Pınar Çuhadar was a Visiting Research Fellow at the University of Bath in 2023–2024.

Souvik Dhar is currently working as Assistant Professor of Law at Brainware University. He has completed his Ph.D. in Law from Amity University Noida. He has successfully passed both the UGC-NET and WB-SET examinations. He has a diverse academic experience. Furthermore, he worked as a Research Investigator at the Centre for Child Rights, WB NUJS, contributing to a UNICEF project focusing on the 'Evaluation of the POCSO Act, 2012 in West Bengal'. His educational qualifications include a B.A. LL.B. from the Department of Law, University of Calcutta, and an LL.M. in Business Laws from Amity Law School, Amity University, Kolkata. Dr. Dhar has also practiced as an Advocate handling cases in consumer rights, banking, civil, and criminal law. He has actively participated, delivered special lectures as resource person. His scholarly contributions comprise numerous articles in reputable journals (including UGC-Care listed journals) and edited books covering diverse legal issues. He is the author and co-author of several books on various legal subjects. He has a total of over 30 publications which includes 15 books. His area of interest includes Health Law, Criminal Law, Corporate Law, and Human Rights Law.

Meenu Gupta is a distinguished academician and legal scholar with over 19 years of experience in teaching, research, and advocacy. She holds a Ph.D. in Law and has been associated with Amity University since 2011. With a strong academic background, she specializes in areas such as Criminal Law, Constitutional Law, International Environmental Law, and Women Laws. Dr. Gupta has authored several books and contributed numerous chapters to edited volumes, alongside publishing peer-reviewed articles in reputed journals. She has presented papers at national and international conferences, focusing on legal reforms, human rights, and environmental law. As a Ph.D. coordinator and LL.M. program leader, she has guided several research scholars. Dr. Gupta is also an active resource person, judge, and chairperson at various legal forums and moot court competitions, showcasing her commitment to advancing legal education and research.

Rena Huseynova is an Assistant Professor at the Department of Digital Technologies and Applied Informatics and the Head of the Department of

Coordination and Organization of Research Centers at Azerbaijan State University of Economics (UNEC). Her research focuses on general economy, digital economy, and knowledge economy. She teaches courses related to these fields and has research papers. Rena Huseynova is an active participant in national and international scientific conferences. She is also a member of the Organizing Committee of several International Conferences. Her technical expertise includes Microsoft Office and various learning platforms. She is fluent in Azerbaijani, Turkish, Russian, and English.

Jipson Joseph has a PhD in Ethics from DVK Bangalore. Currently, he is a Research Scholar in the School of Law at Christ University, Bangalore, India. His research interests are in the fields of ethics, gender studies, constitutional law, human rights, human security, environmental justice, SDGs, Local Self-Government, Developmental policies and global poverty. He has published 2 monographs, co-edited one book, and contributed scholarly articles to many international and national journals and edited volumes including IGI Global Scientific Publishing's edited books.

Georgia Beake Litle is a former practicing attorney and current PhD student in Political Science at the University of Oklahoma. Her legal and professional practice areas include work in corporate compliance at a large international proxy advisory firm, experience with corporate financial audits, practice in complex estate planning, and evaluation of corporate anti-trust litigations. Georgia currently works as a Graduate Teaching Fellow for American Federal Government at the University of Oklahoma. Her research interests relate to the fields of public policy analysis, public law, corporate malfeasance, and comparative politics.

Ananya Pandey is a Research Scholar in School of Law at Christ University, Bangalore. She has her research interests in the field of Constitutional Law, Human Rights, SDGs, Climate Change, Intellectual Property Law and Jurisprudence

Ali Roziqin is a Lecturer in the Department of Government Studies, Universitas Muhammadiyah Malang, Indonesia. He obtained his bachelor's degree from the Department of Public Administration at Universitas Diponegoro, Indonesia. He holds a Master of Public Administration from the Universitas Gadjah Mada, Indonesia. Hisresearch interests are in bureaucracy, public policy and administration, and public sector innovation. He has published papers in the reputable international journals like Sustainability (MDPI), Local Environment (Taylor and Francis), Tourism Critiques, Journal of Science and Technology Policy Management, Journal of the Knowledge Economy, and Public Administration and Policy: An Asia-Pacific Journal, as well as in the IGI Global.

Ulviyya Rzayeva is an Associate Professor at the Department of Digital Technologies and Applied Informatics and the Head of the Center for Digital Economy at Azerbaijan State University of Economics (UNEC). Her research focuses on information systems, emerging technologies, and artificial intelligence. She teaches courses related to these fields and has authored multiple textbooks and research papers. Dr. Rzayeva is an active participant in national and international scientific conferences and has taken part in multiple Erasmus+ programs. Her technical expertise includes Microsoft Office, LOGO TIGER-GO PLUS, SPSS, EViews, and various learning platforms. She is fluent in Azerbaijani, Turkish, Russian, and English and has a basic knowledge of Italian.

Salahudin is senior lecturer in the Department of Government Studies, Universitas Muhammadiyah Malang. He obtained bachelor degree from the Department of Government Studies, Universitas Muhammadiyah Malang, His research interest are public budgeting and finance. He holds Master Degrees from Universitas Muhammadiyah Malang and Khon Kaen University, Thailand. He has completed his Ph.D. in Islamic Politic in Universitas Muhammadiyah Yogyakarta, Indonesia.

Ayu Evita Sari is graduated from the Department of Government Studies, Universitas Muhammadiyah Malang. Currently, she is research assistant on many research project in the Department

Dellannia Segreti is a current PhD student at the University of Toronto and an Ontario Certified Teacher (OCT) at the elementary and secondary level. Her interests lie in equitable and accessible pedagogies, with a focus on Artificial Intelligence (AI), Experiential Learning (EL), research, and technologies.

Susenohaji is lecturer in the Faculty of Vocational Studies, University of Brawijaya. He has research interest are in digital innovation, budgeting, and rural government.

Index

Symbols

A

C

D

E

R

S

T

V

www.ingramcontent.com/pod-product-compliance
Lightning Source LLC
LaVergne TN
LVHW081529300926
849161LV00006B/1352